The Performance Identities
of Lady Gaga

ALSO EDITED BY RICHARD J. GRAY II

The 21st Century Superhero: Essays on Gender,
Genre and Globalization in Film (McFarland, 2011)

The Performance Identities of Lady Gaga

Critical Essays

Edited by RICHARD J. GRAY II

McFarland & Company, Inc., Publishers
Jefferson, North Carolina, and London

Library of Congress Cataloguing-in-Publication Data

The performance identities of Lady Gaga : critical essays /
edited by Richard J. Gray II.
    p.   cm.
Includes bibliographical references and index.

ISBN 978-0-7864-6830-0
softcover : acid free paper ∞

1. Lady Gaga — Criticism and interpretation.   2. Popular
music — United States — 2001–2010 — History and criticism.
3. Popular music — United States — 2011–2020 — History and
criticism.   4. Popular music — United States — Political aspects.
5. Gender identity in music.   I. Gray, Richard J., 1971–
ML420.L185P47 2012
782.42164092 — dc23   2012015220

British Library cataloguing data are available

Front cover image: Lady Gaga, circa 2010 (Photofest)

Manufactured in the United States of America

McFarland & Company, Inc., Publishers
Box 611, Jefferson, North Carolina 28640
www.mcfarlandpub.com

Table of Contents

Preface

On November 1, 2010, Elyse Graham, a journalist for *The American Scholar* magazine, contacted me via email to learn more about my work on Lady Gaga. Three days later, I participated in a telephone interview with Graham. Several of my responses to her questions appeared in an article entitled "Monster Theory" printed in the Autumn 2011 edition of *The American Scholar*. In her article in which she described current scholarship on Lady Gaga, Graham wrote: "Her music videos are surrealist revels, her outfits could make Elton John blush, and her riffs on gender and sexuality have fueled rumors of hermaphroditism. Semiotically speaking, Lady Gaga is a walking court of the Sun King — and her uses of performance and identity drive some scholars wild" (12). Graham's words summarize Lady Gaga's *œuvre* in a way that describes the content of this collection of essays very well.

Our conversation covered a wide range of Gaga-related topics. We discussed my background in language and media studies that had brought me to reflect on a performer whose power centers on the manipulation of signs. We conversed about the early development of a body of work on Lady Gaga — not because Gaga as a subject of study seems strange, but rather, because the study of Lady Gaga seems strangely appropriate. We addressed the following questions: How can the study of Lady Gaga lead us to think differently about our uses of language? Is the "language" of Lady Gaga's *œuvre* more responsive to specifically academic readings than that of others in her field, and if so, what accounts for this? Do academic projects focusing on her work aim to contribute new terms or problems to the field of pop culture studies? Finally, Graham wanted to hear details about the genesis and the progress of this particular book project, and whether I had found, in my capacity as editor, that scholars from different disciplines approached the subject with different kinds of questions in mind ("Interview request, American Scholar"). The short answer to this final question was an unequivocal "Yes."

I am undeniably indebted to Elyse Graham and *The American Scholar* magazine for showing an interest in my collection of essays. The essays included in this collection answer many of Graham's questions. They also raise additional questions regarding the significance of Lady's Gaga's work and how scholars view her songs and performances within a larger context. As Graham wrote following my interview with her:

> One popular angle for critics to take on the singer is French visual theory: power through pageantry, appropriate for the YouTube era's society of the spectacle. Another recurring theme is transgression, Gray says: "This idea of the grotesque, monsters, and fairy tales — not in a Disney sense, but in a scare-the-heck-out-of-you sense. Fairy tales like Grimm or Perrault: a manual for how to conduct your life in a world in which there is danger" ["Monster Theory" 12].

Lady Gaga's work has a clear literary quality. It is precisely because of my love for literature — French literature and theatre, in particular — that I have such a great interest in her work. The reader of this collection will find several chapters referring to Gaga's apparent *francité*. This is not by pure happenstance. How very French, indeed, is Lady Gaga! For the literary scholar, in particular, Gaga's *œuvre* is a gold mine awaiting excavation. Playing on the terms "geology" and "archeology," words that semantically relate to what this collection seeks to accomplish, scholars of Lady Gaga refer to this field of study as *Gagalogy*.

In brief, Lady Gaga's work as a performance artist is a fascinating subject of study. Her *œuvre* has a profundity that the academic world is only beginning to discover. Thank you, Lady Gaga, for your artistry, for your creative genius, and for your courage to inspire others to "embrace their inner monster." Thank you also to my fellow *Gagalogists* for your contributions to this emerging field of study. Most specifically, I would like to thank the contributors of this particular collection for their thought-provoking essays. I would also like to express my heartfelt appreciation to my colleague L. Kip Wheeler for his comments and suggestions on improving the manuscript. Thank you to my friends, colleagues, and students for the support and the numerous emails and Facebook posts on all things related to Lady Gaga. Many of my students are now "Little Monsters" as a result of our numerous discussions. Thank you also to the students at the Institut Jacques Lefèvre, Merville-Franceville, Normandy, France, who helped me to obtain a last-minute ticket to *The Monster Ball Tour* premiere in Paris. Finally, I would be entirely remiss if I did not thank my wife, Andrea, my daughters, Geneviève, Madeleine and Catherine, and my son, Richard. You endure my Lady Gaga obsession every day. *I* am *your* "Little Monster."

Introduction

"I've always been famous, it's just no one knew it yet."
— Lady Gaga

On a warm evening in May 2010 at the Palais Omnisports de Paris-Bercy in Paris, France, in front of more than 17,000 screaming fans, Lady Gaga declared, "If anyone ever tells you that you're not good enough, not pretty enough, not smart enough, you tell them, 'Fuck you! I'm gonna be a star!'"[1] Whether in public appearances, in concert, or in her music videos, outspokenness characterizes pop music superstar Lady Gaga. Born as Stefani Joanne Angelina Germanotta on March 28, 1986, in New York City, Lady Gaga is a performance artist *par excellence* who pushes performance to its very limits. Always controversial, Lady Gaga's *œuvre* inspires her fans to don the moniker of "Little Monsters." In the role of "Mother Monster," Gaga performs a commentary on the social problems affecting the world, including consumerism, racism, sexism, and hatred toward the LGBT community. Lady Gaga has taken the international pop music scene by storm.

Lady Gaga's musical influences include David Bowie, Queen, Michael Jackson, and Madonna. Fashion inspires her songwriting, her live performances, and her music videos. Her debut album, *The Fame* (2008), reached number one in the UK, Canada, Austria, Germany, and Ireland. In the United States, the album peaked at number two on the Billboard 200 chart and topped Billboard's Dance/Electronic Albums chart. The first two singles from the album, "Just Dance" and "Poker Face," became international number-one hits, topping the Billboard Hot 100 in the United States. The album earned six Grammy nominations. In November 2009, Lady Gaga released her second album, *The Fame Monster*. A collection of eight songs, *The Fame Monster* also garnered six Grammy nominations. The album won the Grammy for "Best Pop Vocal Album" and earned Gaga a second-consecutive nomination for "Album of the Year." The album's first single, "Bad Romance," reached number two in the United States, Australia, and New

Zealand and topped the charts in eighteen countries. "Bad Romance" won the Grammy for "Best Female Pop Vocal Performance" while its accompanying music video won the Grammy for "Best Short Form Music Video." Gaga became the first recording artist in U.S. music history with three singles ("Just Dance," "Poker Face," and "Bad Romance") exceeding the four million mark in digital sales. The album's second single, "Telephone," featuring singer Beyoncé, earned a Grammy nomination for "Best Pop Collaboration with Vocals" and became Gaga's fourth UK number-one single. Though controversial, the "Telephone" music video received a relatively positive reception from contemporary critics who praised Gaga for "the musicality and showmanship of Michael Jackson and the powerful sexuality and provocative instincts of Madonna" (McCormick). Controversy also welcomed her next single, "Alejandro." For the music video, Gaga collaborated with fashion photographer Steven Klein. Critics complimented the dark aspects of the "Alejandro" video, though the Catholic League attacked Gaga for a blasphemous use of the nun's habit and the Christian cross.

Lady Gaga's accolades continue to impress fans and critics. In 2009, Gaga began a second worldwide headlining tour, *The Monster Ball Tour* (2009–2011). According to Billboard, *The Monster Ball Tour* grossed $227.4 million, making it one of the highest-grossing concert tours of all time and the highest-grossing for a debut headlining artist (Waddell). With the May 23, 2011, release of her third studio album, *Born This Way*, Lady Gaga continued to climb the charts with the title track, "Born This Way," as well as "Judas," "Edge of Glory," "Yoü and I" and live performances of "Hair." "Born This Way" became the fastest-selling single in the history of iTunes, selling approximately one million copies in only five days (Kaufman). In May 2011, *Forbes* magazine named Lady Gaga the #1 celebrity in the world. At the 2011 MTV Video Music Awards, which aired on August 28, 2011, Lady Gaga won two awards for "Born This Way," including "Best Female Video" and "Best Video with a Message." As of October 2011, Gaga had sold more than 23 million albums and over 64 million singles worldwide ("Lady Gaga to Perform at Belfast MTV Awards"). Lady Gaga became the first musical artist to gain over one billion viral views on YouTube. Lady Gaga is planning a third headlining tour — *The Born This Way Ball Tour*.

Showcasing songs influenced by Electropop music from the 1980s, Lady Gaga's debut album, *The Fame* (2008), treated the life of the rich and famous. With regard to the album's concept, Lady Gaga stated, "*The Fame* is about how anyone can feel famous. Pop culture is art. It doesn't make you cool to hate pop culture, so I embraced it and you hear it all over *The Fame*. But, it's a sharable fame. I want to invite you all to the party. I want people to feel a part of this lifestyle" (Herbert, Ch. 4). Gaga underscored the fact that the artist's fan base holds the power to build the artist's fame. It is for this very reason that Lady Gaga continually tells her fans that it is because of them that she has enjoyed such success. Like popularity, which appears to be based upon a random set of circumstances, fame itself is an artificial construction:

> *The Fame* is not about who you are — it's about how everybody wants to know who you are! Buy it and listen to it before you go out or in the car. [...] I think you've really got to allow artists' creativity to marinate. It took me a while but really delving into myself I finally got it. I couldn't be more proud of it. It's not just a record[,] it's a whole pop art movement[.] It's not just about one song [Herbert, Ch. 4].

The Fame offers a commentary on the structure of fame based on the positive opposition created between the celebrity and the fan base. Without the support of the fan base, fame does not exist.

Inspired by Gaga's personal experiences, her second album, *The Fame Monster*, brought the analysis of fame to an entirely new level by expressing the problems associated with fame through the metaphor of a "monster." On May 22, 2009, Gaga teased her fans by tweeting only the word "Monster." In an interview with *The Daily Star*, Gaga elaborated on her "Monster" theme:

> I have an obsession with death and sex.... Those two things are also the nexus of horror films, which I've been obsessing over lately.... My re-release is called *The Fame Monster* so I've just been sort of bulimically eating and regurgitating monster movies and all things scary.... If you notice in those films, there's always a juxta-position of sex with death. That's what makes it so scary. Body and mind are primed for orgasm and instead somebody gets killed. That's the sort of sick, twisted psychological circumstance [Herbert, Ch. 4].

Gaga further explained that she was obsessed with "the decay of the celebrity and the way that fame is a monster in society" (Carpenter). *The Fame Monster* focused on the darker side of fame. In addition to the re-release of all of the songs included on her debut album, *The Fame Monster* included eight new songs. "Bad Romance" was the first single released on Gaga's second album. Gaga explained the origin of her idea for *The Fame Monster* as follows: "While traveling the world for two years, I've encountered several monsters, each represented by a different song on the new record: my 'Fear of Sex Monster,' my 'Fear of Alcohol Monster,' my 'Fear of Love Monster,' my 'Fear of Death Monster,' my 'Fear of Loneliness Monster,' etc." (Herbert, Ch. 4). *The Fame* and *The Fame Monster* formed two contrasting perspectives: the former focused on the rise to fame; the latter focused on the consequences of fame. By creating a second perspective on fame in *The Fame Monster*, Gaga explored the most haunting recesses of the human experience. Her album treated the theme of the fragility of life and the imminence of death. In an interview with *MTV*, Gaga stated that "I am ready for the future, but I mourn the past, [...] And it's a very real rite of passage — you have to let go of things. You have to mourn them like a death so that you can move on, and that's sort of what the album is about" ("Lady Gaga Gets 'Dark' On The Fame Monster").

On September 16, 2010, Lady Gaga announced the release of her third studio album, *Born This Way*. Gaga offered this assessment of her work: "The album is my absolute greatest work I've ever done and I'm so excited about it. The message, the melodies, the direction, the meaning, what it will mean to my fans and what it will mean in my own life — it's utter liberation" (Sigel). The album's title track was released on February 11, 2011, and the *Born This Way* album was released on May 23, 2011. Unlike *The Fame* and *The Fame Monster*, Gaga's third album showcases a perspective intended to change the world: "I knew I had an ability to change the world when I started to receive letters from fans: 'You saved my life...' ... 'I'm gay and my parents threw me out.' My fans have related to me as a human being and as a non-human being — as a super-human person that I truly am" ("Lady GaGa's New Album Will 'Change The World'"). Intended to shock and awe, Lady Gaga's message resonates in this album: No matter if you are rich or poor, black or white, gay or straight, you have the right to stand up to be counted. Gaga intended to make this album controversial, as she explained to *RWD*: "Everyone tells me I'm arrogant but my music's the only thing I've got, so you'll have to let me be confident about one thing. I suppose that's what you can expect from the album: a lot of hit records that will piss people off" ("Lady Gaga Gets 'Dark' On The Fame Monster"). Society continually forces people to accept certain social labels. Lady Gaga shares Søren Kierkegaard's perspective — "Once you label me, you negate me" — to the extent that even she does not accept fully responsibility for the origins of her ideas, as she told an interviewer at *MTV*: "Beyoncé said, 'Where the fuck do you get these ideas from?' And I was like, 'I don't know Bee, it was just the way I was born" ("Lady GaGa's New Album Will 'Change The World'"). Unlike the dance album label given to *The Fame* — and to a certain extent, *The Fame Monster* — Gaga wanted *Born This Way* to bridge the worlds of pop and rock music. When describing the debut of the song, "Yoü and I," released on August 23, 2011, she explained to *RWD*:

> I wrote the song just to write a beautiful song and I intend to put it on the new album, yes, but it's not totally indicative of the new album sound; it's just a really big rock and roll hit. I do have these hopes that it could be a great crossover record, so I'm going to put my producer's hat on and get it to a place where I feel like it could reach the masses. (Sigel)

Whether or not Lady Gaga's *Born This Way* album holds universal appeal remains to be seen. Nonetheless, there is little doubt that as judged by peers and people "in the business," Gaga is a performance artist to be noticed.

During an interview with *Entertainment Weekly*, Elton John, who collaborated with Lady Gaga in a 2010 performance on the Grammy Awards, characterized the album as follows: "I love her, and I love her ability to write. There's a chance I might do one track with her, but she's so busy and I'm so busy, we can never get together! But her record — it's fucking amazing" (qtd. in "Lady Gaga, Johnny Depp Top Entertainment Weekly Power List"). Comparisons of Gaga's work to that of pop star Madonna have circulated since *The Fame* debuted in 2008. The release of the "Born This Way" single continued to fuel such comparisons as critics noted that the beginning of Gaga's song has the same "feel" as Madonna's #2 hit "Express Yourself" from her *Like a Prayer* (1989) album. During an interview with *MTV News*, Gaga's friend Perez Hilton offered the following evaluation:

> This album is Gaga's *Like A Prayer*, and that is huge praise coming from me, who is, like, the biggest Madonna fan ever....What's amazing about this body of work is that it really is that *Born This Way* is a body of work, where all of the songs make sense together. And it's as if she created this world or co-created this world with her fans, and all of these songs inhabit that world ["*Born This Way* Is Lady Gaga's *Like A Prayer*, Perez Hilton Says"].

Perez's comment acknowledged more than the similarities between *Born This Way* and Madonna's album that pre-dates Lady Gaga's work by more than two decades. His words suggest that Gaga's third album is truly a watershed moment for Gaga. Recognizing the fact that the Madonna aesthetic has informed Gaga's work from the beginning of Gaga's rise toward international stardom, it is noteworthy that Gaga's *Born This Way* album furthers Madonna's dialogue on empowerment initiated in the 1980s. Though Madonna's empowerment message focused primarily on female empowerment, Gaga's empowerment message extends to all people regardless of race, ethnicity, gender, sexual preference, or socioeconomic level. Without any doubt, Lady Gaga performs her message during public appearances, in her concerts, and in her music videos.

While awaiting the opening of *The Born This Way Ball Tour*, Lady Gaga continues to perform. In October 2011, Gaga sang at The Decade of Difference Concert at the Hollywood Bowl celebrating the 65th birthday of former President Bill Clinton and the 10th anniversary of the Clinton Foundation. Stripping down to a nude body suit, Gaga adapted the words of the song "Bad Romance" to "Bill Romance," singing to the former Commander-in-Chief. A humanitarian herself, in November 2011, Lady Gaga announced the creation of the Born This Way Foundation, an organization that Gaga and her mother,

Cynthia Germanotta, direct. The official launch of the Born This Way Foundation occurs in 2012. Lady Gaga continues to produce music videos for songs from the *Born This Way* album and she also continues to prepare for her upcoming television appearances. Gaga tweeted, "Been up all night editing my first TWO films as director! Marry The Night Video + 'A Very Gaga Thanksgiving' the 2nd airing on thanksgiving!" (@ladygaga). On November 24, 2011, *ABC* broadcast her 90-minute holiday special entitled *A Very Gaga Thanksgiving* that included a performance of "The Lady Is a Tramp" with legendary crooner Tony Bennett. Gaga continues to receive numerous accolades. Tweeting in response to the 2012 Grammy Award nominations broadcast on November 30, 2011, Gaga wrote: "I'm humbled + honored to have a Trinity of nominations from the Grammys, including Album of the Year for Born This Way. I love u so much. Paws Up for our album's being nominated three years in a row. I could never do it without you. Together, we were Born To Be Brave" (@ladygaga). On December 1, 2011, *E! Entertainment Television* premiered Lady Gaga's most recent music video, "Marry the Night," a fourteen-minute semiautobiographical creation outlining her rise to fame. Lady Gaga also appeared on the cover and in the pages of the January 2012 edition of *Vanity Fair*.

Lady Gaga and the Concept of Performative Identity

Lady Gaga *is* performance. Whether in public appearances, in concert, or in her music videos, Gaga's performances examine the self "reflected, challenged, codified, cracked up, over baked and served up" (Komitee 1). Transformative and metamorphic in nature, her performances illustrate the birth, life and death of the individual. Gaga's own words support this perspective:

> I begin as a cell and I grow and change throughout the show. And it's also done in what now is becoming my aesthetic, which is, you know, it's part pop, part performance art, part fashion installation — so all of those things are present... It's a story, it's me battling all my monsters along the way. I'm playing all the music from *The Fame*, all the music from *The Fame Monster*. And the stage that I designed with the Haus [of Gaga] is a giant cube that sits. Imagine you were to hollow out a TV and just break the fourth wall on a TV screen. It forces you to look at the center of the TV. It's my way of saying, "My music is art" ["Lady Gaga Plans To Battle Her 'Monsters' During Monster Ball Tour"].

Lady Gaga's "story" reflects both her own personal narrative and the narratives of her spectators as Gaga's performance art serves, in part, to portray our collective experience. When Gaga performs, she performs life scenes that we are too afraid to address ourselves. In a sense, she performs our social reality.

In the field of performance studies, social reality is a representation of human actions. All human forms of expression — religious, artistic, physical — which form the actions of humanity each consist of either great or small performances. Performance studies considers these performances the building blocks of reality. It is, therefore, important to understand how performances function to form our reality. Though performance obviously applies to the performing arts, performance functions in a wider context within the present study. In his book entitled *The Future of Ritual*, anthropologist Richard Schechner writes that "performance's subject [is] transformation: the startling ability of human beings to create themselves, to change, to become — for worse or better — what they ordinarily are not" (1). By means of performance, human beings are born, transformed, and they ultimately die.[2] Schechner outlines seven important functions of performance: To entertain, to make something that is beautiful, to mark or change identity, to make or foster community, to heal, to teach, persuade or convince, to deal with the sacred and/or the demonic (46). Lady Gaga's *œuvre* embraces each of these functions.

While conducting field research in the 1960s, fellow anthropologist Victor Turner noticed a universal theatrical language at play during his study of various cultural rituals. He hypothesized that all groups perform rituals dramatizing and communicating stories about themselves such as coming-of-age ceremonies, exorcism rites, or battle scenes. These "performances," containing a theatrical component, enable the participants to achieve a change in status, to develop coping mechanisms or to engender a new state of consciousness. Turner noted that such performances tended to occur in a liminal space of heightened intensity separate from routine life, much like a dramatic theatre performance. Turner called such situations "social dramas." Turner stated:

> Each culture, each person within it, uses the entire sensory repertoire to convey messages: manual gesticulations, facial expressions, bodily postures, rapid, heavy or light breathing, tears, at the individual level ... stylized gestures, dance patterns, prescribed silences, synchronized movements such as marching, the moves and 'plays' of games, sports and rituals, at the cultural level [9].

In his own research, Schechner had also observed the link between anthropology and theatre in terms of the performative aspects associated with each field. In *Between Theater and Anthropology*, Schechner commented on the characteristics that these two disciplines share such as containing the idea of a transformative act, notions of liminality, and the interaction between performer and spectator. Further, Turner and Schechner noticed the connections between anthropology and stage performance, both of which contain the common notion of fatality.

Fatality is a natural concept. In a sense, there is a hint of fatality in every human action. If every form of human expression is a performance, then every performance is fatal since its expression also exhibits a temporal finiteness. A theatrical representation is a series of orchestrated performances. Further, although it might represent reality, theatrical representations are completely artificial. In *Acting at the Speed of Life*, Timothy Mooney offers the following assessment on the artificial characteristic of the theatre:

> A play is not about me and my little circles of attention. A play is about the great possibility of the universe. My character is a collection of ideas and traits, set into motion to compete, combat and cooperate with other conflicting and agreeing ideas and traits. Whether or not this is a work of "realism," we present those notions to the audience for their consideration. We postulate on their behalf, "What if life were life this?" And we play out the results for them to understand and observe.... Because what we are doing here is *not* life; it is art. And art is artificial. And filled with artifice [9–10, italics are Mooney's].

Therefore, although all human expressions constitute performances, when presented to an audience, such performances are filled with artifice. No matter the level of false reality portrayed in such performances, however, all performances are still representational; they serve to perform or to represent a certain idea, notion, or perspective in front of an audience. In the case of Lady Gaga's *œuvre*, her performances are both representational *and* presentational. In representational theatre, the audience observes the performance while the performer pretends that the audience is not present. The "fourth wall" serves as a barrier between performer and audience. In presentational theatre, in contrast, the performer presents to the audience an expression of his/her character with complete awareness of the audience's presence (Mooney 11). The performer breaks the fourth wall and the audience no longer remains a group of uninvolved observers peeking in through a one-way mirror. The audience becomes performers on stage, implicit in every performance. Nevertheless, the performance must end and no matter what depth of the psyche the performance explored or to what limits of the soul the performance examined, the representation itself is imagined. Lady Gaga's overall message is that fame itself, like any performance, is illusory.

The Collection

This collection of critical essays addresses a range of subjects illustrating the influence and impact of Lady Gaga's *œuvre* through the interdisciplinary framework of performance identity. The essays included in this collection represent the contributions of international scholars from a variety of academic disciplines. There are already many books written on Lady Gaga, including a number of juvenile books, such as Claire Kreger Boaz's *Lady Gaga* (2011) and Heidi Krumenauer's *Lady Gaga* (2011). For general audiences, there is also Sarah E Parvis' *Lady Gaga* (2010), Helia Phoenix's *Lady Gaga: Just Dance, the Biography* (2010), and Emily Herbert's *Lady Gaga: Behind the Fame* (2010). None of these books treats "Lady Gaga" as an academic subject of study. The present collection is among the very first books dedicated exclusively to a scholarly analysis of Lady Gaga's *œuvre*. This collection examines the notion of performance identity through the themes of gender and sexuality, consumerism, visual body rhetoric, homosexuality and heteronormativity, surrealism, the carnivalesque, monstrosity, imitation and parody, human rights, and racial politics. As a collection, these thirteen chapters show the ways in which Lady Gaga performs individual and collective identity.

The collection begins with Mathieu Deflem's essay entitled "The Sex of Lady Gaga." In his essay, Deflem analyzes aspects of Lady Gaga's career from the perspective of cultural questions related to sex, sexuality, and gender. Situated in the sociology of popular culture, Deflem explores Lady Gaga's fame and artistic endeavors in terms of the following (inter)related issues: the use of and meanings associated with sexuality in Lady Gaga's *œuvre*, perceptions of Lady Gaga as a sexy pop star, rumors on the sex of Lady Gaga and the nature of her sexual orientation, the gendered structure of the world of Lady Gaga, and popular perceptions of Lady Gaga as a feminist. A course that Deflem teaches at the University of South Carolina entitled "Lady Gaga and the Sociology of the Fame" informs his essay. The main argument of Deflem's analysis is the notion that sex and gender form relatively important categories within contemporary society, particularly within the world of popular culture and music. Thus, an analysis of the circumstances of Lady Gaga's fame as a popular music artist must explore matters of sex and gender both in terms of the expectations of how men and women should act on the basis of cultural ideas of masculinity and femininity and in terms of social relations involving men and women.

Elizabeth Kate Switaj's "Lady Gaga's Bodies: Buying and *Selling The Fame Monster*" analyzes how Lady Gaga's persona, videos, music, and costumes position her as an artist belonging both to the mainstream music industry and to the more marginalized subcultures of performance art. The primary currency by which she purchases this complex and contested position is the female body. Her own body becomes the ground and the stage that carries her performative costumes, even to the extent of apparently endangering her own health on a long-haul flight when her costume caused her legs to swell. At the same time, Gaga's position as a thin, white, conventionally attractive woman means that her costume and makeup plays at the grotesque and the repulsive rather than actually being repulsive. This effect was furthered, and perhaps made explicit, when she began dyeing her hair blonde. At the same time, Lady Gaga also problematizes the notion of a single, unified female body offered for sale. Her body takes on multiple identities, though she never takes any subaltern identity far enough to endanger her stance as a pop artist. Overall, her work shows the limits and mechanisms of the very systems of celebrity from which she benefits and which she must ultimately serve.

Jennifer M. Santos' "Body Language and 'Bad Romance': The Visual Rhetoric of the Artist" explores the notion of visual body rhetoric in Lady Gaga's smash hit music video for "Bad Romance" that debuted to rave reviews in the entertainment community. But, like much of Gaga's work, the music video has also engendered controversy. In the wake of the fervor of "Telephone," one might forget that "Bad Romance" also captivated audiences for its disturbing depiction of the female form by championing the anorectic body. In some scenes, Gaga's isolated figure seems nearly alien in its thinness; in others, her spine and ribs protrude from beneath white latex. In "Bad Romance," the combination of narrative contradictions and placement of varied body types present a critique of the anorexic body that returns attention to the root causes of anorexia: the realm of the psyche in tandem with the realm of sociocultural conformity. Ultimately, Santos contends that Gaga's "Bad Romance," rather than valorizing the anorexic body, provides a compelling critique of the social and psychological factors that inform body dysmorphia.

Heather Duerre Humann's "What a Drag: Lady Gaga, Jo Calderone, and the Politics of Representation" analyzes Lady Gaga's work through the filter of Judith Butler's *Gender Trouble* (1990). Since the time of its publication, scholars and cultural historians have generally accepted that the socially constructed dimension of gender performativity is arguably most obvious in drag performance. Humann's discussion of drag performance offers a rudimentary understanding of gender binaries by the way it emphasizes gender performance. In her work, Butler recognizes that drag is not necessarily the honest expression of its performer's intent. Instead, she posits that the performance "can only be understood through reference to what is barred from the signifier within the domain of corporeal legibility" ("Critically Queer" 24). Using Butler's theoretical work as a point of departure, Humann examines how Lady Gaga challenges and disrupts normative notions of gender and sexuality by/through her multiple stage/screen personae — including the persona of "Jo Calderone," the male model that Lady Gaga performs. This chapter also explores how Lady Gaga's different incarnations challenge the binaries of man and woman and complicate notions of sexual difference and desire. By/through the persona of Jo Calderone and the other personae she adopts, Lady Gaga pushes cross-dressing into the realm of drag and gender play.

In "Follow the Glitter Way: Lady Gaga and Camp," Katrin Horn explores how Lady Gaga's *The Monster Ball Tour* pays homage to a pivotal scene of gay appropriation of mainstream entertainment ("Follow the Yellow Brick Road" from *The Wizard of Oz*). Gaga's reference forms a part of Lady Gaga's strategic use of camp as a means of queering her persona and performance. Horn claims that Lady Gaga does more than simply referencing these camp predecessors in a meaningless pastiche of styles and stars of the past. Instead, Gaga builds her unique performances on quotations and pop "ready-mades" in order to establish a pop ancestry that she at the same time defies, and a gendered identity that she deconstructs at the very moment of its construction. Besides the "Monster Ball," which in name alludes to voguing balls and to Broadway musicals in its realization, Gaga's reworking of lesploitation flicks in the music video for "Telephone" and specific music videos by Madonna and the film Cabaret in "Alejandro" serve as examples for analysis. Drawing on theories of camp, parody, female masquerade and drag by Jack Babuscio, Pamela Robertson, Judith Butler, and Linda Hutcheon and concepts of diva worshipping and stardom by Richard Dyer, Horn's essay seeks to conceptualize camp as a key component in the understanding of Lady Gaga's music, performance and, most importantly, appeal to an identificatory potential for fans.

Jennifer M. Woolston's essay entitled "Lady Gaga and the Wolf: 'Little Red Riding Hood,' *The Fame Monster* and Female Sexuality" examines Lady Gaga's *The Fame Monster* against the backdrop of the literary tradition of "Little Red Riding Hood." When discussing the cultural implications of the original version of Charles Perrault's classic 1697 tale, "Little Red Riding Hood," Catherine Orenstein suggests, "in the French slang, when a girl lost her virginity it was said that 'elle avoit vu le loup'— she'd seen the wolf." Over time, the literary renditions of "Little Red Riding Hood" morphed, with the heroine becoming less of a cunning burlesque artist and more of a "complete victim" of male violence (Tatar 5). In recent years, some contemporary authors and film directors have shifted the heroine's character back to its autonomous origins while downplaying the notion that she is a passive, weak, and/or helpless female. Woolston shows how Lady Gaga serves as a role model for empowered females. Apart from examining the parallels between the written tales and Gaga's lyrical revisions, Woolston's essay examines issues related to costuming, semiotic signals from music videos, and overall ways in which Gaga plays with (and rewrites) women's sexual attitudes through her performances. Lady Gaga effectively models the notion that surface appearances can deceive.

Richard J. Gray II's "Surrealism, the Theatre of Cruelty, and Lady Gaga" analyzes Lady Gaga's work from a Surrealist perspective. In his essay, Gray posits the notion of a Surrealist Lady Gaga by examining the influences of prominent Surrealist artists including Claude Cahun, Hannah Höch, Max

Ernst, Salvador Dalí, Alejandro Jodorowsky, and Francis Bacon on Lady Gaga's performance identity. Secondly, his essay analyses Lady Gaga's *œuvre* against the framework of an artistic perspective informed by the work of French artist and dramatist Antonin Artaud. Artaud's Surrealist works contained shocking imagery of religious scenes (The Crucifixion), human suffering, and insanity described in his conception of a Theatre of Cruelty, in his notion of an organless body called "Le Mômo," and exemplified in his radio play entitled *Pour en finir avec le jugement de Dieu*. As Gray shows, Lady Gaga's work contains a "shock and awe" technique characteristic of both Surrealist art and Artaud's Theatre of Cruelty. Her music videos contain similar shocking visual texts in which Gaga seeks to reveal the pain that is found inside the individual. Using Surrealism as a foundation of her work and structuring her theatre by adapting Artaud notion of a Theatre of Cruelty, Gaga fragments the viewer's notion of reality thereby forcing the viewing to create an alternative perception of reality. As illustrated in her performances, Lady Gaga's work becomes an examination of contemporary sociocultural, socioeconomic, and sociopolitical issues and a ritual of rebirth and renewal.

In "Rabelais Meets Vogue: The Construction of Carnival, Beauty and Grotesque," David Annandale considers Lady Gaga's performances, whether in concert in the form of music video, as redolent with images fusing sexuality, violence, gore, bodily fluids and monsters. These variations on the grotesque, combined with *The Monster Ball Tour*'s embrace of "freaks," invite an examination of Gaga's art through the prism of Mikhail Bakhtin's theories of the grotesque and carnival. Annandale contends that there is a very close relationship between Gaga's aesthetic provocations and the excesses of Rabelaisian carnival. Gaga's exploration of the grotesque embraces not just the more traditional celebration of the ugly, but interrogates beauty as well. Gaga applies attributes of the grotesque to fashion and stereotypical conceptions of female beauty and sexuality, simultaneously undermining those very conceptions and exposing their constructed nature. Gaga then extends her attack on social roles through the carnivalesque reversals and celebrations of crime present in works such as the music video for "Telephone." As with Bakhtin's carnivalesque, the question arises as to how far Gaga's circus can truly be said to be radical, and whether its subversion might not simply be yet another fashionable image, one enjoyed by Gaga and her fans to the ultimate benefit of a gigantically profitable machine. Gaga's mainstream success, therefore, does not represent a dilution of her subversive grotesque, but rather her carnivalesque transformation of the mainstream itself.

Ann T. Torrusio's "The Fame Monster: The Monstrous Construction of Lady Gaga" proposes that Lady Gaga's appropriation of the term "monster" for her latest album (*The Fame Monster*) and corresponding tour (*The Monster*

Ball Tour) may help to illuminate why she has become both an influential star and a constant source of criticism. Using Jeffery Jerome Cohen's "Monster Theory" as a lens through which to view Lady Gaga, Torrusio argues that since Lady Gaga's monstrous form is a complete fabrication, Gaga has the freedom to constantly reinvent her image. Through this perpetual reinvention, or monstering, she presents herself as a monstrous body of "pure culture" (Cohen 4, 5). Throughout her career, critics have projected various labels onto Gaga in an attempt to categorize her, to compartmentalize her into a specific space in culture. However, due to Lady Gaga's constant reinvention of herself, these labels are highly illusory. In her music videos and in her live performances, Lady Gaga presents herself as a modern shape-shifter, morphing into myriad variations of herself while presenting all the variations as possibly the "true" construction of Lady Gaga. Gaga brings attention to our inability to trust the products of mass media. In another sense, her constant shape-shifting provides her viewers the opportunity to catch a glimpse of themselves. She entices her audience with the notion that the latter are part of the show, affectionately referring to her fans as her "Little Monsters." She presents herself as "Mother Monster" while simultaneously projecting back onto her public its own perverse obsession for fame, smashing the distinction between performer and audience, coexisting in an escapist monsterdom.

Rebecca M. Lush's "The Appropriation of the Madonna Aesthetic" uses the filter of performance theory to better understand and position Lady Gaga against the backdrop of pop star Madonna. As Lush states, the media often-times has defined Lady Gaga in relation to Madonna. Sometimes, the media casts the two pop stars as rivals, such as Madonna and Lady Gaga's *Saturday Night Live* appearance that parodied their media perpetrated rivalry. Other times, the media represents Lady Gaga as Madonna's true heir apparent, after a long stretch of pop hopefuls who often are better known for their tabloid controversies than for their performance successes. Madonna appears to endorse Gaga, seeing herself in the younger pop star. Lady Gaga has constructed her own performance identity by building on the work of the pop culture past in a way that obscures her core personal identity. Her *avant-garde* fashions, for example, render her every entry into public a publicity event. Gaga, unlike Madonna, has become increasingly vocal about her standpoint on hot-button issues surrounding the LGBT community, including "Don't ask, don't tell," helping homeless LGBT teens, and campaigning for gay rights on stage.[3] As a result, Gaga's art has become less flexible and more open to interpretation.

In "Performing Pop: Lady Gaga, 'Weird Al' Yankovic and Parodied Performance," Matthew R. Turner explores the parodic performances of the work of Lady Gaga by "Weird Al" Yankovic, the "King of Pop Parody." As Turner explains, parody itself is often filled with internal contradictions at both the level of the critique of the original artwork as well as at the level of the quality of the parodied performance. In fact, upon more careful critical examination it becomes clear both that "Weird Al" is not the only artist creating "parody" and that Lady Gaga is not his only target. Lady Gaga, herself, creates parody as she examines the pop stars of earlier eras and comments on the work that the latter had created. Critics suggest that Lady Gaga's success is due, in large part, to her imitation of other artists, but her work goes beyond simple imitation. On the level of performance, it is her self-conscious employment and use of parody to which her incredible success owes, at least, a note of gratitude. As a self-professed performance artist, Lady Gaga becomes a nexus of imitation in which she both showcases and expands the limits and the understanding of both parody and performance. Through his own parodies of Gaga's parodic work, "Weird Al" Yankovic highlights this reality.

Karley Adney's "'I Hope When I'm Dead I'll Be Considered an Icon': Shock Performance and Human Rights" illustrates how Lady Gaga uses her performances as a platform for the discussion of civil human rights. As Adney explains, Lady Gaga dressed like Queen Elizabeth I to meet Queen Elizabeth II, she performed with Elton John at the Grammy Awards, and she led Larry King to imitate her appearance. Though these incidents have earned her a permanent place in our collective consciousness and memory, Lady Gaga's shock performance tactics achieve significant results. A self-proclaimed feminist, Gaga says that she cares deeply about the portrayals of women and issues affecting women. Gaga violently challenges tradition through her fashion choices and she encourages viewers to think more about her artistry, her creativity, and her message than her physical form. Her performances, whether on stage or when she walks down the street, showcase awareness for human rights, most specifically rights for women and for members of the LGBT community.

The collection concludes with the co-authored essay written by Laura Gray-Rosendale, Stephanie Capaldo, Sherri Craig and Emily Davalos entitled "Whiteness and the Politics of 'Post-Racial' America" that examines how Lady Gaga's extreme popularity in American culture is occurring at the same cultural moment as conservative discourses about racism (and arguments about Obama-ian post-racism) are gaining increasingly greater control. Examining representations of race and ethnicity in Gaga's music videos, iconographic images, and interviews, the collaborative authors contend that her media prominence is in large part the result of the various ways in which she embodies, deploys and subverts powerful historical discourses about whiteness. Based on experiences using Gaga's work to teach freshmen students in Northern Arizona University's S.T.A.R. (Successful Transition and Academic Retention)

Writing Program, a program focusing on pop culture that includes only lower income, racial or ethnic minority, and/or first-generation college students, and students' nuanced and complex responses, the authors of this essay reveal the ways in which Lady Gaga has both the potential to challenge conservative politics and to undermine crucial strides for racial and social justice.

NOTES

1. The editor of this collection attended Lady Gaga's first The Monster Ball Tour concert in Paris, which took place on May 21, 2010.

2. The music video for Lady Gaga's "Born This Way" underscores this very notion.

3. On September 20, 2011, the United States Congress repealed "Don't ask, don't tell" (DADT).

The Sex of Lady Gaga

MATHIEU DEFLEM

Today, Lady Gaga is ubiquitous. Only a few years after the release of her debut album *The Fame*, Lady Gaga has taken over the world of popular music to become one of pop's most talked-about stars. The case of Lady Gaga's fame deserves attention, not because it is itself the popular thing to do, but because cultural phenomena present questions that we must answer appropriately, even and especially in times of economic and political turmoil. Popularity also need not impede the undertaking of a theme, but caution is certainly in order. A scholarly perspective on the Lady Gaga phenomenon will benefit from a specific formal approach and material subject matter. This paper offers a sociological analysis of the roles of sex, sexuality, and gender as manifest in the career of Lady Gaga that contribute to her fame as a global pop sensation.[1] This chapter, therefore, seeks to clarify questions of sex and gender in the case of Lady Gaga in order to reveal a complex condition whereby Lady Gaga embraces some and yet fights other cultural standards of femininity.

Thematically, this paper will explore a variety of issues related to sex(uality) and gender. Relying on the conceptual understanding of sex as a biological category and gender as a social construction (Wharton), there are many reasons to explore the significance of these issues in the case of Lady Gaga. The analysis works because sex and gender form relatively important categories in contemporary society, especially within the world of popular culture and music. As a minimum, an analysis of the conditions of Lady Gaga's fame as a pop music artist must explore matters of sex and gender, not only in terms of social relations involving men and women but, additionally, in terms of the cultural expectations of masculine and feminine behavior (Cohen).

In terms of its scholarly approach, this paper is rooted in sociology, specifically sociological insights on popular culture that focus on the intersection of music and fame. The fame of Lady Gaga — especially its origins from 2008 onwards — is thus explored analytically in the social context of the contemporary culture of fame in the popular music industry. The case of Lady Gaga deserves such scholarly attention, not exclusively because her fame is spectacular in terms of its size and scope, for the nature of pop star fame has traditionally been global. It strongly resonates on the part of its audience, including fans, non-fans, and anti-fans. Instead, what is peculiarly noteworthy about Lady Gaga is that her fame has occurred at a time when the (popular) music industry has experienced a commercial decline. How, then, has the fame of Lady Gaga nonetheless occurred and how, more specifically, are issues of sex and gender relevant therein?

Music and Fame: A Sociological Perspective

Two principles concerning a sociological viewpoint on music will clarify this paper's approach to the understanding of fame (Bennett; Frith, Straw, and Street; Martin). Firstly, from a sociological perspective, we should not understand music as the organization of sound, but rather as the whole of the social relationships and cultural meanings involved in the production and reception of musical sounds within society. The social or inter-subjective nature of music as a sociological concept pertains to musical performances with regard to the interaction between artist and audience, but it also includes the composition process that involves the relationship of the composer to an existing universe of musical sounds (and their cultural meaning) and the expectations of an audience of listeners. Secondly, the social understandings of and meanings associated with musical sounds are cultural constructs. Relying on now classic insights into the sociology of knowledge (Berger and Luckmann), it is important to recognize from a sociological perspective both that musical sounds do not invoke sentiments and that they do not express ideas on the basis of their inner tonal qualities or any structures of the human mind, but rather that they are established and re-established through socialization within particular communities.

We can extend a constructionist understanding of music to the culture of fame in order to develop a distinctly cultural-sociological perspective. Using the work of one of the founding fathers of sociology, Max Weber, we can explore fame as a cultural phenomenon in terms of the distribution of status. Differentiated from the economic and political categories of class and party, respectively, status refers to the stratification of honor and it relates to lifestyle, privilege and personal qualities of charisma. Though having brought out the distinctly cultural realm of society, Weber's tripartite conceptual scheme largely focused on an analysis of economy and polity for status, as Weber argued, was in relative decline at the dawn of the twentieth century. Sociologists of fame in the modern age went one step further and neglected fame (and popular culture) altogether or explored it in highly reductionist terms. C. Wright Mills, most notably, devoted an entire chapter of his well-known book *The Power Elite* to "The Celebrities," only to conceptualize and denounce celebrity culture as mere power and wealth articulated through the mass media. Even today, such reductionist perspectives to treat fame as a commodity remain popular, but a new cultural sociology of fame (and celebrity) has also begun to emerge.

Harmonizing with cultural perspectives in the contemporary sociology of music, fame (as being well-known) and celebrity (as being acknowledged for being well-known) form cultural constructs that entail a specific social relationship. Fame and celebrity are not qualities of a person or group but are characteristic of a relationship that exists between, on the one hand, the person or group to whom the qualities of being well-known or being recognized for being well-known are attributed and, on the other hand, those members of a community who make such attributions. Like music, we study fame and celebrity sociologically as cultural issues with a focus on their variable meanings and without any preconceived notions with regard to either dynamics or social conditions. As with many cultural issues in society, the degree of fame that an artist attains and maintains within the world of pop and rock music is influenced, amongst other relevant conditions, by issues relating to sex, sexuality, and gender.

Gaga's Sex: Is Lady Gaga Sexual?

This chapter analyzes themes of sex(uality) and gender in the career of Lady Gaga on the basis of news articles, audio and video presentations, and selected representations of Lady Gaga's music and other artistic endeavors. Currently, noting that many of these sources are available online is banal. Less banal perhaps is the fact that there already is an enormous amount of information available about Lady Gaga despite the relatively short period since her debut into the world of popular music. The merit of these sources varies greatly. The main biographical books, in an ever-increasing multitude of such works published these past few years, are Paul Lester's *Lady Gaga: Looking for Fame* (2010) and Emily Herbert's *Lady Gaga: Behind the Fame* (2010), which, despite making the occasional factual mistake, both offer relatively sober and informed analyses of Lady Gaga's career. Ethnographic information on the Lady Gaga community (since spring 2009) serves as an important source of evidence as well. An exploration of questions pertaining to sex, sexuality, and gender in the case of Lady Gaga involves at least the following six topics: 1) the social use and cultural meanings of sexuality exhibited in her work; 2) the perceived sexiness of Lady Gaga as a female performer; 3) the biological sex of the person of Lady Gaga; 4) the sexual orientation of Lady Gaga; 5) the gendered qualities of, and the sexism confronting, the world of Lady Gaga; and 6) the cultural perceptions of Lady Gaga as a feminist icon.

The question of the sexual nature of Lady Gaga pertains to whether or not and to what extent her artistic endeavors contain allusions to sexually-charged themes. The answer is an unequivocal "Yes," simply because Lady Gaga's work displays so much sexuality. This observation should not come as a huge surprise. Not only has sexual display taken advantage of the visualization of music since the rise of the video (Andsager and Roe), but pop and rock music are by their historical nature deeply imbedded in sexuality. After all, the very term "rock 'n' roll" refers to sexual intercourse. It is, therefore, anything but surprising that Lady Gaga describes her work in highly sexual terms. "It's really your job," she said, "to have mind-blowing, irresponsible condomless sex with whatever idea it is you're writing about" (Herbert 131). In the case of Lady Gaga, the sexuality of pop and rock is taken a step further through an explicit and deliberate inclusion of sexual allusions that betray a resolute commitment on the part of the artist to confine herself exclusively to pop and rock history. In her own words, Lady Gaga exemplifies this commitment when she says: "Every artist plays on sex. It's just the context.... I'm a free woman, so I play on sex freely" (Lester 88). Early in her career, in fact, before Stefani Germanotta adopted the Lady Gaga moniker, she deliberately used her sexuality to get attention. Playing in the clubs as an unknown, she recalls, "I didn't want to start singing while they were talking, so I got undressed. There I was, sitting at the piano in my underwear. So they shut up" (Herbert 49).

Among the examples of sexuality in Lady Gaga's work, certain of her songs and/or videos are most striking. Her global hit "Poker Face" dealt auto-biographically with Gaga's fantasies about being with a woman while a man is having oral sex with her. The song "LoveGame" is also autobiographically based on a casual sexual encounter that Gaga had with a man whom she asked if she could ride his "disco stick." Although in her live shows, the disco stick appears as a sort of glowing magic wand held by Gaga while dancing to some of her songs, the reference in the song is clearly to a penis. The music video to the song "LoveGame" is also strikingly sexual in nature, containing lurid dance moves and a semi-naked Lady Gaga kissing both a man and a woman (which caused the video to be censored in some countries and the song subsequently to not be released as a single). Other Lady Gaga songs also explicitly deal with sex: "Monster" and "Alejandro" about casual sexual encounters;

"Teeth" about the joys of pain and sex; "Boys, Boys, Boys" about sexual attraction towards males (during its live performance on *The Monster Ball Tour* the song was morphed into dealing with gay boys); "Dance in the Dark" about insecurity and sex; and the thematically obvious, but musically oddly romantic sounding, "I Like It Rough." Even certain videos that accompany Lady Gaga songs of a less sexual nature feature ample sexuality. The best example in this respect is the video to the song "Yoü and I," which thematically deals with romantic love, but visually involves Gaga as a mermaid having sex with a man.

Lady Gaga's live performances for radio or television and her live concert tours also freely display sexuality. For example, during her performance of the song "LoveGame" on the arena version of *The Monster Ball Tour* (2009–2011), Lady Gaga encouraged the audience to "get your dicks out ... and dance, you motherfuckers!" The dancers accompanying Gaga at her shows also add to the sexual portrayal. When she began her career in 2008, Lady Gaga typically performed with two female dancers in an asexual artsy style that invoked Andy Warhol. Towards the end of 2008, however, three male dancers joined Gaga on stage, who then interacted with Gaga to choreographically visualize the sexual meanings associated with songs like "Poker Face" and "LoveGame." During *The Monster Ball Tour*, the dance group expanded to include about a dozen men and women, further enabling choreographic representations of sex (gay sex included). The wardrobe used by Gaga and her dancers additionally often amplifies sexuality by means of relative nudity, glitter bras, codpieces, S&M-style clothing, etc. Lady Gaga's fans generally respond to her sexuality in similar fashion through a liberal display of (partial) nudity at her shows and a strongly sexualized talk about her, as manifested in fan communications on Twitter, Facebook and in specialized music forums. Strikingly, much of the sex talk directed at the person of Lady Gaga seems to come from non-gay female fans and gay males. Equally striking is the fact that Gaga firmly embraces the sexuality that she receives from her fans, to wit her self-reference as a "hooker" or a "bitch."[2]

Despite its distinct sexual orientation, most of Lady Gaga songs have nothing at all to do with sex. Of the forty-two songs included on Lady Gaga's three major releases — the album *The Fame* (2008) (seventeen songs including bonus tracks), the eight-song EP *The Fame Monster* (2009) and the 2011 album *Born This Way* (seventeen original songs on the expanded edition) — only ten songs deal with sex in more or less explicit ways. The majority of Gaga's songs treat the themes of romantic love (fifteen songs), fun and friendship in her native New York (eleven songs), and a variety of other subjects, including gay rights, immigration, fashion, and freedom, most notably on the thematically wide-ranging album *Born This Way*.

Is Lady Gaga Sexy?

The notion of being sexy or having sex appeal relates to the extent and manner in which Lady Gaga presents herself as a woman within the established standards of feminine sexiness. Such perceptions also reside in the eye of the beholder. In sociological terms, sexiness can be articulated on the basis of the cultural values that are relatively dominant in a community at a given time and place. By conventional standards, Lady Gaga is not or at least not unequivocally sexy, and she does not wish to be a classic beauty, especially not in the sense traditionally understood within the world of pop music. "I am not sexy in the way that Britney Spears is sexy," she once argued, "which is a compliment to her because she's deliciously good-looking. I just don't have the same ideas about sexuality that I want to portray" (Herbert 70). In her own words, Lady Gaga does not want to be "a sexy pop star writhing in the sand, covered in grease, touching herself" (*Elle*). In much of her public conduct and appearance, likewise, Lady Gaga does not present herself as sexy and is also not readily perceived as such. Discussing her sense of fashion and style, she comments: "I just don't feel that it's all that sexy. It's weird ... It's not what is sexy. It's graphic and it's art" (Lester 92). Instead of wearing short skirts, Lady Gaga appears more often skirtless. Few individuals would associate sexiness with a meat dress or other such outlandish outfits. Instead of seeking to invoke sexiness, Lady Gaga says, "I want to cause a reaction. I'm a blonde with no pants ... I love that it shocks people" (Lester 87). The monstrosity that is accordingly often portrayed by Lady Gaga is surely not sexy in a conventional sense (Corona).

Lady Gaga's refusal to be sexy also suggests a statement on her part with regard to what we should consider beautiful and, more broadly, what we should consider accurate in terms of aesthetics. At some of her Monster Ball shows, Gaga has been seen biting the head off of Barbie dolls thrown on stage in order to protest what she holds to be unrealistic standards of beauty. As she fights preconceptions of what female performers have to be and do in order to be successful in music, she deliberately "toys with conventional rules of attractiveness" (Williams). On the covers of her music recordings, Lady Gaga appears only by face, not her entire body, with additional artwork involving the use of artificial facial protrusions and slime to cover herself. As rock star Alice Cooper astutely observed, Lady Gaga is a spectacle not a sex symbol (CNN). Nearly every time that she wears certain clothing or makes a stylistic choice that might otherwise have been sexy, indeed, she does it in a way that is grotesque, even repulsive (Cochrane).

Along with an avoidance of conventional portrayals of sex appeal, Lady Gaga and the community of her fans also seek to embrace a new kind of sexiness. In a very distinct sense, everyone who is part of Lady Gaga's world is considered sexy even when people outside of the Gaga community will likely not, in fact, perceive them as such. In the world of Lady Gaga, everyone is accepted for who they are and who they wish to be even when the mainstream public might judge them to be un-sexy or even unattractive. Related to Gaga's acceptance and embrace of freakishness and monstrosity, the fans of Lady Gaga — also known as her "Little Monsters" — can be tall or short, skinny or fat, or however other might perceive them. At a Lady Gaga concert or in any other form of participation in the Gaga community, however, every monster is sexy and is allowed to feel that way too, in part because of Gaga's dismissal of traditional notions of feminine (and masculine) sex appeal.

What Is Lady Gaga's Sex?

Despite her explicitly gendered stage name and the obvious fact of her biological nature as a female, Lady Gaga has, especially in the early stages of her rise to fame, been confronted with the puzzling rumor that she is a hermaphrodite (Herbert 182–85). As always, the origins of this rumor remain unclear. Several photographs have circulated online that showed a bump between Lady Gaga's legs, but evidence rarely forms the basis of any rumor. The allegation might date back to Christina Aguilera's comment, when she was asked about Lady Gaga after the latter had just begun to make some waves within the world of pop, that Aguilera did not know who Lady Gaga was and did not even know "if it is a man or a woman" (Lester 93).

Lady Gaga's initial responses did little to extinguish speculation, even though her answers could only be understood as ironic. Possibly taking advantage of the notion that "there is no such thing as bad press" and that her rise as a global pop star would surely suffer no damage, Gaga was deliberately provocative: "I have both male and female genitalia, but I consider myself female. It's just a little bit of a penis..." (Lester 94). Likewise, in August 2009, she voiced her happiness about the fact that her song "Poker Face" had reached the top position on the music charts in Japan by tweeting: "I just had to go home and suck my own hermie dick, suckka" (Lady Gaga "Love"). And as late as spring 2011, during her performances of the song "LoveGame" of *The Monster Ball Tour*, Gaga shouted out that she had a "pretty tremendous dick."

Though mostly having fun with and deliberately sustaining the rumor, at other times Lady Gaga has either refused to address the matter or she has openly denied the allegation. While promoting her tour in September 2009, she responded more categorically: "My beautiful vagina is very offended. I'm not offended: my vagina is offended!" (Herbert 185). Her words suggested that her strength as a woman is equated with her having a penis. During an interview with Anderson Cooper for the television show *60 Minutes* that aired in February 2011 on the night of the Grammy Awards, Gaga reaffirmed her female nature precisely by not answering the question directly: "Maybe," she said, and she added: "Why am I going to waste my time and give a press release about whether or not I have a penis? My fans don't care and neither do I" (CBSNewsOnline). Despite its occasional reappearance in the headlines, certainly, by fall 2011, the rumor seemed to have run its course as other issues about Lady Gaga had taken over the celebrity gossip columns.

What Is Lady Gaga's Sexual Orientation?

Like the hermaphrodite issue, the question of Lady Gaga's sexual orientation has been the subject of some speculation, which to some extent Gaga herself has sustained and nurtured. During interviews, Lady Gaga most often flirts with her sexual orientation and responds to the matter with ambiguity. Her responses suggest how she feels about romantic love, both as it exists in her life and how she treats the subject of love in her songs. Most of her songs dealing with romantic love are decidedly negative in tone, for instance, by singing about bad (not good) romance and the possessiveness of her experiencing love as a paparazza. In interviews, she will often deny having a boyfriend, even when she has been romantically connected with several men, most distinctly with Lüc Carl (the subject of all her love songs), who was her boyfriend during her early days in New York and again for about a year until she recorded the music video for her song "Yoü and I" in his home state of Nebraska in July 2011. Nonetheless, Lady Gaga typically justifies the intensity with which she does her work as preventing her from having a romantic partner. "I make love to my music every day," she says, "I'm just not focused on having a boyfriend" (Lester 89). Similarly, she stated in an interview with *Elle* magazine: "I would never leave my career for a man right now" ("Lady Gaga").

On the other hand, Lady Gaga is oftentimes deliberately very provocative about her sex life, which she suggests involves men as well as women. Invoking the theme in her song "Poker Face" of dreaming about being with a woman while she is with a man, she has explicitly admitted to having had sex with women (Lester 91). Yet, arguing to only having been in love with men and only having had boyfriends, her feelings for women would only be physical and not emotional (Herbert 62). In an interview with Barbara Walters in December 2009, she said: "I've only been in love with men. I've never been in love with a woman ... I've certainly had sexual relationships with women" ("How Stefani Germanotta Became Lady Gaga"). More recently, however,

Lady Gaga has even proclaimed that she is bisexual and considers herself to be a member of the LGBT community because of "The b letter," as she stated in a 2011 interview with the LGBT magazine *The Advocate* ("Portrait of a Lady"). However, there is little evidence that Lady Gaga has had many lesbian experiences apart from a few compromising pictures with her friend Lady Starlight (PopCrunch 2009) and some paparazzi snapshots of Gaga flirting with Tamar Braxton, wife of Vincent Herbert, the record executive who originally discovered Lady Gaga on MySpace and who has since served as her A&R representative ("Brew Bits: Toni Braxton's Sister & Lady Gaga"). At best, while her self-identification as 'bi' is not descriptively accurate, we could understand it as a gesture towards the gay community and her accompanying resolute stance on gay rights.

Is the Lady Gaga Community Gendered?

Understood as differential treatment on the basis of sex and gender characteristics, it is difficult to imagine any aspect of social life, including the world of music, which is not "gendered." But the gendered nature of culture can be of various kinds, either involving mere differences between the sexes (indicating sexism) or inequality based on sexual identification, which could be the result of active oppression. It is inevitable that the inter-subjective nature of Lady Gaga's musical exploits suggest that she is a product of her time; she was formed by the social context of both the decade preceding and the decade following the attacks of 9/11. It was from within this complex setting, involving, amongst other things, the Upper West Side of New York, the expansion of the internet, and changes in the music industry, that Lady Gaga developed and practiced her artistic style in its various guises. The social-rationalist theory of meaning earlier introduced in this essay will immediately bring out an element pertinent to the present analysis, specifically the transformation of the rock-oriented stylings of the Stefani Germanotta Band to the electro-pop sounds and performance art of Lady Gaga and the Starlight Revue. Though not absolute in any way, the more typical cultural understanding is (still) such that, all other conditions being equal, pop music is of a more feminine domain in contrast to the masculine world of rock music. As a female pop artist, also, Lady Gaga attracts a fan base that is not only large and remarkably diverse, especially for a relatively young performer, but which is, nonetheless, made up of a female majority.

Gendered differences between the worlds of rock and pop need not necessarily imply sexism, but there are at least some indications that certain gendered cultural pressures were at work in Lady Gaga's initial decision to transform herself (and her music) stylistically. Indeed, according to producer Rob Fusari (who gave the artist her stage name and produced her signature song "Beautiful, Dirty, Rich"), Stefani Germanotta was initially not convinced to adopt the transition towards pop and dance, but was ultimately swayed, not primarily because of aesthetic concerns, but because of a news article about singer Nelly Furtado's transition to dance-oriented pop (Marks). Whatever additional personal and artistic reasons may have swayed her, anticipating success and fame more likely within the world of pop, Lady Gaga began her journey towards global stardom on the basis of her understanding of a distinctly gendered reality, even though she would challenge an elitist understanding of the hierarchical structure of musical genres, proclaiming that "pop music will never be low brow."[3] Lady Gaga's rise to fame thereafter was also eased by the relative vacuum that existed in popular music of the period, which eventually led to the newly vibrant pop world of 2010 dominated by a host of up-and-coming or revived female performers. By spring 2011, Lady Gaga was confident enough in her position to release her album *Born This Way*, recorded throughout 2010, with music that deliberately sought to transcend the sounds of pop to include rock music, thus taking one step further toward her goal of bringing a rock sensibility to pop music.

There are indications that the gendered structure of the Lady Gaga world does not escape criticism. By Lady Gaga's own observation, as a female artist operating within the world of pop and rock she has been confronted with sexism, especially in connection with her liberal use of sexual themes, which, she argues, is much more discussed and criticized than equally sexually explicit material created by male performance artists. "You see, if I was a guy," she said in a 2009 interview with a Norwegian journalist, "and I was sitting here with a cigarette in my hand, grabbing my crotch and talking about how I make music because I like fast cars and fucking girls, you'd call me a rock star. But when I do it in my music and in my videos, because I'm a female, because I make pop music, you're judgmental and you say that it is distracting" (StilettoREVOLT). In response to the sexist pressures Lady Gaga seems to have experienced, she will typically reaffirm her strength as a woman. Simply by speaking so freely about her sexuality and squarely addressing concerns over the differential treatment of female and male pop and rock stars, Lady Gaga seeks to portray herself as a strong female.[4] It is telling that she recognizes sexism but also addresses it head on. As a result, one might argue both that Lady Gaga actively opposes sexism precisely at any time when she is confronted with it and that she adamantly refuses to be a victim of such sexism.

Questions pertaining to sexism within the world of popular music underscore that society often compare female artists to one another. When Lady Gaga was still a relatively unknown performer, media personalities often asked her how she differed or related to performers such as Christina Aguilera and Britney Spears. Further, once Gaga developed her own style and gained visibility, Madonna became the yardstick by which older journalists measured Gaga. And as Lady Gaga's star grew even brighter, other aspiring, young female pop stars were asked to clarify their relation to Lady Gaga. There are certainly obvious reasons of both an artistic and an aesthetic nature that would justify such comparisons. However, we wonder if critics would even pose such questions to male performers, especially within the world of rock music. Being a blonde-haired female alone can, in the world of contemporary journalism at least, readily suffice to justify a comparison among female pop stars. Being male with long hair and tattoos, however, remains an often overlooked characteristic shared by a host of rockers.

Is Lady Gaga a Feminist?

Lady Gaga's feminism relates to her impact on women and the broader cultural perceptions thereof. Harboring a multitude of perspectives on women in society (valuing women as unique, unequal, or oppressed), feminism can signify both a theory or theories referring to a perspective of study and/or a corresponding outlook on life, as well as to praxis, implying an activist attitude oriented at working towards the betterment of women in society and/or a corresponding mode of personal conduct. In other words, the feminism of Lady Gaga refers both to her subjective perspective on such matters and the objective cultural implications of her conduct.

A certain ambiguity exists concerning Lady Gaga's feminist perspective as a result of some of her own explicit statements on the matter that she has made during interviews as she has adopted different perspectives with regard to what feminism is. Her varying perspectives have fueled considerable debate and speculation with regard to her personal thoughts on feminism. In the early stages of her rise to fame, Lady Gaga claimed *not* to be a feminist, much to the discontent of certain feminists (Williams). In a video-taped interview in the summer of 2009, Gaga stated: "I'm not a feminist. I hail men, I love men. I celebrate American male culture, beer, and bars, and muscle cars" (StilettoREVOLT). Elsewhere, she similarly argued, "Even though I'm a very free and sexually empowered woman, I'm not a man-hater. I celebrate very American sentiments about bars and drinking and men buying women drinks" (Lester 47). However, in later statements, Lady Gaga began to view feminism in a different way; she understood that feminism need not imply an anti-male attitude (Feministcupcake). In an interview with the *Los Angeles Times* in December 2009, Gaga said that she was "a little bit feminist" (Powers 2009).

Finally, since her understanding of feminism had changed to encompass a sense of female empowerment, Lady Gaga ultimately affirmed herself as a feminist. In an in-depth article for *Rolling Stone* magazine in 2010, she proclaimed both clearly and decidedly: "I'm a feminist" (Strauss 71).

From the viewpoint of both her conduct and its cultural reception, indeed, it is difficult to deny that Lady Gaga practices a role congruent with feminism. Though working primarily within the world of entertainment and, more specifically, that of pop music, Lady Gaga does not exemplify those roles and styles associated with female pop artists who can be, and often are, more conventionally associated with notions of inequality and patriarchy. Instead, although she is not a feminist activist *per se*, Lady Gaga's work functions as a critique of how society views and values women. In that respect, we should note that Lady Gaga often emphasizes that she is a strong female who is not dependent on anyone, including men. By remaining independent and by "doing her own thing," Lady Gaga factually portrays ideals of feminism, especially the notion that women are free (as free as anyone) to explore their own interests. "She is a 'Free Bitch,'" as journalist Neil Strauss writes (in reference to a line Gaga sings in her songs "Bad Romance" and "Dance in the Dark," "and the audience should be too" (Strauss 68).

Much of Lady Gaga's feminism is distinctly associated with, rather than contradicted by, her distinct sense of sexuality, which embraces sex without yielding to conventional standards of sex appeal and sexuality. Evoking images of monstrosity and tales of sexual exploits of various kinds, Lady Gaga exposes conventional femininity "as a sham" (Cochrane). Through her "blending of the beautiful with the monstrous," as sociologist Victor Corona (11) puts it, Lady Gaga criticizes the role of the conventional female in society by showing, more specifically, that conventional "feminine sexuality is a social construct" (Bauer). And, rather than remaining weak and manipulated, Gaga practices a sexuality that both empowers women and portrays them as strong. The music video to "Bad Romance," for example, visually presents a story in which Lady Gaga is sold into sex slavery only to eventually kill the man to whom she was sold by means of a pyrotechnic bra, ostensibly after, or perhaps instead of, having had sex with him in bed. Lady Gaga interpreted the blazing bra itself—featured during *The Monster Ball Tour*—as a commentary on the fact that female breasts are typically considered as weapons, when to her (as to women in general) breasts are a natural part of life (Lester 91). On the cover of the July 8–22, 2010 double issue of *Rolling Stone* magazine, Lady Gaga also appeared in a machine gun bra.

Understanding feminism as "allowing women to express their sexuality" in ways in which they themselves see fit (Aronowitz), Lady Gaga practices feminism because she is free-spirited and, as she emphasizes time and again, *she* is in charge of her career. As a *de facto* feminist, Lady Gaga has taken ownership of her body and, more broadly, her entire body of work (Cochrane). Even in the earlier periods of her career when she felt the need to take her clothes off to receive attention, Gaga did not view this as giving in to the masculine world. On the contrary, she argues, "I found the idea of taking my clothes off on stage incredibly liberating. I have absolutely no problem with my sexuality and any woman who wants to get more confident about her body should try stripping" (Lester 23). As such, Lady Gaga's sense of sexuality and her particular version of femininity and sex appeal constitute a critique of the popular music industry and of contemporary culture. The female dominance of contemporary pop music is something Lady Gaga welcomes with open arms: "I'm pleased to see that it's mostly women who are dominating the charts" (Herbert 115).

Conclusion

The debate on sex and gender issues in the case of Lady Gaga moved to the foreground of popular discussions in September 2010 when cultural critic Camille Paglia published a condemnation of the new pop sensation entitled wherein she wrote: "Gaga isn't sexy at all. She's like a gangly marionette or plasticised android.... Can it be that Gaga represents the exhausted end of the sexual revolution?" ("Lady Gaga and the Death of Sex"). Needless to say, a multitude of alternate perspectives on Gaga's sexuality and feminism quickly followed Paglia's provocative piece. Yet, we must note that Paglia wrote her essay not on the basis of any feminist concerns, but because of her own perspective on technology and pop music culture. Against the background of an increasing reliance on technology, Lady Gaga is criticized as a star of the current digital age in which, Paglia feels, digitized communications have replaced bodily sexuality. And against the background of transformations in popular music, Lady Gaga receives criticism for her artistic work, which, Paglia thinks, lacks artistic merit. Both observations reflect a nostalgic vision of the past, specifically Paglia's perception of Madonna some twenty years ago. Paglia is thereby indeed both "marooned in the past" (Needham) and completely focused on Lady Gaga as the "icon of her generation" (Paglia). Paglia remains unable to analyze relevant dimensions of a contemporary artist who was not even born in the era in which Madonna had already become a global pop sensation. As such, Paglia stands far from alone in writing about the cultural import of Lady Gaga in terms that betray a lack of the most basic descriptive power, at best being able to reference the "Gaga-savvy daughter" they have at home for the summer (Bauer).

This chapter sought to clarify questions of sex and gender in the case of Lady Gaga in order to reveal a complex condition whereby Lady Gaga embraces some and yet fights other cultural standards of femininity. Liberally relying on sexual themes in her songs and music videos, Lady Gaga ultimately rejects conventional sex appeal. Toying with rumors about her sex and sexual orientation, she both understands the gendered dynamics of the world of popular music and uses them to her advantage. Practicing her art as an independent female and challenging sexism, Lady Gaga presents herself and is also recognized as a practicing "feminist." In combination with other factors, some dimensions of sex and gender directly advance a career in music and contribute to fame, especially by means of an acceptable meshing of show and art, style and substance. But the popular debate and speculations with regard to Lady Gaga's sex, sexuality, and gender also simultaneously reveal and nourish an interest in Lady Gaga as a cultural icon. Controversy also fuels fame.

NOTES

1. I am grateful to Joanna Harrison and Shannon McDonough for their help in the preparation of this essay.

2. As is not unusual for any pop and rock performers displaying a more or less explicit sexual tone, some opposition to Lady Gaga revolves around the purported sexual content of her work. The private group Common Sense Media, for example, uses a video on celebrities as role models that warns against negative behaviors involving sex, drugs, and violence, using references to youngsters singing along to Lady Gaga's "LoveGame" and relying on musical accompaniment in the style of "Poker Face" (Common Sense Media 2010).

3. This phrase originates from Lady Gaga's July 31, 2008 performance of "Just Dance" on the FOX reality television program *So You Think You Can Dance*. Gaga's statement suggests that pop music will never be suitable for a person with little intellectual interest.

4. The idea of the empowered female resonates in her song entitled "Scheiße" from her *Born This Way* (2011) album. In this song, Gaga tells her female listeners that strong females do not need to ask men for permission to do anything.

Lady Gaga's Bodies
Buying and Selling The Fame Monster

Elizabeth Kate Switaj

Lady Gaga is not simply a character played by an actress: "The biggest misconception about me is I'm a character or a persona — that when the lights and cameras turn off, I turn into a pumpkin. It's simply not true. I make music and art and design all day long. Yes, I wash my face and go to sleep but when I wake up, I am always Lady Gaga" (qtd. in Murfett). A performance that never ends becomes an identity and a life; duration may be all that separates a self from a persona. By embodying and maintaining the identity of Lady Gaga, the woman born Stefani Joanne Angelina Germanotta has signaled and purchased her position as both a pop singer and a performance artist. All artists who use the body as part of their art, whether their work is classified as popular or underground, could be said to engage in a similar exchange. What distinguishes Lady Gaga is that she makes these dynamics visible while simultaneously portraying her body as filling unstable boundaries and occupying changing, sometimes contradictory identities. These shifts call the exchange itself into question: if a body that cannot easily be defined is commodified, then exactly what is being sold and bought — or whether the two even match — becomes unclear. Gaga, in other words, benefits from her ability to exchange her body for a position as a popular artist, even as her art reveals and interrogates the dynamics that allow her to participate in this exchange. In these acts of displaying and questioning, Gaga also exchanges her performance of her body for a position as a performance artist.

This almost paradoxical aspect of Gaga's work raises the possibility of a transgressive and subversive art that is at the same time commercially successful. The extent to which Gaga fulfills this possibility manifests through the application of theoretical lenses concerned with issues of social justice, including feminist, anti-racist, and disability theories; that is to say, a critical approach informed by theories that value subversion and change best determines the extent to which Gaga-the-performance-artist challenges the systems of power from which Gaga-the-pop-star benefits.[1] Such a broad base of theory is necessary when addressing the work of an artist such as Lady Gaga who draws from a heterodox set of influences and consistently recreates herself. Within such an approach, feminist theories come to dominate precisely because of the issues surrounding womanhood and the female body on which Gaga's work concentrates (though whether this concentration reflects a deliberate artistic choice or the result of Gaga's own subject position remains unclear). By using this approach to explore and examine Gaga's ways of revealing the systems that allow her to purchase her position as a popular and performance artist, this chapter shows that Gaga's work rarely functions directly as subversive or transgressive; rather, by integrating the revelations of performance art with the reach of popular music and video, Gaga creates conditions that may allow her audience — a broad audience — to subvert and transgress the very systems that allow her to exist.

Lady Gaga, in her role of performance artist, enacts and displays her role of pop star; in doing so, she reveals the necessarily performative nature of gender and other aspects of daily life while also revealing the economics of exchange that underlie celebrity status (including her own status). Gaga herself has hinted at this dynamic in her art: she told Ann Powers of *The Los Angeles Times* in December 2009, "me embodying the position that I'm analyzing is the very thing that makes it so powerful." Embodiment in this case means maintaining her stance as a player in "[c]elebrity life and media culture" (Gaga, qtd. in Powers) at all times. "Lady Gaga is Always Lady Gaga," as the title of a poem by Andrea Quinlan states. To a certain degree, no celebrity can avoid such constant participation; even when a well-known artist attempts to avoid cameras or otherwise to keep a low profile, that very effort becomes part of the public understanding of the individual star. In *Working Girls: Gender and Sexuality in Popular Culture,* Yvonne Tasker notes that "star images are elaborate constructions, characterized by their inclusion of diverse and potentially contradictory elements. In addition to, and indeed, framing, any other specific performances, from movie roles to cameos, to public appearance and interviews, stars always 'perform' their star image" (179); the star image known as Lady Gaga certainly contains contradictions. Two important and interwoven differences, however, distinguish the way she performs her star image from more standard methods of building and maintaining one and thus position her as different from the majority of pop artists: the absence of any aspect of Gaga's star image labeled private or authentic and the way the excesses of her performance make apparent that she is always performing and thus always actively participating in the social constructions that allow her to purchase fame with these performances of her body.

There is no clear distinction between Lady Gaga's on- and offstage personae-selves. She is never seen performing Stefani Germanotta or an offstage version of Lady Gaga.[2] Even her Jo Calderone and Yüyi the Mermaid personae are considered to be alter egos of Gaga, not of Germanotta. Asked by a fan about the distinction between private and public, Gaga replied:

> I believe as an artist, being private in public is at the core of the aesthetic, the message. However, I profusely lie about my personal relationships in an effort to protect that aesthetic and that message. Today people are distracted by unimportant things — like what my diet is, or who I'm fucking. The second part of the question said when is the precise moment when it switches: I would like to be able to say when there's a dick inside me it switches. But it doesn't always. I do sometimes feel that I'm on a stage all the time, and I do feel that life is a stage for my art. When I'm dancing, singing, making breakfast. But there is a moment of freedom, when the stage disappears: when I cry. On stage, off stage, alone or with someone. There's something very honest about that. It has nothing to do with taking off a wig or smearing my lipstick [Interview with Lady Gaga, *In Camera*].

The closest to a private moment she admits to having is one that she might have within a zone or set of actions marked for performance. In other words, she claims she may act or exist in an "offstage" manner even when literally on stage and in costume. This claim blurs the distinction between a public performed self and a private personal one: it makes the "private" part of what is labeled performance. Gaga has also said that, "Every time you see me, it's performance. When I'm sleeping, it's performance" (qtd. in Patch); even the act most likely to be authentic — since sleepers are by definition unaware of their actions — she claims is "performed."[3] Like other pop artists, most notably Madonna, Lady Gaga uses her stage name regularly off stage, instructing interviewers to use it to address her. Even her parents are called "Mama and Papa Gaga," at least according to her friend Justin Tranter (Steele et al. 34).[4]

Unlike these other performers, however, she carries the same level of theatricality with her as she moves through various contexts. Camille Paglia may believe that "[g]oing off to the gym in broad daylight, as Gaga recently did, dressed in a black bustier, fishnet stockings and stiletto heels isn't sexy — it's sexually dysfunctional" ("Lady Gaga and the Death of Sex"), but the truth is that it is neither. Rather, it is the action of a persona-self taking literally the idea that "all the world's a stage." Citing the outfit that Gaga wore to her sister's graduation as an example, Ella Bedard argues that "celebrities are presented as having a public persona [sic] that is revealed during designated instances of performance, but they are also 'caught' by the paparazzi in private leading their 'real' lives with friends, family, and sweatpants. The constancy of Gaga's staged persona works to problematize the false dichotomy between the performers' 'real' and 'artificial' identity." Ella Bedard, however, misses the point of this problematization in concluding that Gaga "is never 'caught' by the camera off-stage since there is no 'real' Lady Gaga behind her performed identity" ("'Can't Read My Poker Face'"). For Gaga, the performed is the real because we are all performers; we were "Born This Way." As Judith Butler argues in *Gender Trouble*, "That the gendered body is performative suggests that it has no ontological status apart from the various acts which constitute its reality" (185). By engaging in a constant performance of her body that can be exchanged for celebrity status, Gaga exchanges her body itself— its reality— for this position.

She also makes this exchange apparent. Gaga's consistent theatricality contributes to the second difference between her performance of a star image and a more usual one: she performs in such a way as to make the performance visible. This visibility leads inevitably to the "misconception" Lady Gaga complained about in the quote with which I began this essay, yet it does not make her a persona, or at least it does not make her any less "real" than anyone else. The precise demarcations between persona and authenticity are, to say the least, slippery, and this slipperiness is part of Gaga's act. Her theatrical actions reveal the performativity of the everyday actions of celebrities and, by extension, of would-be celebrities posting apparently casual images and videos to Facebook and YouTube. It is through this revelation, to a great extent, that she achieves what Ann Powers has observed: "She's tapped into one of the primary obsessions of our age — the changing nature of the self in relation to technology, the ever-expanding media sphere, and that sense of always being in character and publicly visible that Gaga calls 'the fame'— and made it her own obsession, the subject of her songs and the basis of her persona" ("Frank Talk with Lady Gaga"). Gaga's performance of her body is not only exchanged for her position of fame: it ultimately reveals how that exchange takes place both for herself and for those with less far-reaching fame. This revelation, by itself, is not transgressive; it does, however, bring attention to social standards and norms that both may be subverted.

While observers such as Paglia view Gaga's use of high fashion and stage-appropriate attire in everyday situations as problematic, it is precisely by wearing such costumes in seemingly inappropriate contexts that Lady Gaga draws attention to the way in which clothing choice always constitutes part of a performance of a persona or even a self. Clothing always serves as a costume, but we only notice this function when an outfit seems impractical or out of place. Indeed, to call Gaga's clothing choices impractical may be an understatement. In an incident first reported by the British tabloid *The Sun*, the heels-and-crime-tape costume she wore for a transatlantic flight in March 2010 endangered her life. *The Sun* cites an "anonymous airline source" as saying,

GaGa was a high-risk DVT [deep vein thrombosis] case so she was advised to change out of her clothes. But the outfit was so cumbersome she needed help changing out of it. She was particularly miffed about ditching her heels. She was wearing them in memory of her friend Alexander [McQueen] ["Purple Face"].

In a coincidence striking enough to raise the question of whether this incident was engineered, Lady Gaga had said in a television appearance only days earlier, "I would rather die than have my fans not see me in a pair of high heels. I'd never give up my wigs and hats for anything." *The Sun* even included this quote in its coverage of the incident ("Purple Face").[5] A related quote comes directly from Gaga's Twitter: "I'd wear any of my private attire for the world to see. But I would rather have an open flesh wound than ever wear a band aid [sic] in public."[6] The danger of infection is preferred to an interruption of the costume. A Band-Aid, or at least a Band-Aid covering an actual wound, would compromise the performance and thus reduce the value of the body being exchanged. Certainly, Gaga is not the first woman to risk her health for the sake of appearance. Gaga does not rebel against the systems that require women to risk their health in favor of arbitrary standards of appearance; instead, she reveals and revels in their absurdity. She shows that they exist and exist to be transgressed but does not herself violate them.

In Lady Gaga's performance of fame, such risks become if not necessary, then at least a supporting part of an act in which her body serves as the currency with which she purchases both pop stardom and recognition as a performance artist. Risking, or seeming to risk, her health underscores and reveals her willingness to exchange her body. In other words, Gaga's visible willingness to risk the integrity of her body in order to maintain the integrity of her performance situates her body as disposable and thus as an object for exchange. In contrast to those whose bodies are treated as disposable by the global economic system as discussed by Vandana Shiva (5, 45, 63), however, Gaga chooses (or at least seems to choose) disposability and so benefits from the exchanges in which her body is used. Gaga's willing participation subverts exploitative systems that use women's bodies as currency.

Demand for a woman's body as decoration, "art," and a sexual object rises in accord with her ability to meet certain normative beauty standards. As a slender white woman, Gaga, on the one hand, fulfills many of these beauty standards that allow her to appeal to a larger audience of customers. On the other hand, by dressing in costumes that mark her as Other, whether because of their grotesqueness or their appropriation of a subaltern or stigmatized identity, she uses her body as part of a display of alternatives. This enables her to be viewed also as a performance artist; in contrast with the situation of the "image of woman" in patriarchal media described by Laura Mulvey (*Visual* 15), she both bears and makes meaning. That is to say, Lady Gaga makes meaning, and does so in a highly visible way, by transforming her body in order to bear it. When she appears spattered in blood or, as in the "Bad Romance" video covered almost entirely in a white latex outfit reportedly inspired by Max's wolf costume in *Where the Wild Things Are* (Sawdey), she engages in a sort of rebellion against prettiness analogous to what Jeanie Forte describes in "Women's Performance Art: Feminism and Postmodernism":

> Valerie Export, Lydia Lunch, and even [Rachel] Rosenthal have deliberately worked against "pretty" images or conventional aesthetics, frustrating voyeurism, and challenging social conceptions of women as artists. The violence and/or "disgust" factor in these works fuels the exploration of aesthetics as an ideological trap, one which subjugates women in particular but which also dictates the numbed and plastic tastes of dominant culture [268].

Plastic, however, is ubiquitous in Gaga's *outré* costumes, whether they are monstrous or, like her bubble dress (literally) lighter. "Plastic" in the sense of malleable also describes how Gaga performs her body. As Sarah Jaffe, in a startling analysis of the connections between Lady Gaga and twenty-first century American imperialism, describes her, "she is blonde and thin and scantily clad — American as blonde-apple-pie — but also consciously twists and misshapes her body, slathers on makeup and impossible shoes, adds oversized eyes and a protruding spine. She's a female-to-female drag queen, playing with the artifice of Western femininity, showing it for the performance it is, showing the ugliness just below the surface" ("Lady Gaga: Pop Star for a Country and an Empire in Decline"). The plasticity of Gaga's performativity, that is to say, allows her to revolt against prettiness while also benefiting from it — and through this paradoxical performance, she purchases her position as both a popular and a performance artist.

Lady Gaga's fulfillment of mainstream beauty standards and her transgressions against prettiness do not, in fact, conflict. Her ability to exchange her performance of her body for a position suspended between pop and performance art is not as simple as embodying certain qualities that purchase a place in the former and other qualities that purchase a place in the latter. At times, the two sets of performed qualities interact and strengthen the value of each other as currency; on other occasions, the boundaries between them blur. In the resulting grey zone, extreme decorativeness (such as the costume about which Paglia complains) becomes, if not necessarily grotesque, then at least out of line with mainstream aesthetic standards. By maintaining her exaggerated performance of femininity across contexts, Gaga resists the historical tendencies which Mary Garrard has pointed out: "Why is our history ... full of virtuous reversals in which a virile, heroic, or austere style suddenly and dramatically replaces a feminine, lyrical, or luxurious one — David over Fragonard, Caravaggio over Salviati, clean international Modern Gropius over wickedly ornamental Sullivan or Tiffany?" (60). Wickedly ornamental, Lady Gaga's beauty also becomes her ugliness and a sign of engagement in conflict with the history of art, precisely the sort of subversive engagement one expects from a performance artist.

Moreover, to the extent that Gaga's decorativeness meets the demands of normative beauty, the performative aspect of her grotesque costumes becomes more apparent. It becomes clear that she puts on the grotesque rather than being inherently grotesque; her audience of customers can more easily conceptualize (purchase) her grotesquery as a consciously artistic act. Beth Ditto, who openly displays a body considered grotesque because of its fatness, is not considered a performance artist. When Lady Gaga wears video glasses or dances robotically, she comes across as a beautiful woman who plays the cyborg rather than as someone who is a cyborg or who hides her lack of beauty behind technological apparati. She similarly puts on stigmatized identities. In the video for "Paparazzi," she performs disability — cripface — but the speed with which she moves from having to be lifted and placed into a wheelchair to using crutches, along with intercut shots of an apparently able-bodied Lady Gaga rolling around and dancing on a sofa, makes evident that it is only performance, even within the world of the video itself. As Anna Hamilton observes in a blog post for *Bitch Magazine,* "Gaga's disability in this video is temporary, and it's clear that we as viewers are supposed to know that" ("The Transcontinental Disability Choir: Disabililty Chic?").[7] We are also supposed to perceive it as play-acting, something Gaga only engages in within the video world. The perception of Lady Gaga as able-bodied and as normatively attractive remains unaltered, and her performance of disability comes to seem artful in a way that, problematically, would not be available to a woman with actual disabilities. While women with disabilities can and often must make their disabilities part of their art, they cannot make a conscious artistic choice to perform their disability *per se.*[8] Thus, the status and exchange value of a performance that may on the surface seem to subvert the expectations of pop culture regarding women's bodies nonetheless relies on the persistence of a non-transgressive aspect of Gaga's identity.

The choreography of this scene also makes apparent the extent to which whiteness, an aspect of Lady Gaga's fulfillment of mainstream beauty standards, must be performed. The performers playing the role of hired help who lift her from her limousine into her wheelchair and then dance around her as she transitions from wheelchair to crutches are all men of color (though the women who join during the crutch portion include at least one white woman). Their presence contrasts with her Whiteness and so defines it. As Anna Hamilton points out,

Without question, Gaga's "assistants" in this video are amazing dancers; however, save for a few seconds, viewers are not supposed to focus on them. The privileged white woman, of course, is the focus of this video, and people of color are reduced to little more than dancing window-dressing who help Gaga with her "recovery." Given the long history of widespread exploitation of the labor of people of color — in both the public and private spheres — this representation is not particularly transgressive ["The Transcontinental Disability Choir: Disabililty Chic?"].

It might not be transgressive, but it is representative: for Lady Gaga to perform the white womanhood that constitutes part of her normative beauty and thus facilitates her purchase of the position of pop stardom, the performances of people of color must be present, but only in the background and for contrast. Whiteness, that is to say, only exists in contradistinction to people of color, as is suggested by Toni Morrison's argument that the "Africanist character" has been used as "the vehicle by which the [white] American self knows itself as not enslaved, but free; not repulsive but desirable; not helpless, but licensed and powerful" (51–52). There is, however, a striking and problematic similarity between Gaga's use of people of color as backup dancers and (in the video's storyline) servants to display this dynamic and the use of women of color by certain white feminist theorists, as described by Margaret Homans, to justify and add a sense of embodiment to their theories without making their theories relevant or accountable to these women's lives (414). What, it may be asked, is learned about the realities that Gaga's backup dancers face, other than the reality of how they relate to her? Indeed, even this reality is only depicted to a limited degree as the audience never sees how Gaga (or her whiteness) looks through the eyes of her helpers though, as bell hooks points out, "black folks have, from slavery on, shared in conversations with one another 'special' knowledge of whiteness gleaned from close scrutiny of white people.... For years, black domestic servants, working in white homes, acting as informants, brought knowledge back to segregated communities — details, facts, observations, and psychoanalytic reading the white Other" (165). Gaga, for all her outlandish costumes, fails to fully engage this racial Other.

It may also be asked whether the "Paparazzi" music video makes these dynamics apparent by going beyond what is necessary to simply perform whiteness. Certainly, viewers who are already aware of such racial issues and actively engaged in analyzing the media instead of watching passively will notice them. The backup dancers also vogue, an action often appropriated from black gay culture (Lawrence 46–47) by white performers, most notably Madonna (Buckland xix, Dodds 255–56, and Patton *passim*). For an audience familiar with this history, their dancing can serve as a citation. Viewers who are not aware of such issues, however, will most likely not see this or any of the racial dynamics in the display. In the "LoveGame" music video, these dynamics may become a bit more clear to a general audience; as she dances through the New York subway system and a parking garage, Gaga is surrounded primarily (and at times exclusively) by men of color. Though at times they appear to surround her in a threatening manner, she ultimately seems to enjoy their attention and to be in control, whether or not she is wielding the almost parodically phallic disco stick. She meets their gaze with her own powerful and desiring gaze; she is an erotic object not only for the other characters in the videos and for the viewing audience (Mulvey, *Visual* 19) but also for herself. She hangs from a bar in a subway car in order to have the pleasure of lowering herself into their arms. This reversal draws attention to stereotypes of men of color victimizing a white woman, particularly given the addition of scene in which police officers arrest the backup dancers, as if they were in fact a threat, and Gaga makes out with an officer who shifts gender from shot to shot, as if she is grateful for being saved. She performs grateful "rescued" white womanhood, though no real threat existed. The construction of men of color as a threat is shown at once to be false and to contribute to the construction of white womanhood as threatened and fragile femininity in need of saving.[9] On the other hand, it does need to be acknowledged that whiteness, as personified by Gaga, remains central throughout this critique and that, as bell hooks has observed, discussions of race that make whiteness and particularly its socially constructed desirability central are themselves reflective of white supremacy (9–10) and thus neither subversive nor transgressive in terms of race.

Lady Gaga's blondeness also forms a part of her racial identity. Stefani Germanotta was not a blonde, nor was early Gaga. Gaga's blondeness is a performance with certain similarities to Mulvey's description of Marilyn Monroe: "Marilyn's image is an ethnic image; her extreme whiteness, her makeup, her peroxide blonde hair bear witness to fetishization of race. But its cosmetic, artificial character also bears witness to an element of masquerade. Her image triumphantly creates a spectacle that holds the eye and distracts it from what should not be seen" (*Fetishism* 48).[10] Gaga, however, makes the artifice of her blonde-whiteness more explicit. Her literal hair bows — bows made from hair — draw attention to hair as a made, or at least arranged, object.[11] The specific shades of hair she displays through the use of dye and wigs also draw attention to its artificiality. At times, as in the "Telephone" video and on the red carpet for the 2010 Grammy Awards, she wears a wig in a yellow shade reminiscent of the way blondeness is represented in cartoons, which draws attention specifically to the artificiality of her hair's color. She has also appeared in public with hair that mixes platinum tones with violet often enough that the wax figure of her in the Amsterdam Madam Tussaud's exhibits this particular combination. Purple dye, toner, or shampoo is often used to prevent hair dyed platinum blonde from turning orange or brassy, so wearing these colors together draws attention to the fabrication of Gaga's blondeness. Performing, as she sometimes does, with her hair "meticulously bleached so that even the nosebleed seats can see her dark roots showing" ("Lady Gaga Spanks the Planet: She's a Free Bitch, Baby") has the same effect. In an age when thoroughly unnatural hair colors are common enough to go unremarked, maintaining at least a reference to natural or plausibly natural colors does more to emphasize the artifice of hair than pure neon locks ever could. To the extent that a blonde woman is located at the pinnacle of white womanhood, moreover, Gaga's visible performance of blondeness further reveals the constructed nature of whiteness, and this sort of revelation works toward dismantling both racial essentialism and the unmarked nature of the very whiteness which raises her body's value as an object of exchange.[12] Once again, Gaga's performance threatens to subvert the mechanisms that enable the purchase of fame that provides her performance with a large audience.

Gaga has also drawn attention to the effort and restrictions required to maintain the slenderness that similarly helps her to exchange her performance of her body for fame and artistic status while threatening to subvert the standards that allow this exchange to take place. Questioned on the subject, she has claimed that "Pop stars should not eat" (qtd. in Grigoriadis), "It's all about starvation! Pop stars don't eat" (qtd. in Miller), and "I'm on a very strict healthy pop star diet. I don't eat bread, just vegetables and salad and fish. Eating like that is much better for me anyway but on Sundays I sometimes eat pasta" ("Extravagant Lady Gaga Broke, Homeless"). Whatever the truth may be with regard to Gaga's dietary habits, all three quotations describe the regime by which she shapes her body as part of her performance of the pop star role. If she does not eat, it is because pop stars do not or should not eat. If she follows a "healthy" diet, it is one specific to pop stars. Eating forms part of her star formation: it is another performance. The act of making the performative aspect of her normative beauty apparent underlies Lady Gaga's position as a performance artist. By revealing the ways in which her appearance is a performance, her efforts to meet mainstream beauty standards contribute to her ability to purchase not only her position as a pop star but also her claim to being a performance artist.

As a performance artist and a pop star, Lady Gaga not only combines that which attracts and that which repels, but also makes clear that both aspects of her appearance are performed and artificial. Both beauty and ugliness — as she performs them — strengthen each other and her position as a celebrity musician and performance artist. Designer Gary Card, who designed the headpieces Gaga and her backup dancers wore for the 2009 MTV Video Music Awards, calls her "a really interesting bridge between the desirable and the grotesque. She's not at all worried about looking ridiculous or hideous; actually, I think she thrives off it" (qtd. in "Frank Talk with Lady Gaga"). If a single image were to stand for Gaga's duality in this regard, it would have to be the raw meat dress she wore at the 2010 MTV Video Music Awards. By wearing this outfit, she invited people to consider her, literally, as a piece of meat, an object for which one hungers. At the same time, the tendency of raw red meat to harbor microbes makes it repulsive. The meat dress thus makes the repulsive desirable and the desired object also horrifying.

The Fame Monster makes her position as simultaneously desirable and horrifying even more explicit. To a certain degree, the songs on her first studio album, *The Fame*, represent desirability, while the eight newer songs are more troubled and troubling, as Gaga herself noted in a press release: "On my re-release *The Fame Monster*, I wrote about everything I didn't write on *The Fame*. While traveling the world for two years, I've encountered several monsters, each represented by a different song on the new record: my 'Fear of Sex Monster,' my 'Fear of Alcohol Monster,' my 'Fear of Love Monster,' my 'Fear of Death Monster,' my 'Fear of Loneliness Monster,' etc." (qtd. in "Interscope Records"). According to Rosi Braidotti, "If we define the monster as a bodily entity that is anomalous *vis-à-vis* the norm, then we can argue that the female body shares with the monster the privilege of bringing out a unique blend of *fascination and horror*" (81). Gaga's performance of pop stardom then is also a performance of the female body and (white) womanhood that makes such monstrosity apparent in seemingly transgressive fashion.

Still, this (monstrous, white) womanhood sells and is crafted to sell; her performance of gender, even when it seems subversive or transgressive, is thoroughly commodified. It is also revelatory of that commodification: as a performance artist working through the medium of pop celebrity, she makes explicit Yvonne Tasker's description of stardom: "The star functions as commodity, as signifying system, as fetish object and, to some extent, as the space of a narcissistic identification on the part of audiences" (181). Gaga persistently draws attention to her body as a commodity through her songs' lyrics and videos, as well as through the images with which her albums are packaged. "Poker Face" is one of the more obvious examples. The overall lyric arc of the song positions her body and sexuality as commodities, specifically ones she can use to gamble.

"Beautiful, Dirty, Rich" carries this commodification further, combing Gaga's normatively beautiful body with cash and wealth in its lyrics, in the imagery of its video, and in the cover image of the single. The title is repeated throughout, often with "and" following "beautiful," throwing "beautiful" and "rich" into close proximity and association, though the singer also claims to have no money. For both to be true requires that something else function as wealth. The aforementioned proximity of "beautiful" and "rich" suggests that beauty — that is to say, the normatively attractive and able white female body — can fill the gap. This body — Lady Gaga's body — in the video rolls around on a table spread with paper currency. Her body literally becomes part of the pile of cash. Her costume, a hooded red bodysuit with a gold belt, together with the sexually suggestive poses she strikes on the table (including arching her back) remind the audience that her body is commodified particularly in its performance of sexuality. The cover for the single echoes this imagery, showing Gaga in the same costume, with her head tilted back and lips parted, while paper money falls around her.

More dramatically, in the "Bad Romance" video, which Gaga has said shows "how the entertainment industry can, in a metaphorical way, simulate human trafficking — products being sold, the woman perceived as a commodity" (qtd. in Powers), she performs a sexualized dance before a group of men while, on computer screens throughout the room, bids for Lady Gaga appear. As Gaga described the scene that precedes the auction to *MTV News*, "There's this one shot in the video where I get kidnapped by supermodels. I'm washing away my sins and they shove vodka down my throat to drug me up before they sell me off to the Russian mafia" (qtd. in "Lady Gaga Says 'Bad Romance' Video Is About 'Tough Female Spirit'"). The role of the supermodels in particular suggests how this scene functions as an allegory for the fame system's commodification of the female star's body. The use of force may seem out of place. After all, no one literally forced Germanotta to become Lady Gaga in the pursuit of fame. An argument could be made about the coercive power of a culture that (over)values celebrity to create a desire for fame, and certainly such an argument would fit well with the concerns behind Gaga's performances. What may be more to the point, however, is precisely how little power over the celebrity system, and the broader systems in which it is enmeshed, stars have in Gaga's analysis. Consider her statement at the Phoenix performance of *The Monster Ball Tour*: "I got a phone call from a couple really big rock and rollers, big pop stars, big rappers, and they said, 'We'd like you to boycott Arizona because of SB 1070.' And I said, "Do you really think that us dumb fucking pop stars are going to collapse the economy of Arizona?"" (qtd. in "Lady Gaga Protests Arizona Immigration Law in Phoenix"). However one evaluates the degree of choice celebrities have in choosing their roles, once in those positions, they essentially become captives of system(s) that they can neither control nor act directly to subvert, at least according to Gaga, though they can protest, as Gaga noted that she had intended to do at the very same concert.

The auction scene in "Bad Romance" also connects the celebrity system to broader economic systems and implicates the audience in these systems. Product placements (Nemiroff vodka and Hewlett Packard's "Beats" laptop) in the auction scene connect the in-video sale of her body to the literal sales that fuel popular music; by doing so, these placements connect the figurative selling of the celebrity body for fame to the more-literal sales that make celebrity a facet of present-day capitalism. The camera angles, at times, place the viewer in the position of the male potential buyers while, at other times, they provide a broader view. The audience for the video, then, is not only implicated as purchasers or potential purchasers of Lady Gaga's body but also given the opportunity to view the process from a seemingly more objective position; they are invited to participate in the male gaze and to become aware of it. Though Mulvey's 1975 article "Visual Pleasure and Narrative Cinema" sought to use analysis to destroy the male gaze as an experience of pleasure (15–16), Gaga's video seems to suggest that it can be understood and enjoyed at the same time. She sells her body's appearance and performance while also drawing attention to the way in which pop stars' bodies are sold. She is selling both her body and her performance art about the commodification of the body, but doing so in a way that denies pleasure to the audience would detract from her ability to make these sales.

The "Telephone" music video makes clear that the exchanges in which Gaga participates are conducted not only for fame but also, ultimately, for money. By making the product placements excessive and obvious, she makes it impossible for the viewer to ignore them. Brands that appear include: Heartbeats headphones, Viktor and Rolf, Chanel, Diet Coke, Polaroid, Virgin, Miracle Whip, Wonder Bread, and Plenty of Fish. At times, these placements are clearly designed to be noticed and exposed as advertising. The camera lingers on the Virgin phone while Lady Gaga is kissing, fondling, and being fondling by two other prisoners in the yard, thus linking the sexualized body to product placement and economic exchange. When poison receives the same treatment accorded the more legitimate brands, it lays bare the ugliness of these exchanges, yet even this transgression does not subvert the system to an extent that would endanger Gaga's income.

Selling her body for fame and in order to be in a position to promote real brands remains an essential component of Lady Gaga's star formation. What exactly is being sold in these transactions, however, is called into question by the way Lady Gaga's body shifts. To identify these changes and how they create temporary and conflicting ideas of identity is not to say that she escapes identification entirely. Indeed, Judith Butler made the following observation in "Against Proper Objects":

> The normative weight of gender is not suddenly thrown off at the moment in which we imagine ourselves to be fully identified with what we do. On the contrary, it is precisely our sense of gender that is disoriented through such practices: the possibility of reworking normative gender categories is part of the pleasure and

danger of such acts. Although we may posit the heuristic possibility of a world in which acts and identities would be fully separable, it still remains for us to describe what it might mean to live that very separation [3].

Lady Gaga's body consistently maintains its links to white womanhood, ability, and femininity, but what those identities mean and can mean becomes troubled as the terms used to describe her physical self-change from appearance to appearance and within individual appearances themselves. As a result, what it means to sell those identities also becomes disoriented. Her wigs and costumes allow the shape of her body to change, sometimes in a way that does little to challenge the boundaries of identity, as when she appears with absurdly oversized shoulder pads and at other times more dramatically, as when one of the red crosses on her white habit in the "Alejandro" video suggests by its position and shape the possession of a penis. Also, as mentioned previously, Gaga at times takes on different identities, such as disability, but only temporarily.

Indeed, sometimes multiple and conflicting identities appear simultaneously. Most often such paradoxes occur in the contrast between visual aspects of a performance and the lyrics of the song. In her AOL sessions performance of "Paparazzi," as she sings lyrics that are essentially about stalking a star whether as a paparazza or a less culturally authorized figure, she also appears to be terrified and attempting to hide.[13] Such a performance brings out the seeming paradox inherent in a star singing in the voice of a photographer or celebrity stalker. It also collapses the narrative of the official video for the song, in which her body moves from that of an abused partner (when her lover pushes her off a balcony) to that of the abuser (when she poisons him in turn). The "Telephone" music video also includes discord between the body that the lyrics indicate and that which the visual information indicates. She starts out with the stigmatized and abused body of a prisoner, stripped by guards who want to confirm her biological sex, and she is still imprisoned when she begins singing, but she is singing about being in a club and not being able to hear her boyfriend on the phone because of how loud it is on the dance floor. Gaga simultaneously performs the stigmatized and fetishized body of a suspected transgender woman in prison and the more-privileged body of a woman who wants her boyfriend to stop interrupting her night out with her girlfriends. Simultaneously with both these performances, she is continuing to perform her star image, though "Telephone" makes this element far less obvious than "Paparazzi."

As Nancy Bauer observes, "There is nobody like Lady Gaga in part because she keeps us guessing about who she, as a woman, really is. She has been praised for using her music and videos to raise this question and to confound the usual exploitative answers provided by 'the media'" ("Lady Power").

This sort of praise suggests that the fluidity of her bodily performance contributes to her ability to purchase her position as a performance artist who performs her status as a celebrity. So long as she keeps us guessing about her body, we cannot easily define what it is she sells when she sells this performance of her body, but is that uncertainty enough to subvert the systems and exchanges she uses and reveals?

Rosi Braidotti has argued that "[t]he woman's body can change shape in pregnancy and childbearing; it is therefore capable of defeating the notion of fixed *bodily* form, of visible, recognizable, clear, and distinct shapes as that which marks the contour of the body" (79). Lady Gaga's performances expand this notion beyond the area of literal childbearing and beyond the physically visible. By becoming or performing *woman* in multiple other forms, she defeats the idea of fixed bodily form without undergoing pregnancy, and thus she does so without the implied necessity of the participation of a biological male. Indeed, Lady Gaga often makes reference to being celibate and, in an interview with *Vanity Fair,* she said "I have this weird thing that if I sleep with someone, they're going to take my creativity from me through my vagina" ("Lady Gaga On Sex, Fame, Drugs, and Her Fans"). This fear suggests that her avoidance of fixed form has more in common with adolescence than with childbearing, yet rather than fear the changes, she embraces and directs them: it is no wonder she has so many adolescent girls among her fans.

Lady Gaga does not describe her relationship with such fans as one between peers, however. Indeed, it is within the bounds of this relationship that it becomes clear that Lady Gaga also appropriates motherhood, without the sexual involvement of a man into her act (unless, perhaps, that man is also herself, as the introduction of Jo Calderone as a sexual partner for Gaga suggests). She refers to her fans as "Little Monsters" and herself as "Mother Monster." While the name Madonna through its reference to the Virgin Mary alludes to motherhood without sex, Lady Gaga makes the concept integral to her identity and relationship with her fans. Her version of motherhood is entangled in her alternative generativity, her production of an art which emphasizes her own monstrosity. In this way, her use of motherhood reclaims childbirth metaphors for creativity from male artists, but in a way that emphasizes relationships and connections over personal power and which literally embodies aspects of motherhood, such as the shifting body, that male artists have typically ignored.

If such celebration of monstrosity seems transgressive or subversive, however, it should be recalled not only that her embrace of this position contributes to her purchase of a position as pop star and performance artist but also that she often associates monstrosity with mainstream values and institutions. These include the very normative standards of beauty that facilitate

Gaga's purchase of her star position. As Robin James points out, "'Dance in the Dark' emphasizes the grotesque and debilitating effects that the performance of heteropatriarchial constructions of femaleness and femininity has on women's bodies and psyches. The first lines of the song describe the normatively desirable and 'sexy' female body as the 'monster' created by a Frankenstein-esque beauty industrial complex" ("From Dance in the Dark, Little Monsters: On Gaga's Post–Goth Posthumanism"). Similarly, it is no accident that the plasticized monsters of the "Bad Romance" video emerge from what appear to be tanning beds in a bathhouse; the demands of normative beauty create shape-shifting monsters.

More important still in Gaga's *œuvre* is *The Fame Monster*: the phrase serves not only as an album title but also as a description for the dangers of fame itself. This is the same fame which, as her work makes explicit, she purchases with her body in an economic transaction only available to individuals with certain traits. As her videos make clear, only bodies invested with certain degrees of social power, and with the willingness to use that power on other people, can purchase this particular monster. In "Paparazzi," newspaper headlines show Gaga losing status when she is injured and made disabled by her boyfriend and regaining her status when, recovered, she reclaims power by murdering him. Indeed, he throws her off the balcony while playing to the cameras of the paparazzi who play a part in and, in this scene represent, systems of celebrity and fame; he even yells at her (in Swedish) to "[l]ook into the camera," instructing her to use her gaze to serve the desires of the men behind the lenses and the audience they serve. These men, in turn, photograph her prone body in a puddle of blood while calling it "beautiful." In the system within which pop stardom lives and from which Gaga benefits, the products of violence aestheticize and titillate. The photographers, presumably, gain status and career success by documenting violence for these purposes. At the same time, the injunction to look into the camera implicates the cameras recording the video and the pleasure the video's audience takes in viewing the violence of its narrative. Similarly, in "Telephone" the spree killing committed by Lady Gaga and Beyoncé in the diner is followed by a news broadcast about them, evidence of publicity and increased fame. After the murders, moreover, Gaga and Beyoncé appear in American-flag-patterned costumes with backup dancers in matching costumes. Murder makes them all–American girls who are at the center of their social formations: they literally and symbolically lead the dance. Those with higher social status kill, and those who kill gain higher social status. Fame, as an institution, is depicted as both feeding on violence and feeding into it.

If there is transgression here, it resembles the "inverse transgression" which Keith M. Booker identifies as existing in the work of James Joyce, as it "reveal[s] ... the violence and depravity that lie at the heart of certain specific social and political institutions and practices in modern society" (58). That the weapons in the "Alejandro" video belong to uniformed soldiers rather than to rebels underscores how Lady Gaga shows violence to be the domain of the powerful — here, the state, but also, the same racial identity that helps her to meet mainstream beauty standards. As Sarah Jaffe argues, "[s]he's made whiteness itself into an army (in a song where she fetishizes a Spanish-named boy with the crude line 'hot like Mexico')" ("Lady Gaga: Pop Star for a Country and an Empire in Decline"). Jaffe further notes that "[i]ndiscriminate murder is one of Gaga's themes. She reminds us that American culture is drenched in blood, and she couples those images with constant references to her own fame. She seems to ask with each outrageously violent image: since she is famous, can she do whatever she wants?" Fame, beauty, the state, and the racially privileged are all associated with violence, cruelty, and monstrosity in acts of inverse transgression.[14]

The difference between what Lady Gaga does and what Booker labels inverse transgression, however, is that his definition of the phrase requires a condemnation of the violence. Far from meeting this requirement, Lady Gaga at times performs an identification with violence and encourages her fans to do the same. She said in an interview, "I want women — and men — to feel empowered by a deeper and more psychotic part of themselves. The part they're always trying desperately to hide. I want that to become something that they cherish" (qtd. in "Frank Talk with Lady Gaga"). She starts the "Bad Romance" video wearing razor-blade sunglasses. As she describes the creative logic behind them, she invokes as admirable a sort of female strength that is, at least potentially, cruel and violent:

> I wanted to design a pair for some of the toughest chicks and some of my girl-friends — don't do this at home! — They used to keep razor blades in the side of their mouths.... That tough female sprit is something that I want to project. It's meant to be, "This is my shield, this is my weapon, this is my inner sense of fame, this is my monster" [qtd. in "Lady Gaga Says 'Bad Romance' Video Is About 'Tough Female Spirit'"].

In the "Alejandro" video, Gaga herself is enthroned as the ruler of a mil-itaristic regime who dresses in steampunk-inspired fashions and manages to maintain her perfect red lipstick whether watching her soldiers practice wrestling or leading a funeral procession. If the shadows and limited color palette of the visuals imply dystopia, it is still a sexualized dystopia.

Indeed, the results of violence often become beautiful in Gaga's work. Both "Paparazzi" and its sequel "Telephone" reproduce an aestheticization by camera of injury and death. In the first video, in addition to the aesthetic pleasure the photographers take in capturing Gaga's bloodied body in their frames, the main narrative is interspersed with shots of beautiful dead women artfully arranged. These women also appear to wear designer clothes. In the second, the deaths of the patrons in the diner are choreographed, and their final resting positions seem equally artful. Rather than condemn the violence, these videos make it appealing in at least an abstract aesthetic sense. By doing so, Gaga, instead of condemning cruelty, makes it appealing.

In this portrayal of violence as attractive, the limits of subversion within Lady Gaga's self-positioning become clear. If she exposes the violence of the powerful institutions and the economic processes by which a woman's body can be exchanged for fame or other goods both concrete and abstract, she also cannot afford to make those processes unappealing, even when they involve violence or cruelty. To make them entirely unappealing, or to fail to encourage her fans to identify with her no matter what she portrays and performs, would be to lose her audience and thus to lose the status of pop star. Ann Powers notes that, "[i]t's arguable that Gaga could only realize her artistic vision in the center of the pop mainstream" ("Frank Talk with Lady Gaga"). Without that status, she would also lose her ability to make performance art about and out of that position. The exchange would fail.

Nonetheless, the same shifting body that draws into question what precisely is being sold in exchange for pop stardom also draws into question her identification with these processes; she is, after all, at times also the injured body and the body excluded from exchange. "She is both a perfect embodiment of American cultural dominance and subverting what that means at every turn," ("Lady Gaga: Pop Star for a Country and an Empire in Decline") as Sarah Jaffe has argued. Does Lady Gaga overall manifest and glorify or does she reveal and subvert the violence and economics of the fame-system and the larger systems of power and commerce of which it is part? That is not the right question: she, in fact, does both. What she is selling, having used her body and her performance of her body to purchase a position in which she can do so, is a destabilization of categories such as decoration and art, stage and life, pop culture and high culture, celebrity and *avant-garde*, commerce and transgression, victim and perpetrator. Whether this is what her fans, her Little Monsters, are buying, and what they might create in the wake of this disorientation is still being determined, though the numbers of artists and writers inspired by and using Lady Gaga in their work suggests that at least some of them want to do more than "Just Dance."

Notes

1. In contrast with such approaches, see Mulvey's description of Lacan's depiction of sexual difference as leaving woman stranded "within a theory that brilliantly describes the power relationships of the patriarchy but acknowledges no need for escape" (*Visual* 165).

2. For how this distinguishes Gaga from most celebrities, see Vanessa Grigoriadis's discussion of her surprise at finding herself interviewing Lady Gaga rather than Stefani Germanotta, which extends far beyond the issue of what to call her (n. pag.).

3. The following exchange reported by Jonathan Van Meter makes much the same point: "Jimmy Iovine, the chairman of Interscope, actually laughs at me: Whenever I have ridden on a plane with him I have fallen asleep, and apparently I don't move. I sit in my clothes, perfectly still, head straight up, and I just sleep. And then I open my eyes and he's like, 'You scare me the way you sleep.'" It's so perfect, I say, for someone who likes to be.... "Poised? As much as possible?" (570)

4. Germanotta's wholesale transformation into Lady Gaga makes the use of her music in two episodes of *Dollhouse* particularly appropriate. In the series, people who become "dolls" are made (temporarily) into new, different people through cognitive imprinting. At the end of a five-year contract, the "dolls" are given back their original imprints along with substantial sums of money. They exchange their selves and bodies (temporarily) for wealth just as Gaga engages in an exchange for wealth and fame.

5. Also, only a few months later, Gaga told a fan that, on planes, "I sleep in all my glamorous glory!" (Interview with Lady Gaga, *In Camera,* n. pag.).

6. Tweet sent on October 20, 2010 at 10:39 P.M.

7. Interestingly, one of the few things Hamilton appreciates about this portrayal of disability is one of the things Camille Paglia mocks. "As someone who uses a cane, witnessing Lady Gaga's use of shiny silver arm crutches in this sequence makes me wonder if there might be a market for crunk canes (à la the Crunk Cup)," writes Hamilton. Paglia, on the other hand, dismisses these props as "jewelled parody crutches."

8. For an example of how disabled artists integrate their limitations into their work, see the Colors 'N' Motion Dancers and the Axis Dance Company.

9. On the relationship between whiteness and the myth of the Black rapist, see Dowd Hall *passim.*

10. See also hooks' argument that "the obsession to have white women film stars be ultra-white was a cinematic practice that sought to maintain a distance, a separation between that image and the black female Other; it was a way perpetuate white supremacy" (119).

11. D.A. Wallach, who toured with Gaga in 2008 stated that "[o]ne of the first things I remember is her making bows out of wig hair" (Steele et al. 18).

12. Gaga, however, also points to the less advantageous side of this pinnacle position, addressing a list of blonde women who met tragic ends in "Dance in the Dark," beginning with Marilyn Monroe and ending with JonBenét Ramsey.

13. See "Lady Gaga–Paparazzi (AOL Sessions)" on YouTube.com.

14. To the extent that Lady Gaga's work displays this quality, it is particularly fitting that Private First Class Bradley Manning used Lady Gaga CDs to carry away the files he would eventually turn over to Wikileaks; his actions, though more directly than her art, have revealed the cruelty and brutality of powerful contemporary institutions.

Body Language and "Bad Romance"

The Visual Rhetoric of the Artist

JENNIFER M. SANTOS

Lady Gaga's smash hit music video for "Bad Romance"—one of the three contributing to her honor as the first artist with one billion online video views—debuted to rave reviews in the entertainment community, from *Rolling Stone* and *MTV* to *Entertainment Weekly* and *E!*.[1] Indeed, *Rolling Stone* even compared her latest work to Stanley Kubrick and Andy Warhol.[2] But, like much of Gaga's work, "Bad Romance" has also engendered controversy, drawing attention for its disturbing depiction of the female form, seen by some as championing the unnaturally, unhealthily-thin anorectic body. In the most extreme scenes, Gaga's isolated figure seems nearly alien in its skeletal protrusions, with vertebrae so exaggeratedly large that they threaten to puncture the papery layer of skin stretched over them, taking on a nearly-exoskeletal life of their own. In other scenes, her spine and ribs protrude from beneath white latex, connoting, to some, a skeleton—not a person—beneath the skin-tight encasement. In light of these freeze frames, members of the blogging community took Gaga to task only two days after the video's release: *Female-First* chastised the pop star for "setting the wrong example" to "young girls who thing [sic] she's the bee's knees" and, in doing so, joined a conversation about the effect of anorexic representations, like those surrounding Ivonne Thein's earlier (2009) "Thirty-Two Kilos" exhibit, which presents a series of photographs digitally manipulated to amplify models' already dangerously skeletal physiognomies (Ruth).[3] Unlike "Thirty-Two Kilos," "Bad Romance's" combination of narrative contradictions and juxtapositions of varied body types present a critique of the anorexic body that redirects attention to the root causes of anorexia: the realm of the psyche in tandem with the realm of patriarchal sociocultural conformity. Ultimately, I contend that Gaga's "Bad Romance," rather than valorizing the anorexic body, provides a compelling critique of the social and psychological factors that inform body dysmorphia and the more pervasive, insidious patriarchal discourse that makes desirable the eating-disordered bodies that suppress female self-actualization in favor of fulfilling male fantasy.[4]

Beastly Bodies: Visualizing Anorexia

Body dysmorphia — an unrealistic and inaccurate perception of one's own size, often trending towards a self-image of skeletal women perceiving themselves to be "fat" — is one of the many symptoms accompanying anorexia and other eating disorders, which are characterized in the public eye as a relentless drive towards thinness. The psychological community, however, acknowledges that "anorexia is complex and multidetermined, and foils attempts at one-dimensional explanation" (Woody 150). Multidimensional in both its symptoms and its origins, body dysmorphia and the eating disorders that accompany it — most recognizably anorexia nervosa and bulimia nervosa — rarely involve pure physicality, and, increasingly, are recognized as related to the very "bad romances" of interpersonal relationships exemplified by Gaga's hit video: Gaga's exploration of self and Other reflects a burgeoning dimension of eating disordered research.[5] In fact, psychological studies in the first decade of the twenty-first century show that the social "disturbances" once thought to be symptomatic of eating disorders are precipitating causes as well as symptoms: Elizabeth A. Reilly identifies "stresses in close relationships [as] the most common factor *before* onset" of eating-disordered symptoms (378, my emphasis).[6] Increasingly recognizing a social context for eating disorders like anorexia, researchers situate body image issues, along with its related causes and effects, as Mandi Newton and her research team does, "within a socially constructed world," painting a picture of eating disorders that combines biological predisposition with individual and social experiences.[7] The result of the tension between self (internal factors) and the Other (both interpersonal relationships and the sociocultural context that lays the groundwork for those interpersonal relationships) offers a breeding ground for the "monstrous bodies" that have become, as Masud Khan predicted in Twiggy's era, "the typical ailment of our generation" (qtd. in Reilly 375).[8] The result is a sense of the physical self that is monstrous in its dysmorphia, much as extreme cases of anorexia are monstrous in their skeletal thinness.

This monstrosity has resulted in media attention — from news stories to email forwards — that highlight the differences between media stars (especially fashion models) and the average, healthy woman.[9] Often pointing to popular images, like Mattel's Barbie, as emblematic of an undesirable ideal, public interest pieces caution against Western idealizations of beauty that socializes its women to strive endlessly towards a nearly-unattainable ideal in the interests of male fantasy, a fantasy that women, too, internalize as their own.[10] In this view, a happy by-product of perpetual pressure to starve is the helpless woman, quite literally weak and powerless, while the man, like Barbie's mate, Ken, remains virile and powerful.[11] In other words, the relentless trend of "thin-is-in" glorifies "helpless" women and the skeletal models that represent helplessness as an ideal valorized by men and women alike, a trend that Ivonne Thein attempts to expose in all its horrors by showcasing Photoshopped, ultrathin models in exaggerated poses and *haute couture* in her "Thirty-Two Kilos" exhibit. Thein's embrace of the visual rhetoric of the fashion industry (itself representative of a hegemonic patriarchal power structure, established and furthered by men and embraced by women, linking capitalistic culture and female objectification) is meant to be "a critique of the fashion industry and not just weight loss," explains Smithsonian curator Al Miner.[12] Indeed, Thein vehemently disavows the "glamoriz[ation]" anorexia.[13] Yet her choice to avail herself of a static photographic medium associated with an objectifying male gaze has been critiqued as supplying poisonous fodder for the growing community of individuals who celebrate anorexia as a lifestyle choice, self-styled "pro-anas" who themselves resignify Thein's cautionary exhibit as "thin-spiration." Bombarded already with static media images of skeletal models, these viewers and their less-extreme counterparts, so Thein's critics argue, are socialized to see the anorexic body, in all its weakness, as beautiful rather than horrifying. Monsters masquerade as mavens, and those monstrous mavens cultivate relationships with self and Other around eating disorders to such an extent that a common practice of treatment is to encourage patients to name their eating disorders — often "ED"— as a means of disassociating the self from the relationship fostered with the monstrous.[14] Naming ED, such therapists suggest, separates the maven from her monster.

Just as Thein's exhibit may be seen as marrying the maven to the monstrous, one might see Gaga's public persona — and larger *œuvre*— as celebrating such monstrous mavens. After all, Gaga adopts the affectionate appellation "Little Monsters" for her fans, titles her second album *The Fame Monster,* and centers the elaborate narrative of her latest tour around "The Monster Ball." In concert with behavior characterized by naysayers as attention-seeking, Gaga's "monstrosity" might be likened to what Laura Mulvey has identified as a cinematic reification of a gender narrative in which the woman's role is conflated with the "traditional exhibitionist role," where, argues Mulvey, "women are simultaneously looked at and displayed, with their appearance coded for strong visual and erotic impact so that they can be said to connote *to-be-looked-at-ness*" (11). This "to-be-looked-at-ness," a byproduct of male fantasy, reinforces the role of the female body, inseparable from the patriarchal culture that fashions it, as an object that makes normative monstrous bodies as part of a male-centric, female-subordinate narrative embraced by both genders. Yet Gaga's exhibitionism fundamentally flies in the face of normative trends by celebrating difference and deviance rather than likeness and conformity: it almost seems redundant at this stage of Gaga's celebrity status to note her non-normative stance on sexual identity — celebrating LGBTQ — and "freaks" in general.[15] Her representation of monsters, then, paradoxically draws upon recognizable "freaks": in "Bad Romance," costuming, set-design, and choreography recall "Frankensteinian images of creation," vampiric coffins, and claw-like hand movements. From one perspective, these recognizable monsters and their celebration, placed in proximity with scenes of Gaga's own (digitally-manipulated) skeletal thinness, may be read as a valorization of monstrous bodies, a celebration of a body so emaciated that it becomes more (or less) than human: indeed, Gaga's debt to the liberating monsters of Michael Jackson's "Thriller" could well connect a sense of that same liberation with the anorexic body, a freedom from the limits of "ordinary" human constraints.

But from another perspective, one that draws upon the "screen literacy" of her audience and Gaga's own changes to familiar visual themes, presents and represents the female body as part of a self-embroiled in the struggle to negotiate self-actualized individuality while mired in a culture of patriarchal normativity. As *The New York Times* observes, *The Monster Ball Tour* hearkens back to the monsters of "Thriller" with a very different aim than the original: "While the monsters in that classic video are symbols of liberation, Lady Gaga projects something darker than girl power."[16] That "something darker" revolves around a keen awareness of the body as (re)presentational; note that she uses the body's casing, fashion, to "project what [she] want[s] to become," as she tells Anja Cronberg, both in her daily fashion choices and in her music videos and concert tours, where she works with the Haus of Gaga to carefully construct her reinventions of self.[17] Many of these reinventions feature what Ann Powers describes as "physically distorting costumes [which] show that the pursuit of the feminine ideal is far from natural" and far from ideal.[18] Alternately fashioning herself as an *avant-garde femme fatale* and, as critic Daniel O'Brien of *Cracked.com* puts it, "de-eroticizing" a silk nightgown with "mini-helicopter" pads to exaggerate her *gluteus maximus*, Gaga traverses the visual spectrum of the body and monstrosity, establishing a premise of interrogating the very liberation promised by the monsters in "Thriller," the "power" associated with a relationship with ED, and the monstrosity of eating disorders that we will see in "Bad Romance."[19]

Becoming and re-becoming, fashioning and re-fashioning, Gaga's famous visual rhetoric and her *Fame Monster* songs link the monstrous specifically with body dysmorphia as "that something darker."[20] For example, "Dance in the Dark" is, as Gaga explains to *MTV*'s Eric Ditzian, "about a girl who likes to have sex with the lights off, because she's embarrassed about her body. [...] She doesn't want her man to see her naked. She will be free, and she will let her inner animal out, but only when the lights are out" ("Lady Gaga Reveals Real Meaning of 'Dance in the Dark'"). In the darkness, her body no longer matters; or, rather, a male gaze loses the power it so clearly holds over her a type of male fantasy repeatedly playing out patriarchal desires through cinematic representation and narrative (Mulvey 11). Situating darkness as the only way to "liberate" her protagonist, the third-person narrator labels as monstrous "Dance in the Dark's" heroine, dubbing her a "tramp," the very language of subjugation and judgment associated with a male gaze insistent upon an angel/whore dichotomy that seeks to discomfit women's relationship with their sexuality and their bodies. Tellingly, the "liberated" response of "Dance in the Dark's" heroine reveals the extent to which a patriarchal discourse entraps women: experiencing a feeling of liberation only in the dark, the heroine does not escape the male gaze, but more deeply internalizes her experience of it, obeying an urge to hide from the effects it has on the subjective self. Fleeing from the position of object leaves her with a "monstrous" subjectivity (recall that the lyrics label her a "vamp" and a "tramp") that map onto her relationship with her body. The monsters, then, represent her relationship to her body, to her *self*, and to her lover all rolled into one: this "tramp" struggles with her internalization of the socio-psychological complexities lurking within the dark, where monsters breed, by manipulating external circumstances: slaying not the larger monster of the male gaze, but instead her sense of "completeness," her self-actualization, both in her relationship with herself and with her lover.

The Free Bitch: "Bad Romance" as Emancipatory Feminism

The heroine of "Dance in the Dark," distanced from the listener by the third-person lyrics, remains an object of curiosity, the Other so typical of Gothic monstrosities that populate the books and films of popular culture, exploring from a safe distance boundary-bursting non-normative gender and sexuality through such recognizable monstrous bodies as Frankenstein's creature, the Hyde to Dr. Jekyll, Dracula, and various lamia.[21] The monsters, of course, like Gaga's, are meant to be slain in order to re-normalize gender roles and non-threatening bodies, often in the service of "protecting" a helpless heroine from that which lurks in the dark recesses of unrestrained desire and unbridled appetite.[22] The difference for Gaga's "Bad Romance" protagonist, as opposed to her "Dance in the Dark" heroine, is that in "Bad Romance" the protagonist does the slaying: her fire-shooting bra ostensibly indicates that "Bad Romance" is a video articulating the importance of throwing off patriarchal oppression by disrupting the familiar narrative of female captivity (an oppression that can be linked to the anorectic mindset). Certainly, the main plot evokes this narrative of captivity: the heroine, Gaga, is kidnapped by supermodels, forced to drink vodka, and sold to the Russian mafia as a sex slave. Patriarchal parallels seem readily apparent: trafficking in humans makes them objects, commodities, useful only to the extent that they have exchange value — in this case, the exchange is for the male's ability to actualize his self through the female, to fulfill his desire as he evaluates his newest prize, Gaga. Lounging with a glass of vodka as she dances, he wears an expression of *ennui* in his comfort with the *status quo*, content with a narrative that subjugates the female to his wishes. Seemingly, this is a classic case of what Laura Mulvey identifies as a tradition of cinema — based in the pleasures of patriarchy, both in its "fetishistic scopophilia" and "sadistic voyeurism" — that features a repressed, "silent woman still tied to her place as bearer of meaning, not maker of meaning" (14, 7).[23] As a bearer of meaning, Gaga is forcibly stripped, nearly naked, to her physical essence and made to dance for her captors as they assess her value — a monetary value that grows as she becomes complicit in the narrative, no longer sadistically shoved to the front of the dance troupe, but now actively crawling onto the lap of a male captor, erotically gyrating for and on him. It is at this point that her auction price reaches over a million rubles, completing her commodification.[24] Emptied of her own desires and taking on her captor's sense of female meaning, Gaga becomes both an object to be viewed — clad in lingerie and encased in a bubble — and a willing participant in a sadistic male fantasy that slays the male's castration anxiety in her obedience to phallic fantasy. This fantasy "demands a story," a linear narrative propelled by the male to "slay" the castration anxiety made apparent by the very presence of the phallus-less female (14).[25] Yet Gaga confounds the familiar narrative by wresting control away from the male, flaying her captor in a radical rewriting of narrative normativity that rips apart the familiar fantasy.

In so disrupting the familiar fantasy, Gaga undergoes a process created through male expectation in which she alternately resists and conforms to her male captors' desires. Those desires culminate in female self-patrols of physiological "boundaries" of form, shrinking the physiognomy to helpless size as the self likewise shrivels. Nowhere is the male gaze's impact on self and body more apparent than in the scenes of captivity preceding Gaga's actualization of power: in these moments of entrapment, images of Gaga's emaciated form in the bowels of the "Bath Haus of Gaga" flicker across the screen. These images depict an anorexic body alien in its thinness — hunched over, with an enlarged head, protruding vertebrae, and waist leaving little room for the internal organs necessary to life-sustaining digestion; the gloom of Gaga's setting evokes a standard of beauty akin to the predatory Others of *Alien's* Xenomorphs, rather than human women.[26] But as a human woman, she lacks the acidic blood that Xenomorphs use to escape captivity: othered and dehumanized, her physical self remains trapped in a monstrousness associated with the male gaze by virtue of its visual proximity to key parts of a captivity narrative. The first of these images, for example, occurs just over two minutes into the five-minute video, immediately after Gaga has had her final vestiges of agency revoked: she has just been kidnapped, drugged, and stripped. The following thirty seconds witness four subsequent flashes of emaciated isolation, all related to various forced acts (e.g. forcibly stripped by her supermodel captors, violently shoved to the front of the dance troupe) that push her further into the male gaze.[27] In fact, the second iteration of the monstrously skeletal Gaga occurs when she starts to dance with her supermodel kidnappers for her male mafia captors; the third scene, just eleven seconds later, centers on her prominent placement in the male gaze — at the head of the dance troupe. Most compellingly, the final iteration accompanies Gaga's acceptance of normative expectations: the captive Gaga resigns herself to sexually satisfying her captor by giving him a lap dance.[28] The more constraints placed on Gaga, the more scenes of anorectic frailty. This frailty born of a male plot encourages female self-subjugation of body and self by holding up the anorectic body as an ideal born of a trapped self.

Male entrapment of the female maps onto the anorectic body as well as onto the setting where this entrapment is portrayed, recasting that entrapment as only part of a larger narrative of male-inspired self-entrapment of the female. It is not insignificant that these scenes take place in the most constrained of settings — in a shower stall with pipes curving in an enlarged representation of the ribcage that protrudes from exceptionally skeletal bodies. Delimiting the body and its anatomical components, camera angles fixate on *parts* of Gaga's body encased in this image disrupts what Mulvey terms the "illusion of depth demanded by the narrative"; the overarching male narrative is disrupted by the woman-in-peril, so often a prop of male fantasy in both cinema and music videos, through visual effects that heighten the dysmorphically monstrous body (12). The darkness of the Bath Haus, like the darkness of the theater, positions Gaga as self-voyeur, an audience for her own monster movie, who, in the process of looking, witnesses her own destruction, acknowledging that that destruction is both enticing and terrifying, as anorexic patients have described the power of ED.[29] That help-lessness, captured quite literally as she is encased in a bubble, features a lin-gerie-clad Gaga frozen in time and space, incapable of so much as grasping the many gems that hover around her. All the while, the camera circles her, panning her body, as though the audience takes on the role of the mafia mem-bers who lounge in their own encasing (but un-encased) circle around her. Visually, her very self is reduced to her physicality and equated with the many sparkling, but similar gems, from which one could choose. Her objectification is complete; Gaga is nothing more than a collectible. Fittingly, then, the last major representation of anorexia occurs just before Gaga's encasement in this bubble of lingerie and jewels, with one close-up of her face only. In this close-up flash, the body no longer serves as the focal point, and the clearly recog-nizable setting serves as a haunting reminder of the horrors she has endured.

This reminder offers a visual transition between the narrative of norma-tive patriarchal expectation, mapped onto female self-expectation, and the moment of self-liberation from this normative narrative. In the moment of liberation — when Gaga breaks through her encasement in time and space to return to herself, ultimately using a pyrotechnic bra as a symbol of female power, to torch her male captor — viewers witness a cessation of extreme anorectic images. This return to a healthier body bespeaks, in preparation to reclaim self, a burgeoning agency, represented visually by costume colors. From the more typically white costume evocative of the virginal "angel of the house," Gaga's latex and leather turns red with anger and awareness, almost as though her life's blood fights back against a deathly pallor, and she acts out her desire: she slams her fists on the floor, unmasks her face, and stands erect after torching her oppressive nemesis. Indeed, she nearly twirls with glee. Gone are the claw-like hand gestures so often displayed with the entrap-ment of the white costume, a costume that leaves her mouth free for articu-lation but masks Gaga's eyes and the "I" of her personhood. That personhood, that recognition of her *own* desires, was covered quite literally in the color of purity (white) that connotes the virginal "angel" willing to cater to male desire on his terms, much as the rarer black costume — connoting male fantasy for the "bad girl" and ironically emerging as Gaga is made a motionless object — bespeaks a desire by men for women to embrace male desire as their own, to become fully-encased images, as seen in the "bubble" scenes and the metal-lic-orbit costumes interspersed with the encasing bubble depictions. Revealing the body and paralyzing the self, masking and unmasking desire, these cos-tuming choices situate Gaga in the realm of male fantasy until the red-clad persona "freezes the flow of action in moments of erotic contemplation," dis-rupting the male narrative (Mulvey 11).

To disrupt the male narrative, Gaga dons one last time the look associated with masculine desire in the form of a polar-bear pelt. Then she approaches her captor. This time, though, she does not crawl and she does not remain hidden behind a mask: she lowers her sunglasses as she drops the polar-bear coat, directing her own desire by eliminating her male mafia captor through a series of narrative visuals that confounds linear story-telling: only upon reflection — by contemplating the final scene of a charred bed and ash-covered Gaga — can the viewer reconstruct the order of events that bring Gaga to her repose next to a corpse. Her active role in eliminating the oppressor requires active reconstruction of a narrative of emancipatory freedom, itself disrupted throughout the video by a montage of successive cross-cuts comprised of low-angle, medium, long, and close-up shots — scenes that are not, in the words of Kevin Kelly's work on screen literacy, "captured (as in a photo) but built up incrementally" — and held together by a reliance on audience observation of key visual and lyrical juxtapositions.[30] Indeed, it is just this incremental building that Gaga's work privileges: "[t]here is a narrative," she claims, "but the narrative isn't nearly as important as the images are, sewn together."[31] Suturing images, Gaga forces her viewers to do the same, inviting them to step outside the confines of the male gaze. In this freedom, aptly enough, the monstrously skeletal Gaga disappears. We see, then, that freedom from controlling patriarchy implies freedom from at least some of the influences on anorectic behavior. It may be reassuring that Gaga's success in freeing herself — incinerating her indifferent captor with a fire-shooting bra — results in the "healthiest" image of Gaga in the course of the video: lying next to the charred corpse, the presence of curves and a toned musculature return along with her freedom. She even shares with the viewer a post-coital cigarette — not relaxing after possessing the Other, but recuperating after reasserting her own self-possession. Truly, then, Gaga embodies the "tough female spirit" that she aspires to project.[32]

Caught in the Middle: Physiological and Psychosocial Skeletal Snares

One might argue that Lady Gaga visually frees herself from patriarchal oppression to actualize a fuller sense of self that accepts her body. An additional unexplored layer of complexity emerges when one considers that, in the opening scene of the video, Gaga *affects her own kidnapping*. Surrounded by a cadre of super models and various Russian mobsters, Gaga lounges on a throne, draped in gold. Her attire masks a petite physiology with large sunglasses fashioned out of razor blades (another nod, notes Gaga, to the "tough female spirit").[33] The eye, as well as the "I," remains buried by a traditional tool of self-destruction. Almost languidly, one wire-covered finger presses the play button and Gaga is pulled into the world of mafia monstrosities that follow. What should we make of this opening scene?

Is it simply an allegory for the self-denial, the pleasing of others, that accompanies fame (as well as the people-pleasing behaviors characteristic of the anorexic)? Certainly, the theme of her new album supports this premise and Gaga herself speaks openly on her desire for and the perils of fame. She distinguishes between different types of fame. One, more familiar, is "plastic and you can buy it on the street." The other, "the fame," Gaga envisions "not [as] pretending to be rich, [but as] carrying yourself in a way that exudes confidence and passion for music or art or fishing or whatever the hell it is that you're passionate about, and projecting yourself in a way that people say, 'Who the fuck is that?'" Gaga claims that her latest album explores the "fears" (sex, alcohol, love, death, loneliness) associated with this "whole other level of famous" that she experienced on her first album tour.[34] Lurking beneath this list, arguably, is a fear of losing the self, the performance artist who strives to be cutting edge and to make a real difference to her fans, both increasingly challenging goals to achieve when one's name becomes attached to each new trend. Indeed, according to *The New York Times*, there is even a "Lady Gaga of pork products" ('nduja, a spicy salami).[35]

In this darker (but more Kosher) Gagaian world, the artist's "conviction in ideas" can be hijacked by any number of "monsters," even self-imposed monsters.[36] By opening the video with a traditional perspective on fame, a very real image of *self-enslavement* via conformity asserts itself. In contrast to the "tough female spirit," we see a damsel in distress: indeed, among scenes of defiance and forced acquiescence to her kidnappers, flashes of a Gaga in natural makeup, with tear-filled eyes, and the occasional drop rolling down an unmasked cheek indicate the struggling humanity layered beneath the fame, the fashion, and the monstrous. Underneath the façade of power, both the anorexic and Gaga's "Bad Romance" persona lie at the mercy of the Other. Here is the real "Bad Romance" persona, or at least it represents that persona's emotional truth. In her interview with *Vanity Fair,* Gaga claims that "Bad Romance" "is about whether I go after those [sort of relationships] or if they find me" (286).[37] Self-awareness of her romantic patterns breeds monsters, certainly, but also a quest for *more* self-awareness, to question the complexity and effect of those patterns on her life. In knitting together Gaga's personal life and cultural discourse that shapes her personal life through technologies of sight and sound, "Bad Romance" embodies what Powers' has termed Gaga's "multi-pronged campaign for self-awareness" that involves untangling the complex contradictions of self and social discourse.[38] The lyrics of the song bear out this assessment. Although the visual representation indicates a choice-less choice and freedom against all odds, the lyrical significations tell a radically different story.

From a purely auditory standpoint, Gaga is not forced into anything at all. She *desires* the very fetishized scopophilia and sadism represented on-screen as patriarchal normativity. She wants a relationship that can be described only in terms of pain: she craves the monstrosity of her lover's "revenge," his "ugly," his "disease," his "drama," his "horror," his "design" ("Bad Romance"). The most complimentary, or rather, positive entreaty directed towards the object of her affection involves a simple caress, "the touch of [his] hand;" the rest equates love with the horrific and the monstrously unhealthy. Repeating a chorus that both demands and yearns for the divergent desires of "love" and "revenge," Gaga self-selects into oppression, entrapment, and victimization. Indeed, her chorus idealizes a co-created "bad" romantic relationship, and Gaga even includes a Hitchcockian verse desirous of the trapped and/or manipulative women of *Psycho*, *Vertigo*, and *Rear Window*, wherein the healthy relationships of mutually affirming partners is replaced by the very fear, self-doubt, and self-loathing characterizing the anorectic ego.[39] Entrapment meets desire, as Gaga moves lyrically between "want[ing]" and being "caught" in her bad romance. "Caught" she indeed is: both by external circumstances and internal desires, a dangerous combination for those prone to eating disorders. In fact, Frances Connan (et al.) postulates that anorectic women's social relations *vis-à-vis* entrapment increase occurrences of anorectic behaviors and mindsets, explaining that these women who "have little prospect of winning conflicts must resolve social conflict by submission or escape. If escape is barred, an individual becomes trapped in a submissive stance," just as on-screen women are historically represented as historically trapped, in need of saving, or monsters to be subdued (733). In her visual captivity narrative and her narrative pleas for the privilege of being ill-treated, Gaga represents both the helpless heroine and the monster, engaging in the submissive stance that characterizes the discourse of her would-be lover.

While few would define Gaga as submissive in her personal life or music video personae, the flashes of Gaga in natural makeup reveal a pained and helpless woman, unable to achieve the connection, or at least the complete connection, with the object of her desired bad romance. In contrast to the Gaga who spits vodka back at her force-feeding captors or the Gaga who attempts to take ownership of her sexuality during her enslavement, this Gaga sits in uncostumed vulnerability — more naked in these headshots than in lin-gerie, as she quietly cries, exposed in her pain, vulnerability, and insecurity. In fact, Gaga herself has noted that her "lyrics are a way for [her] to talk about how I believe women and some men feel innately insecure about themselves all the time. It's not sometimes, it's not in adolescence, it's always."[40] Her self-identified perpetual insecurity arguably results from the tension of desire for what an overwhelmingly patriarchal society has socialized her to want grating against an attempt to break free from a desire not wholly her own. This tension results in eternal insecurity, perpetual self-doubt and finally, alarmingly manifests as an erasure of self: "Don't call me Gaga," for example, opens "Monster," a far cry from her otherwise insistent assertions of identity in "Just Dance" and "Bad Romance" (as well as in her concert performances).[41] Furthermore, this submission of self to Other conjoins the very social and psychological elements that make up the "perfect storm" for the anorexic: yearning to "just dance," the protagonist cedes to her monstrous mate's preference to have sex, a mate who quite literally ingests ("ate") both her "heart" and her "brain," thus linking lyrically ingestion and physicality with emotion and intellect ("Monster"). These multidimensional, interrelational aspects of the self constitute a theme on Gaga's new album (particularly in "Monster" and "Dance in the Dark"), and "Bad Romance" draws together the emotional and intellectual entrapments to map them onto the body. Indeed, just as psychologists confirm the link between eating disorders and "interpersonal experiences" and "problems of identity or control," so does Gaga's lyrical recognition of a *desire* for "horror" dovetail with the first anorexic scene of the video: it is at the exact moment that Gaga sings about the "horror" that she desires that the audience is introduced to the monstrous skeletal figure that, as previously noted, repeats with great frequency during the thirty-seconds of performance directed at her indifferent captor (195).[42] The monstrous external entrapment (kidnapping) collides with a monstrous internal entrapment: that of unrequited desire and an unfulfilling relationship with ED.

At this stage of "Bad Romance," the chaos of images bombarding the viewer directly mirrors the confusion and turmoil of the anorectic mindset: "the problem," explains Polivy and Herman," is not an inability to *detect* internal states, but rather an inability to *identify* them" (204 my emphasis).[43] Certainly, Gaga's pantomime of a pregnant stomach further indicates this disparity and reemphasizes the seeming contradictions between lyrics and visuals, desire and reality. Arriving at a lyrical recognition of her own emotional truth requires a visual bifurcation of the self: clad in a "scaly" costume of *haute couture* that distorts her form, two identically-costumed Gagas become the visual focus: one, wearing sunglasses, struts claw-shaped-hand first towards a reclining Gaga, *sans* sunglasses, who seems to contemplate the more active figure as she stretches her own hand into a tentative claw-like formation. Yet the powerful, in-motion Gaga's performative prancing actually mirrors her nearly-catatonic *doppelgänger*: it is the motionless Gaga who first fashions her left hand into a claw-like form, making eye contact with the self that struts toward her. Significantly, this is the only eye contact made by the sitting figure, who otherwise stares up and away, into space; it is as though the effort of the glance and the raising of the hand constitutes the limit of her communicative capacity. Unlike the in-motion Gaga, she does not have dark lenses behind which to hide, a mask that allows this ostensibly-more-powerful figure to perform male desire under the guise of fashion. This strutting, sunglassed self quite literally mirrors the motion of the "raw" Gaga, raising her right hand, as though a reflection of the sitting figure's left hand, into a claw, exploring the monstrosity of the message by fashioning more claws for inspection, with one hand, both hands, facing inwards, and facing outwards. Seemingly recognizing the monstrosity of self in her mirror image, the masked Gaga of male performance learns from her unmasked self.

This performing self begins to recognize the separation of her subjective presence from her physical form, her presence as object. Indeed, the lyrics shift from a thrice repeated "fashion" to "*passion*" (my emphasis). In the move from "fashion" to "passion," the external accoutrements (fashion) give way to a recognition of internal emotion (passion). Accompanying the shift in lyrics of the masked-Gaga's approach comes a corresponding scene shift, flickering between the unmasked figure and Gaga's distorted, wide-eyed look of exaggerated innocence at the moment of her kidnapping. Now, though, the innocent male fantasy of naïveté brings her hands to her throat in an act of strangulation, throttling the portion of the self valorized by the male (a valorization she previously embraced herself). In doing so, Gaga's own self, buried beneath a performance of male-defined female sexuality, authorizes her own desire: the unmasked Gaga "pulls the trigger" of the fire-shooting brassiere, via pantomime, gaining emotional control over the rejection implied by her lover.[44] Indeed, the *haute couture* scene's primary narrative presence ends her oft-heard rallying cry in which she self-identifies as a "free bitch." That freedom maps onto the physical self: the final full-bodied anorexic scene occurs shortly before this moment of awareness.[45] The Gaga persona acts on *her* desires, not the desires of another.

What our heroine must achieve for empowerment, then, is not the elusive male prize, but rather self-awareness of her own desire; she must move from a desire to be, as Mulvey puts it, "looked at" as a utilitarian object to a desire to embrace both her own subjectivity and agency. She actualizes her *own* desires, not the male fantasy she is socialized to fulfill, in a climactic choral shift expressing her desire for "revenge" to her desire to not be "friends." The unspoken rejection of *her* desire for a satisfying romantic relationship, sandwiched between the heightened passion of the chorus *en français*, the culturally-recognizable language of passion, accompanies both the costume shift from white to red and an emotional release in the form of a tantrum. The "suppressed anger" of the anorexic achieves catharsis as a newly-empowered Gaga pounds her fists against the ground (Polivy and Herman 197).[46] And, of course, her empowerment extends beyond a tantrum: she acts upon the Other in the raciest plotline of the video to recapture her own sense of agency by incinerating indifference. In doing so, she sheds a polar bear coat — complete with head, maw gaping — that may well represent the weight of a consuming desire that trailed her earlier incarnation of self. As she lays bare the bear, and bares her own emotional truth in a fiery blaze, Gaga attempts to impose on the complexity of her emotional, intellectual, and physical chaos a more ordered self.

The result is, at the video's end, one of the healthiest images of Gaga in the five-plus minutes of "Bad Romance." Her post-catharsis cigarette, however, should not be mistaken for a celebratory conclusion. While the Gaga operating from a position of strength withstands the flames unsinged and the dancing Gaga does a cheerleader twirl of joy just before the lights dim on the carnivalesque narrative, the final scene, as the camera pans back, shows an ash-covered Gaga who wears an expression that very much connotes a need for recuperation. She herself has walked through the fire, depicted as she's half-engulfed in flames, to rise not anew like a Phoenix, but to continue the fight against a socialized desire for her lover's bad romance. Her journey towards a coherent sense of self and away from the monstrously skeletal is not complete: she must regroup, cleanse the residue of an ostensibly-purifying fire, and continue. This sense of cycle and process is born out, as well, by the final repetition of the chorus that again restates her desire for an unhealthy relationship: a bad romance.

Little Monsters, Thinking Monsters: Fan Responses to "Bad Romance"

The catchy chorus and dance beats may well be what keeps her fans returning to the video, netting it well over three million views. Indeed, it goes without saying that all things Gaga pique public interest: all seats on *The Monster Ball Tour* sell out in all venues, attended by what Tom Matlack describes as "a veritable United Nations"; her Facebook fan base broke previous Facebook fan records; and, as *Cosmopolitan* observes, "[e]very snippet of YouTube footage ... ignites instant Internet buzz" (34).[47] Gaga is much more than a cult sensation: her wide-ranging appeal is borne out by *Time* magazine's selection of Gaga for their 2009 list of influential people and Barbara Walter's inclusion of Gaga as one of only ten "Most Fascinating People."[48] While

FemaleFirst and other critics rail against Gaga's "bad influence" (*Fox News* infamously dubbed her "poison for the minds of our kids"), what is more striking is what the fans who have helped place Gaga on these lists make of her visual and lyrical "statements" (285).[49] Of the controversial "Paparazzi" video, where the Gaga-persona's quest for fame ostensibly exploits disability and sanctions murder, fans responded not with protests from the physically-challenged, but rather with appreciation: in her interview with *Vanity Fair*'s Robinson, Gaga recounts that wheelchair-bound fans told stories of the video "chang[ing] their lives"; she is thanked for "giving voice" to these and other individuals unable or unwilling to play the normative role expected of them (330).

In giving her beloved "Little Monsters" a voice, though, Gaga expects them to find their own means of self-expression; she discourages blind mimicry. Genuinely in love with her fans, she tells *Vanity Fair* readers that "[i]t's about loving who you are. I don't want people to love me; I want them to love themselves" (286). She emphasizes the fervor of her loyalty to her fans by speaking openly about her own struggles with her body, with her music, and with her mental state through her now well-publicized foray into drug culture. Reminiscing about her brush with bulimia and cocaine, she asks Robinson to qualify her tale with a message to fans: "if you print that, I do not want my fans to ever emulate that or be that way. I don't want my fans to think they have to be that way to be great. [...] it led to disaster" (329). Indeed, she is clear about the role of the "fantasy of music" as a means for exploring self and affecting change, implicitly valorizing her fans' "screen literacy," as that which provides a truth that, as Kevin Kelly's article on "Becoming Screen Literate" suggests, "you assemble yourself on your own screen as you jump from link to link" (331).[50] Viewers actively engage Gaga's messages, revising for their own purposes Gaga's re-presentations of gender and body: an *a cappella* men's group inserts "Poker Face" into their rendition of "Bad Romance," just after the Hitchcockian verse, seemingly acknowledging "bluff" of a desire that will settle for pain in lieu of a clearer romantic connection (to which the men bow, physically, as they kneel around the primary singer during the revelation that the speaker wants more than friendship); "Badder Romance," a parody described as "sweeping the web" in its viral dissemination, casts a male in the role of the kidnapped Gaga rather than any of the female participants and offers the role of a self-actualized, pyrotechnically-inclined Gaga to one of its curvier participants; and, finally, "Rad Bromance" challenges traditional visions of heteronormative masculinity in rewriting the song to celebrate a platonic friendship verging on homoerotic.[51] Clearly, these screen literate fans appropriate from Gaga their own truths about body, gender, and relationships.

Those less-inclined to *create* media offer similar perspectives: viewers of

"Bad Romance," scrutinizing various scenes — her "ass" as she removes the polar bear coat, her spine in the "Bath House of Gaga" — speculate on Photoshop techniques and purpose. Although some concur with *FemaleFirst*'s critique, as the respondent self-identified as Amy Goode does, arguing that Gaga "exploit[s] our culture[']s objectification of the female form," the more prevalent fan opinion is represented by self-identified anorexic "Amanda," who opines that Gaga's anorectic frailty "demo[n]strates the terrifying things in this world, including mental disease." Indeed, most of her fans are quick to note the monstrous context of the video, making intuitive leaps to the *horrors* of the idealization of such skeletal thinness.[52] Moreover, few parrot back her admittedly-dangerous comment to *Us Magazine* that "[i]t's all about starvation! Pop stars don't eat."[53] Rather, they implicitly embrace Gaga's ostensibly more serious claim that "[e]very minute of [her] life is performance," a performance that valorizes probing and "pushing boundaries" to encourage awareness.[54] And what a performance it is: while it may be dubbed "over the top" by naysayers, it is utterly inimitable. Unlike the fingerless glove craze following Madonna's fame in the 1980s, for example, Gaga's performances deny blind mimicry for the very purpose of encouraging self-exploration and self-expression. Instead, she demands that her "freaks" and "Little Monsters," as she is wont to affectionately call her fans, *contemplate* the veracity — or plasticity — of her antics. Indeed, Gaga herself avers, at least in reference to the recurrent death scenes she stages, that "I can show you so you're not looking for it. I'm dying for you on domestic television — here's what it looks like, so no one has to wonder."[55] Such a perspective might well address the critiques of the bulimic scene featured in *The Monster Ball Tour*, where a white-clad, model-still Gaga serves as a "receptacle," of sorts, for the neon blue bulimic residue of a black-clad counterpart. This mini-movie, with its industrial bass accompaniment during an early costume change, serves a similar purpose: the dark side that looms (literally) over an idealized body image and made toxic (in its unnatural neon blue hue) and destructive, even in the allure of its deviance. Gaga invokes what Laura Mulvey has called the "stolen" image of woman, stealing it back and offering that image to her fans as a means of dismantling a patriarchal narrative of the self within and the body without (18). Gaga's physical representation, her lyrical narrative, and her visual narratives all combine to encourage active thought and dialogue — occurring right now in online forums — about body image and its many influences.

NOTES

1. BBC World Service announced on March 26, 2010 that Gaga "set the record" for online music video hits, with over a billion views of "Just Dance," "Bad Romance," and "Poker Face" (Koch). Only a few months prior to Gaga's record-breaking feat, *The Wall*

Street Journal's John Jurgensen described Gaga as a "digital phenomenon," comparing her MySpace plays (321.5 million as of 29 January 2010) to Susan Boyle's MySpace plays (133,000), a disparity made greater by the fact that Boyle "scor[ed] the No. 2 selling album of 2009."

2. See Daniel Kreps' November 10, 2009 article on Gaga in *Rolling Stone*.

3. Earlier in 2009, Ivonne Thein's "Thirty-Two Kilos," a photo series displaying dangerously thin women in the latest fashion and striking the poses seen by their favorite models, enraged communities of viewers as glamorizing anorexia. Whether one embraces the artist's vision as a horrifying critique of the fashion industry and pro-ana or whether one perceives these images as a celebration of the slender body and "thinspiration," the question of appropriate representation remains much contested. Indeed, a statement from Thein about her anti-ana stance does not inhibit avid anas from appropriating her work as "thinspiration."

4. The author is grateful for the support of family and friends, especially those who put up with the many, many "screenings" of Lady Gaga's music videos and long conversations about those videos. Even more impressive were those who read drafts of the essay while listening to Gaga; these very patient people include C. Kirby Arinder, Elizabeth W. Baker, S. Alan Baragona, Sarah Dean, Alex Hughes, Michael A. Perry, and Susan A. Santos. Additional appreciation is extended to the good-natured members of VMI's class of 2013.

5. Anorexia Nervosa (clinically defined by a refusal to maintain a body weight of at least 85 percent of that which is deemed healthy) and Bulimia Nervosa (defined by cycles of binge eating followed by purging) are the two most widely-acknowledged eating disorders. The DSM-IV also recognizes alternate eating disorders, classified as Eating Disorder Not Otherwise Specified (EDNOS), which can include "bigorexia," or muscle dysmorphia, characterized by a distorted body image that primarily affects men who see themselves as insufficiently muscular. Bigorexia was recently profiled by Simon Rawles in *The Daily Mail's* online venue, *MailOnline*.

6. Reilly is joined in her 2006 exploration of non-parental relationships and eating disorders by Mandi Newton's research team, who in 2005 consider how anorexic women function in romantic relationships, and Anders G. Broberg's 2001 research team, examining "a more general theory of relationships with significant others" as related to eating disordered women. Along with these more inclusive studies comes the perhaps surprising revelation that causes and symptoms of eating disorders influence each other: for instance, Janet Polivy and C. Peter Herman suggest that media exposure to thin celebrities may draw eating-disordered audiences rather than inspiring eating disorders (192). Similarly, Shan Guisinger reports that body image distortion sometimes follows, rather than precipitates, eating disorders: neuroimaging studies, Guisinger explains, reveal that "body image distortion results from specific changes ... only when [the patient is] underweight" (199). See Reilly's "From Calorie-Counting to Relationships" in *Group Analysis;* Newton et al.'s "'An Engagement-Distancing Flux'" in *European Eating Disorders Review*; Broberg et al.'s "Eating Disorders, Attachment and Interpersonal Difficulties" in *European Eating Disorders Review*; Polivy and Herman's "Causes of Eating Disorders" in the *Annual Review of Psychology*; and Shan Guisinger's "Competing Paradigms for Anorexia Nervosa" in *American Psychologist*.

7. Shan Guisinger confirms that "[t]he consensus of the field is that AN [anorexia] develops when psychopathology and social pressures to be thin act in concert with biological vulnerability" (745). See Guisinger's "Adapted to Flee Famine" in the October 2003 *Psychological Review*.

8. Identifying this ailment as "latent anorexia," Khan qualifies the term in an unpublished letter to Geoffrey Gorer as that which does not strictly relate to "true hunger" and the "realistic threat of starvation," anticipating the 2003 cautionary article in *Women's Studies in Communication* that suggests the rhetoric of eating disorders, in emphasizing

extreme cases, marginalizing the more prevalent cases of anorexia (qtd. in Reilly 376). See Reilly's reproduction of Khan's letter in "From Calorie-Counting to Relationships" and Grace E. Lager and Brian R. McGee's "Hiding the Anorectic: A Rhetorical Analysis of Popular Discourse Concerning Anorexia" in the September 2003 *Women's Studies in Communication.*

9. In 2006, Spain drew worldwide attention to the impact of fashion models (who weigh 23 percent less than the average woman) on body image when they banned models beneath the World Health Organization's recommendations for healthy weight. See Juliette Terzieff's "Fashion World Says Too Thin Is Too Hazardous" on *Women's eNews.*

10. Barbie's physiognomy has been refashioned several times to provide more identifiable figures for several eras, but these refashionings have done little to staunch to criticism that follows in her wake. These criticisms explain that the average woman is five feet, four inches tall whereas a life-size Barbie would need to be seven feet, six-inches tall to account for the doll's proportions. It is important to note, though, that while translating her proportions to that of a human woman would make her too thin to menstruate, she would not be forced to all fours in order to support her ample bosom. See Denise Winterman's "What Would a Real Life Barbie Look Like?" in *BBC* magazine.

11. While some feminists, like Naomi Wolf, attribute the onset of eating disorders to a rebellion against patriarchy as suppressing the means of reproductive utility, the larger community consensus (also reached by Wolf) might best be articulated by Susan Bordo: women, argues Bordo, occupy public space that must be "circumscribed, limited" (171). See Wolf's *The Beauty Myth* and Bordo's *Unbearable Weight.*

12. See Rachel Beckman's "'Thirty-Two Kilos': A Stark Look at Anorexia" in *The Washington Post.*

13. Ibid. Beckman explains that "Thein worried about this very outcome [the celebration of her representations]" and emphasizes that her pictures are meant to offer "a critical position."

14. Jenni Schaefer's best-selling account of recovery from an eating disorder, *Life Without Ed*, chronicles her experience recovering from eating disorders, noting in particular the practice of naming her disorder. Notably, Schaefer subtitles her account as a declaration of *independence*, and follows this account with a story of "falling in love" with life after recovery in *Goodbye Ed, Hello Me.*

15. It does bear noting, however, that Gaga's initial rejection of feminism — even as she espoused feminist principles — has given way to self-identification with a feminist discourse: she tells Ann Powers, "I'm getting the sense that you're a little bit of a feminist, like I am" and views her music as, in Powers' words, "a liberating force." Caitlin Moran makes a strong case for the efficacy of Gaga's message, separating her from the "faux-attitude" of many female pop stars and holding Gaga up as a role model, validating "women who are right out there, doing what the hell they want, and who would clearly greet any attempt to criticize their appearance or attitude with wildly disbelieving laughter. Women who are unafraid to express aspects of themselves that seem alarming, unpalatable, uncontrollable or just plain horsescaringly bizarre" (n. pag).

16. Jason Zinoman, for *The New York Times*, notes the parallels between Gaga's "Bad Romance" and Michael Jackson's "Thriller," claiming for Gaga a different kind of independence. See Zinoman's "For Lady Gaga, Every Concert Is a Drama."

17. See Anja Cronberg's interview with Gaga in *H&M Magazine.*

18. Gaga's "commitment to confront the changing notion of what's 'natural,'" suggests Powers, "puts Gaga on the same road traveled by artists she admires."

19. Eating disorders, are, as Polivy and Herman explain, "a domain in which one can gain some emotional control," although those feelings of power are, according to Surgenor (et al.), "unstable and temporary boosts" (196, 140).

20. See Zinoman's "For Lady Gaga, Every Concert Is a Drama" in *The New York Times.*

21. Drawing upon the recognizable monstrosities of nineteenth-century fiction (like Mary Shelley's *Frankenstein*, Robert Louis Stevenson's *The Strange Case of Dr. Jekyll and Mr. Hyde*, Bram Stoker's *Dracula*, Judith Halberstam explains that "the emergence of the monster within Gothic fiction marks a peculiarly modern emphasis upon the horror of particular kinds of bodies," concluding that "plasticity of form comes to define gender, genre, and sexual identity" (3, 62). One might add to this list of monstrously gendered bodies in Gothic fiction the lamia of John Keats' "Lamia."

22. While Gothic — especially women's Gothic — has been characterized as a quest journey, an approach exemplified by Eugenia C. DeLamotte's *Perils of the Night*, Gothic fiction might equally be conceive of women's roles as captivity narratives, given the entrapment and escape that characterizes the journey of any Gothic heroines. The most familiar example is the "Crew of Light" (from Bram Stoker's *Dracula*) whose mission is to save Mina from Dracula, notably after their failed attempt to save Lucy, who moves out of the role of helpless heroine to the desiring woman of insatiable appetite as a vampire who preys on the town's children. Captive to her desires after entrapped by a villain from whom she can only be saved by men who "know better," Lucy's story exemplifies the trope of captivity narratives that abut fear of female desire. Indeed, the critical reception of early Gothic texts likewise focused on fear of female "liberation": reviewers, argues E. J. Clery, fear that women will adopt the interpretative strategies of flighty heroines as their own (114). The popular narrative of early Gothic espoused just such a fear, as cartoonist James Gillray depicts in his (1802) "Tales of Wonder!," in which four women huddle around a candle and a book with expressions of unbridled horror as they listen to a Gothic story unfold; Williams' earlier (1801) "Luxury or the Comforts of a Rum p ford" portrays a lascivious woman, surrounded by piles of books, warming her backside by the fire, one hand holding a well-worn copy of Matthew G. Lewis' notoriously salacious *The Monk* and the other hand slipped beneath her skirts in the act of masturbation. She is "corrupted" by her appetite for reading matter, unleashing her other appetites; Williams, like Gillray, sardonically calls for a containment of desires within the boundaries of literary taste.

23. See Laura Mulvey's "Visual Pleasure and Narrative Cinema."

24. Situating Gaga in the "language" of visual and musical representation, Powers applauds "Bad Romance's" portrayal of what Gaga describes as "the woman perceived as a commodity."

25. Mulvey explains castration anxiety in film by drawing upon psychoanalytic criticism: "the meaning of woman is sexual difference, the absence of the penis as visually ascertainable, the material evidence on which is based the castration complex essential for the organization of entrance to the symbolic order and the law of the father. Thus the woman as icon, displayed for the gaze and enjoyment of men, the active controllers of the look, always threatens to evoke the anxiety it originally signified" (13).

26. Better known simply as "aliens," Xenomorphs appear throughout the *Alien* series and its spin-offs.

27. She is further debased as men pour vodka during her dance, reinforcing her presence as nothing more than an entertaining series of images rather than a self.

28. These scenes occur, respectively, at 2:08, 2:15, 2:26 and 2:27, 2:41.

29. For example, Jenni Schaefer relates her repeated returns to a relationship with ED as an enticing escape from the terrors of abandonment from her support system. See *Life without Ed*, p. 20.

30. See Kelly's "Becoming Screen Literate" in *The New York Times Magazine*.

31. Gaga's commentary on the aesthetics of her videos can be found in Powers' piece. In privileging the suturing of images, Gaga simultaneously articulates the difference between the genres of music videos and film (in the former's less linear flow) and more clearly exposes "the look that defines cinema" for Mulvey (17). This performance artist makes overt the narrative tendencies of visual discourse, breaking the expected boundaries and

reassembling the fragments of those boundaries in new and compelling ways that viewers, in turn, can likewise disassemble and reassemble.

32. See Jocelyn Vena and Sway Calloway's *MTV* report, "Lady Gaga Says 'Bad Romance' Video Is About 'Tough Female Spirit.'"

33. Discussing the glasses with *MTV*, Gaga explains that she "wanted to design a pair for some of the toughest chicks and some of my girlfriends — don't do this at home! — they used to keep razor blades in the side of their mouths," she explained. "That tough female sprit is something that I want to project. It's meant to be, 'This is my shield, this is my weapon, this is my inner sense of fame, this is my monster'" (qtd. in Vena and Calloway).

34. Each song, relates Gaga in a press release publicized by *MTV*'s James Dinh, refers to each of the several "monsters" she encountered with her first tour: "while traveling the world for two years, I've encountered several monsters, each represented by a different song on the new record" (qtd. in Dinh). See also Gaga's discussion of fame in her interview with Laura Barton, of *The Guardian*.

35. See Julia Moskin's *New York Times* piece, "A Dollop of Salami, Spreading from Calabria."

36. See Laura Barton's interview with Gaga in *The Guardian*.

37. Gaga muses on her pattern of romantic relationships, as reported by Lisa Robinson of *Vanity Fair*.

38. Indeed, *Los Angeles Times* writer Ann Powers titles her piece on Gaga "Lady Gaga's Multi-Pronged Campaign for Self-Awareness" and the executive vice president of a rival music label, reports *The Wall Street Journal*'s John Jurgensen, acknowledges the importance of Gaga's "full multimedia package."

39. In her discussion of Hitchcock, Mulvey notes that "[h]is heroes are exemplary of the symbolic order and the law [...] True perversion is barely concealed under a shallow mask of ideological correctness — the man is on the right side of the law, the woman on the wrong" (15). For *Vertigo*, "the spectator's fascination is turned against him as the narrative carries him through and entwines him with the processes that he is himself exercising," much like *Rear Window* features a protagonist burdened with "enforced inactivity, binding him to his seat as a spectator, put[ting] him squarely in the phantasy position of the cinema audience" (16). While Gaga's male spectators, as mafia members, are certainly not on the right side of law as defined by jurisprudence, they do represent the Law of the Father; her *desire* for these emissaries of the Symbolic Order insidiously fortifies as destructively as Norman Bates of *Psycho* does when he seeks to reverse the emasculation he experienced from his mother by murdering women. In some ways, Gaga murders herself to hold on to a desire that patriarchal discourse has inculcated in her, rather than her own desire.

40. *MTV*'s Eric Ditzian makes public Gaga's intent for "Dance in the Dark."

41. Both "Just Dance" and "Bad Romance" repeat Gaga's name in the lyrics; during the 2010 Monster Ball Tour in Arizona, Gaga introduces herself, slowly enunciating "My. Name. Is." before screaming "Lady Gaga" and famously, or perhaps now infamously likens herself to Tinkerbell by telling her fans that she will die without their applause. (Alternately, Caitlin Moran recounts her experience of Gaga's self-identification during the Monster Ball Tour with a slightly different emphasis: Moran's experience features the performance artist's voice roaring "I *am* Lady Gaga!")

42. For an account of the multidimensional aspects of "interpersonal experiences" and eating disorders, see Polivy and Herman. Reilly likewise establishes as "clearly inseparable" the relationship of self and other, and Connan (et al.) hypothesizes that such relationships can fill eating-disordered patients with such horror that they adopt "submissive, avoidant behaviors," restricting their sense of self-actualization as they restrict their caloric intake (380, 748).

43. The failure to identify states of being includes "physiological states (such as hunger

and satiety) and emotional states" (Polivy and Herman 204). Shan Guisinger even theorizes that this inability to identify states, especially physiological states, might lend itself towards an evolutionary explanation for anorexia; though controversial, Guisinger's hypothesis implies that anorexia may serve as a survival mechanism for those in extreme physical or emotional turmoil (199). See Guisinger's "Competing Paradigms for Anorexia Nervosa."

44. See "Bad Romance" at 4 minutes and 15 seconds.

45. Tellingly, Broberg (et al.) reveals that eating-disordered women often share a "fear of abandonment"; Reilly registers "high levels" of rejection as a risk factor for eating disorders; and Polivy and Herman link eating disorders to "(perceived) rejection" (393, 377, 197).

46. Repressed hostility and anger typically constitute shared characteristics of the anorexic's experience: just as Polivy and Herman report that eating disordered women "score higher than controls in guilt, covert hostility, and suppressed anger," so Reilly indicates "[h]igh levels of conflict, hostility" (197, 377).

47. *Vanity Fair*'s Lisa Robinson reports that Gaga's 12 million Facebook fans exceed even "those of President Obama" and Samuel Axon reports that one Gaga Facebook group, totaling "more than 100,000 people initiated National Lady Gaga Day" on January 29, 2010; *Cosmopolitan*'s Christine Spines confirms the sales for *The Monster Ball* tour (282). See also Tom Matlack's contribution to the *Huffington Post* for a description of concert attendees.

48. Claiming Gaga for "Middle America," Caitlin Moran nods to Gaga's appearance on *Oprah;* Lisa Robinson reports Gaga's mainstream media success, noting in addition to Gaga's appearance on lists by *Time* and Barbara Walters her inclusion in *Forbes* as the fourth-ranking celebrity newcomers in 2010 (282).

49. Lisa Robinson's *Vanity Fair* article reproduces *Fox News*' infamous assessment of Gaga.

50. Ibid.

51. Performed by "On the Rocks," the men's *a cappella* version was featured, in a shorter rendition, on NBC's *The Spin-Off;* "Badder Romance," performed by teens, was noticed by Eliot Glazer in its viral spread (an internet circulation also shared by "Rad Bromance.") These adaptation-homages offer non-celebrity perceptions of "the changing nature of the self in relation to technology" that Gaga exemplifies (as reported by Powers).

52. Other respondents agree: "Marissa" notes that Gaga's physical portrayal "is part of the storyline"; Genevieve agrees that it is "part of the rest of the theme of the video. Agreed above with the part of the 'horror' of her new album"; and Jessica says "it's supposed to be horrific. The *Fame Monster* is themed after horror, monsters, the things people shove in their closets. Maybe the point was to shock people and show how hideous anorexia is, not to make her "more beautiful." [...] I truly believe that the point was to cause horror and disgust, not to encourage little girls to obtain the unrealistic body image."

53. Allison Emert's blog for *Examiner.com* repeats Gaga's quote to *Us Weekly*.

54. Fans responded rapidly to this claim, some writing it off as joke and others noting a disconnecting between Gaga's rebellion and the typicality of a celebrity culture fixated on starvation; indeed, Elena Gorgan offers these options in her blog even as she chastises Gaga, but even Gorgan's finger-shaking cannot quell the mystery and discussion inspired by Gaga's commentary. Forcing her audience to think is what Gaga does best: even in the wake of rumors of Gaga's hermaphroditism, Gaga initially allowed the "mystery" of her gender to perpetuate, noting that she "like[s] pushing boundaries" (qtd. in Eager). Likewise, Alexander Cho's "Lady Gaga, Balls-Out" reminds us of Gaga's claim for the performative: importantly, while Cho relegates Gaga's representation of body as "fascist," he acknowledges that she brings to light "pop's own artifice," concluding that "Lady Gaga interrogates the performative nature of gender, sex, and sexuality." By all accounts, Gaga's interrogation of the body in relation to gender and sexuality is overt: cultivating what Caitlin Moran

calls a "second-string career of "being an incident," Gaga walks pantsless, drawing attention both to her body and the clothing that covers it. More often than not, Gaga's pantsless look shows off a body stocking, typically meant, like Spanx(r), to be hidden under clothing. In the words of Philippa Bourke, "shapewear, normally a secret garment, is something Gaga wants to bring out of the closet."

55. See "Lady Gaga: The Singing Sensation on Stress, Sexuality, and Her Romantic Future" in *Elle*.

What a Drag

Lady Gaga, Jo Calderone and the Politics of Representation

Heather Duerre Humann

Lady Gaga (born Stefani Germanotta) is a musician and performance artist who frequently finds herself at the center of controversy — and she seems to relish it.[1] Simply saying that Lady Gaga lives her life in the public eye would be a major understatement, yet the summer of 2010 saw nothing less than a media explosion — even by Lady Gaga standards — in response to a photo shoot she did as her male alter ego Jo Calderone for the September 2010 issue of Japanese *Vogue Hommes* magazine. Indeed, a range of media outlets reported widely on what has come to be known as the Jo Calderone photo shoot.[2] The reason why this photo shoot was the source of so much controversy has to do, of course, with Lady Gaga's fame (or notoriety), but it also stems from the fact that, by posing as a man in a very public way, Lady Gaga calls into question our deeply rooted beliefs about — and indeed, the very nature of— gender. Lady Gaga suggests by so easily donning the (male) persona of Jo Calderone that gender is much more fluid than popular perceptions about it might indicate. Thanks to the internet and other media outlets, these widely-disseminated photos showed Lady Gaga with short, slicked-back brunette hair and dressed in a black suit and white dress shirt — looking convincingly like a man and wearing typical male attire. The Jo Calderone photo shoot reexamines concerns related to embodiment in addition to questions about what it means to perform drag.[3]

This essay will address two key concerns. The first is that our conceptualization(s) of the body must be rooted in historical practices with political, social, cultural, and (often) economic dimensions, and secondly, drag performance raises many questions: is drag about impersonation or does drag offer an alternative lens through which we can view contemporary society's preconceived notions about gender? Indeed, since the time that Judith Butler published her landmark work, *Gender Trouble* (1990), scholars and cultural historians have generally accepted that the socially constructed dimension of gender performativity is perhaps most obvious in drag performance. Butler's discussion of drag performance offers us a rudimentary understanding of gender binaries by the way it emphasizes gender performance, yet, as she argues in "Critically Queer," even Butler recognizes that drag cannot necessarily be considered the honest expression of its performer's intent. Instead, Butler posits that what is performed "can only be understood through reference to what is barred from the signifier within the domain of corporeal legibility" ("Critically Queer" 24).

Using Butler's theoretical work as a point of departure, this essay examines how the wildly popular — and powerful (even by *Forbes*' standards!) — cultural icon we know best as Lady Gaga challenges and disrupts normative notions of gender and sexuality by/through her multiple stage/screen/print personae — including the persona of "Jo Calderone," the male model who is now widely believed to be Lady Gaga herself.[4] This chapter will also explore how Lady Gaga's different incarnations challenge the binaries of man and woman and complicate notions of sexual difference and desire. By/through the persona of Jo Calderone and the multiple other personas she adopts, Lady Gaga pushes cross-dressing into the realm of drag and gender play.

As stated at the beginning of this essay, nothing less than a media storm erupted when Lady Gaga posed as her male alter-ego Jo Calderone for the September, 2010 issue of Japanese *Vogue Hommes* magazine.[5] A wide variety of reporters, bloggers, and cultural critics quickly weighed in on, and speculate wildly about, this latest Lady Gaga controversy. One such reporter was Amy Odell, who discussed the photo shoot and Lady Gaga's new persona in her *New York Magazine* article entitled "Lady Gaga Seems to Be Taking Her Jo Calderone Alter Ego Pretty Seriously."[6] Odell reported on how

> The Internet seems to pretty much agree that Lady Gaga IS this hot new face Jo Calderone, who appears on the September cover of Japanese *Men's Vogue*, shot by Gaga's favorite photographer Nick Knight. Further evidence that Gaga is Calderone exists on Twitter, where this character has a feed that began on June 29, the day the shots began leaking. You'll notice the feed is also clogged with interactions with Gaga's favorite arm barnacle, Perez Hilton [Odell 3].

The *New York Daily News* also printed several stories about the controversy with Kristie Cavanagh, the author of one of these pieces, admitting that "Lady Gaga is such a mistress of disguise; it's often hard to recognize her." In the same article — which features side-by-side photos of Lady Gaga and Jo Calderone — Cavanagh goes on to describe how "the brooding brown-haired looker bears a remarkable resemblance to Gaga, whose middle name is Joanne, leading many to speculate that the photos are in fact of the 'Alejandro' singer in drag" (2).

The internet was also abuzz with rumors about Lady Gaga and the "Jo Calderone" photo shoot. One such example was the online forum *ladygaga.com*, which offered some very interesting insights on the controversy. One individual who posted on this site summed it up as follows:

> My mathematical brain added it up.
> Lady Gaga is a woman.
> Jo Calderone is a Man.
> Lady Gaga and Jo Calderone are the same person,
> but not the same personae [ladygaga.com].

Another respondent on this same site viewed this new persona of Jo Calderone as very much in keeping with Lady Gaga's brand of art:

> It would make sense that Gaga is playing with gender. After all, her Gaga persona is the archetypal hyper-sexualized, hyper-colorful woman; what better way to play off that then to portray a stripped down androgynous man in black-n-white. It may be a one-time fashion shoot or she may have something broader in mind. Remember that she's not just a singer; she's a performance artist and gender is one of the things that such artists can bend and turn inside out in performance pieces [ladygaga.com].

What is particularly interesting about these two posts is that both of the respondents specifically used the term "persona" to refer to Lady Gaga's various stage, screen, and print incarnations. In the case of the former respondent, the use of the term "persona" highlights the conundrum that drag performance both poses and answers: how one person can represent multiple genders. In the case of the latter respondent the post tellingly referred to Germanotta's typical stage persona as her "Gaga persona," thereby highlighting how the performer we know best as Lady Gaga is always already performing her gender. The latter respondent's comments point to the performative nature of Lady Gaga's display of a "hyper-sexualized" female form. In this case, the deployment of the term "persona" reminds us that "Lady Gaga" is no more Germanotta's "natural" form than are any of the other guises she chooses to don. Instead, the adoption of the stage persona "Lady Gaga" is very much a deliberate creation/construction of Germanotta's, one that may have personal dimensions, but that also has a specific artistic end. Therefore, what these remarks ultimately (though perhaps implicitly) suggest is that there is (at least a degree of) ambiguity with respect to gender and an arbitrary, rather than pre-assigned, nature to gender choices.

According to many cultural historians and theorists, this notion is precisely the point of drag performance. As Judith Butler argues in "Critically

Queer," the "critical promise of drag does not have to do with the proliferation of genders ... but rather with the exposure or the failure of heterosexual regimes ever fully to legislate or contain their own ideals" (26). Though Butler's remarks are useful, especially since she links drag with "the failure of heterosexual regimes," it is worth noting that they are directed at drag performance in general, whereas the Jo Calderone controversy deals specifically with the situation of a woman impersonating (and passing as) a man. In other words, the Lady Gaga/Jo Calderone controversy occupies the realm of "drag kings," a phenomenon couched in culturally and historically specific terms differing from that of drag queens.

Laurence Senelick discusses the relationship between the politics of representation of drag and society's attitudes about drag as well as how these issues come into play with respect to drag kings and their performances in his book entitled *The Changing Room: Sex, Drag, and Theatre*. Senelick claims that even as drag queens became more socially acceptable, drag kings remained edgy and controversial: "Once drag queens had become Disneyfied and safe, drag kings (performance artists or nightclub comics, depending on the milieu) seem to have emerged as another dangerous alternative" (483). Key differences that Senelick notes include the group's self-awareness and self-consciousness, especially in relation to drag performers who came before them. He explains: "The increasing self-referentiality, self-protection and self-consciousness of drag, with its special employment agencies and equipment shops, protects its exponents from the instant discard that faced their predecessors. They insist on being winners" (505). Thus, Senelick brings to light is a specific attitude associated with drag kings, one that distinguishes them from predecessors. There is also a deliberate aim in their performances. Indeed, as Del LaGrace Volcano and Indra Wrath (who are also performers) point out in their article "Gender Fusion," there is more to drag than simply putting on clothes; transforming into a drag king "means something more than putting on men's clothes and stuffing a sock down your trousers" (131). According to Volcano and Wrath, the act of transformation, rather than mere impersonation, seems to be central to what these performers are doing. Senelick echoes this sentiment when he cites a popular drag king performer (stage name: Trash) who claims that "she is 'transcending the immediate, the body'" (494).

The point, however, is not always simply to "pass as a man," but often rather to "try to generate enough credibility to put a spin on our habitual ways of viewing things, and on conservative gender norms," as Volcano and Wrath emphasize (131). Thus, though there is inevitability a personal reason for performing drag and a personal dimension to their drag performances, the aim of many drag kings comes across as decisively political as well, for they seek to challenge gender norms and social mores by/through their performances. Kim Surkan addresses the political dimensions of drag, as well as drag king performers' relationship to queer theory, in her article "Drag Kings in the New Wave: Gender Performance and Participation." She argues that "by responding to and revising what has come before, drag kings are creating new performance aesthetics that can be seen as practical applications of theoretical promises familiar to queer theorists" (172). These include, as Rosemary Hennessy points out in her essay entitled "Queer Theory: A Review of the *differences* Special Issue and Wittig's *The Straight Mind*," the disruption of "obvious categories (man, woman, Latina, Jew, butch, femme), oppositions (man vs. woman, heterosexual vs. homosexual), or equations (gender = sex) upon which conventional notions of sexuality and identity rely" (964). As remarks such as these imply, drag has the power to be not only provocative, but also potentially transformative in both personal and political ways. Senelick seems intent on communicating this point as well when he discusses the androgyny associated with drag performance and its political aim: "Its political end is ultimately anarchic, enabling the individual to become a gender Houdini, ingeniously escaping biological determinism and social conditioning" (497).

The Houdini-like (to borrow Senelick's term) nature of drag performance takes on a different tenor — politically, socially, and culturally — when the body "escaping biological determinism" is the female body. Indeed, contemporary feminist discourse has consistently revealed that the female body is defined by, and constantly subject to, various socio-political, cultural, economic, and historical forces. In fact, competing and contradictory politics of representation exist with respect to the female body. In *Gender Trouble*, for instance, Butler emphasizes that "the body is not a 'being,' but a variable boundary, a surface, whose permeability is politically regulated" (177). Moreover, as she argues, "the body gains meaning within discourse only in the context of power relations" (92). Our society's conceptualizations of the female body, thus, not only exist, but are formed by the multiple political forces that seek to regulate it. Indeed, the female body operates, as Sidonie Smith puts it, as a site "upon which the struggle for cultural meaning is waged" (282). Though the female body is subject to these myriad hegemonic forces, it is possible to offer counter-narrative to the dominant cultural messages seeking to define and confine women's bodies.

Drag performance is one possible way to move beyond seeing the female body simply as contested space. As Wendy Harcourt proposes in her piece entitled "Editorial: Lady Gaga Meets Ban Ki-Moon," our society needs "to go beyond statements which position women's bodies as occupied, abused, hated and denied. They are, that is true, but as Lady Gaga and many other women, men, and trans would declare bodies of all genders can be about strength, fun, pleasure, talent and celebration" (Harcourt 143). Lady Gaga accomplishes this precise task in the guise of her male alter ego, Jo Calderone. Posing as Jo Calderone positions Lady Gaga not only as radical, but also as transformative. By adopting this persona, she effectively challenges the heterosexual paradigm and plays with gender binaries. In doing so, she deconstructs them and calls into question their very existence, thereby calling attention to gender at the same time as she does something some people would consider revolutionary: she highlights the arbitrary nature of gender choices. Yet, rather than interpreting Lady Gaga's adoption of the male Jo Calderone persona as a departure from what she has been doing as a performance artist, let us consider it, instead, as an extension of her ongoing political project — and very much in keeping with the type of deliberate creation and construction of herself that she presents in her art and performance.

Through her performance art, Lady Gaga challenges society to think differently — about gender and a range of other issues that she finds important. Lady Gaga states that challenging society to think in a different way is one of her goals. As Lady Gaga herself puts it, "My destiny is to be a liberator and a storyteller in the world" ("Lady Gaga: On the Record"). Part of Lady Gaga's storytelling is both about giving a voice to those who cannot speak for themselves as well as giving a voice to those who can no longer speak for themselves. Sometimes, it is also about bringing attention and awareness to the media and public's fascination with women who have died and have thus been rendered voiceless. She addresses this aspect of her art in a televised interview with Touré where she names and discusses a number of females who have become almost mythic in our perceptions of them — Frida Kahlo and Madame Butterfly, as well as Marilyn Monroe, JonBenét Ramsey, and Sylvia Plath (who all three, according to Lady Gaga, have a "mystique" which surrounds them) — and how they have influenced her and her art ("Lady Gaga: The Lost Tapes"). Indeed, she cites females who died young (such as Monroe, Plath, and Ramsey), and whose deaths attracted a lot of public interest, as inspirations for her September 2009 MTV Video Music Awards (VMA) performance, where she (now) famously bled on stage in front of a surprised audience. There is a clear connection between what Lady Gaga brought to light through her provocative VMA performance and what she accomplishes by donning the guise of the male persona Jo Calderone. In both cases, she gives voice to others and questions not only our society's perceptions, but the underlying values that we take for granted.

Lady Gaga's ability to give voice to others through her art is an integral component of her art as well as part of her political project. Rather than operating separately, the two feed off each other and work well together as part of her performance art. As Kristin M. Langellier outlines in her article, "Voiceless

Bodies, Bodiless Voices: The Future of Personal Narrative Performance," oftentimes "movements to reclaim voice *and* body ground personal narrative performance" (207). She goes on to explain: "the voice needs a body which personal narrative furnishes from social life. A complementary movement applies: the body needs a voice to resist the colonizing powers of discourse" (207). In the case of Lady Gaga, one of the ways she accomplishes the end of giving voice to others is through her adoption of multiple stage, screen, and print personae, including her male Jo Calderone persona. By transforming into "Jo Calderone," Lady Gaga deconstructs gender binaries and questions gender norms and perceptions about gender by embodying (in this case, literally giving a body to) that which she wants the world to see: the fiction of gender. The existence of individuals who do not readily fit into the traditional, prescribed categories of man or woman and the existence of those who, like Lady Gaga, can "try on" a different genders at will, calls into question the very presence of these categories.

Though her project is arguably a political one, Lady Gaga nonetheless seems to have a lot of fun with it — and, indeed, the Jo Calderone guise seems to be all in good fun. Hints of the playful nature of this guise/disguise come in many forms. When asked on the set of the photo shoot about Lady Gaga and being photographed, Jo Calderone, according to a report by the *Huffington Post* went on the record saying:

> "I thought it would be fun to have my picture taken," adding, "I'd love to own my own car shop, I have a bunch of my own 'muscle' cars. Maybe if I take some more pictures I can afford it." When asked of his relationship to Lady Gaga, he explained, "I met her at a shoot Nick Knight was doing. She's fuckin' beautiful, and funny, and interesting. I was a little nervous for Nick to start shooting." She said, "Don't be, baby, you were born this way." I took her out after. The rest is private ["Jo Calderone" 2].

These playful remarks show Jo Calderone to be a personification of male gender stereotypes, as evidenced by his comments about wanting to own a "car shop" and a lot of "muscle cars." The fact that he also takes advantage of the moment to compliment a female's physique (in this case, Lady Gaga, which makes what he says all the more humorous and ironic) and to brag about a female (again, Lady Gaga) responding to him, shows him to be a stereotypical portrayal of a man — interested primarily in women and cars. In a sense, Jo Calderone is a character who respects the dimension of the drag king performance with an exaggerated male form interested in stereotypically male things. However, these remarks also suggest that, for Lady Gaga, the adoption of the persona of Jo Calderone is an exercise in fun (as well as in irony and humor). More evidence that she is having fun with this persona comes from her choice of the name. Jo Calderone is a near-anagram for "Alejandro," a song Lady Gaga says is about saying "goodbye" to her past lovers. The name "Jo" derives from Lady Gaga's own birth name: Stefani *Jo*-anne Angelina Germanotta.

Indeed, inventing names — and having fun with names — is nothing new for Lady Gaga. Many fans know the story of how she came up with her stage name, "Lady Gaga": the name was inspired from Queen's classic hit song "Radio Gaga," and Rob Fusari, a producer who is her former boyfriend and business partner, helped her to create it. Tellingly — and in keeping with her tendency to play with gender — Lady Gaga has said that, at first, she saw "Lady Gaga" as a "burlesque name" (Touré "Lady Gaga: The Lost Tapes"). Knowing that she first associated the name "Lady Gaga" with an art form characterized by its theatricality, a use of parody, and frequent use of grotesque exaggeration, works to remind us not only of the created/constructed nature of the "Gaga" persona, but also that its adoption consisted of playing with the hyper-sexualized female form. Further, Lady Gaga's remark about her name is even more interesting if we keep in mind that the name "Lady" is popularly used as a title for a dominatrix. The moniker "Lady" is, of course, also a common part of a female impersonator's (or drag queen's) name.

For all of the fun that Lady Gaga seems to be having with the Jo Calderone persona, this guise nonetheless remains an effective way for her to challenge gender binaries — and challenging gender binaries is something she has said she wants to do. Moreover, she has often expressed her fascination with androgyny — and, in particular, with androgynous women. When she was asked in an interview about Grace Jones, Lady Gaga replied that Jones is an "inspiration" for her (Touré "Lady Gaga: On the Record"). She further divulged, speaking again of Grace Jones, that in her opinion, "the androgyny of the woman is this kind of fascinating thing that nobody understands or wants to understand unless you are in the beautiful subculture that is my fans and also the gay community — they get it instantly and love it" (Touré "Lady Gaga: On the Record"). The androgyny associated with drag performance has the power to fascinate because of the way in which drag performers can occupy multiple genders at will. In her article entitled "One Body, Some Genders: Drag Performance and Technologies," drag performer Alana Kumbier reveals:

> As a drag performer, alternately king and queen, I inhabit the intersection of some genders (in my daily female embodiment, in the excessive masculinity that I perform in my sleazy macho king persona, Red Rider, and in the excessive femininity I performed as Red Pearl) [192].

Kumbier continues by explaining that these "multiple drag performances also allow me to make specific arguments supporting the denaturalization of gender and desire (as they relate to biological sex) to my audiences" (192–93). Remarks such as these help to illustrate the power of drag as well as the multiple (political, social, etc.) motives behind drag performances.

Ultimately, it is not entirely clear whether Lady Gaga intends her performance as Jo Calderone to be taken seriously (recall all the speculation about whether or not Jo Calderone is indeed Lady Gaga — and keep in mind how convincingly male his looks are), as parody (consider the exaggerated nature of the Jo Calderone persona alongside the comments he made at the photo shoot), or as something else altogether. Regardless of her exact intention, what matters most is that by taking on the male persona of Jo Calderone, Lady Gaga is nonetheless effectively calling into question traditional assumptions about gender. Reading her performance as parody makes sense on many levels, especially when we keep in mind that, as Judith Halberstam points out in her book *In a Queer Time and Place: Transgender Bodies, Subcultural Lives*, "drag king parodies of particularly white masculinity are perhaps the most popular form of drag king performance at present" (134). Yet, even if parody is Lady Gaga's goal, there is still a political end to her performance. If we consider her performance as parody, then "as parody, drag has subversive potential in the sense that it calls attention to the fiction of gender" (Surkan 163–64). Debra Silverman makes a similar point when she notes in her article entitled "Making a Spectacle: Or, Is There Female Drag?" that drag performance "calls into question the 'real' of any single assigned identity; drag is one performance of gender parody" (70).

If, on the other hand, Lady Gaga's intention as posing as a male (Jo Calderone) in the photo shoot is to "pass" as a man, there is a slightly different, although still a deliberately and decisively political, end to her performance. As Amelia Jones strongly argues in her book *The Feminism and Visual Culture Reader*:

> The most critical thing a transsexual can do, the thing that constitutes success, is to "pass." Passing means to live successfully in the gender of choice, to be accepted as a "natural member" of that gender. Passing means the denial of mixture. One and the same with passing effacement of the prior gender role, or the construction of a plausible history [189].

By convincingly portraying a male — befuddling so many and causing so much speculation through her adoption of her male alter ego — Lady Gaga achieves success on the level that Jones describes. By "passing," however, Lady Gaga also successfully challenges the notion that "desire" is heterosexual. Imagine the man (who has always seen himself as "straight") who desires "Lady Gaga" and then realizes *vis-à-vis* Jo Calderone (seeing photos of "Jo Calderone" and hearing about the controversy, for example) that the individual he desires ("Lady Gaga") is as much a deliberate creation as "Jo Calderone" is — one could make a similar argument about a woman who sees herself as "straight" and then feels desire and longing when confronted with the image of "Jo Calderone."[7]

Finally, if we take Lady Gaga's adoption of the male Jo Calderone persona to be something altogether different from either passing as male or as parody, then her drag performance perhaps goes even further in terms of challenging traditional and hegemonic notions about gender and hetero-norms. As Patricia Elliot and Katrina Roen note in their article, "Transgenderism and the Question of Embodiment: Promising Queer Politics," on some levels "both crossing and passing unwittingly reify positions of sexual and/or gender identity" (234). Similarly, parody arguably emphasizes the differences between genders (by exaggerating them), rather than more directly calling into question their very existence. Perhaps, Lady Gaga's intention in posing as Jo Calderone for the photo shoot is primarily to make people re-evaluate gender and desire.

Indeed, challenging people to reconsider the way they think and what they desire is something Lady Gaga has gone on record as saying she hopes to do through her music and performance art. In "The Broken Heart and Violent Fantasies of Lady Gaga," an interview she did with Neil Strauss for *Rolling Stone* magazine, Lady Gaga states that she wants to "seduce people to be interested in something that is uncomfortable" (70). Her adoption of the male alter ego Jo Calderone has succeeded in doing just that, but it has also challenged our society to re-think our views about gender. If she can don the guise of the male Jo Calderone just as easily as she adopts her female Lady Gaga persona — an over-the-top portrayal of the female form — then what does that say about our society's traditional views of— and notions about— gender? If she can challenge our preconceptions about gender, then she can also make us re-think desire, thus calling into question the validity of hetero-normativity and the heterosexual paradigm. Through the persona of Jo Calderone and the multiple other personae she adopts, Lady Gaga pushes cross-dressing into the realm of drag and gender play, but she also make a political statement through her Jo Calderone photo shoot — and her performance art, as a whole.

If there is anything that Lady Gaga's fans — and others who follow her performances — have come to expect from her, it to expect the unexpected, and there is no other arena where she has been more surprising than in her ability to transform. Lady Gaga discusses this herself at length, confiding her thoughts about the power of transformation and how alluring it is to her:

> It is this thing that summons me from the depths of reality and reminds me that the power of transformation is endless. That I (we) possess something magical and transformative inside — a uniqueness and specialness waiting to be exiled from the depths of our identity ["Lady Gaga Confused by Personae"].

It is through her multiple stage, screen, and print performance personae that Lady Gaga is thereby able to tap into the "endless" (as she puts it herself) power of transformation. This power, in turn, allows her convincingly to pose as a man, which gives her a platform to push the boundaries even further. Thus, by adopting the male "Jo Calderone" persona, Lady Gaga accomplishes at least two ends: she forces many people to re-think their assumptions about gender and desire at the same time as she pushes her ability to transform and shift her identity at will to a whole new level.

Notes

1. Lady Gaga has repeatedly referred to herself specifically as a "performance artist." For example, in her lengthy Fuse interview with Touré, she stresses that she views herself in that manner. In this interview, she not only says that she is a "performance artist," but she also emphasizes that her music is "performance art." In this interview, they discussed a number of things including her 2009 album *The Fame Monster*, as well as her music (in general), sexuality and the struggle for gay rights.

2. "Jo Calderone" was photographed by Nick Knight, a photographer who has worked frequently with Lady Gaga. The stylist for the photo shoot was Nicola Formicetti (who is known for being Lady Gaga's stylist).

3. I would like to thank Richard Gray for his insightful comments and helpful feedback on earlier drafts of this essay as well as Madison Humann, Ashley Humann and James Humann for their support and encouragement.

4. In 2010, Lady Gaga was ranked #7 on *Forbes*' list of 100 Most Powerful Women. Further evidence of Lady Gaga's status as a cultural icon resides in the fact that a college-level course centering on her stardom was offered at the University of South Carolina. Called "Lady Gaga and the Sociology of Fame," this 300-level course was taught by Professor Mathieu Deflem. See the article entitled "Lady Gaga studied: Sociology professor says course will be 'challenging'" in the November 2, 2010 edition of the *Atlanta Journal-Constitution*.

5. The publication is sometimes referred to as *Vogue Hommes Japan*.

6. See the August 25, 2010 issue of *New York Magazine*.

7. Though I read Lady Gaga as a deliberate creation of Germanotta's, she insists that Lady Gaga is *not* a character. She was asked in a *Lesbian News* interview "What is the biggest misconception people have about you?" Lady Gaga replied "They think Lady Gaga is a character" (31).

Follow the Glitter Way

Lady Gaga and Camp

KATRIN HORN

Gaga in Garland-land

When Dorothy was not in black and white Kansas anymore and instead hopped, danced, and sang her way along the yellow brick road in bright Technicolor and ruby slippers, a camp classic was born. Closeted "Friends of Dorothy" started using the film as a secret reference to their own homosexuality, while "Over the Rainbow" and its singer Judy Garland became gay icons to such an extent that her funeral indirectly sparked the gay rights movement and that "it is a truth almost universally acknowledged that a single man in the possession of a Judy Garland CD must not be in want of a wife" (Cohan 287).[1] *The Wizard of Oz* thus serves as a prime example of camp's function as queer community building and code-producing artifact from popular culture as well as a defining inspiration for the excessive aesthetics of camp. Queer fans as well as a diverse range of scholars, including Richard Dyer, reveled in the queer meaning and countercultural value of the 1939 musical, claiming the film as either a powerful metaphor of coming out, of the decision between a butch or femme identity or other queer-specific experiences, and thus cemented the iconic film's status as surpassing even that of Judy Garland's legendary Carnegie Hall Concert.[2] Though Lady Gaga has yet to play her first solo-show at Carnegie Hall and her professional career spans merely three years, pop's latest sensation is already notorious enough to raise similar suspicions as Garland about the "wants" of those who own a copy of *The Fame (Monster)* or a ticket to *The Monster Ball Tour*.[3] As a mixture of the outrageous *The Wizard of Oz* and the emotional Carnegie Hall concert (among others), Lady Gaga's "The Monster Ball," in particular, out-camps even Garland's triumphant legacy — a legacy Lady Gaga both playfully and purposefully engages, when she promises her Little Monsters that "The Monster Ball will be a place where they will finally be set free and tells them "...to get to The Monster Ball all you got to do is follow the Glitter Way" (*The Monster Ball Tour*). Though this verbal reference to *The Wizard of Oz*'s "Follow the Yellow Brick Road" might be understood as merely a superficial inside joke for those of her fans old enough to recognize the reference, I want to argue instead that Gaga employs both the intertextual references in her show and her work in general, of which there are plenty, as well as camp and camp aesthetics in meaningful ways. Lady Gaga's fondness for paying homage to earlier stars and icons is widely recognized and is as apparent in her name (taken from a Queen song) as in her commercial collaboration with Polaroid (whose instant-camera was extensively used by Andy Warhol) or her artistic output (such as the Madonna-inspired "Alejandro" video set to a beat reminiscent of Europop-band Ace of Base). Yet by turning her pop concerts thematically into an inspirational journey and visually into the bastard-child of postmodern video installation, a Britney-Spears clip, and a Broadway show, Gaga is doing more than simply referencing these camp predecessors in a meaningless pastiche of another era's styles and stars. Instead, Gaga is building her unique performances on quotations and pop ready-mades in order to establish a pop ancestry, which she at the same time outpaces, and a gendered identity, which she deconstructs at the very moment of its construction. In short, Gaga is employing camp as a strategy critically and politically to queer her persona and performance.

Camp's Queer Revival

Since pop divas like Lady Gaga today, as well as Cher, Annie Lennox or Madonna before, and camp often share the stage, it should not come as a surprise that they also share a common fate, namely that dismissal using tropes and stereotypes, their emphasis on style and their dangerous liaison with mainstream culture. Just as camp, the ironic-parodistic style that originated as a secret code in the Anglophone, gay subculture of the early 20th century, had been discarded by many queers as retrogressive after the Stonewall riots and subsequent emergence of the gay rights movement, Lady Gaga has been accused of having lost her subversive edge when trading the burlesque stages of downtown Manhattan for those of the MTV Video Music Awards.

The (re-)establishment of camp as a valid queer strategy in a Post-Stonewall culture depended upon and was informed by a new approach to the subject matter from queer and feminist perspectives. This revival of interest in camp originated in the 1980s, when, as David Bergmann states, "AIDS and poststructuralist theory [made] camp intellectually and politically respectable again" (9). Among the most important theories for this poststructuralist, queer notion of camp are those by Judith Butler, Pamela Robertson, Linda Hutcheon and Jack Babuscio, whose works helped to shape its conceptualization as a political, critical and potentially transgressive practice.[4] Essentially defined as a parodic device characterized by the four basic features of "irony, aestheticism, theatricality, and humor" (Babuscio 20), camp came to be understood as capable of questioning a given pretext's status as "original" or "natural," and able to open mainstream cultural production to queer readings, hence constituting a queer way of communicating in largely heteronormative commercial surroundings. This strong connection of camp to hegemonic discourses divides it from decisively countercultural queer and feminist techniques and strategies, and also leads to controversy about camp's progressive potential. Although Linda Hutcheon who insists that irony and parody, two important components of camp communication, gain their strength from their "intimacy with the dominant discourse" (*Irony* 89), I posit, however, that camp has the potential to become even more effective when placed in pop-cultural contexts. Despite opposing claims about the dominance of meaningless pastiche in contemporary culture, Hutcheon further argues for the transformative power of parody insofar as parody functions as "repetition with a critical difference" (*Parody* 7). "Critical difference" is produced through irony,[5] which as Hutcheon convincingly argues is not to be confused with ambiguity, as irony adds an evaluative edge. This critical and evaluative ironic effect is not only produced in the interaction between producer and recipient, but also in the interaction between what has objectively been "said" and the "unsaid," which is the implied meaning of this utterance, because "[i]rony rarely involves a simple decoding of a single inverted message; [...] it is more often a semantically complex process of relating, differentiating, and combining said and unsaid meanings" (*Irony* 89). The emphasis on the importance of both context and intertext, which is further stressed through the necessity of "markers" that serve the "'meta-ironic' function" of alerting the audience to the irony ahead (*Irony* 96), makes Hutcheon's concept of irony and parody especially productive for the definition and understanding of camp in pop-cultural contexts. For an analysis of camp, exaggeration and theatricality serve as examples of such markers easing communication between producers and audiences in the same "discursive community [...] constituted by shared concepts of norms of communication," such as gay communities or Gaga's Little Monsters (*Irony* 99).[6] Therefore, the position of Lady Gaga's performances and videos in mainstream discourse and the familiar pictures, ideas and stereotypes make the critique one that functions similarly to Judith Butler's claim for the transgressive power of gender parody: "[...] to make gender trouble, not through the strategies that figure a utopian beyond, but through the mobilization, subversive confusion, and proliferation of precisely those constitutive categories that seek to keep gender in its place by posing as the foundational illusions of identity" (46). Lady Gaga's thus defamiliarizes the familiar, rendering the seemingly normal abnormal, as camp "constantly draws attention to the artifices attendant on the construction of images of what is natural" (Dyer, *The Culture of Queers* 42). Thus, it can question the status of the polar opposite, namely the deviant, as queer pleasure and desire exemplify.

The notion of queer pleasure brings us back to pop divas and the question of why camp artists have such a strong connection to queer fans, while conservative critics dismiss them.[7] As Ken Feil notes, "camp involves a queer parody of dominant culture's deficiencies. This project amounts to a rebellious type of pleasure because it stresses the triumph of queerness against the limitations of the social world" (484). Part of this queer, rebellious type of pleasure in Lady Gaga's pop art stems — in keeping with camp's connection to queer genders — from her how her work defies the notions of essentialism, identity and originality. By refusing to acknowledge any identity behind the endlessly reproduced image of the artist and instead "reducing" her identity to clothes, masks and wigs, she constantly foregrounds the performativity of (artistic) identity and gender performance. In my analysis, Lady Gaga's use of camp strategies and playful engagement with pop culture's tropes makes room for the aforementioned "queer pleasure." Such tropes appear in her live shows, culminating in *The Monster Ball Tour*, and in her music video productions such as the 10 minute-clip for the song "Telephone." This analysis relates Gaga to her pop predecessors such as Andy Warhol, Judy Garland and Madonna, and their respective queer legacy.

Pulp, Performance, Parody — Gaga's Work in Context

The function of camp in Lady Gaga's work can be a means of creative re-signification as well as of critique and transgression. Both strategies would signify a queer surplus value. Among the most obvious tie-ins with queer discourses in Gaga's *œuvre* is the rejection of a stable gendered and sexual identity. Slipping effortlessly between female and male drag, between cone-bras and strap-ons, gay male S/M-sex scenes and lesbian make-out sessions in her videos and public appearances, Lady Gaga refuses to be defined by her sexuality — a fate common to most other female pop stars. Her over-the-top artificiality of her costumes seldom distinguishes between on- and off-stage clothing or private and star persona, which brings to mind Susan Sontag's claim that camp conceives of "being as playing a role" (56). The idea of role-play is central to camp's historic connection to predominantly gay and queer audiences as Jack Babuscio describes. He argues that camp is always closely connected with "gay sensibility" (19), for the development of which the necessity of passing for straight in a hostile environment is one important trigger.[8] According to Babuscio, this experience of passing heightens awareness of the theatricality of everyday life. Richard Dyer picks up this idea and concludes that the "gay sensibility" and consequently camp as well "hold together qualities that are elsewhere felt as antithetical: theatricality and authenticity [...] intensity and irony, a fierce assertion of extreme feeling and a deprecating sense of its absurdity" ("Judy Garland and Gay Men" 163). Even though Dyer refers to the diva-worshipping of Judy Garland and her contemporaries more than thirty years ago, his words transfer easily to Lady Gaga, most notably to her relation to and interaction with fans at concerts.

"The Monster Ball" alludes to voguing balls in its name and to stage musicals. It evokes community, kinship, and non-biological family ties of the freaks and outsiders, in this case known as Little Monsters, into a Broadway show-act. This contradiction between seriousness and the extravagant, between a certain superficiality and deep concern, creates the paradoxical effect Dyer attributes to camp appreciation. Christopher Isherwood describes the anti-ethical quality of camp in his novel *The World in the Evening* (1954), where one of his fictional characters claims "You can't camp about something you don't take seriously" (110).[9] Isherwood frames this definition by the story of isolation that a gay character in a rural area feels, his need for a feeling of connection to others and the search for a way to express himself. The novel "describe[s] camp as strategy of self-identification, [...] by associating it with the politics of marginality and by emphasizing the communal empowerment that the strategy enforces" (Dennishoff 135). "The Monster Ball" borrows this theme and thus becomes one of the most notable examples of the strategic use of camp in Lady Gaga's *œuvre* to achieve queer pleasure. Divided into four acts set in New York City, titled City, Subway, Forest, and Monster Ball, the story of *The Monster Ball Tour* is ripe with over-the-top imagery. A short video introduces each of the four parts,[10] which in stark contrast to the colorful live act itself is shot in either black and white or unsaturated colors. Jarring visual effects such as a gush of turquoise disrupt the almost sterile aesthetic of the interludes, which performance artist Millie Brown ostensibly vomits onto Lady Gaga's dress, or dark red blood pouring from a heart Lady Gaga seems to devour. Staccato-like editing of the clips further emphasize the contrast between these interludes and the playful live-show that make the body of Lady Gaga and other protagonists rhythmically match their house/electro score, distancing the interludes from the pop-centric show. The bodies in these interludes are disjointed or merge into the backgrounds to become inseparable from their environment and unrecognizable as humans. They function as mere stand-ins for lifeless fashion mannequins and as ornamental features for the already highly abstract imagery. Against this extremely artificial and cool background, the live parts of the show, which are characterized by overtly emotional confessions, highly sexualized bodies and intertextual references to both queer-coded and nostalgic cultural artifacts, become even more legible as a camp spectacular, since "camp [...] thrives on mischievous incongruity" (Medhurst 158).

The show opens at its most dramatic with a panic and pain evoking guttural scream by Lady Gaga from the song "Dance in the Dark." As the opening video fades away and the neon signs of the city-scenery appear, Lady Gaga is a shadow on the top of a staircase. The scenery is reminiscent of a rundown former amusement area, a Times Square for has-beens so to speak, where instead of fashionable consumer products, bold letters advertise whiplashes, death cases, and car accidents. BBQ and "good food" are on equal footing with liquor and drugs, as are sedation, implants and dentistry, which all seem to be available at the same place right around the corner of "Hotel (T)Hass."[11] Pop culture's obsession with decay on the one side and beauty on the other, or more precisely the decay of beauty — a recurring theme in Lady Gaga's work — is thus written into *The Monster Ball Tour* from the very beginning. The opening number "Dance in the Dark" picks up this thematic emphasis, as the song is dedicated to a number of mainly female celebrities (with the exception of the legendary Las Vegas entertainer Liberace) who were crushed by their image and the expectations that came with it. Lady Di, Sylvia Plath, Marilyn Monroe, the child beauty pageant participant JonBenét Ramsey, and Judy Garland all died tragically before their time, either by suicide, murder or other "fame-related complications." Gaga also refers to their infamous double-lives, where personal struggles such as bulimia, drug-addiction or homosexuality on the one and public persona on the other hand had to be kept separate at all costs. Matching both this idea of duplicity and the atmosphere of stage design, for most of the song only Lady Gaga's motionless silhouette can be seen behind a gauze screen. At the end of the song, she descends a staircase with handrails made of injection needles in a pants-less purple costume with giant shoulder pads. The scene both evokes and parodies a common show business trope, the classical diva entrance such as Norma Desmond's, the aging star in *Sunset Boulevard*, while the needles serve as a reference to both drug abuse and plastic surgery. "Dance in the Dark" furthermore connects its commentary on fame and public pressure with a more general examination of women's potentially destructive body image. Low self-esteem due to a lack of positive role models and isolation as well as condescending and judgmental messages from a patriarchal environment leaves women feeling either unattractive or slutty. A neon sign literally states this sexy/ugly-divide, but it also manifests in the song succession, which places the bleak "Dance in the Dark" back-to-back with Lady Gaga's breakthrough hit and disco anthem "Just Dance." Positioning Lady Gaga as both the vulnerable protagonist of "Dance in the Dark" as well as the careless drunk party-goer of "Just Dance," *The Monster Ball Tour* not only rejects the rigid distinction between these female archetypes, but through this accentuated role-play foreshadows a burlesque-inspired female mimicry, which characterizes the rest of the show.[12] Furthermore, in this constellation and context, "Just Dance" rises from shallow pop song to sign of empowerment, mirroring Mark Booth's assertion that camp involves "being committed to the marginal with a commitment greater than the marginal [object] merits [in dominant discourses]" (69). In connection to the aspects of gender parody, which are visible in Lady Gaga's stage show, the merit of camp in turn lies in "show[ing] that gender should be a game, something we play at. [...] Camp allows us to not take ourselves too seriously while exposing the violence and oppression implicit in all gender enforcement" (Eisner 262).

Whereas the interludes are full of violence directed at bodies and restrictions against their free movement and expression, the live-show features humorous and playful feminine and queer masquerade that revels in exaggerated stereotypes and the artificiality of gender and social roles. Many of the parodied roles are borrowed from musicals, which is especially noteworthy insofar as Steven Cohan finds "[...] the open acknowledgement in musicals that masculinity and femininity are equally performative, and that this performativity has spectacle as its intent" (xvi).[13] From the *Grease*-inspired "Just Dance" costumes and stage design, *The Monster Ball Tour* develops into a distorted *Wizard of Oz* tribute. Distorted, because the destination is not Auntie Em's farmhouse or another stand-in for a traditional home, but rather the Monster Ball, which is closer do the freak-populated Emerald City than Kansas. Niall Richardson describes the moral of *The Wizard of Oz*, which regards as "one of the most popular road movies ever," as follows:

> [...] Dorothy resolves her Oedipal drama, finds her family and attains traditional subjectivity [...] Dorothy yearns for Auntie Em and her secure home life and, arguably, the film's camp popularity exists because gay men, like Dorothy, feel marginalized from mainstream domesticity and therefore enjoy the fantasy of returning to, and gaining acceptance within, traditional culture [56].

Yet as camp's function in popular culture has changed and taken on more queer than gay connotation, a camp re-telling of Dorothy's adventures must also change the moral of the story — the crucial difference being that "queers resist the regimes of the normal. It implies that we redefine the problem of homosexual liberation so that we no longer fight intolerance but resist normalization" (Escoffier 175). Where *The Wizard of Oz* aimed for acceptance and inclusion by whatever was deemed to be "normal," the story and style of "The Monster Ball" instead do not look or turn back to any kind of traditional home or family and instead head for a place beyond any vision of the normal, where being free in the company of kindred spirits is the goal rather than being accepted by any authorial figure or the heteronormative majority. This vision of freedom, however, is not only projected onto a distant and abstract place at the end of the road. Rather, journey as well as traveler already symbolize freedom from social restraints, as Gaga herself exemplifies who — while impersonating a dominatrix or nun, wearing an orbit or practically nothing — uses the Neo-Burlesque technique of impersonating femininity with a twist, thereby making the undress a tease and consequently a symbol of being in control of one's own body and sexuality. Thus, her performance highlights the artificiality of what has come to stand for "female" much like that of a drag queen, yet with Lady Gaga being a biological woman her critique becomes even more potent as she as the appropriation of drag strategies amounts to a revolt against sexual binaries.[14]

Among the most clearly marked feminine roles in "The Monster Ball" is that of Tinker Bell, the fairy from J.M. Barrie's *Peter Pan*, made famous by the Disney animated film. As such, she quickly gained "family-friendly" nostalgic connotations similar to those of *The Wizard of Oz*.[15] Yet a queer reevaluation of Tinker Bell reminiscent of Dorothy's camp reclaiming has also occurred.[16] Lady Gaga evokes both dimension of the Tinker Bell character when she lies on the stage in a black leather outfit and fake blood smeared over her throat and arms, and then turns to the audience to say:

> "Do you think I'm sexy? 'Cause I think you're sexy.
> [*audience clapping and screaming*]
> I don't believe you. Do you think I'm sexy?
> You know I'm kinda like Tinker Bell. If you don't clap for her, she dies.
> Do you want me to die?" ["The Monster Ball Tour"].

Gaga's reincarnation of Tinker Bell, contrary to the persona established in the well-known film, speaks for herself and actively solicits the attention and validation she needs to survive. The incongruous combination of the sweet and mute fairy's background with her sex-positive and outspoken rendition is both a dismissing comment on the child-woman ideal that Disney's Tinker Bell represents, as well as a gesture symbolic of Gaga's status as a star, insofar as the scene puts the power into the clapping hands of her fans. Thus, the episode further strengthens the communal aspect of the show by parodying the idea of and redefining the boundaries of sexiness queerly to include a rumored-to-be hermaphrodite in a bondage costume. Yet "The Monster Ball" does not completely discard the image of the sparkling and winged fairy, true to Isherwood's dictum that "you can't camp about something you don't take seriously. You're not making fun of it; you're making fun out of it" (110). Fulfilling the expectation raised by the "glitter way" reference to *Wizard of Oz*'s yellow-brick-road in the beginning, the concert features the film's iconic twister in the form of a giant tube of screens, lowered onto the stage.[17]

> "Oh, what's that thing way up in the sky? It's very beautiful but very strange. Is it rainbow? No. Ohh, I don't feel so well. Little Monster ... I'm feeling very strange.
> Oh no, it's a twister!" ["The Monster Ball"].

In this scene, Gaga takes on the role of the naïve child-like woman again, marking the connection to Dorothy as well as the film's queer status through referencing Dorothy's signature song. Yet when Gaga re-emerges from the eye of the storm, her outfit does not resemble Dorothy's dull dress, rather it is an extravagant re-interpretation of the fairy-like Glinda, good witch of the North. The result is the so-called "Living Dress," inspired by Hussein Chalayan and designed by costume designer Vin Burnham, which earns its name from a system of mechanical components that can be remote-controlled to move different parts of the dress, as well as the respective headpiece and wings. During the song "So Happy I Could Die," Lady Gaga merges these two characters, lost Dorothy and Glinda, who is not only a mighty sorceress, but also the decisive figure, who lets Dorothy know about her powers and how she can use them (even if it is only to get home). The episode resonates with the overall story arc of being self-sufficient in one's way to freedom and personal growth, while delivering the most awe-inspiring and show-stopping sight of the evening, or as Isherwood ended his definition of camp, "you're expressing what's basically serious to you in terms of fun and artifice and elegance" (110). Most striking about "The Monster Ball" from a camp and queer perspective is not only its frequent recourse to cultural artifacts with an inherent gay appeal, but even more importantly the underlying seriousness of the show despite its superficial flamboyance and visual extravagance. Illustrating Linda Hutcheon's stand on irony and ambiguity as opposite rather than connected, "The Monster Ball" is never ambiguous in its artistic and political message. The show takes a firm stand towards what is to be expected at the end of the glitter way. It reveals in the monstrous community despite or maybe even because of its frequent tongue-in-cheek moments and humorous components. The rejection of any normalizing authority regarding gender, sexuality and morals is never compromised. This relates queer Lady Gaga back to gay Judy Garland, who was just as likely as Lady Gaga "to share the insider jokes [...]. The one thing Garland never kidded, however, was 'Over the Rainbow.' She knew the complex and highly personal associations the song had for many in her audience, and she never distanced herself from those emotions" (Jennings 100). Lady Gaga follows a similarly appreciative rationale not only in her live-shows of which "The Monster Ball" is a prime example, but also in her inter-views, tweets and music videos. The latter rely equally heavily on camp, yet due to the less direct mode of communication, they add to the aforementioned "triumph of queerness" not so much through community-building aspects. Instead her music videos serve to even more overtly criticize modes of repre-sentation and hegemonic discourses on gender and sexuality. As is the case in "The Monster Ball," Gaga's videos feature a plethora of intertexts with specific queer and gay resonance to that effect. Yet it is not only of interest what they refer to both visually and narratively, but more importantly, how these texts are recycled and infused with an additional evaluative and critical edge — which, as previously mentioned, signifies meaning-making as compared to mere humor and meaningless pastiche.

Camp achieves this edge by "laying bare the devices." Via the over-the-top exaggeration of images and structures as well as a foregrounding of the artificiality of the presented, camp renders the mundane incredible. This is the basic premise, for example, of "feminist camp" as Pamela Robertson sug-gests in her book *Guilty Pleasures-Feminist Camp from Mae West to Madonna.* Robertson, one the most influential scholars to apply Butler's idea concerning gender parody to a camp analysis of popular media, advances the argument that women can — despite camp's historical roots in predominately gay male subculture — "reclaim camp as a political tool and rearticulate it within the theoretical framework of feminism," since "camp offers a model for critiques of gender and sex roles" (6). The basis for this re-articulation is her model of female masquerade, where the "credibility of images of the feminine can be undermined by a 'double-mimesis' or 'parodic mimicry'" (10). Though Robertson herself limits her discussion of this parodic mimicry to straight women and does not go into the possibility of lesbian camp at length, her work still constitutes an important reference point for thinking about female queer viewing practices. Robertson argues that camp functions not only as a distancing device for female spectators, but also as a way to enhance the pleas-ure that they can derive from cultural products, which may not at first appear to either liberate or to empower. Camp allows for both the potentially misog-ynistic, homophobic, or merely normative mainstream entertainment on the one hand and the critical distance toward depictions on screen/video/radio on the other, to coexist and interact with one another.

Camp can be a form of "detached attachment" in the audience, which is made possible by camp's overthrowing of hierarchies of form and content. The seemingly trivial form produces an altogether new content and thereby a new level of potentially resistive consumption. A camp reading thus relies on the audience' ability to not only notice, for example, the clichéd and repetitive narratives of Mae West's films or their reliance on old-fashioned sexual innuendo, but also how their use of excessive style functions as an evaluative marker of distance to the employed norms.[18] This is, of course, not only true for moments of spectatorship itself, but has a lasting effect and will — like all consumption of art — influence future encounters with similar images, sounds and stories. Consequently, Lady Gaga's choice of pre-texts is significant for her camp reading and its critical potential, especially with regards to pop cultural texts and concepts. One particularly interesting example for such "laying bare" and "over-performing" strategies is the setting and theme of her collaboration with Beyoncé for the song "Telephone." The video is a remake of lesploitation-films, drawing on the clichéd and sexualized images from a string of "girls behind bars"–B-movies.[19] Like other exploitation films, most prominently the genres blaxploitation and sexploitation, the lesploitation-film was constructed around minority issues and fringe topics presumably for the titillation and viewing pleasure of the white straight male. The lesploitation-genre in particular was based on the objectification of women's bodies and female — especially lesbian — sexuality, the trivialization of violence against women, and the impossibility of meaningful bonding among women.[20] Since these characteristics are to varying extents still defining features of current pop culture, the combination of this theme with the collaboration of two of the most successful and influential contemporary female pop artists is revealing. With lesploitation, the creative team behind "Telephone" chose a theme that has already been re-appropriated by queer, namely lesbian audiences. The process is comparable to the on-going cult-success of 50's gay and lesbian pulp novels whose colorful and sensationalistic covers can be seen as an inspiration for the sets and costumes of "Telephone." Pulp's cultural significance as camp, however, stems from the interaction between the attention-grabbing covers and even shallow literary quality with their often serious content:

> Even as these texts were instrumental in creating certain stereotypes (or, conversely, archetypes) of queerness, which were often internalized and made iconic — for better or worse — by the gay and lesbian audiences, their very lack of respectability allowed them to perform the iconoclastic function of presenting, if only obliquely, subversively positive images [Smith 1999 xxi].

In portraying the lesbian femme in "Telephone," whose image was made popular in mainstream culture by exactly these pulp novels, Lady Gaga also adds another significant component to the ever growing array of gender performances expressed in her photo shoots as well as on stage and screen, ranging from hyper-femininity to androgyny and conflating lesbian femme and drag queen, stud and true lady.[21] Complementing the recurring habit of gender parody in Gaga's *œuvre*, the "Telephone" video emphasizes the potential for queer pleasure in the genre in several ways: it casts butch performance artist Heather Cassils as the object of the protagonist's desire who defies both genre and cultural norms through her female masculinity; it installs two female bodybuilders as guards, who, however, are not either sadistic or lonely outsiders like their counterparts in the original texts; it brings the female gaze into the foreground via shots of female onlookers.[22] Perhaps most importantly, the video adds the lesbian happy ending most of the traditional lesploitation films lack, when Gaga and Beyoncé drive off into the sunset together. Tavia Nyong'o summarizes the appeal of this approach by stating that "what is innovative about "Telephone" is its upending of the heterosexual fantasies that underpinned both the archive of mainstream representation and so many of its intentionally offensive and transgressive alternatives" ("Iphone"). Another important source for the "rebellious type of pleasure" (Feil 484) one can derive from the video lies in its over-the-top visual design, which at times produces a narrative counteracting or at least complicating the plot and the stereotypes it employs. Having Lady Gaga arrive in a low-cut latex-suit, for example, sporting stripes otherwise known from early prison uniforms, undercuts the supposed innocence and naïveté of the "new girl," which the normative "girls behind bars"-storyline requires. The clothing accentuates how "Telephone" deviates significantly from the genre's original plot line: the new inmate is actually already known to be guilty, since the audience has witnessed the character's cold-blooded murder of her abusive boyfriend in the "Paparazzi" video to which "Telephone" serves as sequel. While wearing a yellow Mickey-Mouse-costume, which mocks the infantilizing tendencies of pop culture, and drinking her signature tea, a symbol of both aristocracy and aloofness, the main character "Paparazzi" had shown no sign of remorse or guilt during the poisoning. Whereas the lesploitation film tries to uphold the image of the ultimately available and seemingly — at least in the beginning — tamable young girl, "Telephone" instead starts with Lady Gaga as an established criminal. In other scenes, the video does not directly contradict but rather exaggerates what the lesploitation-genre accepts as a given: the glamorization and sexualization of life behind bars. The effect, however, is everything but reassuring for the originally implied straight male viewer, if one takes a closer look for example at the cage-dance sequence. It occurs as one of only three dance-parts in the ten-minute long "Telephone" short film and thus resembles the occasional dance-number in film musicals. In the first of these three scenes

Gaga dances seductively in the prison hall, her movements mimicked by scantily clad and conventionally attractive female backup dancers. Their dance choreography is, however, interrupted by scenes depicting Lady Gaga as the victim of a crime, or rather her body as a living crime scene as she is wrapped in "crime scene, do not cross" barrier tape, whose limbs still move rhythmically to the music in a fashion to what could be seen in "The Monster Ball" interludes.

The unsettling combination of violence against and the objectification of the female body repeat in the other two dance sequences as well, once when Gaga and Beyoncé dance in a pool of dead bodies and again when Lady Gaga prepares poison for a mass-murder. In all three scenes, Gaga represents a stereotype of women's conventional presentation in the media: the sexy stripper, the devoted housewife, the chaste Wonder Woman. All three figures are constituted through costume, hair, setting, and makeup in a way that underlines their constructedness and through their close connection to violence in the video, also their inherently oppressive nature. While thus subverting the allure of conventional ideas about gender identity and desire, the video at the same time makes room for positive depictions of queer desires and gender performances, which the genre — and by extension today's media — often tries to repress. The genre of the lesploitation film especially lends itself to the discussion of gender expressions and women's depiction in popular media, because

> while men do appear [...], this is a [...] genre, where relationships between women are paramount. Differences between women are stressed, as if to take the place usually occupied by gender: differences between butch and femme personae, differences in age, differences between types of crime (particularly prostitution versus everything else), physical differences [Mayne 127].

These various kinds of differences between female protagonists are reflected in "Telephone," where men appear only in minor roles as such as backup dancers, diner guests and as another abusive boyfriend, this time Beyoncé's, who is quickly killed. Women, however, are represented in all shapes and sizes and several constellations of power, antagonism, friendship and desire without being devaluated or played off against each other. Rather than using the wardens' nonconforming bodybuilder-physique to divert from Lady Gaga's own rumored sex deviation, the video stresses the connection between these different kinds of women as gender outlaws. At the same time, the video portrays as attractive what heteronormative culture would reject, such as androgynous and muscular Heather Cassils or curvy women of color in the prison yard, while placing conventionally attractive women, such as Gaga's female dancers or even Beyoncé herself in situations and contexts that diminish or problematize their potential sexual allure. Thus "Telephone" inverts the power dynamics of media reception, where the empowering or queer reading of such products as lesploitation films are relegated as "readings against the grain" or appropriations. Here, by contrast, any straight reading would be forced to justify itself as a valid re-appropriation. This is especially visible if "Telephone" is compared to the preceding collaboration between these two performers, Beyoncé's "Video Phone." Based on their lyrics, the two songs can be opposing treatments of a common theme in pop, namely the supposed availability of women. "Video Phone" invites the implied male partner to make use of advanced communication technology in order observe (and control) Beyoncé at will, while "Telephone" reminds him that even smartphones can be switched off and that Gaga defines the conditions of her availability herself. These contrasting messages are mirrored in the respective videos, as "Video Phone" consists almost exclusively of dance sequences by either Beyoncé alone or supported by Lady Gaga, whose male onlookers, albeit slightly abstracted through their heads merging with lenses and cameras, feature prominently in the video. Thus, the video's art direction further underlines the privileging of the male viewing pleasure already laid out in the lyrics. "Telephone" in turn complicates questions of the gaze, in part by adding a narrative in which women are the driving force rather than ornamental accessories. The only intradiegetic video of Gaga is showing her leaving the prison as if strutting down a runway. The other "recordings" are Polaroid pictures that Gaga takes of herself and Beyoncé. These can be read in two ways. On the one hand, they are blatant product placement for a brand for which Gaga has recently been chosen as Creative Director, thereby underscoring her status as influential business woman even inside the narrative of the music clip. On the other hand, the Polaroid Pictures refer to another iconic, if again unusual, road movie, namely *Thelma & Louise* (1991). As such, the pictures of Gaga and Beyoncé are not meant to be seen primarily by men. In reference to the intertext that they evoke, they are instead taken to capture a moment of female bonding. But whereas a picture is all that remains of the heroines in the original road movie, in Telephone the Polaroids serve to capture the fleetingness and spontaneity of a moment, which in contrast to *Thelma & Louise* does not stand for defiance through self-annihilation, but for triumph repression. Thus "Telephone" pays homage to and positively retells a watershed-story of 90's progressive "girl power" culture, while also manipulating its idea about women and their limited access to freedom and mobility.[23]

A similar method is used in the video's treatment of another film that also combines the genres of rape-revenge and road movie, both flawed in their usefulness for creating filmic spaces for women. Quentin Tarantino's *Kill Bill: Vol. 1* is referenced not only through the story of an abused woman who goes on a killing spree, but also through the use of film's most iconic prop, the Pussy Wagon. Yet "Telephone" brings the Pussy Wagon closer again to its original meaning as a ridiculous, but ultimately endearing "chick magnet" from the musical *Grease* than the negative connotations it took on in Tarantino's film, where it serves a constant visual reminder of the female protagonist's sexual exploitation.[24] While Tarantino used the Pussy Wagon as a cynical joke at the women's expense, "Telephone" makes the car exemplify freedom, mobility and unity between the female couple. This re-signification is further underscored visually, as the pink and yellow pickup with huge flame ornaments in *Kill Bill* is a comment on the owner's lack of taste and a kind of comic relief. In the stylized, bright colored aesthetics of "Telephone," however, the car blends in — its literalized purpose written onto the car perfectly complementing Gaga's and Beyoncé's figurative costumes. The reclaiming of the car as a feminist space, or rather the subversion of the car as a predominantly masculine space in film and popular media is additionally achieved via Lady Gaga's wearing of an otherwise out-of-context leopard-print catsuit. The costume evokes the one worn by Shania Twain in the video for her song "That Don't Impress Me Much," another version of the independent woman favored by 90's pop culture. Yet whereas Shania Twain's progressive image of modern womanhood depended on her free choice of which ride to take as a hitchhiker, "Telephone" has Lady Gaga dance in front of a pickup truck that either she or "Honey B" (Beyoncé's character in the video) owns. By connecting "Telephone" aesthetically with these references to patriarchy, heterosexuality, and pop-cultural ideals of femininity, the narration strengthens the queer subtext, as the already implicit romantic pairing of its leading female character is positioned in relation to and opposition with patterns of heterosexual gender relations. Thus, the visual allusions suggest reading Gaga's and Beyoncé's characters as in a relationship, which ties in with the significance of Beyoncé's ethnic marking as correlating to lesploitation's treatment of race, as Judith Mayne suggests that "[...] the opposition of black women and white women is eroticized" in the genre (138). "Telephone," however, does not limit itself to a lesbian reading, but stresses the queer performativity of gender and sexuality by tying in the lesbian couple with Gore Vidal's most famous literary (and later filmic) creation, the transsexual character Myra Breckinridge. According to Dennis Altman, the film *Myra Breckinridge* (1970) "was part of a major cultural assault on the assumed norms of gender and sexuality which swept the Western world in the late 1960s and early 1970s [...]" (132). Its titular character is introduced into the world of "Telephone" via the quoting of its most iconic costume, namely the stars and stripes bikini outfit revived by Gaga's and Beyoncé's costumes in the video's third dance sequence. Especially given Gaga's own precarious status as multi-gendered woman, the reference is both daring and humorous, as it creates an string of gender deferrals: Lady Gaga poses as a hermaphrodite, who passes as a woman, who is playing a lesbian that is mimicking a transsexual man, who passes as a woman modeled on the asexual Wonder Woman. A reading of the *Myra Breckinridge* original comes to the conclusion that "[...] through its camp conventions the novel queers these heterosexual acts, reminding us of the queers who exist in its margins — and who must be erased by the end" (Eisner 267). Yet the contemporary performance of Myra, as well as of numerous other icons, figures, and characters from the above mentioned films and texts, lack any tragic components, specifically a tragic ending, which changes their function entirely. Gender deviants in "Telephone" no longer serve as foils against which to posit the "healthy" alternative, a heteronormative lifestyle. Rather, they are represented as the alternative themselves when what dominant discourses with much media support have deemed "good" and "normal" is exposed as artificial and/or oppressive. In outrageous costumes, wigs and masks, the music video's protagonists, above all Gaga herself, enact the significance of camp

> as a "queer performativity," through which a subjectivity is enacted that takes not the heterosexist imperatives of sexually and ideologically self-reproductive, marriage-sanctioned, sexuality as its exemplary performative act (as in what we might label "orthodox," or "straight" performativity), but rather the queer deviation, and demystification, of those very imperatives [Cleto 32].

Reveling in the seemingly shallow and stereotypical, exaggerating known forms and conventions, and taking sexism and objectification to its extreme, Lady Gaga's work achieves to place an ironic, demystifying parody at the heart of pop culture. Via camp, it re-appropriates mainstream discourses and makes room for the unsettling, disturbing, and in turn, empowering and queer. This use of camp "operates as an aggressive metamorphosing operation, attacking norms of behavior, appearance, and art to revel in their inherent artifice" (Klinger 135). Just as the "Telephone" video's "prison for bitches" — i.e. the gender deviants and unruly women — cannot actually contain its transgressive inmates, so mainstream media discourse, too, is unable to hold its inherent queer potential at bay as the video, and Gaga's artistic output generally shows.

Gaga for Pop's Giants: The Truth Isn't Out (There)

Lady Gaga's rootedness in a pop ancestry made up partially of other "unruly women" was beautifully demonstrated when she appeared at the 2010 MTV Video Music Awards ceremony for what was to become one of her most shocking appearances in a dress made entirely out of raw meat. As she climbed the stairs to the stage to accept her award for "Bad Romance" as Best Video of The Year, she handed her meat purse to Cher, who was dressed in a fishnet costume reminiscent of the one which had received similar reactions of outrage and critique twenty years earlier — at the time the see-through dress even got her strongly homoerotic video for *If I Could Turn Back Time* banned from *MTV*. Standing side by side on the *MTV* stage in dresses emblematic of the evolution of what is and has been deemed "shocking" on national TV, Cher and Gaga served as a stunning visual reminder of the at times paradoxical demands of the entertainment industry. Award shows and video productions continue to expect its female stars in particular to look sexy, while at the same time never to transgress the rather arbitrary line of decency and good taste. Insofar as "[...] camp is a method by which the hegemony is queered, denaturalized, and thus, subverted through *over-articulation*" (Devitt "Girl on Girl" 32, emphasis mine), both Cher's overtly revealing vintage fishnet costume, as well as Gaga's quite literal interpretation of the demand for more "naked flesh" are critical responses to pop culture's interpolation.

Lady Gaga and her work appear even more firmly in line with a pop ancestry via the defiance of any notion of artistic or gendered "truth" and assumed authenticity. The connection to this exact pop history in turn influences how critics read her and underscores the community-strengthening code character of her persona and performances. As she herself acknowledged in numerous interviews, her art would be unreadable, maybe even unthinkable without prominent predecessors ranging from Pop Art and Glam Rock to feminist camp icons.[25] Of course, a critique of her work should not depend solely on those names referred to in magazines or referenced in style and attitude. Yet taking into account that figures such as Andy Warhol, Grace Jones, David Bowie, Queen, Madonna and Cher and texts like *Caged Heat*, *The Wizard of Oz* or the films of New Queer Cinema that heavily influenced the aesthetics of "Alejandro," for example, considered an important part of contemporary queer discourse and identity, her references to these pop icons cannot be underestimated in their appeal to and identificatory potential for her fans.

Yet, were Gaga's work limited to simple imitation and quotation, the sum of it would amount to mere pastiche, and thus actually diminish the critical potential of her work. Instead the references together with her exaggerated aesthetics function in a similar way to Linda Hutcheon's meta-ironic markers, as they suggest the question to the performance's audience that Sedgwick describes as the camp-realization in contrast to kitsch-attribution, "What if the right audience for this were exactly me?" (qtd. in Tinkcom 46). This establishment of a specific queer context enables her strategic use of camp, in which the methods of former practitioners of camp are updated. The use of allusions is essential even, since "if camp 'is' something, it is the crisis of identity, of depth, and of *gravity*. Not a stable code, therefore, but rather a discourse produced by the friction with and among other discourses [...]" (Cleto 34).

The invention of the Candy Warhol-character for the interludes of the first concert tour, aptly titled *The Fame Ball*, exemplifies this process of combining different references and discourses to create meaning not at either end of the given spectrum, but in the interplay between the different points of reference. The figure presents itself as a combination of pop artist Andy Warhol and his transgender muse and actress, Candy Darling. By merging creator and creation in Lady Gaga as Candy Warhol, the creative minds behind The Haus of Gaga, take Warhol's idea that everyone can become famous to the logical extreme that anyone can make themselves famous, while at the same time The Haus can be understood as an advancement of Warhol's factory. Whereas the name "factory" still kept the private and public sphere apart by alluding to the difference between living and working spaces (Lobel 44), the Haus disclaims such traditional notions and brings the concept of actively produced identities even into the most private spaces when re-named Bath House of Gaga in the video for "Bad Romance." A critical approach to fame and the role of celebrities reflected in this re-working of Warhol also appears in the music of Gaga itself. Her use of Auto-Tune is specifically interesting in this regard, as this technique is most commonly used in pop music to digitally enhance the quality of a performer's voice.[26] Yet as Gaga's voice does not necessarily need digital enhancement, her extensive use of Auto-Tune in some of her songs, such as "Just Dance," adds another feature to her conscious performance of pop. The technique has become one significant part of pop music and has often been pointed out as a sign of to the demise of "real stars/real talents." For Gaga, however, altering her voice with Auto-Tune is not the last straw she is clinging to in her attempt to strike the right tone, but merely another form of masquerade, which further connects her Cher, who introduced the extensive use of Auto-Tune in one of her biggest hits, "Believe" (1999). In her discussion of the song, its technical aspects, as well as its success among gay fans, Kay Dickinson establishes the combination of Auto-Tune and female pop-voices as one way of expressing camp aesthetics aurally, as it expresses "a certain delight in the inauthentic, in things which are obviously pretending to be what they are not" (34). Lyrically, this notion resurfaces in Warhol's quotation about celebrity culture, "I love Hollywood. They're beautiful. Everybody's plastic, but I love plastic. I want to be plastic," in one of Lady Gaga's most overtly meta-referential songs, "Paparazzi." The integration of Hollywood iconography as the hallmark of celebrity, fame and glamour is as paramount in Gaga's work as it had been in Warhol's, whose images "force viewers seriously to consider what happens beneath the iconography of commodity fetishism" (Dyer, J. 34).

It is important to note, however, that glamour itself may already contain subversive elements as historically, "[...] in many contexts a desire for glamour represented an audacious refusal to be imprisoned by norms of class and gender, or by expectations of conventional femininity" (Dyhouse 3), hence the connection of many female camp icons from Mae West, Greta Garbo and Judy Garland to Cher and Madonna to glamour. Lady Gaga's outlandish clothes as well as her frequent collaborations with well-known artists have helped to establish an equally glamorous image, which combine with her almost daily change of style and leads to frequent comparisons with the Queen of Pop, Madonna.

Pamela Robertson, whose discussion of Madonna's subversive value remains rather ambiguous, nonetheless accounts for Madonna's "cumulative image from her varied and multiple performances [...] as a kind of meta-masquerade" (125–26). Though Robertson relates this masquerade only to Madonna's feminist value, it connects to Judith Butler's remarks on performative subjectivity and how they relate to Warhol's practice of producing similar, but never identical images and portraits. Pop-divas' constant self-reinvention as well as Warhol's varying copies, while formulated on different levels, have in common that they leave "a trace of difference to queer subjectivity" (Dyer, "The Metaphysics of the Mundane" 55). They alert their audience to the fact that "formative matrices, such as political systems or discursive structures, cannot completely articulate the subject" (55). In an interview accompanying a photo shoot, in which she is seen without a bra, but with the silhouette of a strap-on clearly visible beneath her pants, Gaga illustrates his theme and comments on the press' obsession with the "truth" about celebrities and personal identity — as if there was such a thing:

> Y'know, we always laugh when we get some major magazine and they're like *[high-camp voice]*, So, the art direction of the shoot is: we want the worlds to see *the real you*. [...]. That's like saying *[whispers conspirationally]*, "We know you're full of shit. But it's fine, *we* get it. So let's just cut the bullshit for one shoot. 'But you don't really wanna get to know me or photograph my soul, you want to do some version of what you already think I am and then expose something that you believe is hidden. When the truth is, me and my big fucking dick are all out there for you. But I'm not angry, I'm laughing. The joke is not on me, it's on *you*'" [Patterson 52].

Thus elevating a sex-toy to the status of identity signifier, Gaga once again articulates the "[...] opposition between authentic subjectivity and inauthentic society" (Suárez 134) that has been shown as characteristic of her work and camp in general. Toying with gender parody, identity politics, artistic integrity and hegemonic sanctioning of the aforementioned, Lady Gaga's camp becomes both a mode of making room for queer humor, and subsequently pleasure, as well as a vehicle for serious critique of those hegemonic discourses that oppress alternative models of meaning-making. To accept Gaga's invitation "to follow the glitter way" thus means both to follow and acknowledge pop's equally glamorous, entertaining and subversive predecessors as well as to open oneself to radically new spaces for artistically and politically authentic expressions of queerness.

NOTES

1. For an exploration of how gay culture and resistance in the 60's was connected to Judy Garland and her status as gay icon, see Patricia Juliana Smith's "Icons and Iconoclasts."

2. For more on Garland's Carnegie Hall Concert, see Jennings.

3. Lady Gaga has performed a duet at Carnegie Hall with Sting for the *Rainforest Benefit Concert* in May 2010. For more information on the history and lasting influence of Judy Garland's performance at this venue, see Wade Jennings' article.

4. This queer notion of camp continues to exist side by side with colloquial understanding of camp as merely cultish appreciation of trash-phenomena, mostly influenced by Susan Sontag's quote: "The ultimate Camp statement: it's good because it's awful" (292).

5. Irony itself is not without its critics especially in postfeminist contexts. Rosalind Gill, for example, criticizes: "Most significantly, however, in postfeminist media culture irony has become a way of 'having it both ways,' of expressing sexist or homophobic or otherwise unpalatable sentiments in an ironised form, while claiming this was not actually meant" (165).

6. Linda Hutcheon makes very clear in her argument that the producer of the text may not necessarily be the *intentional* producer of irony, when she states "there is no guarantee that the interpreter will 'get' the irony in the same way as it was intended. In fact, 'get' may be an inaccurate and even inappropriate verb: 'make' would be much more precise. [...] this productive, active process of attribution and interpretation itself involves an intentional act, one of interference" (*Irony* 11). Yet she stresses that irony is a form of communication, not of reading against the grain. The community-specific meta-ironic markers either are or are not embedded in a text/utterance and can insofar only be read as intentional code for irony by the interpreter.

7. Numerous examples for this distinction include a diverse spectrum of people, ranging from Oscar Wilde, Andy Warhol, David Bowie to New Queer Cinema and Madonna.

8. "I define the gay sensibility as a creative energy reflecting a consciousness that is different from the mainstream; a heightened awareness of certain human complications of feeling that spring from the fact of social oppression, in short, a perception of the world which is colored, shared, directed, and defined by the fact of one's gayness" (Babuscio 19). Jack Babuscio's seemingly essentialist notion of gay (male) identity as the producer of camp is softened by his own acknowledgement that gay sensibility is not limited to gay identified men and that "this is not [...] to plead for the application of any narrow sociological analysis" (36). He also explicitly mentions the usefulness of camp for women (28).

9. Via the *The World in the Evening* (1954) character Charles Kennedy, who is confiding in the narrator about his relationship to Bob Wood.

10. This description refers to the second "re-vamped" version of *The Monster Ball Tour*, which has been performed from late 2009 until the end of the tour in 2011. The first leg of the tour had different stage design, other interludes and even slightly different costumes.

11. The name of the Hotel is written in a way that allows for both a reading as "*thass*," a derogatory noun for the body part between thigh and ass, as well as the German word for *hate*, since Lady Gaga is known for incorporating European languages such as French and German into her work (i.e. "Bad Romance," "Scheiße").

12. One insightful discussion of the relation between (Neo)-Burlesque and femininity is Debra Ferreday's "Showing the Girl."

13. Stated even more bluntly: "By focusing on the gender ideal as a matter of aesthetics, mainstream musicals propound a view whereby femininity, say, is not an innate quality guaranteed to women but instead a special effect available to anyone with the proper skill and accessories" (Whitesell 273).

14. Devitt defends the use of the term "drag queen" to describe female-bodied performers who perform femininity, arguing that a definition of drag that relies on a "binary sex-based concept of crossing not only belies the rich wealth of gender identities that inform contemporary gender performance and drag but also reifies the naturalness of that binary" (Murphy 25).

15. According to the Library of Congress "[...] *The Wonderful Wizard of Oz* has become America's greatest and best-loved homegrown fairytale. The first totally American fantasy for children, it is one of the most-read children's books."

16. As a fairy, which used to be a pejorative term for "gay," Tinker Belle's connection to gayness is so established that Sean Griffin decided to use her in the title of his monograph on the relationship between the Walt Disney Company and their gay and lesbian fans and employees *Tinker Belles and Evil Queens*.

17. Lady Gaga explains the appearance as follows: "And so, as my friends and I travelled further and further down the glitter way, we ran into a magical angel with a beautiful black harp. And she said that she knew just the music to play to get us closer and closer to The Monster Ball."

18. For a more detailed analysis of films which are considered camp, see Barbara Klinger's book, in which she speaks of Sirkian melodramas as "mass camp." Another example from the Classical Hollywood era would be the successful Freed Unit at MGM and their musicals (Tinkcom 36–72).

19. The genre of women-in-prison films reached its first heyday in the 50s according to film scholar Judith Mayne: "Throughout film history, there have been periods of ebb and flow of the popularity of the women-in-prison film. The genre was popular in the 1950s and less so in the 1960s; it re-emerged in the 1970s, and again in the late '80's and '90's. [...] Genealogies of the women-in-prison film usually cite *Caged* (1950) as the prototype of the genre [...]. In tracing the history of the women-in-prison film, one finds an interesting tension between the respectable, social problem film and the exploitative B-movie" (116–19).

20. One notable exception is *Caged Heat* (1974), a later example of the genre, which actually anticipates the positive ending of "Telephone": "The film ends triumphantly, with the women successfully riding off into the sunset and the villains dead. However one feels about describing films from popular genres as 'feminist,' this is surely a conclusion that celebrates female solidarity" (Mayne 136).

21. "Historically, the term *femme* applied to and was adopted by lesbian and bisexual women; a *femme*, therefore, was a gay woman who 'looked' like 'a girl' or who identified with femininity. Over the course of the last three decades, however, the term has undergone a kind of postmodern renovation, resulting in its redefinition as a more broadly conceived *queering* of conventional/straight femininity and its adoption by people who are not necessarily female-born or female-bodied: transwomen, transmen, genderqueers, and even

butches. In other words, femme is now more commonly understood in queer communities as an act of gender — something one does to or with femininity, a means of both being queer and 'doing' femininity, an invested but critical *performance*" (Devitt 5).

22. "Female Gaze" is used here in reference to and contradiction with Laura Mulvey's concept of the male gaze, which she defined as governing most films (and other audiovisual media).

23. For an analysis of *Thelma & Louise* as itself already a parody and appropriation of filmic conventions, as well as of its subversive potential, see Birgit Däwes.

24. "You know that I ain't bragging, she's a real pussy wagon — greased lightnin," lyrics of the song "Greased Lightning" from the movie *Grease* (1978).

25. See interviews with Sylvia Patterson and Stephen Fry.

26. For a discussion of this trend, as well as its development see Josh Tyrangiel's article for *Time Magazine* entitled "Auto-Tune: Why Pop Music Sounds Perfect."

Lady Gaga and the Wolf

"Little Red Riding Hood,"
The Fame Monster *and Female Sexuality*

JENNIFER M. WOOLSTON

Lady Gaga was born Stefani Joanne Angelina Germanotta on March 28, 1986. As a fledgling recording artist, she has experienced an impressive level of worldwide success. "She [Gaga] debuts her videos on YouTube; in March 2010, she becomes the first artist in history to generate one billion hits, and by February, her album *The Fame* went diamond, having sold ten million copies worldwide" (Callahan 13). Gaga's second album *"The Fame Monster* debuted at number five on the Billboard Hot 200 and went to number one in eight countries" (Callahan 199). Gaga has become immensely popular in a rather short period. Powers writes, "[t]his is all happening not because Gaga is cute or takes off her clothes but because (to use one of her favorite words) she is a monster — a monster talent, that is, with a serious brain" ("Lady Gaga's Multi-Pronged Campaign for Self-Awareness").

Gaga's fans are many and celebrities occasionally bestow acolytes upon her. In a *Rolling Stone* interview, blogger Perez Hilton noted that Gaga has become "the new princess of pop!" (qtd. in Hiatt "New York Doll" 58). Gaga has posed on countless magazine covers, and "[i]n *Vogue's* December [2009] 'Arts' issue, the master of exhibitionism stars as a high fashion wicked witch alongside stage actor Andrew Garfield and model Lily Cole, who play 'Hansel and Gretel,' respectively" (Hintz-Zambrano). Gaga is no stranger to fame — at least not in the Warholian sense. However, it should be noted not all of the publicity surrounding Gaga has been good and, perhaps unsurprisingly, *Star Magazine* was one of the first media outlets to question publically the singer's hidden messages. The magazine asked readers, "[w]ith hoods, hair-pieces, headdresses and masks, Lady Gaga has created a public persona that doubles as a wall of secrecy. Her wacky façade has won her fame, fans, and millions, but just what is she hiding behind it?" (Cronin 42). Gaga writes (or co-writes) all of her own music, and this feat aligns her with the feminist theories of author Hélène Cixous. Women must write themselves into the world, reject male representations of the self, and express their longings without fear. Gaga does all of this repeatedly. Audiences might be surprised to learn that a large bulk of *The Fame Monster* is in dialogue with the classic fairy tale "Little Red Riding Hood." Aside from examining the parallels between the written versions of "Little Red Riding Hood" and Gaga's lyrical revisions — this essay will examine related costuming, semiotic signals from music videos, and overall ways in which Gaga plays with (and rewrites) women's sexual attitudes through her performances. Just as the wolf could embrace the visual disguise in the literary renditions of the tale, Lady Gaga effectively models how surface expectations often betray.

Part of what makes Lady Gaga's self-penned lyrics throughout *The Fame Monster* so exciting is the way in which she fearlessly and unabashedly expresses women's desires. Gaga's writing (and subsequent vocalized performance) speaks very directly to the feminist tenants of French theorist Hélène Cixous. Cixous defined masculine writing as separate from that of the feminine — and she applies the phrase *écriture féminine* to this unique theoretical position (Alphonso 253). "Understood psychoanalytically, masculine writing is rooted in a man's genital and libidinal economy," summarizes author Rosemarie Putnam Tong within *Feminist Thought: A More Comprehensive Introduction*, "which is emblemized by the phallus. For a variety of sociocultural reasons, masculine writing has reigned supreme over feminine writing" (199). Cixous pointed her theories to a system of binary opposites that frame masculine writing. These opposites manifest themselves as either the sun or the moon, black or white, high or low. These collections of seemingly polar binaries are always understood in such a way that one piece of the dyad takes precedence over the other. Cixous asserted that the male-female division is the inception of these binary thoughts. The male is often associated with the more favorable term out of the pair of words, while the female is often viewed as the inferior. Women are therefore living in a man's world constructed and shaped by man's terminology.

Cixous dared women to create a new world. Within "The Laugh of the Medusa," Cixous called women to write by urging:

> [w]omen must write: her self: must write about women and bring women to writing, from which they have been driven away as violently as from their bodies — for the same reasons, by the same law, with the same fatal goal. Woman must pull herself into the text — as into the world and into history — by her own movement [257].

Women must write themselves back into history by unapologetically expressing their wants, needs, and desires. Cixous felt that female desire was multi-faceted. By harnessing their fluid sexuality, women can create a genuine space for themselves within Western identity. Cixous said that women's writing was akin to breast milk. It is a fluid life force (Cixous 263). On the contrary, male writing is done in rigid dark ink. Cixous felt that this sense of rigidity mirrors the stiffness of the phallus. Cixous suggested that males are incapable of writing with the same fluidity as females. Furthermore, Cixous maintained that male writing was akin to "masculine masturbation," whereby the authors assert their sexual fantasies about women through the printed word and ensuing limited representation (Cixous 265). Male writing offers no space for authentic representations of women. Women are the only ones who can claim their place within the world by writing about both how they feel as well as what they know. This writing will be the "locus and means" of the social shift that will occur when female desire is openly expressed (Sellers xxix).

Female writing embraces the task of negating the traditional system of male control. The patriarchy does not exist in a separate sphere from poetics and aesthetics. The power structures surrounding patriarchy are as real for Cixous as the bodies that she urges to write. Cixous believed that the very act of writing created by a woman drawing from her own flesh and blood gave her strength. Cixous openly stated that women needed to "break out of the snare of silence" (262). Women can reclaim some of the power that men have held over their heads historically by expressing their sexual longings on paper. Women can transgress their limitations and create a "volcanic" eruption of the binary gender system within Cixous' view (269).

Gaga seems well acquainted with the power present in expressing herself through her music. One biographer noted that during a 2009 leg of her tour in Japan, Gaga "tattooed a quote from Rilke's *Letters to a Young Poet* on the inside of her upper left arm: 'In the deepest hour of the night, confess to yourself that you would die if you were forbidden to write. And look deep into your heart where it spreads its roots, and answer, and ask yourself, must I write?'" (Callahan 90). The message contained in this tattoo seems to echo the pleas of Cixous — as a woman, Gaga must write in order to share her experiences with others and, in turn, the writing allows her and her listeners to move away from the inferior status often socially imposed upon females. Additionally, Lady Gaga seems seasoned in the notion of the male-female social power division as espoused by Cixous. Some journalists and bloggers famously seemed to take pleasure in speculating on whether or not Gaga was really born with a male appendage. Gaga offered a theory about the pervasive social rumors that she was a hermaphrodite by noting, "[t]he idea that we equate strength with men, and a penis is a symbol of male strength, you know — it is what it is" (qtd. in Callahan 189). Rather than take noticeable offense to the rumor, Gaga swiftly identifies its root in the social fear of unabashed female sexuality. Gaga has expounded on the topic by saying, "'I'm a free woman, so I play on sex freely. But I am not the first pop artist in history to be sexual.' She talked about her fire-breathing Pyro Bra and said it was meant to be a comment on the fact that female sex-parts are regarded by the media, and men in general, as 'weapons'" (qtd. in Lester 91). Here, viewers will note that Lady Gaga incorporates the notion of Cixous' engendered eruption of expression as a part of her stage show — the bra in question shoots out sparks and pyrotechnics from its nipples.

Lady Gaga comments on her newly embraced position within the feminist movement by telling an interviewer, "'I'm getting the sense that you're a little bit of a feminist, like I am, which is good,' she said. 'I find that men get away with saying a lot in this [music] business, and that women get away with saying very little.... In my opinion, women need and want someone to look up to'" (qtd. in "Frank talk with Lady Gaga"). What Gaga fails to mention here is that women also desire someone to speak on their behalf and express their inner desires publically. Gaga, is, in a sense, a vessel through which women's yearnings publically manifest. Rather than tokenize her comments about feminist aims, she continued to speak out about it. Gaga has expounded on her views by noting:

> [y]es. Yes I am. I am a feminist. I reject wholeheartedly the way we are taught to perceive women. The beauty of women, how a woman should act or behave. Women are strong and fragile. Women are beautiful and ugly. We are soft spoken and loud, all at once. There is something mind controlling about the way we're taught to view women. My work, both visually and musically, is a rejection of all those things. And most importantly a quest. It's exciting because all *avant-garde* clothing and music and lyrics that at one time were considered shocking or unacceptable are now trendy. Perhaps we can make women's rights trendy. Strength, feminism, security, the wisdom of the woman. Let's make that trendy ["Push(back) at the Intersections: Lady Gaga and Feminism"].

Gaga, quite literally and intentionally, performatively erupts as a sexualized, unapologetic, and uninhibited female vocalist. She is a mouthpiece, in one sense, for female audience members. As a result, Gaga's lyrical expressions often puzzle male critics. Lester comments on the song "Bad Romance" and Gaga's sophomore album by asking, "[v]ery interesting, but what did it all mean?" (122). Throughout several costume choices and much of *The Fame Monster*, Gaga addresses, challenges, and ultimately revises the classic fairy tale "Little Red Riding Hood."

Lady Gaga aligned herself with the earliest recorded version of the "Little Red Riding Hood" tale by stating, "[m]y grandmother is basically blind, but she can make out the lighter parts like my skin and hair. She says, 'I can see you because you have no pants on.' So, I'll continue to wear no pants, even on television, so my grandma can see me" (qtd. in Herbert 98). Here, Lady Gaga's grandmother can identify her visually by her lack of clothing. In the 1885 version of "Little Red Riding Hood" entitled "The Story of Grandmother," the wolf similarly tells the girl to take off all of her clothing. She must remove "her bodice, her dress, her skirt, and her stockings," and each time, the wolf says, "[t]hrow them into the fire, my child. You won't be needing them anymore" ("The Story of Grandmother" 11). Here, readers may notice that Lady Gaga's grandmother and the fictional wolf seem aligned in the desire to see her without full clothing on. Fewer wardrobe pieces separate Lady Gaga from other young female performers. Additionally, in Charles Perrault's 1697 version of the tale "Little Red Riding Hood," the young girl addresses the cross-dressing wolf by stating, "[g]randmother, what big eyes you have!" (Perrault 13). Of course, the wolf then replies, "[t]he better to see with, my child!" (Perrault 13). The lack of full attire, then, becomes the way in which the viewer visually identifies Lady Gaga. Lady Gaga embraces this audience gaze as a way in which her family can notice her and an avenue through which viewers can enjoy her performative body.

Perrault ends the famous tale with a moral warning aimed at "young girls," who are, "pretty, well-bred, and genteel," that states, "watch out if you haven't learned that tame wolves are the most dangerous of all" (13). This warning applies to Lady Gaga in the sense that she embodies the type of woman that Perrault describes. The young Stefani Germanotta attended school at the conservative (and expensive) New York–based Convent of the Sacred Heart with luminaries such as Nicky Hilton (Herbert 15). Perrault's warning seems to echo the notion that young women must watch their conduct around men — and however docile, a monster is still capable of (eventual) savage beguilement. Conversely, part of Lady Gaga's appeal is how she turns this warning on its head. Along this line of thinking, readers may recall that Aesop famously penned the fable entitled "The Wolf in Sheep's Clothing." In the fable, a wolf famously wears the pelt of a sheep in order to lure a young lamb away from a flock with the sole intention of devouring it as a meal (Aesop 125). Of course, the wolf is successful, and Aesop presents readers with the sage moral "[a]ppearances are deceptive" (125). This fable relates to Gaga in the sense that she openly (and actively) embraces the idea of duality. Gaga plays with the concept of being the self-reflexive prey to carnivorous wolves on a famous magazine cover. "Posing on the September cover of *Vogue Hommes Japan*, the boundary-pushing singer [Gaga] wears nothing but pieces of raw meat strung together to create a dress-like design. The only thing redder than her shocking look is the color of her lipstick" (Everett). Of course, after appearing in the meat-bikini for the Japanese *Vogue Hommes*, Lady Gaga shocked American audiences by wearing a similarly designed dress made completely from raw meat at the 2010 MTV Video Music Awards. Lady Gaga commented on the *Ellen DeGeneres Show* that the dress' symbolism was rooted in the idea that the dress, "has many interpretations.... If we don't stand up for what we believe in and if we don't fight for our rights, pretty soon we're going to have as much rights as the meat on our own bones. And, I am not a piece of meat" (qtd. in "Lady Gaga Explains"). On one hand, Lady Gaga links her meat-dress to a larger social issue. On the other, she plainly plays with the idea of metaphorically tempting wolfish predators. It may not come as a surprise that the most well-known portion of fairy tales such as "The Story of Grand-mother," is the section where the wolf makes his intentions to eat Little Red Riding Hood quite clear. The line, "[t]he better to eat you with, my child," has become almost synonymous with the notion of the slavering creature that lurks in the woods seeking out victims ("The Story of Grandmother" 11). Gaga twists the idea of equating the female with the victim by wearing the meat-dress in the public eye, commenting upon its alleged symbolism, and then denying that she is aligned with any type of subaltern visual or physical objectification.

Lest this analysis seem like too much of an analytical stretch, Lady Gaga has directly aligned herself with the fairy tale "Little Red Riding Hood" through one of her more famous costume choices. In a photo essay about the many outfits worn by Gaga, one author discusses her red-cloaked leotard by writing, "innocent little Red no more — Gaga belongs in a more risqué version of the fairy tale with her tight red leotard, silk hood, lacy tights and leather gloves. We're pretty sure she's not going to grandma's house in that getup" ("Lady Gaga's Extreme Looks"). This same visual homage to "Little Red Riding Hood" can also be seen on the cover of the promotional single for the song "Beautiful, Dirty, Rich." Interestingly, Lady Gaga wears the ensemble throughout her music video from the same song. In the music video for "Beautiful, Dirty, Rich" Gaga wears the red leotard and hood while lying upon a pile of money. She also later burns the money and eats it, all while wearing the telltale costume (Lady Gaga "Beautiful, Dirty, Rich Video"). Furthermore, Gaga invites fans to emulate this artistic foray into the fairy tale realm by offering a similar red-headscarf to visitors of her official online merchandise store. Under the Lady Gaga Halloween costumes tab, fans can purchase a red headscarf to "top off" their Gaga-inspired look ("Lady Gaga Headscarf"). Not only is this accoutrement closely modeled after the "Little Red Riding Hood" scarf that the star famously wore in her "Beautiful, Dirty, Rich," music video, but its inclusion on her official online store further supports the notion that it is a seminal part of her performance art to date.

"Little Red Riding Hood" would become a critically overlooked leitmotif throughout Lady Gaga's widely popular second album. When discussing this album, *The Fame Monster*, Gaga notes, "I would not add, nor take away from any songs from this EP. It is a complete conceptual and musical body of work that can stand on its own two feet" (qtd. in Lester 129). "Bad Romance" is the first song on *The Fame Monster*, and biographer Lester notes that the song included, "a verse in French ... to add mystery and exotic spice" (122). What Lester fails to recognize here is that Gaga is immediately aligning herself with the mythology surrounding the classic fairy tale. When discussing the cultural implications surrounding Perrault's 1697 French publication of "Little Red Riding Hood," Catherine Orenstein discusses the cultural implication of the story by noting, "in the French slang, when a girl lost her virginity it was said that elle avoit vu le loup[sic] — she'd seen the wolf" ("Dances"). When Lady Gaga sporadically sings in French" during "Bad Romance" she invokes the sexually charged chorus, while simultaneously (and quite surreptitiously) inscribes herself into one branch of the historical origins of the famous fairy tale. "Little Red Riding Hood" is indeed a complex story when viewed through the lens of historical adaptation, revision, and re-appropriation. Scholars will note that the earliest recorded version entitled "The Story of Grandmother," featured a cunning sexually charged young burlesque artist who manages to evade the wolf by asking to use the bathroom — and therein escaping his clutches (Tatar 5). Marshall notes, "[t]he tale foregrounds Little Red's sexuality as she undresses and climbs into bed naked with the wolf.... Here, it could be argued that Little Red's feminine body invites the sexual advances of the wolf; however, it is that same excessive body through which she frees herself" (263). Fans of Gaga will note here that the singer is well versed in the art of the striptease. Gaga herself admits, "'I have a strong sense of my own sexuality,' she said, without shame. 'I love the naked human body and I have huge body confidence. I was working in strip clubs when I was 18'" (qtd. in Lester 22). Of course, "Little Red Riding Hood" later, under the revisions of Perrault and the Brothers Grimm, morphed into a tale about a young victim of male violence who was either eaten by the wolf (Perrault 13), or saved from the belly of the beast by a heroic huntsman (Grimm and Grimm 15). Still later, and perhaps most interestingly, the character of Little Red Riding Hood became the mistress of her own salvation. In Thurbers' revision of the tale, the girl "took an automatic out of her basket and shot the wolf dead" (17). Dahl's version is penned in a similar vein, where the heroic young woman finishes the tale by showing passers by her "lovely furry wolf skin coat" (22). Each culture and time period has revised the fairy tale. One single solitary version does not exist. In *Little Red Riding Hood Uncloaked: Sex, Morality, and the Evolution of a Fairy Tale*, Orenstein argues, "Little Red Riding Hood's perennial popularity is due in part to her ability to adapt to the times. Every year, reincarnations of the old story pop up in print, on television, on billboards and advertisements, in children's games and adult jokes" (6–7). Since Lady Gaga uses images from the fairy tale throughout *The Fame Monster*, a closer examination of the album's lyrical message will yield a deeper understanding of the revision of the story that she is creating here.

Early in "Bad Romance," Gaga tells listeners that she desires their repulsiveness and maladies. Thus, Lady Gaga announces her intentions of becoming involved in a sexual relationship with something that is both conventionally unattractive as well as unhealthy. The terminology here could quite literally reference a monster-figure, while the notion of illness invokes the possible infection by whatever strain of gruesomeness that the lover carries (be it physical and/or mental). Gaga alerts audiences to the fact that the object of her affections may indeed terrify some while simultaneously noting that this individual has a plan in mind (Lady Gaga "Bad Romance"). This nod to an intended model of behavior may refer to the basic plot of "Little Red Riding Hood," where the wolf usually plans to devour the young girl. Gaga begins to complicate the narrative here by telling listeners, that she is an unencumbered "bitch" (Lady Gaga "Bad Romance"). Lady Gaga's use of the term "bitch" begins to blur the line between her human characteristics and her potential alignment with the wolf-figure. In terms of strict denotation, the word "bitch" refers primarily to "the female of the dog." Some listeners may be surprised to learn that despite many levels of scientific nuance, "wolves are related to dogs" (Coppinger and Coppinger 41). Therefore, it follows then, by calling herself a "bitch," Lady Gaga aligns tenuously herself with the female incarnation of the wolf. Some have read this linguistic play as a feminist move on the part of the singer. "As she [Gaga] puts it over and over in the show, she is a 'free bitch,' and the audience should be too: free not just of society's pressures to conform but also of letting the men in their lives control or define them" (Strauss 68). Gaga is a free agent — be she embodying Little Red Riding Hood, the wolf, or a hybrid character in-between. "Bad Romance," Gaga noted, was her way of saying, "'I want the deepest, darkest, sickest parts of you that you are afraid to share with anyone because I love you that much'" (qtd. in Lester 123). Clearly, Gaga is well aware of the dark nature of the album and the ways in which is speaks to the duality of human nature. Although the obvious links present between Gaga's lyrical content and the fairy tale may seem scant at this point in the album — each song will continue to hark back to the same story in different ways.

The second track on the album, "Alejandro," speaks to the history of "Little Red Riding Hood" in an equally subtle manner. In "Alejandro," Gaga directs the listener not to address her by name, therein aligning herself with the nameless daughter featured in "The Story of Grandmother" (10). Gaga is nameless, yet she refers to three men in the song by their given names. Lady

Gaga musically tells Alejandro, Roberto, and Fernando that she isn't to be infantilized. Here, Gaga seems to shun purposefully the notion of being babied, and moves away from the "little girl" featured in the early tale ("The Story of Grandmother" 10). Lady Gaga clearly embarks upon a musical and conceptual journey here — without the aid of male figures such as Alejandro, whose name means "defender" (Bolton 413), Roberto, whose name means "one who is bright with fame" (Bolton 605), or Fernando, whose name means "a courageous voyager" (Bolton 477). By turning her back on these men (and their symbolic place as protectors) she appears to be quite openly rejecting the character of the huntsman who saves Little Red Riding Hood from the wolf's stomach, skins him, and goes home with the pelt (Grimm and Grimm 16). Gaga may even be equating all men with wolves here, declaring her independence from the potential threats they present by rejecting them from her space. Gaga's lyrics reveal her desire for complete autonomy during her sojourn in the metaphorical wilderness.

Additionally, within the music video for "Alejandro," Gaga visually aligns herself even further with the character of Little Red Riding Hood. Towards the beginning of the video, Lady Gaga is presented with a (presumably human) heart from a person walking in front of a coffin. This is a telling scene because in "The Story of Grandmother," a cat warns the girl not to "eat the flesh and drink the blood of granny" that the wolf attempts to present to her as innocuous meat and wine (10). In the same vein, Gaga spends much of the "Alejandro" video either dressed as a nun in a red-vinyl habit, or cavorting around a bed with a host of male dancers who are all scantily clad (and quite sexualized). One may wonder how these images may relate to the tale and the answer lies within the notion of a moral choice. Tatar points out, "both Perrault and the Brothers Grimm remained intent on sending a moral message, and they did so by making the heroine responsible for the violence to which she is subjected. By speaking to strangers (as in Perrault) or by disobeying her mother and straying from the path (as in the Brothers Grimm), Red Riding Hood courts her own downfall" (6). Lady Gaga modernizes this notion of a fall from grace by showcasing herself as a religious figure in the video — by eating a rosary on-screen in a nun's habit she appears to be showcasing her internalization of moral codes and messages, while simultaneously choosing to abandon this sanctified position by provocatively dancing, rolling around in/near beds, and being touched by scores of half-dressed men. Through "Alejandro," Gaga rejects the idea of safety, and enters full-throttle into a world of sex, temptation, and wolves. Gaga does not appear to be scared — in fact — she seems to be somewhat excited by the allegorical journey.

The Fame Monster's third track, appropriately entitled "Monster," seems to be Gaga's first unquestionably direct acknowledgement of her usage of fairy tale imagery. The singer tells listeners that a male physically consumed her heart and continues to elaborate by noting that the male in question is wicked, camouflaging himself as a human when in reality he is a wolf, and gazes at her with sinful eyes. First, by representing the male as cannibalistic, Gaga directly calls to mind the fairy tale wolf who desires to eat Little Red Riding Hood. Additionally, when Gaga claims that the male is secretly a wolf, she is aligning him with the villain in "Little Red Cap" who eats granny, "put on her clothes and her nightcap, lay down in the bed, and drew the curtains" (Grimm and Grimm 15). Here, the wolf must disguise himself in order to trick Little Red Cap into sharing his bed. Rather than lambast the man in the song, Gaga seems to both embrace and court the monster. His stare rivets her. Gaga seems enthralled and eager to learn more about his motives. The wolf in the song (unsurprisingly) lives up to type when the artist notes that he presents her with a slavering grin, and informs her that he wishes to devour her. Of course, Gaga tells the wolf to remove his paws from her body. Once the trickster makes his intentions to eat Gaga known, she verbally rejects his advances. However, as the song progresses, the wolf seems to win as Lady Gaga notes that there is a creature in her boudoir who strips her of clothing and consumes her heart and brain. Rather than heeding warnings from authors like Perrault who note that some wolves are "tame, pleasant, and gentle, following young ladies right into their homes and chambers" (13), Gaga seems interested enough in the wolf's advances to court her own demise. The wolf consumes Gaga, but instead of dying, she seems to become a hybrid of the two. She lives, but without a heart or brain — she seems to be driven by base desires rather than feeling or intellect. She transforms into what Beckett calls "The Riding Hood Wolf" (199). At this point of *The Fame Monster*, Lady Gaga begins to shift away from being solely a young girl, and turns instead into a walking, talking, she-wolf.

The next song on the album, entitled "Speechless," is a quiet nod to the fact that the singer is changing into a "Little Red Riding Hood" inspired wolf-woman. In the song, Lady Gaga sings that someone has left her wordless. The wolfish man from "Monster" has muted the human aspect of the singer's mentality. Gaga is becoming lupine. During the song, Lady Gaga repeatedly wails. What listeners may not notice, at first blush, is the way in which this refrain mirrors (albeit musically) the howling of a wolf. Gaga can no longer deny her animal nature — which is why it begins to surface during the chorus. When the singer notes that she cannot write music anymore and refuses to sing it is reminiscent of her lack of human speech. Gaga cannot express herself fully through human words. Instead, she must incorporate her growing animal nature into the album's conceptual framework.

The idea of the she-wolf is not unique to Lady Gaga or to the album

The Fame Monster. In 2001, as a part of a Pepsi One commercial, actor Kim Cattrall appears dressed as "Little Red Riding Hood." What is remarkable about this televised advertisement is that once the actress zeroes in on a nearby male, "she narrows her gaze. Suddenly her eyes flash lupine yellow and she gives a mental howl" (Orenstein *Little Red Riding Hood* 170). This creation most recently appeared in Shakira's 2009 album entitled *She Wolf.* The message conveyed in both the television advertisement and in the song is similar. Sometimes the woman, with all her requisite beauty, can also be a beast. Through crooning a musical wolf-howl throughout "Speechless," Gaga appears to be admitting to listeners that she, too, is becoming a Riding Hood wolf.

"Dance in the Dark," Gaga's next track on *The Fame Monster*, follows the narrative arc by prominently featuring a she-wolf character. Lady Gaga refers to a woman dancing in a club by noting that the woman is moving through moonlight and howling at a man. Gaga further elaborates that the woman is a vixen who exhibits amazing prowess on the dance floor. By singing about a woman who dances in the moonlight — replete with howling — Gaga fully acknowledges the idea that women can be both beauties as well as beasts. The darkness here may remind readers of the woods — a place that certainly instilled fear in a young Little Red Riding Hood — but a marker of freedom and sanctuary to the character of the wolf. The woman in the song who enjoys partying in the dark symbolizes someone who embraces their nature when nobody else is looking. Gaga herself noted that the song "Dance in the Dark" focused on a girl who was not completely comfortable during a sexual encounter (Lester 133). Gaga explained, "'[s]he doesn't want her man to see her naked.... She will be free, and she will let her inner animal out, but only when all the lights are out'" (qtd. in Lester 133). By referring to an inner animal here, Gaga quite tellingly agrees with the assertion that the woman in the song is a she-wolf. This woman is a hybrid that Gaga celebrates. Additionally, Gaga expands the song's focus to include other notable women cut from the same (dualistic) cloth.

In a nod to famously distressed superstars, Lady Gaga invokes Marilyn, Judy, and Sylvia as a call to other wild and gorgeous ladies, while also noting that Diana will always be remembered by the populace. These lines address Marilyn Monroe, Judy Garland, Sylvia Plath, and Princess Diana. Gaga, quite impressively, seemingly identifies these popular iconic females as previous wolf-women. She-wolves, as part of their nature, are less afraid of death and the dark sides of humanity than their counterparts are. These women seem to court death just as much as they experience life. Marilyn Monroe, despite being a world-renowned cinematic beauty, wrote poetry that expressed her disillusionment with life. In 1958, Monroe sent Norman Rosten a poem that she had authored, which read, in part, "Help I feel life coming closer/When all I want to do is to die" (Summers 201). Monroe's life would be full of private pain, and at one point during her career, she was committed to a mental hospital due to her depression and suicidal expressions. Similarly, in the 1940s actor Judy Garland made national headlines when she attempted to kill herself by cutting her own throat with a shard of broken glass (Fricke 77). Additionally, Plath's name became so synonymous with suicide, one author contends, "Sylvia Plath has become (probably) the most famous suicide of the 20th century" (Baker 195). While audiences may not quickly align Princess Diana's character with suicide, one biographer notes that the famous figure did indeed talk about the subject quite frequently. Brown notes that Diana spoke to friends about (seemingly illogical) suicide attempts, such as "slashing herself with a lemon slicer" (202). Despite the focus here on the tortured female persona — Lady Gaga moves to valorize these popular women in her song when she proclaims that all of these women will metaphorically join her cavorting to the music. Rather than condemn these superstars and their links to death, depression, and darkness, Lady Gaga places them on a mythic pantheon with herself and other she-wolves. These creatures are their happiest in the wooded darkness. Here, that same darkness (and the taste of freedom experienced therein) aligns with the "wilds" of a modern dance floor.

During the song, "Telephone," Lady Gaga continues to explore the joys and freedoms that wolf-women feel on the dance floor. Lady Gaga (and featured guest Beyoncé) beseech the listeners to cease calling as they wish to stop cerebral activity while grooving at a dance club. Here, Gaga eschews contact with the outside world in favor of the uninhibited outlet of dancing. The heart and brain that the wolf-man previously took from Gaga appears to be re-instated and fully functioning as she pursues her personal pleasure here. Gaga is no longer without speech nor is she howling. Instead, Gaga refuses to speak. This, as listeners can surmise, is her autonomous decision. In the music video for the song "Telephone," Gaga enters a women's correctional facility, where the prisoners (as they lick the bars, paw at her in the exercise yard, and smell her hair) appear to be representations of wolf-women. Furthermore, while in the prison, Gaga is shown wearing pieces of crime-scene tape as a makeshift bikini-outfit. The implication here is that Gaga possesses a dangerous body, and may, in fact, be lethal to others. Beyoncé, arriving in the "Pussy Wagon," bails Gaga out and decrees, "[y]ou've been a very bad girl. A very, very bad, bad girl Gaga." Rather than chastising Gaga, Beyoncé appears to be acting as a mirror reflection — in the next scene both women proceed to enter a diner and poison everyone in it. Both women then proceed to dance in outfits festooned out of the American flag — therein invoking a sense of liberty from those around them, who would seek to dominate, control, or restrain their animalistic natures. Following this scene, Gaga is showcased in a leopard-print cat suit, as homage to her animal side, dancing wildly. By collaborating with Beyoncé here, Gaga's message seems to be that wolf-women are indeed dangerous — but they also crave the companionship of others like them. By using the "Pussy Wagon" prominently in this video, the singers poke fun at the notion that men in American culture relegate women to a subservient status. Instead of pandering to the vulgar classification of the patriarchy, Gaga and Beyoncé illustrate the idea that, while they may possess female genitals, they can also express a bestial side.

In, "So Happy I Could Die," Lady Gaga notes that she feels so much bliss in a dance club, while drinking red wine, that she is ready to embrace death. In Grimms' version of the tale, Little Red Cap is given "a bottle of wine" for granny, and is warned not to leave the path, lest she "fall and break the glass" and lose the alcohol (14). Rather than produce the liquor for another, Gaga keeps it for herself, drinks it, and proceeds to dance the night away in happy abandon. Gaga does not need to worry about delving off of the woodland path and/or about dangerous predators. Rather, she herself contains both the historical innocence/beauty of the young girl as well as the sexual appetite of the ravenous and rakish wolf-figure. Here, Lady Gaga is saying she is the viewer (enjoying her gazing at the nearby female), the drinker, and perhaps, the sexual aggressor. Gaga must, here, come to terms with herself in a moment of actualization. In the wilderness of the dance floor, Gaga recognizes the wolf-woman she has become and refuses to misrepresent herself any longer. She notes that in the quiet of night, despite falsehoods and tears, she can feel satisfaction by touching herself. By stroking herself, and perhaps her metaphorical wolf-pelt, Gaga is engaging in a moment of self-acceptance and self-soothing. Lady Gaga realizes that it will be difficult to maintain her dualistic nature, and alludes to upcoming death when she tells audiences that she is so content that she would welcome death. These words appear to foreshadow the end of the album, as the singer alludes to a calm acceptance of her spiritual/ghostly side.

Gaga's final track, "Teeth," seems to welcome death with both arms. Here, Lady Gaga instructs the listener to taste her flesh, bite her, and bare their teeth without fear. Gaga baits the (presumably male) figure with this plea to be devoured — showing audience members that she is consciously embracing the act; Gaga is not a victim here whatsoever. Instead, she serves as a role model for empowered females — she is the author of her own destiny. She takes risks with abandon. Lady Gaga tells the wolf here that she will accept them despite any bondage they may place her in, addressing the fact that she will likely (despite her permissiveness) become the monster's prey. This line connects to "The Story of Grandmother" because the wolf ties the young girl up with woolen ropes before allowing her to venture outside to use the bathroom (11). Rather than appearing helpless, Gaga chooses to accept the restraints placed upon her, while offering up her unwavering affections. Lady Gaga does not shrink away from the wolf's mouth, but begs him to exhibit his fangs while also admitting that she finds religious salvation within him. Gaga has come to terms with her bestial nature and wishes to be sacrificed by another wolf. Her sole belief, according to the lyrics, is in the primal exchange yet to come. The song's lyrics harken back to the way in which Gaga aligns herself with the she-wolf community in "Bad Romance." Now, it seems, Gaga is both free to make her own decisions, as well as hardened enough to accept their consequences. Gaga moves full circle within the album, from naïve girl to monster to willing prey. As previously stated, Gaga's position throughout the album is one of strength. Lady Gaga notes, "I am not a victim. And my message is positive" (qtd. in Strauss 72). Gaga gives herself to the wolf during "Teeth," and continually baits him to open his mouth. She quite vocally wants to be devoured. Gaga becomes the quintessential Red Riding Wolf when she demands to be eaten by the wolf. In this moment, Gaga expresses self-awareness, her dual nature, and her fascination with death.

Along these same lines, in the music video for "Teeth," Lady Gaga stars as "The Photographer," who collects men's photographs, and then their teeth, in glass mason jars. Audiences are shown several bottles of teeth, crudely labeled with the handwritten names "Alejandro," "Fernando," and "Roberto." Gaga then (amidst choreographed dancing), picks up pliers and attempts to remove teeth from a handsome young man who is tied to a bed. At the close of the video, the same man (hiding a jar labeled "Lady Gaga" and a pair of pliers behind his back), surprises the star by knocking on her door, and then pushes her down on a bed. The door then closes and audiences are left to speculate the ensuing action. The implication is that the aggressor, Gaga, will now be in the position of her prey — meeting a similar fate.

Gaga's *The Fame Monster* album "ended up with not one but two covers, which delighted her because she was keen for them to convey the yin and the yang of the pop business: the stylishly slick surface beneath which lay the dark reality" (Lester 131). Here, the album's dual covers belie the notion that the music will deal with the complexities of the human condition. Gaga channels this narrative through her revision of "Little Red Riding Hood." Orenstein writes, "[l]ike a prism that refracts light and delivers the spectrum of the rainbow, 'Little Red Riding Hood' splits and reveals the various elements of human identity. The truth is that in the real world, as in the fairy tale, we are a little bit of everything: a spectrum of possibilities, interwoven and interrelated" (Little Red Riding Hood 244). Each of us can be a beauty as well as a beast. A topsy-turvy doll crafted for children in the 1960s–1970s easily encapsulates this notion: "On one side it is Red Riding Hood and when you turn the dress inside out it is Grandma. When you lift Grandma's bonnet on the back there is the Wolf dressed in Grandma's clothing" ("Little Red Riding Hood Topsy"). The idea of one person embodying a multiplicity of characteristics is nothing new. Orenstein writes that "[e]ach of us carries within an intuitive understanding of what it means to be wolf, Grandma, woodsman, and Little Red Riding Hood" (Little Red Riding Hood 245). Gaga seems to understand the idea of channeling various facets of her persona quite well, for "when she emerged from a plane at Heathrow in August 2009, it was with fangs and fake nails attached..." (Herbert 193). Once again, Gaga embraces the notion of being a self-aware she-wolf. Gaga appears to be, here and throughout the album, one part beauty and one part beast.

Gaga builds upon this notion of multi-faceted identity construction throughout *The Fame Monster*. Gaga states, "'I guess what I am trying to do is take the monster [celebrity culture] and turn the monster into a fairy tale'" (qtd. in Powers). What Gaga coyly references here — without explicit admission — is the fact that this album rewrites and revises the classic tale "Little Red Riding Hood." Gaga takes the notion of "wolf as monster" and revises it through her lyrics and music videos. Gaga collectively expresses women's desires and fluid natures when she rewrites the well-known tale from a (somewhat) new, and decidedly edgy, perspective. Gaga asks an interviewer, "I want to be a legend. Is that wrong?" (qtd. in Strauss 74). While the answer to Gaga's question remains unclear at this historical juncture — by rooting much of her work in the immensely popular and historically enduring "Little Red Riding Hood" — the songstress appears to be well on her way to achieving her goal.

Surrealism, the Theatre of Cruelty and Lady Gaga

RICHARD J. GRAY II

No musical performer in the world displays a more profound expressive nature than Lady Gaga. Since her arrival in the celebrity spotlight in 2008, Gaga's means of self-expression exemplified in her fashion selections have made her the object of extensive criticism. Arguably, the most controversial of her performative costuming choices was the raw meat dress that she wore to the 2010 MTV Video Music Awards. Gaga's performance texts have become increasingly more vocal, underscoring current issues such as those pertaining to the LGBT community ("Don't ask, don't tell") and the need for self-expression and liberation. From the "Bad Romance" music video in which Gaga suggests that women should stand up for their rights, to the "Born this Way" video in which she advocates an acceptance of all people, Gaga's performance identity serves as a visual metaphor for the establishment of an equality transcending gender, sexual preference, financial status, and race. As a performance artist, Lady Gaga writes herself into a long narrative of Surrealists, including Marcel Duchamp, Claude Cahun, Hannah Höch, Max Ernst, Salvador Dalí, Alejandro Jodorowsky, and Francis Bacon. Her *œuvre* also reflects themes and theatrical structures embodied in the work of Surrealist artist and playwright Antonin Artaud. This essay has two core objectives. Firstly, it explores the influences of Surrealism on Gaga's performance identity. In doing so, this essay traces several prominent Surrealists whose work has impacted Lady Gaga's performance identity. Secondly, this essay also examines Lady Gaga's *œuvre* against the backdrop of Antonin Artaud's manifestos on the Theatre of Cruelty published in his book entitled *Le Théâtre et son double* (1938). As this essay illustrates, the Surrealist footprint in Lady Gaga's work is both evident and significant. Known for her use of parody and imitation, Gaga's reinvention of Artaud's conception of a Theatre of Cruelty for a twenty-first century audience merits examination.[1]

Deconstructing the Surreal Lady Gaga

Lady Gaga is the living embodiment of twenty-first century Surrealism. Surrealism began in the French *avant-garde* theatre of the 1910s. An experimental form of theatre, the *avant-garde* focused on challenging socially and culturally acceptable boundaries. The word "Surrealism" itself appeared for the first time in a March 1917 letter from author Guillaume Apollinaire to Belgian writer Paul Dermée:

> Tout bien examiné, je crois en effet qu'il vaut mieux adopter surréalisme que surnaturalisme que j'avais d'abord employé. Surréalisme n'existe pas encore dans les dictionnaires, et il sera plus commode à manier que surnaturalisme déjà employé par MM. les Philosophes/All things considered, I, in fact, believe that it would be better to adopt the word surrealism than the word surnaturalism that I had initially used. Surrealism does not yet exist in dictionaries and it would be easier to manage than surnaturalism that has already been used by Gentlemen Philosophers[2] [qtd. in Livi 115].

Apollinaire's experimental play entitled *Les Mamelles de Tirésias* of that same year, in fact, carried the subtitle *un drame surréaliste*/a Surrealist drama. In his *Manifeste du Surréalisme* (1924), André Breton, the leader of a group of literary Surrealists, defined the Surrealist movement as a "automatisme psychique pur, par lequel on se propose d'exprimer, soit verbalement, soit par écrit, soit de toute autre manière, le fonctionnement réel de la pensée/pure psychic automatism by which one proposes to express either verbally, in writing or by any other means the real functioning of thought" (328). Surrealism emerged from post–World War I Dadaism with Paris, ultimately, serving as the epicenter of the Surrealist movement. Dada, in contrast, was defined as an artistic movement *and* as a cultural movement. Both movements were generally known for their manifestos and graphic art works. The Surrealist movement expanded during the Interwar and post–World War II periods and many prominent European artists of the age began to self-identify as Surrealists. Surrealist art exhibitions and performances became a common occurrence throughout the coming decades.

Surrealist inspirations permeate Lady Gaga's performance identity. Max Ernst's painting *Men Shall Know Nothing of This* (1923), one of the most well-known and significant pieces of the early period of the Surrealist movement, was inspired by Sigmund Freud's study of the delusions of Daniel Paul Schreber, a judge suffering from *dementia praecox* whom Freud had treated. Schreber had fantasized about becoming a woman and Freud interpreted Schreber's fantasies as an effect of the "castration complex." As depicted in the painting, the foregrounded image of two pairs of legs denoted Schreber's latent hermaphroditic desires. Ernst's inscription on the back of the piece stating "the two sexes balance one another" suggested that Schreber's desires to possess both male and female genitalia might be natural. Willow Sharkey explains the artistic link between Lady Gaga and Ernst:

> Gaga's mother monster imagery—on the one hand, a writhing evil body twisting in excruciating pain, and on the other hand, a perfected image of split-screen symmetry, which together comprise an intermingling of supposed oppositions—brings to mind Ernst's project: a sensitive meditation upon finding the humanity in those that Freud's psychoanalysis would deem the insane other, on finding the balance within imbalance, the joy in pain, the human in what has been designated inhuman ["Manifesting Love: 'Born This Way' and Surrealist Art"].

The ability to find joy in pain is central to understanding the surreal Lady Gaga. As literary scholar Joseph Campbell stated in his book entitled *Reflections on the Art of Living* (2011), "Find a place inside where there's joy, and the joy will burn out the pain" (Ch. 1). This concept is the central notion that Gaga puts forth in the "Born This Way" music video. Just as the birthing procedure is full of pain and fear, it is also a naturally beautiful act. And in the same way in which the Surrealists used techniques to displace the viewer's perception of reality, the "Born This Way" music video fragments the narrative in order to alter the spectator's perception of reality. To accomplish this task, the artist sometimes depicts the human form in androgynous or monstrous ways.

Claude Cahun, a noteworthy Surrealist who exemplified androgyny in her art, served as a basis for Gaga's own androgynous performance identity. Born as Lucy Schwob in Nantes, France, Cahun began to photograph herself under the name "Claude." Cahun's self-portraits became the visual representation of how she had hoped that outsiders would perceive her. By masking her face in her portraits, as Lady Gaga does in her own performances, Cahun masked her gender and her sexuality, emphasizing her androgynous nature. Claude Cahun's self-portraits questioned society-established gender identity boundaries. Gender neutralization became a central component of Cahun's work. As Morganne Maselli states, by altering her gender in her own portraits, Cahun implied that "in every form of self-representation elements of masquerade are involved, whether it be physically masking one's identity, or emotionally" ("Masking the Human Face in Dadaism and Surrealism"). In Surrealist and Dada depictions, in particular, the female body often underwent gender neutralization. In Dada artist Hannah Höch's photomontage entitled *Mutter: Aus einem ethnographischen Museum* (1930), for example, Höch created the epitome of androgynous depiction. Höch's motherly figure included female breasts, but her facial features remained masculine in nature. Her right eye with long lashes and makeup was the only feminine trait on her face. Behind what looked like an African tribal mask, the overall lack of visual equilibrium reflected a monstrous construction. Lady Gaga certainly acknowledges the importance of monstrosity and masquerade as a component of her own performance identity. She has stated, "We infer based on something's lack of ordinariness that it is disgusting or somehow linked to something inhumane, in some cases one might say uncivilized" ("The World of the Body According to Lady Gaga"). Gaga has also stated that she intentionally wears masks and sings in a lower register in order to seem more androgynous. It is possible that by incorporating both maternal characteristics and the notion of patriarchal authority, Höch's masked *Mutter* inspired Gaga's "Mother Monster" notion ("Androgyny in Dada and Surrealism: From Marcel Duchamp to Lady Gaga").

In her music videos, Gaga challenges the limits of the display of explicit and raw imagery. Beginning in 2010 with the release of the music video to accompany the song "Alejandro," Lady Gaga's own brand of Surrealism more fully emerged. Directed by Steven Klein and choreographed by Laurieann Gibson, the "Alejandro" music video featured ultramodern costuming, stylized dance choreography, and the typical "WTF? Moments" for which Lady Gaga is well known. In what might look like a Nazi propaganda film, the performance superstar morphs into a series of characters including a latex nun, a female version of U2's Bono, and Madonna, the "Material Girl" — complete with a machine gun bra that Gaga later wore on the cover of the July 2010 edition of *Rolling Stone*. Controversial and immediately decried by the Catholic League as blasphemous, in the "Alejandro" music video, Gaga swallows a rosary, gyrates with her gay dancers, and wears a red phallus-shaped mark on her crotch, most likely addressing the rumor that she was a hermaphrodite. Like the 2009 "Bad Romance" music video that also, at the end, showed Lady Gaga lying in bed with the charred skeletal remains of her lover, the ending scene of "Alejandro" depicts Gaga lying in bed before it culminates by showing Gaga's white face morphing into a white ghost as the film — and Gaga's face — catches on fire inside the film projector. In her music videos, Gaga unmistakably resist any attempts to hold up a mirror to reality. As Steven Klein explained, "We combined dance, narrative and attributes of surrealism" ("'Alejandro' Director Breaks Down Lady Gaga's Racy Video"). Through her Surrealist lens, in fact, Gaga unites the consciousness and unconsciousness in order to challenge the spectator's understanding of reality.

Building upon the initial Surrealist footings established in "Alejandro," Lady Gaga's single "Born This Way" unmasked a profound Surrealist foundation. The promotional advertisement for the "Born This Way" music video showed the "Mother Monster" giving birth while sitting above the Earth. Gaga acknowledged that twentieth-century Surrealist painters, in fact, had inspired the "birthing" idea presented in the music video. Gaga said, "It's very inspired [...], especially in the beginning, [by] Salvador Dalí and Francis Bacon. The surrealist painters. It's this story about the birth of this new race;

a race that bears no prejudice and a race that's primary ambition in life is to inspire unity and togetherness" ("The Birth of a New Race"). "Born This Way" was born into a world still wrestling with marginalizing policies such as "Don't ask, don't tell." Cultural anxieties regarding gender identity continue to permeate contemporary society. Performance superstar Elton John, called "Born This Way" a queer anthem, intended to find joy in an otherwise painfully marginalizing experience. Throughout the song, Gaga speaks about the idea of acceptance. Whether you are a "Jesus freak," a racial minority, or involved in a same-sex relationship, the gospel that Gaga preaches in one of love for yourself and for your fellow human beings. Gaga first performed "Born This Way" at the Grammy Awards on February 13, 2011. During her performance, she emerged on stage from an egg-like capsule. This visceral image originated from Salvador Dalí's statue called *Geopolitical Child Watches the Birth of the New Man* (1943). The beginning of the performance shows her being born, symbolizing a release from the restrains of her past. In the music video, in contrast, Gaga moves from being born on stage to giving birth herself.

Another Surrealist influence on Lady Gaga's work was a painting entitled *Exquisite Corpse* (1934) created by Surrealists André Breton, Valentine Hugo, Paul Éluard and his wife, Nusch Éluard. Their painting portrayed the anxieties that humans feel regarding depictions of the gendered human body. The Zombie dance sequence in the second half of the "Born This Way" music video echoes the emotional state evoked in *Exquisite Corpse*. A throwback to Michael Jackson's music video "Thriller" (1982), Gaga's mirroring of Zombie Boy (Rick Genest) represents a beautiful construction of the monstrous body. Gaga transforms the dead body signifying the unknown, the hopeless, lifelessness, and death itself into an object of beauty. Through the zombie dance sequence, Gaga shows us that poignancy, pathos and pain ultimately lead to the discovery of the beauty found within our agonizing life experiences (Matthews). The last scene of the "Born This Way" music video depicts Gaga's face, still in her zombie makeup, trapped inside a pink triangle. Her monstrous appearance recalls the work of another Surrealist artist that Lady Gaga has cited, in fact, as an influence for the "Born This Way" music video: the Irish-born painter Francis Bacon and his dark self-portraits, in particular, his painting entitled *Self Portrait* (1973). By referencing Bacon's presentation of a face as a monstrous, yet still human-like depiction, Gaga once again emphasizes the process through which "pathologized or stigmatized objects may become subjects" ("Masking the Human Face in Dadaism and Surrealism"). Tracing the path of life from the pain of childbirth (the egg or vessel) to the suffering of death (the zombie), Gaga consciously roots the "Born This Way" music video in the universal life-to-death struggle. Her efforts to mix pleasure and pain illustrate the fact that the past and the present are inextricable. Human consciousness regarding the relationship of past to present resists reification. By evoking Surrealist imagery, Gaga creates a complex understanding of the life and death cycle reflected in all human experience.

Lady Gaga's performance work is also grounded in Surrealist representations of the 1960s. On May 24, 1965, Surrealist artist Marcel Duchamp appeared in front of a crowd of more than 2,000 spectators at the American Students and Artists Center near Montparnasse in Paris. As the performance began, the curtain rose to reveal a white stage with a black car parked at the very center. Deafening guitar feedback squelched from the loudspeakers. A band of topless women painted head-to-toe in bright colors and brandishing strangely-shaped weapons attacked the cars on stage. Dressed in a black leather uniform and a white crash helmet, artist Alejandro Jodorowsky emerged, and like Ozzy Osbourne before a colony of bats, he decapitated two white geese by hand before throwing the blood-gushing heads into the front row of spectators. The performance peaked as he beat the topless women with the headless birds while twenty pounds of meat hanged from his leathered body. Forty-five years later, Jodorowsky suggested that Lady Gaga might have copied his meat suit for her appearance at the 2010 MTV Video Music Awards.[3] He also questioned if the new millennium really needed to return to Surrealism:

> I liked Lady Gaga's meat dress. It was funny. But I did that first in my Panic performance. Maybe she has seen what I've done — I don't know. I like to think her song Alejandro was written for me. Her music is interesting. It's interesting because it's very free. But it has no meaning because what she's singing has no hope. It is without hope. It's only about revolution, which isn't enough. We need a re-evolution right now, not a revolution. We need something new. Lady Gaga has a lot of energy and that is fantastic, but she is using old Surrealist images ["AnOther Thing I Wanted to Tell You: Alejandro Jodorowsky on Lady Gaga & Surrealism"].

Jodorowsky also noted that Surrealism had served a necessary purpose in the post–World War I period. Like the work of German philosopher Immanuel Kant, Surrealism bridged the gap between rationalism and the subconscious. By the early 1960s, however, Surrealism had become too intellectual and romantic. It had ceased to "shock and awe." Jodorowsky added: "I needed to go further than Surrealism, and that's why I formed Panic. Surrealism — in particular with Salvador Dalí — was all about ego. It was all about extreme individualism. And it's the same with Lady Gaga" ("AnOther Thing I Wanted to Tell You: Alejandro Jodorowsky on Lady Gaga & Surrealism"). We should, perhaps, consider Gaga's *œuvre* to be a combination of Surrealism and Dada. Both movements shared an *avant-garde* approach to making art and a fascination with sexually androgynous human beings.

With its use of raw imagery and blended contrasts, Gaga's music video creation, "Yoü and I," brings her Surrealist perspective to a new level of visual representation and performance. Here, Lady Gaga depicts a host of characters explaining the formation of individual identity. The "Yoü and I" music video bases its visual representational argument on ostensibly opposing images. We see a Cyborg Gaga walking down a hot Nebraska state highway. Left on an abandoned road in the middle of corn country, the Cyborg Gaga is the epitome of *haute couture*, yet strangely enough, she is entirely synthetic, robotic, and artificial.[4] The music video also portrays a mad-scientist lover and the Frankenstein Gaga-mermaid that the mad scientist creates. There is also the Jo Calderone alter ego, a throwback to the movie *Grease* (1978), and Farmgirl Gaga, the stereotype of the innocent farmer's daughter. These last two characters form a couple contrasting with the cruel, decadent coupling of Mermaid Gaga and her Frankenstein-like creator. Finally, there is the blue-haired "pleathered" Gaga who dances and sings in a barn. We have already seen her outside of the music video setting, as she will appear again, in part, in the "Marry the Night" music video. In the "Yoü and I" music video, Gaga creates binary character oppositions initially appearing as stark contrasts to one another. Upon closer examination, however, these characters are, in fact, inextricably linked to one another at such a level that they ultimately become indistinguishable from each other. As the narrative illustrates, Cyborg Gaga returns to her hometown after have been transformed by the "Big City." Though the cliché "You can never go home again" certainly comes to mind, Gaga suggests that though Cyborg Gaga might have changed drastically through technological innovations, she is still a "hometown girl." This particular narrative, arguably, also applies to Lady Gaga herself. Once again, Gaga comments on the synthetic nature of her own fame. No matter the success that she has enjoyed over the last several years, she is still Stefani Germanotta, "that girl from NYC." The depiction of the Jo Calderone alter ego is self-explanatory. He *is* Lady Gaga. He is Gaga's own artistic creation in all its feminine masculinity. Gaga alone *performs* Jo Calderone. Finally, Jo Calderone completes Farmgirl Gaga's dream of finding a worthy partner. In similar fashion, Mermaid Gaga and her winged mad-scientist Frankenstein-like lover also form a complete union. This particular union builds upon Gaga's unique notions of monstrosity. Their monstrous combination is entirely natural: he exhibits bird-like characteristics and she is clearly a mermaid (half woman/half fish) of his own construction. Though cruel in nature, their relationship is one of co-necessity. This relationship based upon cruelty and violence forms an interesting commentary on the existing dialectic. Mermaid Gaga's pain and suffering are reflected in the misery of Cyborg Gaga whose high fashion shoes cause her feet to bleed as the latter walks down the Nebraska highway. Here, the joy and the pain exuded are inextricable. The return home is the greatest pain that Cyborg Gaga will ever feel.

Like the "Born This Way" music video, the "Yoü and I" music video builds upon Gaga's statement on identity formation. Gaga suggests to her viewers that Farmgirl Gaga, Calderone Gaga, Mermaid Gaga, blue-haired "pleather" Gaga, and Cyborg Gaga are not five different characters, but rather that these different "Gagas" are, in fact, part of the same "Gaga." Through its Surrealist imagery, "Yoü and I" conveys Lady Gaga's identity politics in which Gaga questions whether we should yield to the identities placed upon us or if we should strive to explore the multiple identities found within each of us. In the Preface to his *Phenomenology of Spirit*, Hegel wrote,

> Further, the living Substance is being which is in truth Subject, or, what is the same, is in truth actual only in so far as it is the movement of positing itself, or is the mediation of its self-othering with itself. This Substance is, as Subject, pure, simple negativity, and is for this very reason the bifurcation of the simple; it is the doubling which sets up opposition, and then again the negation of this indifferent diversity and of its antithesis [the immediate simplicity]. Only this self-restoring sameness, or this reflection in otherness within itself— not an original or immediate unity as such — is the True [10].

There are similarities between Gaga's and Hegel's perceptions of identity. Hegel maintains that an authentic identity is based upon both internal and external perceptions that, in fact, form one another. There is always a point in which a person thinks that they know who they are, but they are not really sure how others perceive them. Lady Gaga, in contrast, seeks a state of authentic identity in which we can "just be."[5] In the "Yoü and I" music video, Gaga visualizes Hegel's explanation of "this substance is, as Subject, pure, simple negativity." Thus, identity is a matter of transcendence and transformation often occurring in painful ways. Cyborg Gaga must complete her long journey home. This journey leaves her ankles covered with blood. Through an apparent rape by the mad scientist, Mermaid Gaga's monstrous metamorphosis occurs. In the Jo Calderone alter ego, however, Farmgirl Gaga simply seeks a greater understanding of herself. The blue-haired "pleather" Gaga sings and dances Gaga into existence. In short, these multiple "Gagas" reflect Lady Gaga's perception of her own authentic identity and they serve as a model for Gaga's fans to look beyond the surface narrative in the search for their own unique identities.

Antonin Artaud, the Theatre of Cruelty and Lady Gaga

Nineteenth-century poet Charles Baudelaire stated, "J'ai pétri de la boue et j'en ai fait de l'or"/"I have petrified mud and from it I have made gold." In her *œuvre*, Lady Gaga plays the role of a twenty-first century alchemist ("Épilogue"). In his collection of poetry entitled *Les Fleurs du mal* (1857), Baudelaire explored the relationships that exist between beauty and evil, between happiness and an unattainable ideal, between pleasure and pain, and between the poet and his readers. Lady Gaga, too, seeks to show the relationships existing between good and evil, the path to happiness, the link between pleasure and suffering, and the mutual relationship between performance artist and his or her fan base. Building upon the *Grand Guignol*-style of theatre, Gaga's work embraces Antonin Artaud's Surrealist notion of a Theatre of Cruelty functioning as an intense physical attempt to expose the metaphysical and sacred dimensions of theatre. The very life and work of Antonin Artaud resonates in Lady Gaga's performance identity. Gaga's performance identity itself becomes an Artaudian act of cruelty.

Antonin Artaud (1896–1954) — actor, poet, theatre director, genius, madman — was fired from most of the positions that he had held in traditional theatres. Incarcerated in an insane asylum for an extended period time and in generally poor health, Antonin Artaud had only two years from the moment that he left the asylum in 1946 to make a definitive theatrical statement concerning his concept of the Theatre of Cruelty that he had outlined in his book entitled *Le Théâtre et son double* (1938). In *Antonin Artaud: Man of Vision*, Bettina Knapp summarized Artaud's Theatre of Cruelty as follows:

> The Theater of Cruelty was to be a theater which aimed to activate man's magnetic nervous system to such an extent as to enable him to project his feelings and sensations beyond the usual limits imposed by time and space. This kind of theater would make it possible for audiences to have a powerful metaphysical experience while watching the spectacle on stage. After undergoing such an emotional upheaval, the spectator would feel cleansed and purified, ready for rebirth and renewed life [106–7].

Artaud's theatre consisted of illustrating the "universal forms of life," the characteristics that all human being hold in common. Artaud acknowledged that the theatre could not create reality, but only fashion its own constantly changing perspective that surpasses human understanding. Through an analysis of the repressed forces of man, man would ultimately learn to free himself from the very characteristics that define his humanity. If the theatre could lead the spectator back into man's world of dreams and primitive instincts, he would be submerged in a vicious and inhuman world, one which would reveal his hidden psychoses. Artaud underscored the importance of modern psychoanalysis in which the patient finds a cure by evaluating his psychosis from the outside. Lady Gaga's *œuvre* reflects a parallel exploration of the soul and the search for a cure to her (or our own) psychoses.

Until the publication of *Le Théâtre et son double* in 1938, the only live performance of Artaud's Theatre of Cruelty had been his May 6, 1935 adaptation of Percy Shelley's *The Cenci*. It was a box office failure. Artaud had centered his version of *Les Cenci* on the idea of a theatre in the round, believing that this format created closer contact between actors and spectators than that of the traditional proscenium theatre. The performance of *Les Cenci* used mechanical devices to create an acoustic chaos: harsh and cacophonous sound effects, revolving stage sets, flashing lights to represent storms, unusual vocal effects, etc. The moderately-conservative Parisian theatre-going audience of the Interwar period had not prepared itself for Artaud's brand of theatre based on cruelty, violence, incest, and rape, nor the fact that his characters spoke with bizarre and unnatural voices. Artaud's production of *Les Cenci* foreshadowed the sound effects that he would use twelve years later in his radio play entitled *Pour en finir avec le jugement de Dieu* (1948). As Richard Gaffield-Knight explained in "Antonin Artaud: In Theory, Process and Praxis," "Artaud wanted his audience to experience theatre the same way it would if it viewed a painting or a sculpture, or an approaching hurricane, i.e., viscerally. By exploring the void within himself, this embodiment of Surrealism was probing a place within himself that had no center, circumference, or metaphysical limits" (Ch.1). Artaud's concept of the Theatre of Cruelty is fully preserved in *Pour en finir avec le jugement de Dieu*. In the course of developing his radio play, Artaud described gruesome and fear-provoking death rituals. In the audio recording, in particular, he blended a well-developed lexicon of made-up words with intermittent groans, shrieks, and screams. Artaud also invented a dictionary of onomatopoeias to explain the dissociation of meaning from language. The use of percussion both punctuated Artaud's screaming and divided the sections of the text; the improvised musical component to this work raised it to the level of a frenzied, haunting music drama. From the apparently random mixture of mysterious statements, hysteria, clown voices, chattering xylophones, and the low, tortured delivery of the actresses emerged a true post-apocalyptic vision of a ruined Europe and a haughty articulation of the crisis of faith characterizing France since the Interwar period. Initially banned because of its scatological, anti–American, and anti-religious references and pronouncements, French radio stations did not broadcast Artaud's radio play until 1973.

For Artaud, the theatre presented two immovable obstacles: the first was the external pressures of audience, critics, and spectators; the second, the actors themselves. In Artaud's last extant letter, written February 24, 1948 in response to the cancellation of the broadcast, Artaud expressed the importance of the theatre:

> Je voulais une œuvre neuve et qui accrochât certains points organiques de vie, une œuvre où l'on se sent tout le système nerveux éclairé comme au photophore avec des vibrations, des consonances qui invitent l'homme A SORTIR AVEC son corps

pour suivre dans le ciel cette nouvelle, insolite et radieuse Epiphanie/I wanted a
new work which hangs on to certain organic points of life, a work in which one
feels the entire nervous system lit up like a candle jar with vibrations, and conso-
nance, which invited man TO LEAVE WITH his body to follow in the sky this
new, strange, and glorious Epiphany [*Œuvres complètes* XIII 130–32].

Artaud believed that the theatre of his era had become a preserver of culture, devoted to a narrow range of societal problems, which remained unresolved. Gaga's *œuvre* critiques contemporary music and performance in a
similar fashion. Artaud sought to present theatre as a myth, as Oscar Brockett
explained in his book entitled *Century of Innovation: A History of European
and American Theatre and Drama since 1870*: "The great myths are dark, so
much so that one cannot imagine, save in an atmosphere of carnage, torture,
and bloodshed, all the magnificent fables which recount to the multitudes the
first sexual division and the first carnage ... in creation" (qtd. in Brockett 225–
26). Human restoration was possible through the exploration of the cruelty
contained in myth. What, then, was Artaud's definition of "cruelty"? As used
by Artaud, cruelty did not signify "blood" or "carnage," although a performance might very well use these elements. The word "cruelty" must be understood in a philosophical sense. To be born, to live, and to die are all acts of
cruelty. Artaud wrote:

J'emploie le mot de cruauté dans le sens d'appétit de vie, de rigueur cosmique et
de nécessité implacable, dans le sens gnostique de tourbillon de vie qui dévore les
ténèbres, dans le sens de cette douleur hors de la nécessité inéluctable de laquelle
la vie ne saurait s'exercer; le bien est voulu, il est le résultat d'un acte, le mal est
permanent/I employ the word cruelty in the sense of an appetite for life, of cosmic
rigor, of implacable necessity, in the gnostic sense of a living whirlwind that
devours the darkness, in the sense of that pain apart from whose ineluctable necessity life could not proceed; good is desired, it is the result of an act; evil is permanent [*Le Théâtre de la Cruauté* 159].

Finally, he also believed that theatre had the capacity to heal people of psychoses. It was through the "playing out," the outing of these psychoses, that
healing is possible. This same "playing out" appears throughout Lady Gaga's
œuvre.

After a stay of several years, Artaud left the psychiatric facility in Rodez
in 1946. To eliminate Artaud's delusions and odd physical tics, his doctor,
Gaston Ferdière, had administered fifty-eight electroshock therapy treatments
and numerous insulin injections. Ferdière believed that Artaud's habits of
crafting magic spells, creating astrology charts, and drawing disturbing images
were symptoms of mental illness.[6] Though controversial, it was during these
electroshock treatments — in conjunction with Ferdière's art therapy — that
Artaud began to write and to draw again after an extensive period of inactivity.

Described in his book entitled *Artaud le Mômo* (1947), during his stay in Rodez, Artaud developed his vision of an organ-less body, eviscerated and naked that he called "Le Mômo," which Gregory Whitehead described as "the pure energy of direct brainwave transmission, born from an occult synthesis of needles, electricity and a cacophony of irrefutable inner voices" (90). Complete with abrupt sounds, noisy jolts and grotesque imagery, Artaud's "Le Mômo" depicted the disembodied individual.

The sound poetics defining much of his work shocked his audience in the same way that Artaud's own electroshock treatments at the insane asylum had shocked him. To shock the audience, after all, was one of the main goals of Artaud's Theatre of Cruelty (Nelson 29). His "text" was no longer only exclusively written or spoken language, but rather any form of human expression including clothing, body movements, voices, and sounds became "text." In a second manifesto published in *Le Théâtre et son double*, Artaud spoke of actors who had forgotten how to scream (194). Herbert Blau wrote that "without the old totemism of beastly essences, the false theatre of mimesis has forgotten more than that. For the scream would seem to be an effraction of memory — the break, the tear, the rending — which is the definitive trace of theatre's birth in the primordial rupture of things" (106–7). Artaud's scream vocalized the condition of the organ-less body. The scream is a reactionary spasm. It represents the entire body trying to escape from its very self. Like Artaud, Lady Gaga's uses a "shock and awe" approach in her own performances. She also uses the scream, for the scream is the reaction conveyed in the charred skeletal remains of Gaga's lover at the end of the "Bad Romance" music video. Though silent, the scream is the spectators' reaction at the end of Lady Gaga's 2009 MTV Video Music Awards performance of "Paparazzi." We scream in horror as we see bright red blood dripping down Gaga's costuming as she ultimately ends her own life by hanging herself on stage. The scream is also the reaction depicted at the end of the "Alejandro" music video when the director shows Gaga's white face morphing into a phantom as the film — and Gaga's face — burns inside of the film projector. As a viewing public, we scream when we look at Gaga's meat dress. In a sense, the scream signifies the intense pity that the meat evokes. Finally, we scream at the birthing process depicted in the "Born This Way" music video. In her music videos, Lady Gaga visualizes her scream. She illustrates the body beaten down by fame, attacked by the rules of society to which the individual must always conform.

When visualized against the backdrop of Artaud's organ-less body, Lady Gaga's meat dress, in particular, gains a deeper meaning. It represents the biblical Crucifixion scene: the ritual human sacrifice of Jesus Christ himself. Ritualistic and sacrificial in nature, Gaga's 2009 MTV Video Music Awards performance of "Paparazzi" and the meat dress that Gaga wore in 2010 recall the setting portrayed in *Pour en finir avec le jugement de Dieu* in which Artaud suggested that both God's judgment of man and man's judgment of God were at issue (Nelson 213–14). Artaud's radio play, in fact, questioned the very nature of the Church and the existence of God. Part of Lady Gaga's recent work is grounded in religious imagery. Like Artaud, who was repeatedly condemned for the supposed atheistic views conveyed in his radio drama, Lady Gaga also receives constant criticism for her depiction of religion in her work. Some viewers have even labeled the music videos to "Alejandro" and "Judas" as "blasphemous." Rodney Clapp offers an enlightened perspective defending accusations pertaining to the supposed blasphemous nature of Gaga's work:

> Whether she intends to or not (and however sacrilegious such songs as her "Judas" may appear), Lady Gaga reminds us that Jesus came among us as a misfit, born into a feed trough.... He ended up beside the most despised of the despised, crucified naked on a humiliating Roman cross.... Jesus when he lived on this earth was widely despised and rejected, treated like a monster. And if that Jesus is the Jesus who calls us to be like him, even to be a part of his body, then Christians are the original little monsters [45].

By linking her performance identity to religious imagery, including the idea of man's judgment of his fellow man, and by connecting herself to the image of hanging racks of meat (meat dress), Gaga permitted the viewer to interpret her work in many ways. One possible reading suggests that society is a deranged executioner murdering those who are unwilling to convert to a certain world view or way of life (like Christianity). Another possible reading suggests that the meat represents the raw nature of Gaga's performance identity that she must constantly reinvent before society has the opportunity to taint it. A third reading suggests that Gaga is consumed by her fame, left to rot and die when society no longer has any use for her.

Lady Gaga's theatricality as a whole echoes the essential elements of theatre that Artaud had outlined in his manifestos on the Theatre of Cruelty: Spectacle, Costumes, Language, Lighting and Staging. Artaud's conception of spectacle centered on physical elements perceptible to the audience including cries, shrieks, screams, magic, bizarre music or sound effects, and vibrant colors (*Le Théâtre et son double* 144). As a performance artist, spectacle and costuming have been Gaga's prime focus. While performing at college bars, Gaga noticed that she had to do something special to attract the audience's attention away from the rest of the bar scene. Gaga explained: "I was once playing at a crowded college bar and it was packed with fratty drunk NYU students, they wouldn't shut up and I couldn't play until everybody got quiet, so I took my clothes off, that shut everybody up, that blew their minds"

(Goodman 27). Beyond the obvious display of nudity, the "shock and awe" factor caught the audience's attention that particular night. In similar "shock and awe" fashion, Gaga began her performance at the 2009 MTV Video Music Awards by first lying on the stage floor surrounded by her dancers all scantily clad in white jumpsuits, herself wearing a white jumpsuit and a white wolf-like mask. Slowly, she began a rendition of her song "Poker Face" before transitioning into "Paparazzi." Channeling her "Inner Artaud," a blood-stained Gaga performed a ritual culminating on stage in her own death by hanging. Likewise, in her music video "Born This Way," Gaga performs a birthing ritual complemented with music transitions, an intense use of lighting, and *haute couture.*

Costuming, in fact, also played an important role in Artaud's concept of The Theatre of Cruelty, As Artaud explained: "En ce qui concerne le costume et sans penser qu'il puisse y avoir de costume de théâtre uniforme, le même pour toutes les pièces/Where costumes are concerned, modern dress will be avoided as much as possible without at the same time assuming a uniform costuming that would be the same for every play" (*Le Théâtre et son double* 148). Lady Gaga embraces Artaud's philosophy on costuming more than any other contemporary pop superstar. Whether in a meat dress or in a dress made of miniature Kermit the Frog stuffed toys, Gaga never wears the same outfit twice. In her music videos, Gaga dons a range of thought-provoking costumes, from the pyrotechnic bra that she wears in "Paparazzi," the white spiked-headed bodysuit and the silver orb in "Bad Romance," the futuristic black helmet with dual monocles, the red nun's habit, and the machine-gun bra in "Alejandro," the zombie costuming and nude bodysuits in "Born This Way," the jeweled-crown, cape and bishop's garb in "Judas," to the haunting black dress, hat and sunglasses of Cyborg Gaga from "Yoü and I." Always alluring, often controversial, Lady Gaga continually rewrites Artaud's definition of innovative costuming.

For Artaud, language and music also formed important elements of the Theatre of Cruelty: "Il ne s'agit pas de supprimer la parole articulée, mais de donner aux mots à peu près l'importance qu'ils ont dans les rêves/It is not about suppressing articulated language, but rather giving words nearly the same importance as they have in dreams" (*Le Théâtre et son double* 145). In the same manner in which Artaud repeated used onomatopoeias, Gaga's use of foreign languages (French in "Bad Romance," Spanish in "Alejandro," Italian in "Born This Way," and pseudo–German in "Scheiße"), in particular, forces her audience to speculate on her intended meanings. This element speaks to the very way in which Gaga writes her lyrics and her music. Each of her songs is grounded in the combined performance aspect of the juxtaposition of words and music. Gaga stated, "I like my songs to be small performances in themselves, having a clear beginning, middle and end. I want the audience to be able to see with their ears" (Goodman 32). Gaga's technique plays on one of the essential notions of Artaud's radio dramatic composition: the visualization of the aural element of theatre. In "Le Théâtre de la Cruauté," Artaud also cites the use of music as an important element of his theatre: "Ils seront employés à l'état d'objets et comme faisant partie du décor/They will be used as objects and as part of the set (*Le Théâtre et son double* 146). Artaud also outlined the use of shrill, unusual, or uncommon instruments in his manifesto that are reflected in Gaga's work. In a similar fashion, Lady Gaga uses music and musical instruments — including kazoos, violins, cellos, and harps — as a part of her performance identity. Her Salvador Dalí-inspired piano and her use of Keytars (half-keyboard/half-guitar) have become iconic. Each of Gaga's musical instruments is a performance element of her show.

The use of stage lighting and stage space were also central to Artaud's concept of a Theatre of Cruelty. Artaud found that stage lighting during his era was rather limited, offering the director little flexibility. He maintained that lighting should bring out emotional responses within the spectator such as fear, joy, or sadness (*Le Théâtre et son double* 147). Lady Gaga's live performances exemplify Artaud's notions of proper use of lighting and setting. In her performance of "Paparazzi" at the 2009 MTV Video Music Awards, through changes in stage lighting, Gaga illustrated the transition from the depiction of an upper-class Victorian age by employing warm candlelight tones to a death scene emphasized though the use of strobe lights and waves of red lights flooding the stage. In the last moment of her performance, the stage flooded in red light — representing the blood issuing from her chest — before turning completely black as the final beat of the song sounded. Artaud also comments on the use of stage space: "Nous supprimons la scène et la salle qui sont remplacées par une sorte de lieu unique, sans cloisonnement, ni barrière d'aucune sorte/We will remove the stage and the auditorium that will be replaced with a unified space, without partitioning or any sort of barrier" (*Le Théâtre et son double* 148). Artaud also referred to a removal of the theatrical "fourth wall," the invisible barrier serving to separate actors from spectators. In Artaud's theatre, the spectators *were* actors on stage, each contributing his perspective to the performance at hand. If not literally, Lady Gaga's Theatre of Cruelty places her audience at the center of the performance.[7] Gaga's portrayal of fame as a bidirectional relationship between performance artist and fan base is evident in her stage performances. In order to break the theatrical "fourth wall" as much as theoretically possible, in her performances of *The Monster Ball Tour*, Gaga employed a long stage runner extending from the center of the main stage into the audience. The fact that Lady Gaga has always maintained that her performance identity is not a persona certainly suggests that a theatrical barrier between performer and audience does not, in fact, exist.

As Lady Gaga continues to develop her own Surrealist vision, her performance art harkens back to Artaudian inspirations. In a teaser trailer entitled "Marry the Night: The Prelude Pathétique," introduced in a tweet posted on November 15, 2011, Gaga depicts her own attempt to cruelly fragment our view of reality. Directed by Gaga herself and nearly two minutes in length, the teaser trailer for "Marry The Night," the initial track from her *Born This Way* (2011) album, summarizes well Lady Gaga's perspective on her Theatre of Cruelty. As the image of a brunette Gaga fades in, Gaga's own voiceover begins: "When I look back on my life, it's not that I don't want to see things exactly as they happened, it's just that I prefer to remember them in an artistic way. And, truthfully, the lie of it all is much more honest because I invented it" (@ladygaga).[8] As a close-up of her face fills the screen, Gaga continues to speak: "Clinical psychology tells us arguably that trauma is the ultimate killer. Memories are not recycled like atoms and particles in quantum physics — they can be lost forever. It's sort of like my past is an unfinished painting, and as the artist of that painting, I must fill in all the ugly holes and make it beautiful again." The camera pans out a little to reveal that Gaga is laying on a gurney: "It's not that I've been dishonest, it's just that I loathe reality," she says as two nurses push her down a long hospital corridor. Still delivering her monologue, Gaga adds, "For example, those nurses, they're wearing next season Calvin Klein and so am I. And the shoes? Custom Giuseppe Zanotti. I tipped their gauze hats to the side like Parisian berets because I think it's romantic and I also believe that mint will be very big in fashion next spring." As the nurses stop the gurney to allow them to open a door in front of them, the performance artist adds, "Check out the nurse on the right. She's got a great ass. [pause] Bam." The next shot shows several other patients. "The truth is, back then at the clinic they only wore those funny hats to keep the blood out of their hair," Lady Gaga says. "And that girl on the left, she ordered gummy bears and a knife a couple hours ago. They only gave her the gummy bears; I wish they'd only given me the gummy bears." The teaser trailer ends with the two nurses pushing Gaga into a mental ward leaving fans to speculate on the fate of their Mother Monster.

Gaga's voiceover explains *her* reality, without which the viewer only sees a lifeless woman lying on a hospital gurney being pushed down a long hallway toward a large room. The spectator would not notice that the white nurses' uniforms and Gaga's inmate's garb were, in fact, designer dresses, nor would they notice that Gaga, in reality, was wearing Italian designer shoes. In the next line, Gaga reveals her own fashion sense — and her *francité* — by offering a commentary on spring 2012 *haute couture*. Next, she entertains rumors of her bi-curiosity and/or bisexuality by commenting on the *gluteus maximus* of one of the nurses. Offering a glimpse at the pain and suffering of the mental hospital setting, Gaga deconstructs the "funny hats" that nurses traditionally wear, suggesting that a nurse's cap, in fact, has an application that is arguably more practical than it is fashionable. Finally, as Gaga and her gurney roll into the large room of the mental hospital, Gaga contrasts her mental ward experience with that of another patient who only received gummy bears. The mental hospital scene depicted in the teaser trailer recalls events from the life and work of Antonin Artaud, a creative genius whose mental and physical illness cut short his life.

On December 1, 2011, *E! Entertainment Television* broadcast Lady Gaga's newest music video, "Marry the Night." The presentation began with the above-mentioned teaser trailer showing Gaga being rolled on a gurney in a mental ward. Leaked on the Internet several hours before the 8:00 P.M. premiere, "Marry the Night" is a fourteen-minute semiautobiographical music video opus directed by Gaga herself outlining the performance artist's failures on the road to stardom. Playing on the *Girl, Interrupted* motif, "Marry The Night" is painful and poignant. Ultimately, we witness Gaga's "hissy-fit throwing, destruction-wreaking, soul-baring nekkidness, a scene that Gaga called 'the most honest moment' in the whole video" ("Watch Lady Gaga's Music Video Premiere of 'Marry the Night'"). With tears flooding her eyes, Gaga tells her nurse — who calls Gaga a "morphine princess" — "I'm gonna be a star. You know why? Because I have nothing left to lose."[9] As the camera pulls away, the nurses and the other patients in the ward seem to go about their routine and a piano begins to play. An abnormal laugh accompanies the piano music. Next, the viewer sees a stage on which Lady Gaga, in Surrealist pointe shoes, is performing a dance recital in an empty recital hall. Then, the scene moves to Gaga's apartment. Lying topless on her bed, she receives a call from her director, whose words are oddly subtitled in French, who apparently gives her some bad news, "But, I'm an artist," says Gaga. "What do you mean give up?" She starts to destroy everything in her apartment. Next, we see her dying her hair blue and she begins to sing the opening lines of "Marry the Night." "You may say I lost everything," adds Gaga in a voiceover, as we see her wearing a bedazzled denim outfit. Gaga continues, "But I still had my BeDazzler and I had a lot of patches, shiny ones from M&J Trimming, so I wreaked havoc on some old denim. And I did what any girl would do — I did it all over again." Next, we are outside. A full moon shines down on Gaga, wearing all-black pleather. She is sliding though the right T-Top of a Pontiac Trans-Am when the song finally starts (after about the nine-minute mark of the music video). The car explodes and Gaga remains dancing and singing in the aftermath of the explosion. In the next scene, Gaga is at a dance studio, dressed in 80's clothing, dancing in an apparent throwback to the 1980's television series *Fame*. Here, we witness her metamorphosis; she transforms herself from the ballerina of an earlier scene to a pop backup dancer. As she dances both in the studio and on the street, the video cuts in and out to Gaga naked in the bathtub of her apartment. The moments leading up to her breakdown are portrayed through short scenes depicting Gaga's full range of emotions. As the video comes to a close, we see a handwritten message on Gaga's hand reading, "Interscope Records; Hollywood, CA; 4 P.M." The final shot of the music video shows Lady Gaga surrounded by flames. She is wearing the latest *haute couture* before the scene ultimately fades to black.

In the "Marry the Night" music video, Lady Gaga becomes the embodiment of Artaud's "Le Mômo." She gives a uniquely "organic" performance. As she explores her rise to fame, her performance body is stripped naked (quite literally), scraped clean, and turned inside out. We see her at her very weakest moments, exemplified in the nakedness of her desperation. As "Le Mômo," Gaga reflects "the pure energy of direct brainwave transmission, inspired from the merger of needles, electricity and a cacophony of irrefutable inner voices" (Whitehead 90). In this form, Gaga gives voice to the prosthetic language of the disembodied. Further, in the music video, Gaga's voice, and her voice coupled with the music, percussion and words reflect a constant tension between sanity and irrationality, between artistic control and reckless abandon. Her voice, combined with the rushing images, communicates a state of emotional and psychological turmoil that intentionally undermines the sense of the music video itself. Moving beyond the limit of words, mere utterances of the body that fail to fully express the hidden psychological state of its being, in an Artaudian sense, Lady Gaga suggests that we seek understanding in the metaphysical. Like the Russian Futuristic poets Velemir Klebnikov and Alexei Kruchenykh, the leading practitioners of Zaum poetry (заумный язык) who sought to undermine the conventional meanings of words that permitted sounds to generate their own array of meaning or even the invention of new words based entirely on sound, Gaga's opus performs a similar function. In the "Marry the Night" music video, Gaga creates a metaphysical cacophony; a sometimes unpleasant combination of jarring sounds that combined with flashing imagery creates a visual and musical dissonance. Shrill sounds, alternative language, spectacle, lighting and costuming formed the essence of Artaud's Theatre of Cruelty signifying the move toward an alternative way of describing the psychotic energy living inside the organ-less body. In similar fashion, Lady Gaga's rise to fame depicted in the "Marry the Night" music video electroshocked Gaga's own performance identity.[10]

Conclusion

By appropriating a Surrealist foundation as a component of her performance identity, Lady Gaga fashions a new means of fragmenting the spectator's perception of reality. Inspired by the works of Surrealist artists including Claude Cahun, Hannah Höch, Max Ernst, Salvador Dalí, Alejandro Jodorowsky, and Francis Bacon, Gaga explores a new reality seeking to depict the individual not as a reflection of external perceptions, but rather as the emergence of one's true essence. Gaga's Surrealist *répertoire* contains a variety of elements including the depiction of androgynous individuals who challenge the notion of heteronormativity, the use of futuristic, unnatural, and distinctively bizarre costuming, and the use of a range of "characters" serving to illustrate the creation of a new, authentic identity in which we can all "just be." Through an exploration of Gaga's own performance identity, the pop superstar writes — or sings and dances — a commentary on the socio-politics of the new millennium, an age in which, until a few short months ago, one could neither "ask" nor "tell." Gaga's "shock and awe" approach to performance serves as a tribute to twentieth-century Surrealist artists who through their drawings, paintings, plays, or stage performances also sought to challenge the *status quo* of their own age.

This essay also used Antonin Artaud's concept of a Theatre of Cruelty elaborated in his book entitled *Le Théâtre et son double* (1938) as a backdrop against which to study the *œuvre* of Lady Gaga. Characterized by a violent physical attempt to expose the metaphysical and sacred dimensions of theatre, Lady Gaga uses Artaud's Theatre of Cruelty as a structural framework for creating her visual representations. Lady Gaga's performances appropriate theatrical elements that Artaud had outlined in his theatre manifestos: Spectacle, Costumes, Language, Lighting and Staging. Spectacle remains at the very core of Gaga's performance identity. Through the use of risqué and extravagant costuming, innovative language, sounds and music, imaginative uses of theatrical lighting, and a manipulation of the traditional theatrical space, Gaga's spectacle reaches an Artaudian level. Further, her performances form powerful metaphysical experiences during which her audiences undergo an emotional upheaval serving to cleanse and purify the spectator who is then ready for rebirth and renewed life. The music video to "Born This Way" and Gaga's performance of this song at the Grammy Awards on February 13, 2011 reflected Gaga's purificatory rite of passage.

Through her *œuvre*, Lady Gaga ascribes her own name to a long list of important Surrealist artists who redefined the boundaries of acceptable art. Gaga's performance work certainly shocks the spectator, but more importantly than simply shocking the viewer, it forces the viewer to reexamine notions of reality. Painful and cruel by its very nature, Gaga's art advances Antonin Artaud's definition of cruelty that he called "appétit de vie ... dans le sens de cette douleur hors de la nécessité inéluctable de laquelle la vie ne saurait s'ex-ercer/an appetite for life ... in the sense of that pain apart from whose ineluctable necessity life could not proceed" (*Le Théâtre de la Cruauté* 159). Pain is an inevitable fact of life. Without pain, we could not understand the concept of pleasure. Lady Gaga shows her fans that the exploration of pain ultimately leads to the discovery of the beauty found within our unbearable life experiences. In this beauty is found a love for all that transcends socio-cultural, socioeconomic, and sociopolitical barriers.

NOTES

1. I am grateful to Chad Airhart for his help in the preparation of this essay.

2. All English-language translations included within the present article are mine.

3. In 1987, Canadian artist Jana Sterbak wore an infamous meat dress. In 2006, Sterbak created a Flank steak and black button thread on polyester resin structure called "Chair Apollinaire." The reference to Surrealist Guillaume Apollinaire cannot be a coincidence. Further, Sterbak plays on the English and French meanings of the word "chair." In French, the word *chair* means "flesh." Therefore, Sterbak had literally created a chair made of steak.

4. The "Yoü and I" music video recalls the French Decadent movement of the late nineteenth century inspired by the poetry of Charles Baudelaire and exemplified in Joris-Karl Huysmans' novel *À Rebours* (1884) and in Auguste Villiers de l'Isle-Adam's novel *L'Ève future* (1886).

5. The notion of an authentic identity is one which poses its own philosophical questions. Is an authentic identity even a theoretical possibility? Do all human beings not, in some way, assume identities that others have created? How, then, can one forge an authentic identity? This essay, therefore, must acknowledge this potential paradox.

6. In modern clinical terms, Artaud likely suffered from schizophrenia. He also suffered from an undiagnosed case of rectal cancer.

7. Gaga, in fact, specifies the physical dimensions of her concert performances: "Stage Requirements: 2 (two) extensions from down stage should go through the audience. The dimensions for these platforms should be 5w x 20l..." ("Lady Gaga's Technical Rider" 3). Artaud preferred a theatre in the round. Artaud's staging format, however, cannot be applied fully to Gaga's stage performances since her shows take place in concert halls and arenas.

8. All citations in this paragraph originate from Lady Gaga's voiceover to "Marry the Night: The Prelude Pathétique."

9. These citations are taken from the full-length version of Lady Gaga's music video entitled "Marry the Night," released December 1, 2011.

10. During Lady Gaga's first *The Monster Ball Tour* concert in Paris, which took place on May 21, 2010, Gaga addressed her fans regarding her difficult start in the music business. Before the release of her album *The Fame* (2008), Gaga often performed in New York City clubs in front of relatively small groups of people.

Rabelais Meets Vogue

The Construction of Carnival, Beauty and Grotesque

David Annandale

In the wake of Lady Gaga's appearance at the 2010 *MTV Music Video Awards*, where she sported attire made out of slices of raw meat, BBC News Magazine printed an article entitled "Five Interpretations of Lady Gaga's Meat Dress." The meanings attributed to the dress varied from a feminist commentary on the objectification of women — "It's a clever play on women being viewed as chunks of flesh" ("Five Interpretations of Lady Gaga's Meat Dress") — to an ironic statement on the nature of fashion, to the possibility that there is no meaning at all, and that the dress is merely the latest shock-for-shock's-sake tactic of an attention-grabbing pop star. The variety of evaluations here, suggesting that Lady Gaga, as an artist, might be everything from fiercely intelligent to merely media-savvy, is unsurprising, given not only the provocative content of her performances and appearances, but also what might understandably seem like an incoherent mix of elements. Her clothing is outrageous to the point that "over the top" is a sadly inadequate descriptor. Her videos and performances are rife with violence, murder, blood and monsters, which seems at odds with the catchy dance hooks of the music itself. One might well ask, how can (or should) one connect the dancing-at-the-nightclub lyrics of "Telephone" with the women's prison film conventions and diner slaughter of its video? For that matter, what do dancing Fascists in stiletto heels have to do with the vaguely ABBA-esque romantic complaint of "Alejandro"? And what bearing does any of this have on Gaga's Gay Rights activism?

If the answers to the last two questions are purely and simply "nothing" and "none," then one might conclude that Lady Gaga's art is indeed the aforementioned incoherent mix, perhaps interesting because of the collision between disparate subjects, but otherwise something of a dead end. This conclusion would be a mistake. It would, in the first place, ignore the rigor with which Stefani Germanotta maintains the Lady Gaga persona. "I'm Gaga," she says, "and I live and breathe it every day" (Robinson 329). In "Lady Gaga and the Death of Sex," Camille Paglia writes, "Going off to the gym in broad daylight, as Gaga recently did, dressed in a black bustier, fishnet stockings and stiletto heels isn't sexy — it's sexually dysfunctional. And it's criminally counterproductive, erasing the cultural associations from that transgressive garb and neutering it. The gym-going Madonna, to her credit, has always been brutally honest about publicly showing herself in ratty gear with no make-up" (Paglia).

I would argue that Paglia's reading is incorrect on a number of levels, as I will subsequently show. But the point to emphasize here is that Paglia's example demonstrates the extent to which the Gaga persona exists at all levels of reality. To put it another way, the stage extends all the way from the stadium to the gym. If Gaga is always there, if Germanotta "lives and breathes" a persona every day that is recognizable as such, then a certain unity appears amidst the chaos. The fashion, the behavior, the music, the performances, the grotesqueries and the violence come together to form a subject as specific and identifiable as a fingerprint.

This chapter's contention, then, is that the range of interpretations that Lady Gaga invites, and her chaotic, disruptive artistic collage, are part and parcel of an aesthetically and ethically coherent strategy, one that also includes (in fact, embraces) a meaningful meaninglessness. The meat dress is merely one tactic among many that make Lady Gaga a strikingly successful embodiment of Mikhail Bakhtin's conceptions of the carnivalesque and the grotesque. We should emphasize the word "embodiment" here because Gaga uses her physical reality as an integral component to her art, an art that takes the form of a performance that flows without division from music, to video, to live performance, to political activism, and to even the most mundane public appearance.

Lady Gaga's carnival is unending. Partly because of this quality, her work counters one of the principle criticisms leveled against Bakhtin: that carnival, by virtue of being contained within a limited space and time, is little more than a social safety valve, and is therefore ultimately a conservative support of the *status quo*.[1] Furthermore, Gaga sometimes deploys carnival and the grotesque in ways that Bakhtin does not anticipate, but which are very much in keeping with Gaga's social and artistic context. A case in point is her application of the grotesque to the worlds of beauty and fashion. In so doing, she provides a specifically feminist turn on Bakhtin, and so corrects a significant lacuna in his work.

Little Monsters and Paparazzi at the Carnival

Bakhtin writes that carnival "is syncretic pageantry of a ritualistic sort" (Dostoevsky 122, emphasis his), which is as good a description of any of a rock concert, with the phenomenon's fusion of sound, light, spectacle and participation. All of these elements appear in Lady Gaga concerts, but she gives them a particular direction and focus. For example, on May 30, 2010 at London's 02 Arena, Lady Gaga performed "Paparazzi." As the song begins, she is attacked by some sort of gigantic, tentacled angler fish. It is, she cries out, "the Fame Monster." Turning to the audience, she exhorts, "Come on, Little Monsters. Help me kill him. I can't kill him by myself. Get out your cameras. Take his picture!" ("Attacked by the Fame Monster"). Over the course of the song, she is consumed by the Fame Monster, but ultimately sends it packing, thanks to the combined forces of the audience's flash cameras and her Roman candle brassiere. Beyond the spectacle, it is worth underscoring the performative, ritual role the audience undertakes here, becoming part of a mini-narrative unfolding on the stage (Gaga has just been abandoned by friends while on the way to the Monster Ball, setting up something along the lines of a "Little Red Riding Hood" scenario). Familiarity between participants and a purpose to the revelry are crucial features of Carnival. Bakhtin writes that Carnival "marked the suspension of all hierarchical rank, privileges, norms and prohibitions. Carnival was the true feast of time, the feast of becoming, change, and renewal. It was hostile to all that was immortalized and completed" (*Rabelais and His World* 10). Further, carnival has

> a characteristic logic ... of the "inside out" (*à l'envers*), of the "turnabout," of a continual shifting from top to bottom, from front to rear, of numerous parodies and travesties, humiliations, profanations, comic crownings and uncrownings. A second life, a second world of folk culture is thus constructed; it is to a certain extent a parody of the extracarnival life, a "world inside out." We must stress, however, that the carnival is far distant from the negative and formal parody of modern times. Folk humor denies, but it revives and renews at the same time. Bare negation is completely alien to folk culture [11].

Bakhtin might as well have written these descriptions after having attended "The Monster Ball."

The first of the Bakhtinian carnivalesque reversals one might consider is Gaga's hailing of the audience members as "Little Monsters." Once again, the use of a negative term "monster" as a mark of praise is hardly unusual within the concert setting. Gaga's use of "Little Monsters" is, arguably, not significantly different from, for instance, the use Rob Halford, lead singer of Judas Priest, makes of "Metal Maniacs" in his performances. Indeed, there are many carnivalesque elements in any given pop or rock concert. Gaga's "Little Monsters" is, however, a somewhat more wholesale reclamation, in that, unlike "Metal Maniacs," "Little Monsters" is not a new coinage: the term pre-exists as a description of unruly children. Furthermore, Gaga's use of the word "monster" has a fluidity in keeping with what Bakhtin identifies as carnival's hostility to the finalized and the nailed-down.[2] The Little Monsters are good, "The Fame Monster" is bad, and "The Monster Ball" is good. Categories, definitions, and evaluations blur and fuse.

Other reversals are more specific to "Paparazzi" itself. Gaga turns the tables on the Fame Monster, moving from victim to victor, standing triumphantly while fountains of sparks blaze from her chest. The method by which the audience assists in her victory is significant: the Little Monsters must take the Fame Monster's picture. The implied reading is that the photo-snapping voyeurs of yellow journalism cannot stand to have the gaze redirected back at themselves. The lyrics also reverse the audience's expectations. The narrative of the stage show notwithstanding, the song is not exactly about being subjected to the paparazzi. Rather, the narrator is paparazzi. Being a paparazzo becomes a metaphor for being a stalker. The ostensible lyrical content and its stage embodiment thus seem to be at odds with each other, a feature of so many of Lady Gaga's songs that it is difficult to believe the consistency of approach can be coincidental.

Reversals — visual, of hierarchy, of victim and victimizer, of lyrics and performance — recur in the video for "Paparazzi." Here, an abusive (and camera-aware) boyfriend drops Gaga from a rooftop. Her career and fame (which appear to be one and the same thing) plummet with her actual drop. She is crippled, and confined to a wheelchair, though we then witness her dancing resurrection intercut with subliminal shots of her elegantly attired corpse hanged, shot, suffocated, overdosed, etc. At the conclusion of the video, she poisons the boyfriend, and confesses to the murder, becoming even more famous (and therefore successful) than before. The latent menace of the lyrical content is at odds with the gentle romance of the melody, but this menace is itself far outdone by, and thus collides with, the cascading images of violence and death of the video. The audience reverses its reactions to the song, and reverses them again, depending on what aspect it notices first.

As ever, Gaga's physical appearance plays a crucial role in the reversals. As her resurrection begins, opaque glasses conceal her eyes. Eyewear is a leitmotif in the videos which we will consider later in this chapter. For the moment, it is sufficient to indicate the reversal of the gaze that the glasses signify: Gaga, who is the unknowing subject of the camera's look while she and her lover cavort precariously on a balcony, now gazes back at the camera while blocking its view of her eyes. One of the most striking reversals, however, happens with makeup. When the moment comes for her revenge, Gaga is made up (and dressed) as Minnie Mouse, her lipstick creating the illusion of a tiny, pursed mouth. This illusion is shattered when, as she pours poison into a glass, she bares her teeth in extreme close-up — Disney's passive female mouse transforms into a snarling predator. The female figure, Laura Mulvey argues, presents a problem to the male spectator, in that she "connotes something that the look continually circles around but disavows: her lack of a penis, implying a threat of castration and hence unpleasure.... [The] woman as icon, displayed for the gaze and enjoyment of men, the active controllers of the look, always threatens to evoke the anxiety it originally signified" (13). The means of dealing with this anxiety involve "investigating the woman, demystifying her mystery" (13), "the devaluation, punishment or saving" of the woman (13), or the "complete disavowal of castration by ... turning the represented figure itself into a fetish so that it becomes reassuring rather than dangerous (hence over-valuation, the cult of the female star)" (13–14). All of these strategies construct the woman as the passive recipient of the male gaze. In this moment, however, Gaga takes that passive figure first to caricatured levels — the little mouse — and then, with the baring of the teeth, confronts the gaze with the terror of castration, thus evoking the very fear that her makeup pretends to assuage.

The pattern in "Paparazzi" — reversals of up and down, positive and negative, vulnerability and strength, life and death — recurs throughout Lady Gaga's work. Also present is another pattern, an integral component of the reversals, but that also, for both Gaga and Bakhtin, has its own distinct and vital identity: the boldly grotesque. As one might expect, Gaga's grotesque reverses and blurs the signifiers of "beautiful" and "ugly." However, the grotesque, for both Gaga and Bakhtin, indicates the unfinished and the transforming. This quality gives the grotesque a subversive charge.

Grotesque Transformation

For Bakhtin, the grotesque is a necessary and inevitable part of the dissolution of hierarchy, and the free and familiar contact of carnival. "In grotesque realism," he writes,

> the bodily element is deeply positive. It is presented not in a private, egotistic form, severed from the other spheres of life, but as something universal, representing all the people.... The material bodily principle is contained not in the biological individual, not in the bourgeois ego, but in the people, a people who are continually growing and renewed. This is why all that is bodily becomes grandiose, exaggerated, immeasurable [*Rabelais and his World* 19].

Similarly, Gaga's body is exaggeratedly open and displayed. Furthermore, she realizes that this body is not only the possession of Stefani Germanotta, but also that of the fans. Gaga says:

> If I were to ever, God forbid, get hurt onstage and my fans were screaming outside the hospital, waiting for me to come out, I'd come out as Gaga. I wouldn't come out in sweatpants because I busted my leg or whatever.... I don't want people to see I'm a human being. I don't even drink water onstage in front of anybody, because I want them to focus on the fantasy of the music and be transported from where they are to somewhere else [Strauss 70].

The result might seem paradoxical (though so does "grotesque realism") in that, according to Maureen Callahan, "She's posited herself as none of her peers have: a blank slate, a creature of self-invention, an object of emotional projection and wish-fulfillment.... Gaga's [mystery] seems born of genuinely feeling like the misfit she's claimed to be. She seems human" (Callahan 17–18). Following Bakhtin's argument, however, resolves the paradox. The elimination of all human traces of the bourgeois ego makes the body human and universal — the blank slate and object of wish fulfillment that Gaga offers to her fans.

Gaga's sense of duty to image and her responsibility to her fans would appear to be a logical consequence of the intense relationship between her and her audience: "It borders on the kind of hysteria once reserved for the likes of Judy Garland or Michael Jackson, but the difference is that Gaga really, really seems to love them just as much right back" (Robinson 286). As proof of that love, Germanotta must strip the more earth-bound, mundane aspects away from Gaga. "Lady Gaga" is a fantasy, but a physical one, a bodily conduit for the music, a being in the service of the collectivity of the Little Monsters. This collectivity might better be called a "multitude," in the sense defined by Michael Hardt and Antonio Negri. Following Bakhtin, they describe their multitude as featuring "a constant dialogue among diverse, singular subjects, a polyphonic composition of them, and a general enrichment through this common constitution.... This is the logic of the multitude that Bakhtin helps us understand: a theory of organization based on the freedom of singularities that converge in the production of the common" (Hardt and Negri 211). Gaga and her fans, then, do not construct a monologic narrative together, but rather a polyphonic fantasy of meanings that speak to the specific needs of the individuals that the multitude create.[3] For the fantasy to be as accessible and universal as possible, its avatar needs to be in a state of perpetual transformation.

According to Bakhtin, perpetual transformation is an essential characteristic of the grotesque body. It "is a body in the act of becoming. It is never finished, never completed; it is continually built, created, and builds and creates another body. Moreover, the body swallows the world and is itself swallowed by the world" (*Rabelais and His World* 317). Similarly, Lady Gaga's visual appearance always fluctuates, a one-woman fashion parade of garish, impossible costumes, while her body is torn open, broken and remade by the violence on-stage and on-screen. The line between clothing and body blurs: "Her outfits often morph the shape of her frame so that she looks less like a female human being and more like a sexualized creature" (Goodman 118). The meat dress, of course, is a particularly literal case of body and fashion becoming one, but so too are the costumes that are not actually made of flesh. The ones on display in the video for "Bad Romance" are cases in point.

Early in the video, Gaga emerges from a coffin-like pod, labeled "Monster." Her latex bodysuit covers her head, peaking in a crown, and covers her eyes, leaving only the lower half of her face visible. The pod is reminiscent of the hibernation chambers in *Alien* (1979). The alien itself is a being whose lack of eyes are as disturbing as its exaggerated jaws. Gaga's jerky movement and coiled posture are those of a praying mantis. She is indeed the monster. But the monster is also sexual. The Alien is a grotesque, predatory creature, but it also sports a phallic head, drools KY Jelly, and its movements are sinuous and fluid. Gaga's costume distorts her, shapes her into a monster, but it also emphasizes her body, aggressively sexualizing her. The sexual/monstrous image simultaneously draws the viewer's attention to the contradiction and shows that the two forms, in fact, are not contradictory.

This costume is, of course, only one of many that Gaga sports over the course of the video. Her appearance transforms every few seconds. One moment she is wearing nothing at all; the next she is draped in an entire polar bear, and in the next she is parading in the most painful Alexander McQueen fashions imaginable.[4] The video becomes a fast-forward demonstration of the mutability defines Lady Gaga's physical incarnation: "'She took direction from Madonna,' says *MTV*'s Gateley, 'but she's done it even more brilliantly. Madonna would change images every year, every two years. Lady Gaga changes her image every week'" (Callahan 89). Each costume, each look, each image has its reading (or readings), each its complex of significations. The global effect is Bakhtin's endless becoming, the only certainty being that the incarnation of the moment will be supplanted in the next. Gaga's body swallows the world, and is swallowed by it, in its absorption of, and by, innumerable references contained in the looks. Many of her looks and costumes recall or replicate those of (among others) David Bowie, Grace Jones, Dale Bozzio, Björk, Marilyn Manson, Isabella Blow and, especially, Madonna (Callahan 85–88). While the question of whether it is a matter of homage or plagiarism (see "Dissenting Opinion"), the sheer number of influences turns Lady Gaga into a pop culture Legion.[5] There is no longer one stable identity (the body has been swallowed by the world), but the entire world now explodes from this one point.

In literature, the function of the carnival-grotesque is "to consecrate inventive freedom, to permit the combination of a variety of different elements and their rapprochement, to liberate from the prevailing point of view of the world, from conventions and established truths, from clichés, from all that is humdrum and universally accepted" (*Rabelais and His World* 34). Bakhtin's description is very much in line with the fantasy construction Gaga wants her concerts to be. It also provides a way of reading her strategies of appropriation. What is important is not simply that so much of what Gaga looks like or refers to is recognizable, but also that there is so much that is recognizable. The sheer number of elements collides and, as Bakhtin argues, this creates new combinations, new assemblages, and new meanings. In some instances, the liberation from established truths and clichés involves appropriating them and turning them on their heads. The video for "Telephone" embodies this strategy.

Stealing the Fantasy

Storytelling is an important part of Gaga's work, whether in the form of monster battles in concert, the stories in the videos, or the mythology of Gaga's life.[6] Furthermore, she writes her own music. The video for "Telephone" is very much her vision. According to Callahan's interviewees, "She was basically co-directing it" and "[the concept] was largely hers" (Callahan 210). Narratively, then, in "Telephone," Gaga subverts the women-in-prison film. This staple of exploitation cinema is an apt one for Gaga to appropriate, since, to return to Mulvey, it is difficult to imagine a type of film more blatantly geared toward the male gaze and male fantasy than the women-in-prison film.[7] Gaga subjects the genre to so much exaggeration that its fantasy collapses and reverses. She then reconstructs the fantasy for her own purpose.

The conventions of the women-in-prison film all appear accurately: victimization of the new inmate; lesbianism; extremely feminine inmates at the mercy of brutal, masculine-coded guards; brawls; and copious female flesh. The credits, meanwhile, signal the video's grindhouse inspiration through their retro-70s font. But the video imitates its models so precisely only to make the differences stand out all the more. Variations creep in to trouble the fantasy. Gaga's nude body is strategically covered by police tape, the words "DO NOT CROSS" barring the male viewer's access, as well as implying "do not cross this woman." The fight scene is not only far better choreographed than any of its antecedents (and thus is a copy that is superior to its original), but it also has a brutality to some of its blows that is a far cry from the scratching and hair-pulling typical of the exploitation film. In fact, the bone-crunching impacts are more reminiscent of the brawls in the male prison film, which has its own set of conventions. A similar blurring occurs when Gaga walks into the exercise yard. The spectacle of menacing, weight-lifting prisoners with bulging biceps is a common prison film trope, but again, in the male prison film. The bodies and hair styles of the inmates here blur gender distinctions, and the briefly glimpsed body shapes are, in keeping with Bakhtin's bodily grotesque, grandiose and exaggerated. When the lesbian embrace occurs, Gaga's androgynous partner (Heather Cassils) does not in any way resemble the male fantasy figure that would be fulfilling the equivalent role in the traditional women-in-prison film.

Meanwhile, Gaga herself, as the new inmate, is far too confident and imperious to be a victim, even if she appears in a blindfold and chains in the exercise yard. She responds willingly to the other inmate's caresses — something the conventional version of Gaga's character, which is invariably heterosexual, would never do. Thus, the clichéd sexual assault scene vanishes at the moment it appears. But the game does not end there: The other inmate caresses Gaga's crotch, but then moves her hand to her true target: Gaga's cell phone, which she holds still for a moment, so the camera can clearly see the Virgin logo. The blatant and ham-fisted product placement becomes parody, exaggerated to the point that the viewer is more aware of the fact of the product placement than of the product itself. The lesbian assault scene of a women-in-prison exploitation film turns into a cell phone commercial. The adage that sex sells is given a ludicrous literalization. The result of carnivalesque combination is that each element, by virtue of the juxtaposition, becomes an object of withering irony.

Another primary characteristic of the new prisoner in the women-in-prison film is that she is usually either innocent, or, if guilty, a victim of circumstance. This is not the case with Gaga's character. What she has done to be thrown in prison in the first place is not specified, but in the second half of the video, when she leaves prison in the company of Beyoncé, she poisons the entire clientele of a diner, right down to a Great Dane.[8] While Beyoncé poisons her boyfriend presumably out of revenge (and he certainly comes across as criminally rude), Gaga seems to have no motivation other than the sheer hell of it. The scene of the deaths is, of course, grotesque. James Parker notes its "John Water-esque" quality as "fried food falls in lumps from people's mouths," and asks, "What does it mean, the image of an aproned Gaga turning a diner into a vomitorium? It means gaga, it means gagging, it means nothing. Or rather, right now, somehow, it means Pop" (Parker). So Gaga's name itself is enacted on the screen, and becomes an expression of the grotesque. Carnival still reigns supreme, as morality inverts and the energetic dancing and infectious beat invite the viewer to celebrate the murders.

The celebration carries on through to the video's final image, an image that is yet another carnivalesque combination. Callahan describes the conclusion as "swiped from Thelma and Louise" and summarizes it as follows: "[Gaga] and Beyoncé, wanted by the police, engage in a high-speed chase before probably driving off a cliff" (209). While Callahan is right about the reference, she is wrong about the implied ending: the video ends with the words "To Be Continued" and irises out by means of a "_" symbol. Furthermore, the vehicle driven is not the convertible from *Thelma & Louise*. It is, as Callahan points out, the Pussy Wagon from Quentin Tarantino's *Kill Bill: Vol. 1*.[9] A vengeful female reclaims the truck in the film from an abusive male, and here it is the chariot of the narrative's pop amazons. In short, everything about the ending implies a revision of Thelma and Louise's finale. This particular sisterhood need not preserve itself by going over a cliff.

Granting the carnivalization at work in Gaga's art, the question that then arises concerns its value. Does it have any effect beyond its frame? Does it, to return to Parker, mean anything more than "Pop"? Does it mean anything at all? In other words, we have returned to the issue that haunts the Bakhtinian carnival: whether carnival has a truly subversive potential, or whether it is merely a safety valve, a release of circumscribed, officially sanctioned anarchy whose function, in the final analysis, is the maintenance of the *status quo*.

Real or False Transgression

Clair Wills writes, "So it appears a mostly compensatory gesture when critics enthuse about the 'carnivalesque' they find in the latest (post-) modernist novel.... What seems to be lacking in this textual carnival is any link with a genuine social force.... [Peter Stallybrass and Allon White] point out that literary carnival doesn't possess the same social force as actual carnival may once have done. Displaced from public sphere to the bourgeois home (let alone to the novel read by its fire), carnival ceases to be a site of actual struggle" (85). One might simply shift the scene from a book read by the fireplace to a video watched on YouTube on a home computer, or to a song listened to in the even more private sphere of the iPod, in order to see that the issue is very much the same with Gaga's work. The question of whether Lady Gaga's carnival is in any real way transgressive is the same question that confronts Bakhtin's conception of carnival. The principle argument for carnival being, in the end, a conservative, rather than subversive, force, is that it is both temporary and authorized. As Caryl Emerson explains,

No one doubted that Bakhtin's image of carnival was utopian fantasy. It had long been a matter of record, stressed by cultural historians both East and West, that real-life carnival rituals — although perhaps great drunken fun for the short term — were not necessarily cheerful or carefree. In its function as society's safety valve, as a scheduled event that worked to domesticate conflict by temporarily sanctioning victimization, medieval carnival in practice could be more repressive than liberating [164–5].

The displacement of carnival from the street to artistic representation would appear to compound the problem, since "the textual commodities of the textual carnivalesque ... are still no more than static products" and there "is always some kind of dichotomy between the carnivalesque discourse of the text and the social power of its actual equivalent — the rock festival, the grunge concert, the mosh pit, the all-night party: the realities of being and doing" (Brottman 19). Carnival is not only a time-limited event, it also reinforces the power structures it purports to undermine by channeling the energies that would threaten them into a sanctioned and meaningless release; and its artistic representation, by virtue of the unchanging nature of a literary object, remains at an even further remove from any effective action.

Lady Gaga's carnival is not a literary one, and with her concerts, at least, if one accepts Brottman's equivalence between the rock concert and carnival, she avoids the problem of represented carnival. Nevertheless, the charge of phony transgression has also been leveled at her: "Her weirdness threatens no one. This allows the viewer to have a 'transgressive' experience without being required to think. Gaga's act purports to be about many things, but at bottom it satisfies the common demand that 'every artist ... shall pat [the viewer] on the back and tell them that thought is unnecessary.' All else is marketing" ("Dissenting Opinion"). This comfortable transgression sounds rather like the "compensatory gesture" that Wills describes (85): the opportunity to feel radical and chic while putting absolutely nothing on the line. Moreover, Paglia sees "a monumental disconnect between Gaga's melodramatic self-portrayal as a lonely, rebellious, marginalized artist and the powerful corporate apparatus that bankrolled her makeover and has steamrollered her songs into heavy rotation on radio stations everywhere" ("Lady Gaga and the Death of Sex"). In other words, Gaga's carnival is for the ultimate benefit of a gigantically profitable machine. The revolution has been sponsored.

To begin with Paglia's objections, it is perhaps worth noting that part of her critique is based on Gaga's socio-economic background, which leads her to make assumptions about the nature of certain elements of Gaga's carnival, specifically her relationship with her fans. Paglia writes, "Although she presents herself as the clarion voice of all the freaks and misfits of life, there is little evidence that she ever was one. Her upbringing was comfortable and eventually affluent, and she attended the same upscale Manhattan private school as Paris and Nicky Hilton" ("Lady Gaga and the Death of Sex"). Here, Paglia assumes that no one who has had a financially secure upbringing can be a misfit. She also sees presumption and condescension in Gaga's attitude towards the fans: "She constantly touts her symbiotic bond with her fans, the 'little monsters,' who [sic] she inspires to 'love themselves' as if they are damaged goods in need of her therapeutic repair" ("Lady Gaga and the Death of Sex"). Paglia ignores what it is like to be an adolescent, and the fact that, at that age, everyone is a misfit, everyone is damaged goods. Much of Gaga's audience, on the other hand, is either living through this truth, or, at the very least, has not forgotten it. Gaga's demographic-crossing appeal speaks to the misfit and the freak of every (self-) description, and the fans welcome the embrace of the performer who celebrates any and all characteristics that have led to whatever degree of alienation, isolation and self-doubt they may be experiencing.

As for the carnival's corporate backer, there is no denying that Interscope profits enormously, and thanks to the nature of its contract with Gaga, it profits even more the further the carnival spreads: Interscope "gets a cut of the artist's profit from everything — licensing, downloads, endorsements, T-shirt sales. Gaga's deal with Polaroid, MffIAffIC, and any other company? The label gets a cut" (Callahan 153). It is possible, however, that the exploitation runs both ways: "Back in 2008, she said she knew exactly what she was doing: 'People frown upon the major label system,' she said. 'I, on the other hand, am using it to my advantage. I want to create something huge and amazing'" (154). Without wanting to push the idea too far, it is nonetheless interesting to consider, in this light, the lawsuit brought against Gaga by Rob Fusari, her former producer. According to Callahan, what one entertainment lawyer "finds most interesting is that Fusari, the industry veteran, is essentially claiming that this very young girl exploited him" (127–28). Time will tell to what degree Gaga can be said to be exploiting the industry, and whether or not who is exploiting whom in this case has any bearing on the position of the audience, but the point here is that the situation is more complex and interesting than Paglia believes.

More important, however, is the audience's perception, because it is here that the carnivalesque can have its strongest impact. Whatever the "reality" might be behind the Lady Gaga phenomenon, perception determines the reality of the phenomenon. As argued above, Gaga's never-complete, perpetually becoming body and image are her offering to the fans. The fans, in turn, find in the construction that is "Lady Gaga" the support they need, depending on their context. Callahan provides one example in Japan, where "the increasing socioeconomic power of women ... causes existential anxiety" (222). She explains: So you can see what a Lady Gaga might mean to young Japanese women. "She's everything to us," says a twenty-nine-year-old superfan who goes by the name of Junko Monster, "we have nothing except for Gaga." "She said to us [that] we're precious," says Megumi Monster. (222–23) Being valued is what the fans take away from their relationship with the star and because of her mutability the fans feel this valuing no matter what their specific context. It is enough for them to feel excluded in some way by their society, to be a freak, to be a little monster, to then feel included by Lady Gaga.

The perception created by the interaction between artist and audience extends beyond the concert, CD or video, and here we find the answer to the objection that carnival is time-limited, and thus ineffective. Lady Gaga's carnival does not end. This is, again, why Paglia is wrong to lambaste Gaga for appearing in character even when going to the gym. In fact, it is crucial that Gaga never break character. In this manner, Gaga spreads the carnival to every corner of her life and demolishes the spatio-temporal boundaries of the concert performance.[10] Of course, it is simply not enough for Gaga to be Gaga at all times. The effectiveness of her carnival depends on more than her serving as a blank slate for the projected hopes and desires of her fans. No doubt the most visible way in which she has pushed the transformative potential of the carnivalesque is through activism on behalf of Gay Rights, and most notably campaigning for the repeal of the "Don't ask, don't tell" legislation. Her involvement with the gay community dates only from around the launch of her first album — "part of the prerelease strategy was establishing Gaga not only in the gay community but as of it" (Callahan 119, emphasis hers) — and thus an uncharitable reading would see the reasons for this involvement beginning and ending with corporate strategy. But whatever the origins of the relationship, its embrace by star and community has made it genuine. Writes Jack Halberstam, "Can you hear me? Listen up: I am gaga for Gaga." Just as telling is the title of an Advocate editorial — "Gaga: We've Found Our Fierce Advocate" (the wording castigating President Obama for failing to live up to his promise to be just that) — and a piece that concludes that "Lady Gaga has been a more visible force for DADT repeal than almost every politician in Washington combined" ("View From Washington"). The image has become reality with a vengeance. Precisely how much impact Gaga ultimately had in the success of the repeal will be for others to determine, but that she did have an impact seems hard to deny, and so one might point to this historical moment as an example of carnival's potential being realized.

Taking a position opposite to that of Stallybrass and White, Wills points out that for Bakhtin himself, "in order for popular carnival to become politically effective it must enter the institution of literature. In *Rabelais and His World*, Bakhtin argues that it is only in literature that popular festive forms can achieve the 'self-awareness' necessary for effective protest" (86). However,

Wills goes on to say that "'artistic awareness' is never fully theorized by Bakhtin ... what seems to be at stake is a juxtaposition of 'official' and 'non-official' modes of communication ... the power of carnival to turn things upside down is facilitated by bringing it into dialogic relation to official forms" (87). Further, and most crucially with regards to Lady Gaga: "It is only by bringing the excluded and carnivalesque into the official realm in a single text that the concept of public discourse may be altered (so texts written solely in the vernacular would be too far outside the official realm to have an effect)" (87). This is precisely what has occurred in the case of Gaga's "Don't ask, don't tell" activism. Gaga brings her carnival into direct exchange with official discourse through "having discharged soldiers escort her to the Video Music Awards, exchanging tweets with Reid's office about the vote, tweeting an explanation of a filibuster, and instructing her 'little monsters' [via YouTube] to call their senators" ("View From Washington"). She speaks her truth to power, and always in character. Because the carnivalesque Gaga is omnipresent, and Stefani Germanotta has disappeared, Lady Gaga is all the more powerful and effective. The official realm listens because it knows who she is, and the carnival follows her direction because of the continuity she has created. Thus, Lady Gaga is far more impact than Stefani Germanotta alone ever could have. And though Germanotta reappears in name at the conclusion to the YouTube call to arms "A Message from Lady Gaga to the Senate," when Gaga recites the phone call she will make, the visual appearance belongs to Lady Gaga. Furthermore, the name Germanotta will acquire force in the phone call only when it is accompanied by "also known as Lady Gaga" ("A Message from Lady Gaga to the Senate Sept 16 2010").

Wills and Bakhtin emphasize the textual carnival, and Gaga, too, adds a textual element to her performative carnival, in order to give it direction, purpose, and effect beyond the concert itself. Her shows come complete with a manifesto. Callahan quotes the speech that comes near the close of the performance: "It is in the theory of perception that we have established our bond, or the lie I should say, for which we kill. We are nothing without our image. Without our projection. Without the spiritual hologram of who we perceive ourselves to be, or rather, to become, in the future" (219). There is both a precision to the tactic and a deliberate vagueness (or perhaps, more accurately, openness) to the content. Once again, one can see the emphasis Gaga herself places on becoming. As well, the image is of crucial importance, since it comes to define reality. Whatever the present reality is, the image is insisted upon until it becomes the reality. And so, as we have seen, how Gaga came to be involved with the gay community hardly matters. It is the image of her involvement that has come to have greatest import.

Gaga's image is also crucial in the realm of fashion, and it is here that her carnival-grotesque addresses what Bakhtin omits. One of Bakhtin's examples of the grotesque body comes from the "Kerch terracotta collection [where] we find figurines of senile pregnant hags. Moreover, the old hags are laughing" (*Rabelais and His World* 25). As Russo argues,

> for the feminist reader, this image of the pregnant hag is more than ambivalent. It is loaded with all of the connotations of fear and loathing associated with the biological processes of reproduction and of aging. Bakhtin, like many other social theorists of the nineteenth and twentieth centuries, fails to acknowledge or incorporate the social relations of gender in his semiotic model of the body politic, and thus his notion of the Female Grotesque remains, in all directions, repressed and undeveloped [219].

Lady Gaga's version of the female grotesque goes far beyond Bakhtin's while still remaining true to his conception of the excessive, never-completed body. We have already seen Gaga's sexual grotesque from the opening of the "Bad Romance" video. There is also the birth scene at the beginning of the video for "Born This Way," with its kaleidoscopic breaking up of Gaga's body into mirrored fragments and a delight in bodily fluids worthy of David Cronenberg. Meghan Vicks underscores the monstrous side of the grotesque that Gaga creates by way of her sexuality: "she transgresses the normal bounds of the pop icon ... by hyperbolizing and making monstrous the extreme sexuality of that role.... She makes horrific the sveltely thin yet curvy figure of the pop starlet by wearing outfits that distort, exaggerate, and sharpen those sexualized contours of the female body" ("The Icon and the Monster: Lady Gaga is a Trickster of American Pop Culture"). However, what should not be lost sight of is the other side of the equation. Gaga does make the sexual monstrous, but she also makes the monstrous sexual and desirable. The viewer may well find Gaga's visual incarnations bizarre, destabilizing and disturbing, and even disgusting. The responses may indeed include fear and loathing, but of a qualitatively different sort than that which would greet the pregnant hags. Gaga's agenda is more disruptive than repulsive. She describes her look as sexy, "But I don't think anybody's dick is hard, looking at that. I think they're just confused, and maybe a little bit scared" (qtd. in Goodman 135). The ambivalence is important, and makes her relationship with the fashion industry an ongoing, developing commentary on the representation of women.

The nature of Gaga's correction to Bakhtin's grotesque can, I think, be seen in Brian Massumi's interpretation of Deleuze's and Guattari's "becoming-woman." This he describes, in rather carnivalesque terms, as "carrying the indeterminacy, movement, and paradox of the female stereotype past the point at which it is recuperable by the socius as it presently functions, over the limit beyond which lack of definition becomes the positive power to select a trajectory (the leap from the realm of possibility into the virtual — breaking away)" (87). And this, precisely, is what Lady Gaga does. She embodies "a femininity done right and over done to the point of parody" ("You Cannot Gaga Gaga"). She is such an exaggeration that it becomes impossible not to see the objectification of women in the high-heeled, sexualized displays. The fashions are so extreme — models have refused to wear the armadillo shoes she dons in the "Bad Romance" video ("Three Models")—that they become graphic illustrations of the bodily distortions the industry mandates (even as designers flock to provide ever more outlandish attire for Gaga).[11]

Gaga takes the female stereotype to the point of self-destruction. It can no longer function as a signifier for "woman."[12] But it is not enough to demonstrate how women are victimized by the images imposed on them. Gaga takes the painful, extreme image and, having exposed it for what it is, makes it her own. To return once again to "Bad Romance," Gaga explains that the video "explores how the entertainment industry simulates human trafficking, the woman as commodity" (qtd. in Goodman 25). And while Gaga is indeed displayed, then sold to a rather sinister male figure, she emerges triumphant. The bed where the transaction is completed erupts in flames, and the video ends with a smirking Gaga beside the incinerated corpse of the man who sought to own her. The sparking bra is there again: her sexuality, far from being controlled, has destroyed her would-be victimizer.

Conclusion

There is, finally, one more tool that Lady Gaga uses to give her carnival a sense of purpose. This tool is her glasses. More often than not, they are opaque, and they are ubiquitous. No matter how exposed Gaga is, no matter how much her body is offered up as a spectacle, again and again this barrier rises, concealing her eyes from the viewer. The glasses, though, are just as outlandish as the rest of the costume, and so draw attention to the very thing that they are concealing. Something, it would seem, is being held back. Some aspect of self, of identity, is preserved.

Even more importantly, however, the viewer remembers Gaga's gaze. Early in the video for "Alejandro," for example, Gaga appears, shrouded in darkness, her gaze trained on the spectacle that is about to unspool before her, a spectacle in which she is also a participant. The expected carnivalesque reversals are here again: the dancers wear high heels and their movements are coded feminine, but they are male. Fascist fashions are exposed for the fetish they are, the sinister deflated by being associated with that which it would choose to suppress (homosexuality). In the shots of sexual coupling, Gaga adopts both male and female positions. The entire carnival is staged for the benefit of the watching Gaga. It is she who calls it into being and who directs the revels. The active gaze in this spectacle is explicitly and centrally female, as if Gaga responds to the very problem Mulvey sees lying at the heart of the cinematic experience. The spectacle on display is, precisely, a spectacle — an elaborate performance for the presiding Gaga — and is overtly erotic. This fact further emphasizes visual pleasure

But if Gaga, the woman, seizes the active gaze and controls the events, she leaves open the end to which the revels are directed. The actions in the video are suggestive, but subject to multiple readings. The same is true with many of her lyrics. The nonsense lyrics that open "Bad Romance" have just enough recognizable sense that they must mean something, even if that something is mysterious. She wants her fans to be empowered: "I want women — and men — to feel empowered by a deeper and more psychotic part of themselves" (qtd. in Goodman 44). Like the lyrics, the concealed gaze is one more variation of the blank slate. But the barrier is also a screen on which the Little Monsters can project the images of their liberated desire, until, through the power of the unfettered, unbounded, unending carnival, image becomes reality. As we have seen, the nature of this "reality" might itself be subject to debate, as one grapples with differing empirical and psychological realities. That Lady Gaga has had some effect on the former seems very likely; it would be difficult, I would contend, to maintain that she had no influence on the repeal of "Don't ask, don't tell." As for the psychological realities of her fans, the enthusiasm and self-empowerment are impossible to ignore. The longer term will determine the ultimate effectiveness of Gaga's carnival. But its potential is enormous.

NOTES

1. See, for example, Umberto Eco, who argues that because of the limits of time and space, "comedy and carnival are not instances of real transgressions: on the contrary, they represent paramount examples of law reinforcement. They remind us of the existence of the rule" (6).

2. "The grotesque body, as we have often stressed, is a body in the act of becoming. It is never finished, never completed; it is continually built, created, and builds and creates another body" (*Rabelais and his World* 317).

3. Thus, when a male Japanese fan states, "[M]aybe I could be Lady Gaga. Maybe I could create something. Maybe I have something. To be inspired is important" (Callahan 224), the narrative he has constructed for himself via the agency of Gaga is not the same as the lesson of empowerment experienced by female fans — "She said to us [that] we're precious" (Callahan 223). Both narratives, however, have originated in the same collective event.

4. "Fashion of his Love" from *Born This Way* is "about the relationship she shared with the late designer" ("Lady Gaga Writes 'Love Song' to Alexander McQueen") testifies to the role his fashions have played in the visual performance of her art.

5. She contains all of these influences in a single entity, and this visible presence of the

multitude-in-one is thus a defining characteristic — perhaps even a paradoxical uniqueness — of the construction that is "Lady Gaga."

6. The mythology consists of the conflicting stories about how her name came to be, how her meteoric rise to fame transpired, how much of a misfit she truly is, and so on.

7. Of interest here is Jonathan Demme's directorial debut *Caged Heat* (1974), which is an early attempt to bring feminism to a form that would, at first glance at least, appear to inimical to such a project.

8. Michelson suggests that the video is a sequel to "Paparazzi," beginning with the result of that story's murder.

9. It is fitting that this reference should be to another recycler and re-inventor of popular culture.

10. If one were to argue that the impact of the carnival in the rock concert is limited by the fact that the concert has a set duration and location, and thus discount any possibility that the emotions triggered by the performance have any lasting effect, then one is still faced the performing persona existing outside the concert, and continuing to act in a carnivalesque fashion, thereby denying the end of carnival.

11. Among these designers are Vivienne Westwood, Thierry Mugler, and Hussein Chalayan (who designed the bubble dress) (Goodman 140). McQueen was "Lady Gaga's most important fashion collaborator" (Goodman 140).

12. Gaga's femininity, exaggerated to the point of deconstruction, has something of the drag performance about it. This, along with her embrace of the gay community, is, perhaps, yet another reason for the rumors, spreading in the wake of a blurry concert image (Callahan 189) that Gaga is a hermaphrodite. The implied message would seem to be that a woman who defies the acceptable definitions of "woman" cannot possibly *be* a woman. Gaga's drag king persona "Jo Calderone" further complicates and interrogates gender identity.

The Fame Monster

The Monstrous Construction of Lady Gaga

ANN T. TORRUSIO

Since her debut album in 2008, Lady Gaga has developed into a powerful star and cultural icon. Yet, despite her success, she faces constant condemnation from critics who view her work as a sensational side show with little substance. Perhaps part of Lady Gaga's marketability is her ability to simultaneously expose the values of American popular culture and to function as a warning sign that undermines the culture's entire value system. A site of paradox, Lady Gaga constantly dazzles and disgusts a fixated public. In this sense she is a monstrosity; she is a text that embodies our biggest anxieties and desires. The monster, etymologically *monstrum,* was both a warning sign and a revelation. Seneca identified the *monstrum* as "a visual and horrific revelation of the truth" (Staley 113). In his essay "Monster Theory (Seven Theses)," Jeffrey Jerome Cohen asserts that monsters' bodies are cultural products and "disturbing hybrids whose externally inherent bodies resist attempts to include them in any systematic structuration. And so the monster is dangerous, a form suspended between forms that threatens to smash distinctions" (6). By using Cohen's "Monster Theory" as a lens through which to view Lady Gaga, I argue that because Lady Gaga is a complete fabrication, she has the freedom to constantly reinvent her image.

Through this perpetual reinvention, or "monstering," Lady Gaga presents herself as a monstrous body of "pure culture" (Cohen 4). Throughout her career, critics have projected various labels onto Gaga in an attempt to categorize her, to compartmentalize her into a specific space in culture. However, due to Lady Gaga's constant reinvention of herself, these labels have ultimately been fleeting. In television interviews, music videos and live performances, Lady Gaga presents herself as a modern shape shifter, morphing into myriad variations of herself while presenting all the variations as possibly the "true" construction of Lady Gaga. By doing this, she calls attention to our inability to trust the products of mass media. In another sense, her constant shape shifting provides her viewers the opportunity to catch glimpses of themselves, and to promise that they, too, can become famous. Cohen warns that to step out of the bounds of our sanctioned social spaces is to risk walking into the world of monsters that flourishes at the margins of the world (12). Like gargoyles that drape the periphery of old cathedral roofs such as that of Notre Dame de Paris, monsters teeter on the edges of culture, and Gaga's insistence upon remaining at the borders of the possible is in part what makes her so alluring to her fan base. She shows her fans what exists beyond the sanctioned boundaries of society and entices them to follow; what lies beyond these boundaries, she implies, is not ostracism, but adoration. Affectionately referring to her fans as "Little Monsters," she tantalizes her audience with the notion that, if they follow her, they will become part of the show. She presents herself as "The Fame Monster," whose greed for fame has destroyed the woman she once was, while simultaneously projecting back onto her public its own perverse obsession for fame. Paradoxically, she both promises it and undermines their fixation on it. Gaga avoids systematic structuration by smashing the distinction between performer and audience, forcing both to coexist in an escapist monsterdom.

Gaga and the Elusive Confession

In 2009, Barbara Walters voted Lady Gaga as one of the "Most Fascinating People" of the year. While a montage of images from Gaga's recent career fills the screen, Walters discussed Gaga's success, concluding with a compliment for Gaga's conservative fashion dress during their prerecorded interview: "When I met Lady Gaga, she was not in one of her outlandish costumes, instead in her platinum hair and serious Chanel suit, she was quite a lady, and not gaga at all" (Walters). The camera then depicted previously filmed footage of the pair walking onto an empty stage toward two chairs facing each other. Gaga was indeed wearing what appears to be a black Chanel skirt suit with a frilly white blouse and dark round sunglasses. Her arm was tightly linked in Walters' arm. There was a pronounced unsteadiness in Gaga's stride, as if she could not quite walk on her own in her black platform heels, and must hold on to Walters for support, who appeared more than pleased to help. As they took their respective seats at stage center, Gaga offered to shed her sunglasses for the interview: "You know, I don't take my glasses off for many interviews, but I'll take them off for you" (Walters).

Walters thanked Gaga for removing her glasses and asked her to address some popular misconceptions about herself. After refuting the rumor that she was artificial, she continued, "I aspire to be a teacher to my young fans, who feel just like I felt when I was younger.... I want to free them of their fears, and let them know they can create their own space in the world." Walters made several inquiries about her past and asked whether Gaga knew as a young child if she was going to be a performer. Gaga responded, "I had this dream, and I really wanted to be a star ... I was almost a monster in the way that I was fearless with my ambitions." Two notable moments in the Walters' interview address her physical body and sexual orientation. The Walters' interview also addresses the question surrounding the rumor that Gaga is a hermaphrodite:

> "You know," Walters begins, "there also is this strange rumor that you are part man and part woman. You've heard this rumor?"
> Gaga, looking straight ahead of her, responds quickly with a "Yes."
> "True?" asks Walters.
> "No," responds Gaga, thereby squelching a rumor that circulated the Internet and radio waves for a year. She concludes with the assertion: "I portray myself in a very androgynous way.... I like pushing boundaries."

Walters also sheepishly inquires about the "muffin" line in Gaga's hit single "Poker Face," leading the discussion to address rumors regarding Gaga's bisexuality. When asked if she has had sex with a woman, Gaga initially gasps and claims "My goodness!" as she readjusts herself in her seat. However, she eventually confesses that she has had "sexual relationships" with women.

Despite Gaga's responses to Walters' line of questioning, the rumors surrounding Gaga's biology and sexuality remain a popular topic of discussion. Alleged photographs of her male genitalia have gone viral and YouTube videos with titles such as "Lady Gaga is a hermaphrodite with proof pictures" have been viewed hundreds of thousands of times and continue to spark debate among fans and critics alike. The perverse desire for the public to label Gaga as abnormal or malformed is not unlike the rumors that circulated about Marilyn Monroe having six toes on one foot, a falsehood that continued to make its way into publications like the *Weekly World News* as late as 2001. It is as if an ogling public feels compelled to conjure up freakish physical attributes to stars they find especially compelling, perhaps in an attempt to categorize them as "not like us." Although the exact origin and motive behind Gaga's rumored hermaphroditism remains a mystery, the public's continued discussion of Gaga's purported hermaphroditism only further establishes her relationship with monster culture.

In Michel Foucault's *Abnormal,* the second of Foucault's lectures at the Collège de France to appear in English translation, he examined the legacy of the monster and the evolving conceptualization of the monster through time. Foucault speculated that from the Middle Ages to the eighteenth century, the monster was essentially a mixture of the animal and human realms, "the man with the head of an ox, the man with a bird's feet — monsters.... It is the mixture of two individuals: the person who has two heads and one body or two bodies and one head is a monster. It is the mixture of two sexes: the person who is both male and female is a monster" (63). Foucault described the period from the Middle Ages to the eighteenth century as a time when hermaphrodites were executed simply on the grounds of hermaphroditism. The very condition was condemnable. One of the last reported instances occurred in 1599. The hermaphrodite was burnt alive after it was determined he/she could only have both sexes as a result of having relations with Satan (Foucault 67). The desire to stigmatize the anatomical anomaly continued through the sixteenth and seventeenth centuries, although hermaphrodites were still subjected to intense social regulation. By the seventeenth century, hermaphrodites were not executed simply for being "born that way," but they had to choose and document which sex with which they would legally identify.

In *On Monsters and Marvels,* a text written by the sixteenth-century French surgeon Ambrose Paré, his explanation of the legal regulations placed upon hermaphrodites articulates this point:

> Male and female hermaphrodites are those who have both sets of sexual organs well-formed ... and both the ancient and modern laws have obliged and still oblige ... to choose which sex organs they wish to use, and they are forbidden on pain of death to use any but those they will have chosen.... For some of them have abused their situation, with the result that, through mutual and reciprocal use, they take their pleasure first with one set of organs and then with the other: first with those of a man, then with those of a woman ... [27].

The historical threat posed by hermaphrodites was the ability to experience too much pleasure. The excess of pleasure posed a threat to the *status quo,* and the inability to categorize and compartmentalize the human body threatened the very structure of the state.

Foucault also cited the 1765 trail of Anne Grandjean to emphasize the shifting cultural beliefs about monstrosity and its link to hermaphroditism. Foucault noted that Champeaux, the man who chronicled the trial, contended that Grandjean's monstrosity was not found in the fact that she was a suspected hermaphrodite, but rather because she loved a woman as woman — the gender under which she was officially registered. "[I]t is this monstrosity" Foucault concluded, "which is not a monstrosity of nature but a monstrosity of behavior that calls for condemnation" (73). In the Modern period, however, our understanding of monsters enters a new stage. "Monstrosity ... is no longer the undue mixture of what should be separated by nature. It is simply an irregularity, a slight deviation, but one that makes possible ... the monstrosity of character" (73). In the later part of the eighteenth century, Foucault argues for the emergence of "the monstrous nature of criminality ... the moral monster" (74–5). In other words, monsters morph from natural transgressions into moral monsters and criminals. Actions define monsters' anatomies.

Even today, the curiosity and debates over Lady Gaga's sexuality and rumors of her hermaphroditism stem from the legacy of the public's desire to restrict or confine the parameters of an individual's sexual activity and that a deviation from those pre-established categories legitimizes labeling one as a monster. Even after Gaga blatantly discounted the rumor that she is a hermaphrodite, her ambiguous and scandalous confession of having "sexual relations" with other females creates a modern case study not unlike that of Anne Grandjean. What is puritanical about America tries Gaga for monstrosity of character and condemns her as a moral monster. Her confessions, ironically, also solidify her position at the crossroads of culture and at the borders of the possible.

Borderline Positive: Gaga and Illness

A few weeks after her interview with Walters, Larry King interviewed Gaga on his television program *Larry King Live*. The interview took place while Gaga was touring in England and the majority of interview was depicted with a split screen with King's torso on the left and Gaga's on the right. For the interview, Gaga sported a white button-down shirt rolled up to her elbows, thick black sequined suspenders and thick solid black tie. Her hair was short and platinum, slicked back. On the whole, her costume was rather masculine, a far departure from the Chanel suit that she had worn for her interview with Barbara Walters. For her interview with King, Gaga also wore the same round sunglasses that she had worn for Walters. On the other side of the split screen, King wore a black button-down shirt with white suspenders and a black tie with white polka dots. His sleeves were also rolled. The split screen created a striking juxtaposition between the two individuals — Gaga looked as if she were a photographic negative of King, the same look with the colors inverted. Like the Walters' interview, King's questions revealed his interest in the rumors that had been circulating about Gaga's physical body. King mentioned the rumor that Gaga had Lupus and he asked her if she had been diagnosed with the disease:

> You know ... Lupus is in my family, and it is genetic, and ... it's funny cause my
> mother told me the other day that my fans were quite worried about me because

I did talk about the fact that I was tested for Lupus. The truth is, I don't show any signs, any symptoms of lupus, but I have tested borderline positive for the disease. So, as of now, I do not have it, but I have to take good care of myself [King interview].

Gaga's response casted her in a threshold of an able/disabled body or a body defined with its disease. Her body inhabits a space that is both able-bodied: "I don't show any signs, any symptoms of Lupus," while potentially marked with a specific disease. Gaga also responded by carefully placing her fans at the forefront of the answer: "my mother told me other day that my fans were worried about me." By doing so, she showed her fans that she possessed a privileged awareness about her body and health. Her response alluded to the idea that she has handed her body over to her public, allowing them to project onto her what they want or need to project. The way that she positioned herself as "borderline positive" for Lupus created a situation not unlike the rumors that she was a hermaphrodite, rumors of her bisexuality, and — although not discussed during her interviews with Walters or King — accusations that she was a rabid drug user and an extreme dieter. Indeed, Lupus is commonly known as "the great imitator" because the disease's symptoms mirror many other diseases. The diagnosis situates her body at a unique crossroads that defies categorization.

Part of Gaga's ability to receive myriad meanings is her ability to shape-shift literally before the eyes of her public. For instance, in the music video for "Bad Romance," one of the top-selling singles from her 2009 album *The Fame Monster*, Gaga retransformed herself in nearly every shot. Aside from a variety of costumes changes, which includes a bodysuit of red vinyl covering every part of her body — except her mouth — and a white fur dress that ends in a train with a bear's head still attached, Gaga literally changes shape throughout the video, challenging us to determine which one is Gaga's authentic body. Some of the more extreme examples include a shot in which a single backlight illuminates her frighteningly thin body with each vertebra practically breaking through her flesh, and another shot where her eyes are digitally enlarged like a Japanese anime character. Even the basic concept behind her hit single "Poker Face" lies in the inability to identify an authentic person behind a consciously crafted projected image. The album cover to *The Fame Monster* depicts a curly haired platinum blond Gaga on the outside, while the inside cover contains a long, straight dark haired Gaga; both images were sold simultaneously.

Gaga's shape shifting, particularly in the context of *The Fame* Monster album, harkens back to a marketing strategy employed by Tori Amos for her *Strange Little Girls* concept album from 2001. The album, consisting of nothing but cover tracks, was issued with four alternative covers depicting Amos as the various personae she created for each song. Fans could choose which album cover to buy based on which persona they identified with most, or select one based on which cover they thought looked best. In a similar way, Gaga constructs herself in so many different ways that she allows her public the option to gloss over the versions of herself we find unpalatable in favor of other images we are willing to accept. This is an important characteristic of Lady Gaga's "performance."

The paradox of Gaga's performance, as Kathryn Leedom points out in her critical essay entitled "'Grab Your Old Girl With Her New Tricks': Lady Gaga and Reflective Performance," lies in her ability to be "extremely unique and yet reminiscent of many various people." Gaga's performances are a barrage of radically different looks. They invite us to project onto her performance whatever meaning we want: we can choose to embrace certain allusions to different performers while dismissing others, and we can determine for ourselves if these allusions are artistic tributes to various performers of the past or ironic commentaries on the social conditions under which these former stars appeared and thrived. It is perhaps due to Gaga's ability to carry out this type of performance that many critics consider her an artistic genius.

In a 2009 critique of American culture entitled *Empire of Illusion: the End of Literacy and the Triumph of Spectacle*, Chris Hedges addressed how the celebrity interview constructs an illusion of intimacy and its effect between the celebrity and the remote viewer:

> The celebrity interview or profile, pioneered on television by Barbara Walters and now a ubiquitous part of the news and entertainment industry, gives us the illusion that we have intimate relations with celebrities as well as the characters they portray. Real life, our own life, is viewed next to the lives of celebrities as inadequate and inauthentic. Celebrities are portrayed as idealized forms of ourselves. It is we, in perverse irony, who are never fully actualized, never fully real in celebrity culture [19–20].

In her interviews with Barbara Walters and Larry King, Gaga fostered this sense of intimacy between herself and her fans by constructing both interviews as confessions of devotion to her fans. In her televised interview with Walters, Gaga gushed, "I can't say enough about my Little Monsters, my beautiful fans." In her interview with Larry King, she confessed that she could not believe how, when she looks out at 17,000 people, they "know" her songs and they "know" her name. The simple fact that Gaga is not Gaga complicates this statement. During such interviews, Gaga also exploits her ability to transform her appearance to mirror physically her hosts. Kathryn Leedom refers to this effect as "reflective performance" that enables her to function "as a mirror for consumer culture and her audience." When the two women sit facing each other, Gaga bears an uncanny resemblance to a younger, perhaps idealized, version of Barbara Walters. Gaga also provides Walters with the formula for an ideal interview. For example, Gaga mimics the pattern of a successful Walters' interview by making confessions about her turbulent past, addressing problems in her family while shedding tears. In Gaga's interview with Larry King, she employs a similar tactic. Even her posture and mannerisms seem to imitate King's own movements throughout the interview, calling attention to our inability to trust the products of mass media.

During her interviews, Lady Gaga affirms the instability of her identity while underscoring its performity as well as the performity of the interviewers' identity. Gaga's physical display of mirroring her hosts usurps the interviews, which reminds the audience of the meta-theatricality of the interviews and exposing the latter as mere "performance." Furthermore, Gaga's reflective performance bears an uncanny resemblance to her interviewer as she plants herself somewhere in between the interview and the interviewee; she performs *for* and *as* the interviewer, positioned in the cultural crossroads of the monster figure. In other words, the structure of the televised personal interview underscores her ability to occupy the same subject position as the monster, a projection signifying something other than itself. Occupying this position enables Gaga to criticize this culture while simultaneously playing into it and she uses her interviews as a carefully crafted event.

"I'm your biggest fan": Gaga and the Paparazzi

Although Lady Gaga has used televised interviews to underscore her identity as performance, Gaga's music videos provide her both the space and the authority to have unrestricted play with her identity and her relationship with the public. In the music video "Paparazzi" from *The Fame Monster* album, Gaga presents herself as a monstrous body created by the paparazzi, a microcosm of the general public. The video begins with Gaga kissing a lover on her balcony until she realizes he has set them up for the paparazzi to view. When she resists his embraces, he pushes her over the railing. As she falls to what we perceive to be her death, paparazzi leeches hound her and snap photos of her crumpled body on ground while shouting "beautiful!" and "Right here! That's it!" Newspapers then fill the screen with headlines such as: "Lady Ga Ga Hits Rock Bottom," "Lady is No More Gaga!" and "Lady Gaga is OVER." The paparazzi are portrayed as unrelenting harpies who manage to take a literal event, Gaga's falling to her apparent death, and undermine and misconstrue it into a figurative fall from public grace. Later in the video, Gaga poisons the boyfriend who threw her from the balcony. The action is followed by a voiced-over confession from Gaga: "I just killed my boyfriend." Although

Gaga's motive initially appears to be revenge, perhaps Gaga actually kills her boyfriend to show her devotion to the paparazzi. After her confession, another series of headlines flash across the screen: "She's Back!" and "We Love her Again!" The announcements are coupled with a scene of her fighting her way through the paparazzi to get into a police car that drives her to jail.

Historian Daniel Boorstin's pioneering text *The Image* (1961) evaluates the modern notion of fame as the state of being "a person who is known for his well-knownness" (57). He also addresses the creation of a "pseudo-event," or an event staged only so it can be reported, such as a photo opportunities and press conferences (57). Boorstin's analysis of fame as being a result of being "known" and the impact of pseudo-event are still applicable today. Celebrity gossip eclipses professional achievement. Gaga's "Paparazzi" video critiques the media's ability to create celebrity out of nothing more than "well-knownness" by ironically demonstrating that events with tangible consequences — the attempted murder of Gaga and the revenge poisoning of her boyfriend — have little to do with popularity or fan loyalty. Even authentic events receive the gloss of a "pseudo-event" in an attempt to control it and package it for public consumption.

At the end of "Paparazzi," an arrested Gaga poses for her mug shot, but the scene takes an notable twist when we overhear an off screen photographer directing her to strike several poses for the camera, reconfiguring the mug shot as yet another publicity photo.[1] The scene underscores Gaga's constant attempt to break free from culturally constructed spaces. Generally speaking, the arrest functions as a method of regulating social norms that remove undesirables from public view; however, in the video, it ironically reinforces her position in the public's eye. In other words, the incarceration of her body causes her image to resurge into the public eye. Other videos literalize the portrayal of Gaga getting a public break in "Paparazzi." For instance, "Telephone" featuring singer Beyoncé depicts an imprisoned Gaga, and yet even while imprisoned Gaga manages to maintain her agency. During the video, Gaga walks out into the prison courtyard wrapped in chains, initially appearing more confined than the other prisoners. A closer look reveals the key wrapped in the chains, showing her fellow inmates as well as her viewers that she still has the ability to break out of her physical constrictions. Gaga also uses her agency to obtain a cellphone, which ultimately becomes the means of her bailout/breakout from prison.

Gaga continues the theme of breaking out of culturally prescribed boundaries in the title video from her latest album *Born This Way* (2011). In "Born This Way," the cinematography reveals what initially appears to be Gaga's face, but is actually a painted mask on the back of her head. But her authentic face appears just as artificial as the mask, leading the viewer to wonder which face, if either, is genuine. Like the Roman Janus face of transition, the monsters of our culture are consistently planting themselves at a crossroads, resisting our categorization, denying us the security of pinpointing their subject position. The video also depicts Gaga perpetually being birthed from herself like a set of Russian Dolls. In this way, she is depicted breaking out of the confines of her own body, reproducing herself again and again. The repeated imagery of breaking out of the boundaries of her physical body and the boundaries constructed by societal norms serves to strengthen her self-conscious positioning on the margins of culture. The image of her perpetual rebirth reinforces her monstrous ability to always escape the grips of a public that constantly tries to learn who the real Gaga is. Like an ancient map that depicts sea monsters in uncharted waters, Gaga embodies the dangerous spaces that exist on the margins.

"A Devoted Jester": Escape to Monsterdom

Gaga's latest stage production, *The Monster Ball Tour*, effectively uses monsters both to criticize the cultural hierarchy as well as to reinforce her relationship with her fan base. During interludes at her concerts, Gaga reads the "Little Monster Manifesto," which articulates this point:

> So, the real truth about Lady Gaga fans, my Little Monsters, lies in this sentiment: They are the kings. They are the queens. They write the history of the kingdom, and I am something of a devoted Jester. It is in the theory of perception that we have established our bond. Or, the lie, I should say, for which we kill. We are nothing without our image. Without our projection. Without the spiritual hologram of who we perceive ourselves to be, or to become rather, in the future. When you're lonely, I'll be lonely too. And this is The Fame [Manifesto of Little Monsters].

With her verbal announcement, Gaga creates a hierarchy in which she occupies the subject position of jester. Her fans become the kings and the queens who, she claims, will record the history. On the surface, the statement empowers her fans because it indicates that her very existence depends on her fans' willingness to include Gaga in the culture's collective consciousness. However, the jester, a member of the court identifiable by ridiculous behavior and flamboyant costuming, is the only member socially sanctioned to publicly make a mockery of the court. Historically, the jester gets away with undermining the state, pointing out its flaws. Furthermore, the jester exists solely as a performance, requiring the court for his audience. Cohen contends that the danger of a monster lies in its ability to always escape (5). The monster's "threat," he claims "is its propensity to shift" (5). The position of the monster only exists in relation to the cultural moment that creates it, therefore is it constantly being reinvented, returning in "slightly different clothing, each time to be read against contemporary social movements" (5). However, like the Fool in Shakespeare's *King Lear*, when the social system of the court completely falls apart, the jester simply disappears.

In addition to her "Little Monster Manifesto," her performance of her song "Paparazzi" attempts to underscore her relationship with her public. The lyrics of the song juxtapose against her on-stage battle against the giant "Fame Monster" which looks like something between an Angler fish and an alien with tentacles, destabilizes her position as pop icon. The effect of the performance creates myriad layers of meaning. In one reading, she is a fan pursuing the attention of an unidentified star, in another reading, she is a pop icon singing from the perspective of a relentless public, and yet in another reading, she is a woman so obsessed with fame that the concept has become personified, a physical form she must publicly battle. Every night during her live show, Gaga is victorious, barely escaping the clutches of the monster that wants to consume her.[2] Gaga has made an art out of escaping and escapism. Like the monster that always shifts right when we believe we have it pinpointed, she escapes into the darkness of the margins.

Ironically, it is in part her constant suggestion of escape and the sense of escapism offered by her performances that bonds her to her fan base — her "Little Monsters." During her interview with Larry King, Gaga stressed this bond with her fan base through her often flamboyant dress, and she reinforced the notion that her image is a connection or hologram that links her to her fans, stating that she "[tries] to create [costumes] that are quite easy for my fans to replicate.... Some of them not so much. But some of them are very easy for my fans to replicate, and that bonds us in a way. It's quite nice to have this connection to them outside of everything else" (King interview). Gaga indicates that by replicating her style, her fans can bond with her and even become close to her. To have this bond exist "outside of everything else" also indicates a pure, unadulterated link between them.

A recent *ABC News* broadcast evidenced the belief in this bond from her fans' perspective. Several fans — labeled by *ABC* as "super fans" — interviewed in succession, all proclaimed themselves as Gaga's "biggest fan." One super fan, who created several Lady Gaga-inspired costumes concluded, "She's just the real deal" ("Meet Lady Gaga's Little Monsters"), revealing Gaga's conscious desire to connect with her fans through costume replication that ironically creates a "real" bond between them. All of the fans interviewed espoused the overwhelming belief that Gaga's love for them is sincere and that she inspires them to seek out and discover their own unique goals and dreams. A strange conclusion, considering the segment ended with several super fans dressed like Gaga and replicating a dance routine memorized from one of her music videos. The resulting image is more of a Lady Gaga look-a-like contest than it is a group of young men and women on the verge of discovering their own unique ambitions. The interviews with the super fans make it difficult to imagine what would motivate their ambitions if they did not follow Gaga, and it is more difficult to imagine them casting off the "super fan" label in order to become labeled and defined by their own experience and success.

For many of her "super fans," Gaga has created a perfect come-as-you-are subculture. She instills in her "super fans" the belief that they are important, beautiful and unique; they will find their place in the world in the cultural margins. Gaga's belief that they are really kings and queens who write history is interpreted as a promise that they also can be famous, as power, fame and wealth become inextricably tangled when fantasy and reality become blurred. Ultimately, once we examine Lady Gaga through the lens of "pure culture," this criticism of her fan base is far less of a critique of Gaga's professional motives and more of a criticism of the culture that we created in which figures like Gaga can easily thrive. Like Elvis in the 1950s and the Beatles in the 1960s, Gaga is a product that came into being at precisely the moment when a new generation of consumers was breathless with anticipation for something or someone on which to attach its hopes and dreams. Gaga's fans always perceive her adoration for them as genuine, and it is possible that they may well be correct. However, it cannot be ignored that her well-cultivated relationship with her fans has made her one of the most powerful celebrities of our time, an icon that has lured her "Little Monsters" into the margins of culture

Regardless of her sincerity, Gaga's efforts to acknowledge publicly her adoring fan base have created a marketing sensation. Kathryn Leedom underscores the outcome of this paradox: "Mirroring her fans' love has the benefit of securing her position in fame" ("Grab Your Old Girl with Her New Tricks"). Gaga inhabits the world of celebrity culture, which is designed out of fantasy and deception in order to make a profit. Gaga's message is profoundly powerful because she assures her public what they want to believe about themselves is true. Her image promises that those with the rather abstract desire to "be a star" can reach their goals. Her sympathetic assurance that, in the past, she has felt the same pain and alienation that her young fans now feel projects her as a mentor for the young masses who willingly misinterpret Gaga's statements as a recipe for success and fame. Like a flattering mirror, Gaga promises to reflect back at her fans their idealized selves. Ironically, only through Gaga's performance — a performance created for a consumer audience — can we hope to represent our real self and create a space that Gaga assures us is not a space that exists only in fantasy, but a place where we coexist with Gaga as stars.

Notes

1. This video aired during the period when Lindsay Lohan and Paris Hilton, two celebrities also known for their "well-knownness," smiled for their mug shots, conveying to the public that there were no real consequences for their actions and that this was all just part of the show. We stare at our celebrities as icons, but we also stare at them as oddities in the curio cabinet, monstrosities we ogle.

2. Interestingly, she manages to kill the "Fame Monster" at the end of the song with sparks from her notorious pyrotechnic bustier originally known for being worn at the end of her "Bad Romance" music video.

The Appropriation of the Madonna Aesthetic

REBECCA M. LUSH

The press and her fans have consistently remarked upon Lady Gaga's penchant for weirdness. Whether she wears a dress made of meat or places jewels in her tea cups, her appearance and actions always create a media sensation. Lady Gaga has been no stranger to controversy and headlines, but the meat-dress, in particular, ushered in a new level of media attention and criticism while drawing more questions about who Lady Gaga is, especially since her every move seems to be an elaborate, *avant-garde* performance. What did the dress mean? Was the ensemble really made out of meat? And then there is the more generic and frequently espoused question of what she was thinking. Was she making a statement about the media sexualizing images of women and treating them like a "piece of meat," a common euphemism to describe the objectification of sexual bodies? Or was the dress indeed linked more closely to Gaga's stand on the "Don't ask, don't tell" debate since, as she said without fully explaining how her choice of metaphor, meat, made a statement for gay rights? Surely, a performer as astute as Gaga is wary of taking the artist's word as a definitive statement of meaning and purpose. Gaga's meat-clad presence at the 2010 MTV Video Music Awards both showed her undeniable success in music and entertainment (winning eight awards in total for her videos), and her status as a harbinger of controversy, albeit one that most will admit to not fully understanding. Gaga's success leads her supporters to praise her as a performance genius while her controversies often lead her detractors to dismiss her for lacking substance, nothing but superficial pop sheen.

Yet, such episodes in Gaga's highly documented, although young career, reach the heart of the great Gaga debate: is she original or is she just an expert assembler of past cultural references? The idea behind the meat-dress was

173

obscure enough — part of the *avant-garde* world of fashion and art sculpture by Jana Sterbak, although the dress was designed by Franc Fernandez — that the average viewer, or "Little Monster," would not have had a ready referent for its antecedent. The bizarre outfit seemed original, but then again perhaps what would have been more surprising to the media and the audience was if her outfit was not unusual, but mundane; being different can begin to look the same. To those that see her as original, Gaga strives to step outside of the boundaries of the mainstream, using her musical talent and eye for haute-couture visuals to separate herself from the pack of Ke$has, Rihannas and Britneys. Gaga's outlandish performance identity promises substance by creating questions for her audience to parse out. To those who deem her another product of savvy marketing, she is simply the most effective at commercializing and peddling her "brand," gathering much of her material from the careers of those who have gone before her. To detractors then, Gaga's promise of substance is just that (a promise), finding instead a charade of performance poses that ultimately confer no meaning to work.

Gaga assembles a performance identity by building on past cultural referents, much like her predecessor Madonna, and I compare these two iconic pop performers in order to assess how the meaning of celebrity and celebrity performance has changed from the emergence of Madonna to the emergence of Gaga. This essay addresses the rhetorical place of visual quotation, specifically the meaning inherent in Madonna's self-reflexive performances during her *Sticky & Sweet Tour* and her music video career, and Gaga's co-opting of the Madonna aesthetic for the Monster's Ball Tour as well as for her own music video releases. The analytic apparatus of performance and gender studies shows that Gaga repeats the performances of others to construct a performance identity that is sexually ambiguous but also ambiguously provocative because the emphasis remains on the artificiality of performance. The juxtaposition of Gaga and Madonna raises provocative questions about how to locate meaning in an iteration divorced from its initial context and how each performer's differing approach to copying and re-appropriation reveals a generational shift in how the meaning of celebrity forms through reuse and repetition. Gaga has described her entire career as a sociological study of fame and this academic approach to her music and performances allows her to emphasize the highly constructed nature of all aspects of life — both public and private. Gaga's use of copying, in particular, shows her perspective on fame and artistry as social constructs by building on cultural symbols and works from the past.

Like Madonna, Lady Gaga has built a career in dance pop while courting controversy through her sexuality and alignment with liberal politics. Also like Madonna, Gaga uses a variety of cultural referents, some not always identifiable to those under twenty-five who constitute the largest section of her fan base, which gives her a sense of originality even when she borrows from the work of others. Both artists "perform" their copying. They model recognizable ideas, events, or people from previous moments in pop culture. As argued by performance studies scholar Joseph Roach, among others, performance enables the notion of repetition. The repeated performances of celebrities such as Gaga and Madonna enable both singers to make their copying an indistinguishable part of their celebrity persona. The framework of performance studies allows us to question the very construction of a performance, what tools are necessary, and how artists assemble the performance tools of others to create new performances by repeating past performance tropes. The interplay between past, present, and future ensures the longevity of a performer's career and work, and in the case of Gaga her use of the past enables her to reach across generations.

A comparison of Gaga and Madonna offers the chance to consider two strategies of celebrity and cultural appropriation and the implications of those differences. Although the connection of Gaga with Madonna is by no means new, the visual aesthetic each performer has recently embraced on stage reveals both their commonalities and fissures. Comparing Gaga to Madonna distinguishes Gaga as unique from her predecessor while uncovering the meaning inherent in Gaga's dizzying bevy of performance and fashion oddities. Whereas Madonna's career has been celebrated as a pioneering brand of feminism with a post-modern appreciation for appropriation of narrative and symbol, Gaga's career emphasizes the constructed nature of identity and blurs the antecedents used. Gaga's strategy troubles copying by making the audience work to separate the strands of the pop cultural past she has combined. The distinction between Madonna's and Gaga's type of copying shows the shift in the place and consumption of popular culture as a result of changing social and entertainment technologies, placing Gaga at the helm of the Digital Age.

Madonna copied and combined styles or visual tropes from others and re-contextualized what she quoted to make it her own; Gaga copies Madonna's copying without overt reinterpretation. Madonna created an image based on appropriation and reinterpretation of images from the past that demonstrated a depth of cultural references, many of which she used to stir media controversy and raise what she often referred to as "provocative" questions about a number of social issues surrounding gender, power, and sexuality. By contrast, Gaga copies Madonna and her host of referents but, despite Gaga's explanation to her fans and the media that her *œuvre* addresses similar social issues, she ultimately comments more on the process of performance and place of fame in identity construction. Gaga exposes the limits of representation and meaning-making, a pop culture post-modern crisis, without delivering a coherent narrative on her pet social issues in her songs or performances. Gaga's copying of Madonna and others contributes to her image as a popular figure who is heavy on metatheatricality without the same expanse of social contextualization that Madonna consciously builds.

Media coverage of Lady Gaga often acknowledges her debt to Madonna. Lady Gaga and Madonna have even participated in the media's comparisons of the two pop superstars. They appeared together on Saturday Night Live and parodied their media-perpetrated rivalry by dancing side by side, with Madonna, cast as the older generation, interjecting at one point "what the hell is a disco-stick" making reference to Gaga's chart hit "LoveGame," but also her inability to understand the younger performer. Other times the media emphasizes a sense of a pop singer family tree and represents Lady Gaga as Madonna's true heir apparent, after a long stretch of pop hopefuls, most notably Britney Spears, who are now better known for their tabloid controversies. For example, Spears' fall from her place as Madonna's apprentice, as evidenced by their performance of the "Like A Virgin/Hollywood" medley on *MTV* which included "that kiss," to her current status as subject of speculation about her mental health with a very public discussion of her father having conservator rights over her estate. Gaga, on the other hand, appears to have a ringing endorsement from Madonna herself who says that she sees herself in the younger pop star, which, in classic Madonna fashion, pays compliment to Gaga while predominantly elevating Madonna to the place of originator and mentor. Yet, what remains unspoken in media coverage of Lady Gaga in relation to Madonna is how both performers use past references from popular culture and formulate them into something different and new that then becomes inextricable from each woman's performance identity. Madonna's identity as a performer has been constructed on copying images of past pop culture phenomena, particularly Marilyn Monroe and Marlene Dietrich. As a result, Madonna's success has inspired later celebrities to do the same, most recently Lady Gaga.

Postmodernists and scholars of popular culture have long studied Madonna's output. Performance theory scholarship on Madonna provides a productive critical approach for assessing Lady Gaga. Lady Gaga emerges as a litmus test for Madonna's use of copying because for all the similarities cited between the two performers (ranging from a shared Italian-American identity, making dance and pop music, and having significant followings in both the gay, lesbian, and trans-sexual communities), Lady Gaga's career is still unique because of her different approach to questions of performance and cultural copying. Gaga's difference enables one to better understand Madonna's approach to copying. Madonna's assertion that she sees herself in Gaga chronologically positions the two women. Madonna, despite a successful career to this day, came from an American pop music scene that was devoid of social networks or reality programs where "average" people enter televised talent contests and emerge with record contracts and a number one hit single. Lady Gaga's discussion of fame in her lyrics and her performances speaks to an awareness of how socially constructed the world is for people of her generation as more people enter online social networks and develop different personae on the screen. Fame, as presented by Gaga, represents a type of fantasy life, but one she asserts to be real, just as social networks and online exchanges have the paradoxical status of being simultaneously imaginative and non-tangible, but also construct an important part of people's day-to-day experiences.

Before analyzing the intricacies of copying and performance, we must first consider the appeal each singer generates as a prominent celebrity. Performance theory scholar Joseph Roach has most recently defined successful, iconic celebrities as possessing "It," an unspeakable sense of that *je ne sais quoi* that attracts both men and women to a single star. Building on the writings of classic Hollywood figure Elinor Glyn and the discussion of the original "It" girl, silent film star Clara Bow, Roach defines and analyzes the characteristics of "It." For Roach, "It" includes a sense of physical attraction that may not depend on beauty but also includes a host of effortless, yet contradictory qualities that tantalize and mesmerize watchers, such as "strength and vulnerability, innocence and experience, and singularity and typicality" (Roach 8). However, more important to a consideration of Madonna and Lady Gaga and their relationship to performance copying is the concept that exceptional celebrities (ones in possession of Roach's "It") manifest "public intimacy (the illusion of availability), synthetic experience (vicariousness), and the It-Effect (personality-driven mass attraction)" (Roach 3). Madonna and Lady Gaga both rely on sexual images that provide a false sense of availability, invite fans vicariously to experience their lives (most notably through endorsed product lines), and attract legions of wannabes and "Little Monsters" wherever they go. Copying as a key element in constructing a performance persona thus would seem to contradict some of the innate qualities of "It," as "It" would seem to embody originality. But therein lies the complexity of celebrity appeal, the combination of the fabulous or glamorous with the mundane. In fact, the contradictions *per se*, the give and take between relatable experience and performative possibilities that generate "It," and the media fascination with both Lady Gaga and Madonna explain their celebrity appeal.

Sexuality informs these performers' stage identity and cements their place as figures of controversy as described by the "It-Effect." Feminist cultural-critic Camille Paglia has recently argued that despite using sexual imagery, Lady Gaga is not sexy and can even be seen as the symbol for the death of sex, the poster child for what Paglia has dubbed "Generation Gaga," or those who entered adolescence in the Digital Age. Paglia argues that for all her exhibitionism, Lady Gaga does not convey a meaningful sexual identity despite her scantily clad appearances, noting in particular a lack of emotional register on her face in many of her photographs and videos — a numb and even distant approach to sex. Madonna, on the other hand, has been championed by Paglia as a feminist who enjoys sex, a female performer who saw the power in using her sexual identity to make a statement about women's rights, which in turn has brought her a host of controversy as well as success. The sexual identity of these performers links to how each woman represents her own brand of "public intimacy." Madonna has mimed all manner of sexual activities on the stage over the years, even including her infamous masturbation scene in her performance of "Like A Virgin" during the Blonde Ambition tour. Gaga likewise has mimicked sexual acts in her videos and on the stage, yet as Paglia points out her often placid, expression-less face, so like the masks she often wears, renders her asexual. Within the context of performance copying, the lack of genuine sexual expression in Gaga's work draws attention to the work's status as a copy, which, I argue, elevates it to the position of aesthetic production. Gaga's work thus copies a sexual aesthetic, not a sexual expression.

In the context of the post-modern conundrum of where one locates meaning when everything has already been said, the realm of the aesthetic becomes a logical extension. Madonna crafted a stage presence that relied on an interplay of sexual boundary-pushing, which brought with it an additional wink and nod to the Catholic symbolism of her first name. Placing sexually charged women at the forefront of society, not because she is placed there through male objectification, has been Madonna's main claim to feminist fame. Gaga has crafted a stage and performance identity that uses the language of sexuality not to convey ideas of sexual boundary-pushing but rather to comment on the process of artistic production. Indeed, Gaga presents herself first and foremost as an artist. In this sense, the "Bad Romance" video becomes a prime example of the Gaga sexual aesthetic. Gaga's sexually inflected scenes narrate the horrors of human trafficking, but can ultimately be read as a self-reflexive exercise in meta-commentary: the nature of music marketing as the selling of an empty sexual expression. Instead of working against Gaga's ability to construct meaning, as Paglia argues, her vapid approach to sexual expression draws attention to the result of an overly saturated sexual market. Gaga thus makes an artistic statement rather than a political one. Madonna shocked audiences because the entertainment world did not expect the level of explicit sexual performance in popular culture that she provided. In the wake of countless starlets with widely circulated sex-tapes and more than two decades worth of scantily clad women in music videos, there is little shock value in revisiting moments from Madonna's early career. This is why Gaga's copying of Madonna's sexual button-pushing becomes a post-modern exercise in finding new meaning in such exposure when as a culture we encounter exposed and grinding bodies daily on the internet, on television, and on film.

It is this cultural environment that separates and distinguishes the kind of performance copying between Madonna and Gaga. The online community fosters video and media sharing. These enable users access to multiple genres to express their identity — thus, Lady Gaga, whose name embodies performance theory and reference to a song by the British band Queen, incorporates different cultural borrowings that still make her appear to be unique because she blurs the antecedents in her combination of them. Madonna, by contrast, used her borrowings consciously — she needed her audience and the media to see precisely what she was borrowing for the full meaning to be conveyed. The video for "Material Girl" was an obvious homage to Marilyn Monroe's performance of "Diamonds Are A Girl's Best Friend" from the film *Gentlemen Prefer Blondes* (1953) and succeeded predominantly because the borrowing from Monroe was part of Madonna's message: she was the new Marilyn. Madonna understood both what Marilyn Monroe symbolized (the original blonde ambition, sex, and stardom) and how she placed herself in relation to that past narrative. In contrast, Lady Gaga's borrowings often function to blur their antecedents, not in the deceptive sense of plagiarism, but in the sense of community identities, they allow her to appear "original" despite her reliance on the pop cultural past.

Madonna has maintained her presence in popular culture and media through her penchant for "re-invention." Madonna has made a career of appropriating images and concepts from past entertainment and art movements or figures and reassembling them to reflect a specific context that usually changes with each new studio album. For Madonna, using past images is her language for cultural commentary and perhaps paradoxically this use generates a new and unique part of popular entertainment culture. The unique meaning attached to Madonna's quotation of past cultural images is best illustrated in how she is able to even quote herself and separate her interpretation from its initial source. As a result, Madonna equates her performance creations with the classics of pop culture she draws from, reifying an important aspect of the Madonna formula: control. In her 2008 *Sticky & Sweet Tour*, Madonna performed the song "She's Not Me" from her last studio album while battling a number of dancers dressed as her most famous past alter egos. This performance demonstrated Madonna's assemblage of visual tropes and symbols from others to create something new and quintessentially "Madonna." She mock-fought four of her most recognizable phases from the earlier part of her career: Material Girl, Like a Virgin, Open Your Heart, and Blonde Ambition.

Madonna's battle with her Material Girl *doppelgänger* within this performance context was not misinterpreted as her source material from Marilyn Monroe, which showed how her copy has diverged from its point of origin and has come into its own as an important event in popular music culture. The segment works within the lyrical context of the song "She's Not Me," best summarized as the failed attempts of a woman to copy Madonna's clothing, hair choices, and intellectual interests; Madonna differentiates the copying of the character in her song by stipulating "she doesn't have my name she'll never have what I have" ("She's Not Me"). The song thus criticizes the copier and those who fall for the imitation — a meaning reinforced by Madonna removing the four dancers dressed like her. This performance clearly critiques those who copy, reminiscent of the flock of "wannabes" that constituted her main fan base in the mid-1980s to the wave of other celebrities copying her including Kylie Minogue and Britney Spears, and, now, Lady Gaga. Indeed, the criticism of this brand of copying is reinforced by how Madonna attacks her look-a-likes. She systematically strips them of the accessories that define that style: gloves, heels, bridal veil, and bra and attacks the copier with the iconographic pieces, or performance props, that create the copy. Included in her attack is a taunting of the copied poses. The copied pose precipitates Madonna's stripping the wannabe of the defining article of clothing; her action symbolizes the ensemble's "Madonna-ness" — as she does so she shouts "Wannabes!" establishing herself as the original.

Madonna retains relevance and longevity in the fleeting world of pop music by changing images — she thus is always in search of new cultural and artistic contexts to reinterpret and bring into the Madonna brand. The different phases of Madonna can be replicated simultaneously on stage and in print. They suggest the multiplicity of performance personae she has crafted: they can all be identified as "Madonna," but yet she maintains a unique identity reflective of the era in which they were created. Madonna has thus recently interrogated the nature of copying providing a post-modern, meta-critical layer to a career that feminists and performance critics within academia have already analyzed. Instead of providing academics with more fodder to deconstruct her career, Madonna's recent foray into self-reflection provides a way for scholars to analyze the aging pop icon in relation to the younger generation of performers. Madonna's meta-commentary on her relationship to copying allows one to see more clearly how her copying differs from that of Lady Gaga, who is the current focal point of pop music culture. What emerges, in particular, is how Gaga's copying of Madonna separates the women from different generations. Madonna's positioning of herself as the object of copying may seem to be just another narcissistic moment from a less-than-shy star, but more importantly demonstrates how Madonna "owns" her pop cultural copying, paying homage to its status as appropriation, but one with a subsequent unique attachment to Madonna.

Madonna constructed a performance persona by drawing on various strands of popular and artistic culture, re-packaging them to pose what she has referred to as "provocative questions" about social conundrums and prejudices. In doing so, she has often presented her different incarnations, or "re-inventions," as authentic parts of her core identity; for example, her foray into Kabalah and mystical studies manifested itself in the introspection of Ray of Light. However, despite Madonna's avowal of the authenticity of her re-inventions, she remains the queen of ambiguity. The controversial music video for "American Life" clearly expressed Madonna's anti-war sentiments but left her representations of President George W. Bush more ambiguous and open to interpretation. Leaving key aspects of her material vague leads to unanswered questions, which then lead Madonna to emphasize the symbolism in her choices of cultural copying and her desire to forge a career that will be viewed as artistic, but also one with social relevance. Madonna has stated that the role of the artist is to make statements for people to question and reflect on as opposed to give them a direct answer or stance on a particular issue. In this formulation Madonna assumes the role of auteur.

In comparison, Lady Gaga has constructed her performance identity by building on the work of the popular culture past in a way that deliberately obscures her core personal identity. Her *avant-garde* fashions, for example, render her every public entry a publicity event. Gaga even incorporates tabloid speculation about her personal life into the overt artistic performances of her videos. For example, the speculation about her being intersex is openly discussed in the jail scenes of the "Telephone" video, which reduces personal speculation about the performer to part of the performance to be consumed. Gaga, unlike Madonna, has become increasingly vocal about her stand on hot button issues surrounding the LGBT community, including "Don't ask, don't tell," helping homeless LGBT teens, and campaigning for gay rights on stage. As a result, Gaga's art would appear to be less malleable and open to interpretation. She endorses a particularized reading to her artistic output, such as her admission that the "Alejandro" music video symbolically represents the "Don't ask, don't tell" situation and her anger about it. Yet, like the meat dress, when one tries to connect metaphor to message, the ability to reconstruct Gaga's meaning is fraught with contradictions.

In spite of Gaga's very pointed claims of the meaning behind her art, she never provides for the audience an explanation of how her metaphors work — she provides the guise of specificity of claim without explaining her choices in lyric, image, or performance to construct that claim. Gaga's artistic claims have provided two kinds of reaction; the naysayers who see Lady Gaga as lacking substance, since oftentimes the process of connecting image to metaphor is less clear, or those who say that like Madonna, Gaga is an auteur of a different sort, one who provides a red herring of explicit interpretation only to show the audience the ambiguity, and often contradiction, of meaning within her work. For example, the phrase "Little Monsters" that Gaga uses as an affectionate term for her fans is, in one sense, a diminutive version of how she sees herself that she then applies to her listeners. As she explains, the term embodies her sense that she is an outsider who appeals to other outsiders, those who feel that they are not embraced by mainstream society. If Gaga is the big monster, then all of her fans become Little Monsters which also implies a sense of copying or following and hierarchy. Despite Gaga's insistence that she is an outsider, the fact that there are legions of "Little Monsters" weakens the notion of an outsider culture since the "counter-culture" appears to have gone mainstream. Conversely, Gaga's notable speculation on the experience of fame in songs such as "Paparazzi" makes it more difficult to fully commit to Gaga's explanation of her phrase "Little Monsters"—the sense of stalking and media oppression emerge all too clearly in the term, especially when compared to the giant puppet Gaga referred to as the "Fame Monster" that chases her across the stage during a segment of *The Monster Ball Tour*. Indeed, it would seem that being a "monster" is not always about celebrating individuality, but also about how the individual feels pursued by others.

Likewise, Gaga's inclusivity of her fans with her success leads to double meanings as well. Gaga has made a habit of accepting awards or addressing fans during her shows from an inclusive perspective that acknowledges their participation and enabling of her success. Yet, unlike the scores of performers who have come before her who have also often thanked their fans for support or acknowledged that their fan support enabled them to reach career milestones, Gaga takes this formula in a new direction. She exclaimed "We did it Little Monsters!" when accepting her Moonman awards at the 2010 MTV Video Music Awards. She also frequently tells her audience that she exists for them and that together they create her concert performance because without them she would not be able to perform. This distinction is ultimately what characterizes her use of cultural copying within her work; copying becomes a collaborative process that occurs under the moniker "Lady Gaga."

Gaga's androgynous performance identity is inherent in her stage name, and the idea of androgyny itself embodies contradictions: it yokes together opposing qualities within one entity. Although Madonna's given name has enabled her to stir up controversy, the fact that it is her birth name makes her performance persona a combination of fortuitous circumstances combined with carefully chosen material. By comparison, "Lady Gaga" is the stage name for the performer born as Stefani Joanne Angelina Germanotta, which makes the relationship of the artist's marketed name to her material very different. The official narrative of the performer's name is that "Gaga" comes from the Queen song "Radio Gaga," and "Lady" the result of a serendipitous auto-correcting program on her text messaging system. The Gaga myth unites the pop culture past with 21st century technology. Yet, "Lady" seems to be a more likely antecedent from her theatrical friend "Lady Starlight" known in the nightclub circuits, and as part of the larger context of gender performance theory that undergirds much of Gaga's presentation of androgyny ("Who's That Lady?"). Gaga embraces androgyny — costume and performance create gender. As shown in the "Telephone" video, gender is a social construction, which makes Gaga's essentialist rallying cry "born this way" to describe the orientation of the LGBT community a rather limiting perspective that excludes some members of that community and contradicts her focus on life as performance. Yet the very contradiction between essentialist and performative ideologies is consistent with other tensions between Gaga's specific claims and the nature of her performance actions.

Comparisons between Madonna and Gaga reached a new level of scrutiny upon the release of Gaga's video for her single "Alejandro." The song on its own had already been garnering attention from online communities that it sounded like Madonna's single "La Isla Bonita"; however, the video saw a cornucopia of Madonna references that previously had just bubbled under the surface in the Gaga canon. The "Alejandro" video may have a notable aesthetic debt to Madonna's earlier video "Like A Prayer," but the two short films could not be more different in how they address the controversies that they embody. In "Like A Prayer," Madonna emphasized the performativity of social identities, and as a result implied that most prejudices are the result of social constructions as opposed to essentialized differences among groups — the burning crosses and racial tensions the video portrays are later revealed to be part of a stage play, creating a twice removed filtering mechanism for the viewer. Viewers of "Like A Prayer" watch a performance of a performance that raises questions about the performer's perception of the social issues that she includes. The very ambiguity within Madonna's controversial material is what fuels an array of public responses to her ranging from those who praise her artistic and marketing genius to those who denigrate her as crass and exploitative of minority groups. By contrast, the "Alejandro" video's meta-theatricality recalls the religious imagery of "Like a Prayer" and alludes to the voyeurism of Marc Caro and Jean-Pierre Jeunet's art-house film *City of Lost Children* (1995), but instead of drawing attention to questions of artistic form, Gaga claims to use the familiar imagery to make a clear statement about gay rights that reflects her construction of her own performance identity as a crusader for equality.

The "Alejandro" video was a collaboration with photographer Steven Klein, previously known for his provocative and dark photo-shoots with Madonna for *W* magazine and her tour programs, and the video bears this aesthetic — dark and atmospheric, utilizing props common to the Madonna shoots such as metal-work bed frames. The song itself does not match the visuals that the video imparts. The same could be said of other videos released from her *The Fame Monster* album. The music video for "Bad Romance," which addressed the serious issue of human trafficking, had, in fact, a tenable connection to the lyrics of the song. "Alejandro" hardly seemed the obvious material for the military and religious symbolism employed in the video. Yet the video shows a variety of military, religious, and sexual symbols and scenes, which fit rather disjointedly together. However, the most consistent aspect of the video is how it reminds the viewer of key imagery from Madonna performances — it is as if the video were Gaga's official announcement of being the next Madonna in the same way that a debutante's ball debut announces her entrance into society. Gaga's use of religious imagery in particular echoes Madonna's "Like a Prayer" video and her concert performance of "Oh Father" from Blonde Ambition, while the men dance marching in the video recalls the "workers" of Madonna's reinterpretation of Metropolis for her "Express Yourself" video.

Director Klein has stated that the "Alejandro" video represents the struggle between good and evil, which is why the religious imagery is key: Gaga becomes a nun at the end and retreats into a world of isolated contemplation; hence the film burns out her eyes and mouth first to represent the end of her communication with the outside world ("Lady Gaga's 'Alejandro': Video's Religious Imagery Gets Mixed Reactions From Fans"). Critical responses to the video do not find Klein's narrative description quite as obvious upon viewing. Indeed, if Gaga becomes a nun by the video's end, she is certainly a nun with a more-than-colorful past. Yet to return to the question of cultural copying, or what one could also refer to as cultural quotation, the video recalls a number of historical as well as cultural contexts — it presents many possibilities without committing itself to a direct and coherent narrative, despite Klein's description and Gaga's explanation that it represents her anger over "Don't ask, don't tell." The very fact that the video is a composite of prior visual references shows how Gaga relies on cultural copying to construct her visual presence. The video at once recalls images of *City of Lost Children* as Gaga wears an elaborate facial contraption that allows her to be a voyeur, in addition to Madonna imagery. The swallowing of the rosary is a new take on Madonna's "sins of the flesh" in the "Like a Prayer" video, and the men carrying the latex-habited Gaga provides a visual counterpart to Madonna's fall into the church of "Like a Prayer" — both videos show the singers' bodies suspended in midair and rely on religious imagery to convey the conflicted relationship between sacred and secular.

Gaga's assemblage of images in the video reflects a fragmented narrative experience that complicates the ability to locate meaning. However, whereas Madonna's video, like many of her videos, held the status of a mini-movie with a complete narrative about inter-racial romance and the added twist that it is all a stage play performed by Madonna, the actress, and the rest of the cast, Gaga's video does not offer that same sense of continuous narrative. Even in her videos for "Paparazzi" and "Telephone," which contain a linked narrative, the action is never direct as in the early Madonna videos — the use of frequent cuts between shots, which help to mimic the upbeat tempo of the dance music especially in "Telephone," mean that we receive a fragmented visual experience, and it is this very fragmented, hyper-action that best showcases Gaga's visual quotation of Madonna. Gaga's latex nun costume with a strategically placed cross over her crotch copies Madonna in the sense that the relationship between sexual expression and Catholicism closely associated with her is immediately evoked, even though Madonna has never worn a latex habit in her performance career.

The scenes of Gaga riding over a man in the metal framed bed also recall Madonna's photo shoots with Klein. The earlier photos focused on Madonna and her yoga-trained body in a multitude of seemingly impossible poses, many of which appear sexual. The attention was on Madonna's body and conveyed a sense of auto-eroticism further underscored by the dark lighting that created a sense of loneliness. Gaga's video also has that same atmospheric dark loneliness but because she is not alone in the bed, the emphasis shifts from the lone performer to how Gaga interacts with the actor. Gaga certainly takes center stage in these segments in the sense that she controls the movement, but like with the previous quotations the meaning behind her riding the man in the larger narrative of the video becomes less clear — if we follow Klein, is this representative of the dark or evil she has to fight within herself (the inability to overcome sexual temptation), or does Gaga domineer over a man who represents the evil Klein speaks of, or is it something else? The metaphor as usual is unclear, but the viewer does see its visual antecedent in the earlier Madonna/Klein collaboration. And despite the eight-minute length of the music video, a singular narrative still does not emerge; instead, the video exhaustively catalogs past visual referents.

The ultimate moment of Madonna copying in "Alejandro," however, comes towards the end of the video where Gaga appears wearing a machine gun bra — an obvious correlative to Madonna's conical bra designed by Jean Paul Gaultier. Whereas the Gaultier bra was inspired by women's lingerie from the 1950s that forced the breasts to assume a pointy shape, Gaultier's bra exaggerated the visual aesthetic of the 1950s and added the context of the breasts as a weapon. The sharp angularity of Madonna's conical bra made her breasts not the objects of sexual pleasure or display, but her breasts as dangerous, sharp, cutting, and intrusive objects. Gaga's machine gun bra takes the metaphor behind Madonna's costume a step further, literalizing the metaphor of breasts as weapons. The larger meaning in Gaga's reformulation of this visual moment is less clear — does it refer to a new sense of feminism, or a sexual assertiveness? The good versus evil narrative the video's creators espouse does not have a clear relationship to these visual symbols.

Gaga's use of Madonna is a new model for creating celebrity identity that suggests a shift in the place of pop culture celebrities in the age of online gossip blogs and daily-posted candid photos of stars doing mundane tasks. For all of the criticism that Madonna has faced — that she is an egocentric performer and that she creates controversy to call attention to herself rather than to the issues that she claims to be discussing — her model of mimesis and then subsequent re-contextualization indicates an increasingly obsolete model of celebrity performance identity. Gaga's copying of Madonna enables her to reinforce ideas about herself that in turn reinforce the media's coverage of her.

Gaga constructs a performance identity by relying on extreme opposites: covered body versus exposed body, good versus bad, famous versus unknown. Her videos consistently emphasize celebrity culture and scenes of consumerism: photographers follow her in "Paparazzi." Thus, Gaga's songs and videos explicitly address her conflicted identity as creator and consumer. The parade of commercial products in the "Telephone" video ranging from Miracle Whip to Diet Coke could be seen as the danger of consumerism since it leads to a literal poisoning that ultimately jeopardizes Gaga's and Honey B's (Beyoncé's video alter ego) ability to avoid altercation with the law. Regardless, Gaga emerges as the ultimate consumer in all facets of her stage and cultural presence, a celebrity who has built her presence by consuming and then performing the pop cultural past. Since she has constructed a performance identity that relies on the above mentioned binaries, it results in an ambivalent employment of the popular images and figures she copies — binaries can only be sustained if Gaga does not account for the full range of context and meaning of their original uses. Thus, Gaga copies the visual iconography of Madonna. She does so in order to comment on herself and her place as a recording artist and not on specific hot button issues that we have come to expect from Madonna despite Gaga's cries of social activism. The emphasis on the individual performer and her status as a celebrity is a post-postmodern variation of Madonna's performances and cultural copying. Madonna borrowed from past pop cultural tradition to forward the idea that although she merely reused the established tools, she could still create meaning from them. With her excessive inclusion and awareness of audience, Gaga draws attention to the art of performance or the performer as artist, as well as to the performer's status as a performer.

New social technologies have increased the place of audience in the lives of celebrities, and Gaga takes full advantage of the performance power of Twitter — frequently tweeting updates about her life and career to her little monster followers. On December 31, 2010, she tweeted, "YOU'VE CREATED THIS MOMENT. YOU IMAGINED ME." This tweet echoed earlier Gaga "double-talk" about the audience's role in establishing her career. It is this relationship to the audience and Gaga's hyperawareness constant performance that creates the Gaga-paradox. She asserts her authenticity in the most contrived and performative moments, yet because she markets herself as a collaborator between herself and her Little Monsters, it is no surprise that she sees the use of cultural copying an authentic and original process.

Lady Gaga's reliance on the Madonna aesthetic will likely continue to foster discussion in the future. The importance of copying in the artistic output of pop stars such as Lady Gaga gains a renewed sense of purpose when one considers how fans seek to imitate or copy facets of these stars in their own lives. According to pop culture legend, the term "Wannabe" originally described the throngs of teenage girls in the mid–1980s who wanted to be Madonna — copying her signature fashion sense as well as her devil-may-care attitude reflected in her film appearances such as *Desperately Seeking Susan* (1985). Lady Gaga has also been the subject of young fan adulation and imitation, due in part to her extreme hair, makeup, and clothes (aspects that fans isolate as unique to Gaga become the features that through copying bring fans closer to the performer), but due to online opportunities provided by sites such as YouTube, fans can post videos of themselves performing Lady Gaga's songs or recreating her videos in tribute. If imitation is truly the highest form of flattery, then once day fans and critics may also speak of a historic Lady Gaga aesthetic.

Performing Pop

Lady Gaga, "Weird Al" Yankovic and Parodied Performance

MATTHEW R. TURNER

Shortly after Lady Gaga, the new "Princess of Pop," burst onto the musical scene, her work became nearly ubiquitous. That kind of popularity breeds imitation and at the same time becomes fodder for criticism, critique, and parody. The most obvious parody of her work was created by the "King of Pop Parody," "Weird Al" Yankovic. "Perform This Way," from "Weird Al" Yankovic's 2011 album entitled *Alpocalypse*, is a comical critique of Lady Gaga's "Born This Way" and a parody of not only the song, but of Lady Gaga as a cultural phenomenon. As "Perform this Way" exemplifies, parody itself is often fraught with internal contradiction. On one level, there is critique and deconstruction of the original artwork. On another level, however, the parody becomes a kind of homage succeeding largely because of the strengths and popularity of the original. This paradox complicates and expands the concept of parody. In fact, more careful critical examination reveals that "Weird Al" is not the only one creating this parody and Lady Gaga is not the only target. Lady Gaga *also* participates in parody as she looks at the pop stars of earlier eras and mines and comments on their work. Though some critics suggest that Lady Gaga's success is due in large part to her imitation of other artists, her work goes beyond mere imitation and moves into the realm of parody. It is this self-conscious employment and performance of parody that is at least partially responsible for her incredible success. As a self-professed performance artist, Lady Gaga becomes a nexus of parodied performance, revealing and expanding the limits and the understanding of both parody and performance.

One of the defining modes of the current era is comic or parodic. Much of popular culture is self-conscious and self-referential. References to exterior

188

pop culture and events enrich texts while at the same time fraying their originality and internal coherence. We can define parody as a comical imitation. Parody is often lighthearted in nature, unlike more purposively critical forms such as satire. The origin of the Greek word for parody, *parodia,* originally meant, "counter song." Linda Hutcheon suggests that although traditionally this has led to a fairly narrow definition of parody, a broader interpretation is necessary. "The prefix *para* has two meanings, only one of which is usually mentioned — that of 'counter' or 'against.' Thus parody becomes an opposition or contrast between texts ... one text is set against another with the intent of mocking it or making it ludicrous" (32). She furthers her idea by expanding the definition beyond its traditional boundaries: "However *para* in Greek can also mean 'beside,' and therefore there is a suggestion of an accord or intimacy instead of a contrast. It is this second, neglected meaning of the prefix that broadens the pragmatic scope of parody in a way most helpful to discussions of modern art forms" (32). Indeed, it is this expanded definition of parody that provides the foundation of our exploration of the function of parody in the works of both "Weird Al" and Lady Gaga.

In order to understand how Lady Gaga is both an object and performer of parody, it is important to regard her as an icon of pop culture. Her image is based on her perception in mass culture but also by her own professed self-definition. Born Stefani Germanotta, she has created an image of herself as Lady Gaga. She takes great pains to control this carefully crafted image and her goal is to have the world believe that she has, in fact, become this image. Nothing is as disappointing in an idol as prosaic reality, so Gaga has endeavored to remove such elements from her personal history. Maureen Callahan stated that "her high school and college friends attest that she was a normal, well-adjusted teenager with mainstream interests" (84). Lady Gaga posited herself "as none of her peers have: a blank slate, a creature of self-invention, an object of emotional projection and wish-fulfillment" (Callahan 17). Her ability to have a relatively anonymous past is a direct result of her incredibly rapid rise to fame. This lack of surveillance allowed her an unprecedented opportunity to control her own image. During her transformation, she made sure to remove her normal pictures from Facebook, helping keep that part of her old life out of the public realm. She was very aware of her potential to rise to fame and how important controlling her image would be in that journey.

One of the central elements of her image is the idea of the artist as genius. Lady Gaga has told interviewers that she learned to play the piano by ear at age four, much like the renowned musical genius Mozart. Lady Gaga's story, however, is a fabrication, part of her constructed image. To a certain extent, the truth of the statement is irrelevant because for Lady Gaga, the image becomes reality. Douglas Wolk has argued that, "What Gaga is selling is a perfectly mannered façade" (58). Another important aspect of her image is the idea that she has *become* her image, which also helps to erase her past by making it irrelevant. Gaga has said that "the largest misconception is that Lady Gaga is a persona or a character. I'm not — even my mother calls me Gaga. I am 150,000 percent Lady Gaga every day" (qtd. in Scaggs 34). The idea that the person is indistinguishable from the image is not new, as Callahan described: "From Marilyn Manson and Alice Cooper, Gaga stole the scary makeup, the androgyny, and the construct that she is Lady Gaga 24/7, that this alter ego long ago subsumed her former identity, that she is never off-duty" (87). While there is no novelty in this pop culture construction, she is remarkably committed to it.

Her commitment to her character and careful control of her image are all part of her pursuit of fame. When speaking to an interviewer from *Rolling Stone*, Gaga said the following with regard to the material that the former was planning to use: "Use the stuff that's going to make me a legend. I want to be a legend. Is that wrong?" (qtd. in Strauss 74). This focus on fame and apparent lack of depth have invited critique as a counterpoint to the hordes of adoring fans that she has amassed. Stephen Marche has stated that "Lady Gaga's greatest achievement as a celebrity and an artist is her self-consciousness about the ephemerality of fame, so why hasn't she already vanished?" (80). The answer to this question is provocative, and while it is unclear how long she can maintain this level of popularity, some qualities no doubt have helped her to obtain and maintain her fame. She is clearly talented as a musi-cian and singer, with a compelling stage presence and a broad streak of nar-cissism. Gaga is also unafraid to exploit her sexuality to further her career goals and craft her image. Lianne George argues that an "overt, fluid sexuality is part of her shtick, but her aim is never to look conventionally attractive" (47). These qualities, of course, are shared by many other aspiring artists. However, one trait that sets Gaga apart from many of her peers which is largely responsible for her early and continuing success is her incredibly strong work ethic.

Elizabeth Barfoot Christian has suggested that Lady Gaga personifies "Baudrillard's theory of simulacra and simulation, where the image has replaced the original" (209). This assertion requires scrutiny not only because it speaks to the modern idiom of the image-obsessed world, but also informs the idea of parody relating to Lady Gaga. Jean Baudrillard describes simulation in these terms: "It is the generation by models of a real without origin or reality: a hyperreal" (169). This hyperreality is what Lady Gaga has become. She is a model of a thing that never existed and has no origin. In her own words, she wants "to fight so hard for it every day that the lie becomes the truth" (qtd. in Callahan 52). When the lie of Lady Gaga becomes the truth, then it also becomes the perfect mass-market commodity. It is easy to package and distribute and in the digital era that means bits and bytes in the electronic ether with neither form nor substance. Much like her music files offered for download on iTunes, Lady Gaga is a digital product. As Baudrillard explained: "The real is produced from miniaturized units ... and with these it can be reproduced an indefinite number of times. It no longer has to be rational, since it is no longer measured against some ideal or negative instance" (170). Having no reference point, Lady Gaga, as an image, is free from mundane considerations such as reality. Indeed, in the digital era, she never has to age, but can endlessly recycle her image (and as we will discuss, others' images as well) in an infinitely recursive loop of artistic production and reproduction.

Lady Gaga is "on a mission: to prove that Lady Gaga is art and that her art is not a mask. It is her life" (Strauss 66). The danger inherent in the merging of artistic life with real life is the existential conundrum that produces when the art is deconstructed or unmasked. This is where Lady Gaga becomes subject to parody: "Now that we've reached the phase of desperate reproduction, and where the stakes are nil, the simulacrum is maximal — exacerbated and parodied simulation at one and the same time — as interminable as psychoanalysis and for the same reasons" (Baudrillard 187). The simulacrum is no longer a distorted image of reality, but according to Baudrillard's theory, becomes real in itself. Parody pulls Lady Gaga's free-floating image back to earth as it points out the image's construction and internal incongruity. No matter how hard Lady Gaga has tried to wipe clean the previous script of her life, like a palimpsest, some faint lines of the previous script are still visible, both in her life and her recycling of performance art and pop culture.

On one level, the danger of parody's knife is very tangible. Lady Gaga's image initially hides the real person that is/was Stefani Germanotta. Lianne George argues that "for Lady Gaga, outward trappings are the whole point. Her MO is pop star as illusionist. To see beyond the image is to kill the effect" (49). If the real is revealed, then the illusion disappears and she suddenly becomes human and mortal and fallible reality loses the intrigue that has brought Lady Gaga's fans to her. The other peril of parody is perhaps ultimately even more dangerous. In speaking of the Iconoclasts who tried to destroy the images of God, Baudrillard argues that "their metaphysical despair came from the idea that the images concealed nothing at all, and that in fact they were not images, such as the original model would have made them, but actually perfect simulacra forever radiant with their own fascination" (172). Just as the Iconoclasts feared about the use of the image of God, perhaps the mask that is Lady Gaga actually contains nothing at all. It is its own image and when that is removed there is nothing left for Lady Gaga or for her legion of fans. This is the danger of becoming one's own artistic expression.

Perhaps, though, we can better understand Lady Gaga as a poser, someone who wants the trappings of art without all the hard work of intentional artistic expression. Seth Walls argues that Lady Gaga shows no appetite "to bear the risk of intending to mean something.... Instead, she is content to give us thesis and antithesis, because the contrast sparks commentary (and, yes, her fame)" (57) and that she ultimately "offers no synthesis" (57). There is a sharp divide among critics over Lady Gaga's art, whether it is unimaginative and derivative. Her music is catchy, but unoriginal at its best and banal at its worst. The music, however, is only a small part of Lady Gaga, and there is a disconnect between the narrative content of the music and the narrative of spectacle and performance that her music videos and live performances become. Ultimately, though, these issues of the quality and artistic integrity of Lady Gaga's work are not central to the concept of parody. For parodies of Lady Gaga's work to exist, it is sufficient that they be popular. The kind of parody, of course, may depend on these issues of the quality of artistic expression, but not the inevitability of the parody itself.

Successful parody requires a complex understanding of the parodied text, the system in which it is operating, and current trends in popular culture. Since 1983, "Weird Al" Yankovic has worked as a professional recording artist and parodist and is the "most successful comedy recording artist ever" (Bliss 5). As Jo Ann Lloyd states, "Weird Al" has spent many years "making music, making fun of music, making fun of people making music" (13). "Weird Al" is well practiced in the art of parody, he understands the world of fame in which popular artists live, and he has long looked at that world with a critical eye. "Weird Al" understands *how* to parody this world. "Weird Al" represents the artist as genius. His lyrics reveal an exceptionally witty and intelligent man and his biography supports such an assessment. Yankovic received straight As in high school, graduated as valedictorian and then went on to enroll in college when he was only sixteen years old. In 1980, he graduated with a degree in architecture from California Polytechnic State University, San Luis Obispo. Yankovic began to play the accordion when he was just seven years old. Despite his long career in the music industry, "Weird Al" has remained remarkably different from many of his musical peers. In commenting on the 1997 *VH-1* documentary on his life he stated,

> Those documentaries usually chronicle the ups and downs of bands. How they made it big. How they fell off the charts. How they got caught up in drugs and alcohol. And then how they got cleaned up and made a comeback. For my piece, the worst that could be said was, "Well, the last album sold a few hundred thousand less copies" [qtd. in Bliss 5].

"Weird Al" is anomalous in the pop world. He has avoided many of the pitfalls that come with fame and money and thus is simultaneously a part of that world *and* separated from that world.

"Weird Al" and Lady Gaga share some surprising similarities. While Lady Gaga has admittedly been around only a short time, she exhibits some of the same attention to detail and the desire to constantly re-imagine herself and her music that "Weird Al" does. Both are talented musicians, singers, and composers, who can write popular music. Both "Weird Al" and Lady Gaga have forged identities for themselves based on difference. They also have devoted hordes of fans who dress up for concerts and follow them on tour. Both prize their fan bases and use social media to keep in touch with them and maintain their popular images. Finally, they also parody other artists. While there are some interesting similarities between the two artists, there are also clearly defined differences. "Weird Al," for instance, has never attained, nor will ever attain, the level of popularity enjoyed by Lady Gaga. "Weird Al" tends to appeal to an intellectual niche audience. Lady Gaga does appeal to segments of intellectuals; however, she also relies heavily on the masses for her popularity. Furthermore, "Weird Al," does make a clear separation between the character he performs when he is on the stage and who he is in real life. Jeff Bliss described "Weird Al" as follows: "Off stage, the 'King of the Parodies' is low-key and thoughtful, a stark contrast to the 'Weird Al' persona that has earned him near-cult status and record sales in the millions" (3). "Weird Al" also has created a bit of separation between work and home life, for he does not anxiously work to create new material as Lady Gaga has done since 2008. In fact, prior to the release of "Perform This Way," "Weird Al's" last studio album was his *Straight Out of Lynnwood* album in 2006, which was well before Lady Gaga had arrived on the national scene. While Lady Gaga has been described as working frantically on her tours producing new material, "Weird Al" treats tours very differently. "When I'm on the road, my brain is kind of on vacation. I don't find myself scrawling lyrics while I'm on the tour bus. I don't resent the touring. It's a break from working on albums" (qtd. in Bliss 4). This perspective is ultimately important for "Weird Al's" parody to be successful. "Weird Al's" simultaneous participation in the world of popular music and his abstaining from many of its vices makes him uniquely qualified to speak in an authentic voice while maintaining the necessary critical distance to create a successful parody.

Additional characteristics of parody are worth noting. For instance, while parody often attacks an inferior product, such is not always the case. Parody can be distinguished from satire precisely because it does not attempt to moralize or act as a social or artistic corrective. Further, the parodied text is not necessarily inferior to the parodying text. In order for a parody to be successful, it must follow the original text closely enough to be recognized as a parody. However, if the parody is too close to the original, it is seen merely as imitation. Thus, parody must have a certain critical ironic distance in which it recognizes and addresses any risible flaws or elements of the original. By pointing out the construction and weaknesses of the original text, parody opens the door for change and ultimately reinforces the original through the repetition of the structural elements of the original. Parody goes beyond mere reinforcement; it also builds on the original as it layers new meaning into the artistic work. After listening to "Weird Al's" parody, "The Saga Begins," one can never listen to the parodied text of Don McLean's "American Pie" in quite the same way. One can still appreciate the artistry of the original as well as the artful re-imagination of the parody and therefore experience both versions simultaneously when listening to either one. In the case of "The Saga Begins," the parody relies mainly upon the music and rhyme scheme of the original. The story recounts the plot of *Star Wars: The Phantom Menace*, and beyond the incongruity of associating the original music with the Star Wars universe, the parody has relatively little to say about the original text. It is mainly a vehicle for the parody. In the case of "Perform This Way," however, "Weird Al" is not only using the song as a starting point to showcase clever lyrics, but his song actively comments both on Lady Gaga's original "Born This Way" and on the whole phenomenon that is Lady Gaga.

"Weird Al's" parody begins with the title of his song, "Perform This Way." Close enough to "Born This Way," comparison becomes inescapable. "Weird Al" also refers to Lady Gaga's most defining element: her self-definition as performance artist. One of the biggest critiques about Lady Gaga has been that for all her talk of musical and stylistic originality, neither her style nor her music are particularly original. Marche states, "Isn't Lady Gaga just Britney Spears spackled with art-school clichés?" (79). "Perform This Way" speaks to this same issue and suggests that for all of Lady Gaga's eccentricities, she sells nothing more than an empty pop culture version of performance art, which ultimately undermines the original meaning of her song. Lady Gaga is really just a "performance" herself and, therefore, her message to her fans in this song becomes a hollow lie masked by a fantastic image.

After Lady Gaga emerged from a giant plastic egg at the 2011 Grammy Awards to sing "Born This Way," Alison Powell asked in an interview, "So, how is it that no one is laughing, really, at her?" (63). This somewhat untimely question rose just a month after "Weird Al" had released his single, "Perform This Way," which unquestionably parodied Lady Gaga. "Weird Al" has said, "My main goal is just to be funny and to try to get people not to take themselves too seriously. I suppose it could be argued that a few of my songs make a statement of some sort, but primarily I'm just going for laughs" (qtd. in

Lloyd 14). "Weird Al" works to deflate some of the pretention in Lady Gaga's songs and performances laughing at her expense. In discussing Lady Gaga's pretention to high art in her song "Just Dance," Daniel Nordico said, "I guess I was a little skeptical. I thought it was a little high-concept for a pop song about being drunk at a club and dancing" (qtd. in Callahan 142). It is pretension such as this that "Weird Al" mocks. His mockery, however, is not necessarily mean-spirited. The relationship of "Weird Al" to those he parodies is frequently a complex one and Lady Gaga's case is no different. At one level, he mocks and comically critiques a musical artist, but being parodied by "Weird Al" is now seen as a milestone or a "rite of passage" for artists, which shows that they are now successful enough to merit "Weird Al's" attention. The manager for rapper T.I. explained this notion to his client when they discovered that "Weird Al" wanted to do a cover of one of T.I.'s songs: "This dude did Michael Jackson, and now he's asking to do you? ... For sure, it was definitely a validation and a certification you have a real hit" (qtd. in Itzkoff AR16). In Lady Gaga's case, the road to accepting the honor of a "Weird Al" parody was not a smooth one. One of Lady Gaga's managers requested the lyrics and then a completed track of the song as a precondition of approval.[1]

"Perform This Way" functions as a parody on several levels, the first level of which is clearly textual. "Weird Al" is known as a musical parodist, but the parody is mostly of the text, not of the music itself. "Perform This Way" is no different. "Weird Al" parodies the words, but his music is almost identical to the original. "Weird Al" targets not only the song itself, but the entire entity and phenomenon that is Lady Gaga. Another level of parody, as became evident with the release of "Weird Al's" video for "Perform This Way," is a visual critique of Lady Gaga. In many ways the visual elements of the video make a much more trenchant commentary on Lady Gaga than the lyrics do. I will examine both textual and visual elements to illustrate how "Weird Al's" parody addresses Lady Gaga and her work.

The "Perform This Way" music video opens with a beautiful blond woman in a skimpy bikini emerging from a large plastic egg in much the same way that Lady Gaga did at the Grammy Awards. Her back is turned to the camera until it pans up to show her head. She turns around to reveal "Weird Al's" face digitally placed on a female model's body. Part of the humor, of course, is the incongruity of what is obviously a male head and face attached to a female body.[2] "Weird Al's" lyrics here are telling as well. He sings, "My mama told me when I was hatched, act like a superstar" closely parodying Lady Gaga's lyrics. Because the line is very similar to the original it effectively sets up the comic parody. Lady Gaga, a woman whose background was a nearly blank slate before she hatched, fully formed, into the pop cultural scene, was also hatched when she unveiled "Born This Way" at the Grammy Awards.

"Weird Al" also points out that we cannot all be born superstars, but Lady Gaga certainly acted like one until she became one. By suggesting that one "act" like a superstar, he is also pointing out the ridiculousness of Lady Gaga's Lake Wobegonian assertion that everyone "is" a superstar. His next lyrics then encourage the fledgling superstar to "Save your allowance, buy a bubble dress and someday you will go far." Here, he suggests that for Lady Gaga, the clothes make the superstar, a contention that few would completely discount. "Weird Al" also specifically references her bubble dress, which she copied from the designer Hussein Chalayan ("Lady Gaga" 60). We can sort much of the rest of the parody into five basic categories of critique on the phenomenon that is Lady Gaga: fashion, pretention as a performance artist, narcissism, self-serving tendencies such as the pursuit of money and fame, and pretention to artistic and musical originality.

One of the most obvious targets of parody in "Perform this Way" is the idea of Lady Gaga as a fashion icon. "Weird Al" begins his video by wearing the same sexualized black and white bikini outfit that Lady Gaga wears in her video. He is also wearing leather-spiked gloves, a nod to the gay and lesbian aesthetic of the New York club scene to which Lady Gaga consciously marketed herself. Throughout the course of the video, "Weird Al" wears an increasingly more bizarre series of outfits modeling the trajectory that Lady Gaga herself underwent as her fame and influence grew. These outfits include for instance, a unicorn hat, a pointed nod (pun intended) both to Lady Gaga's song "Highway Unicorn" and her own personal interest in unicorns. He also wears a spiked dress, the impracticality of which "Weird Al" points out by poking a backup dancer in the eye. He wears a nun's habit to point out the provocative religious imagery that Lady Gaga includes in her videos and costume choices. "Weird Al" dresses up in the skeleton makeup that Lady Gaga sports in her "Born This Way" video, but he pairs this image with the line "Cause every day is Halloween for me." Here, he undercuts Gaga's pretention to high fashion by removing her outfits from that world of fashion to the world of prosaic Halloween costumes. Another costume he wears is the crime scene tape that Lady Gaga wore for her "Telephone" video. He dresses in cheese, bees, a whipped cream bikini, a gold lamé straight jacket, a peacock costume, and in a hat shaped like the Taj Mahal with a cloak made out of octopus arms. By showing the increasingly more bizarre and outrageous costumes that Lady Gaga wears and then by suggesting that she would refuse to break this somewhat outdated fashion rule, "Weird Al" brings her image down to earth and creates a humorous incongruity.

Several of "Weird Al's" outfits straddle the worlds of performance art and high fashion. For one such outfit, "Weird Al" wears a porcupine on his head, an oblique reference to Lady Gaga's Lobster hat that was first worn in

1998 by Isabella Blow. "Weird Al" points out the ridiculousness of this kind of outfit even though Lady Gaga tries to use it to associate herself with the world of high art. "Weird Al" also uses this moment to tie back into the original music and lyrics which closely resemble Lady Gaga's original lyrics.

The most interesting outfit unifying the worlds of fashion and Lady Gaga as a performance artist was, arguably, the outfit made out meat which she wore at the 2010 Video Music Awards, a provocative throwback to a dress made of meat created in 1987 by the artist Jana Sterbak (Sterbak). Although "Weird Al" could let the incongruity of a dress made out of meat stand as its own "joke," he decided to turn it into a play-on-words. "I strap prime rib to my feet, cover myself with raw meat. I'll bet you've never seen a skirt steak worn this way." This is a particularly effective play-on-words as a "skirt steak" is an actual cut of meat. The tie between the skirt steak as a cut of meat and a skirt made of steak allows the audience to view the outfit in a comic context and therefore provides a critique of Lady Gaga's fashion sense and pretention to high art. "Weird Al" does not stop his attack on Lady Gaga as a performance artist. He sings, "I'm strange, weird, shocking, odd, bizarre," words that have been used to describe performance art and modern art in general. His character dances awkwardly with contrived hand movements at the beginning, calling into question the unusual, but smoothly choreographed and packaged dance moves that Lady Gaga often uses. He wraps his intestines around his neck and sets fire to himself. These are exaggerated performance art techniques that rely heavily on gore and pyrotechnics that Lady Gaga has incorporated into her stage performances. All of these behaviors in a normal or non-performative human interaction would be considered a form of insanity, which is why "Weird Al" consistently insists in the song that he is not crazy, but that it is, in fact, a performance.

"Weird Al" also questions the painfully transparent practice of artists singing a portion of their music in another language (usually European) in an effort to appear cultured and educated. Lady Gaga employs this technique by singing in French in "Bad Romance," in Spanish in "Alejandro," in Italian in "Born This Way," and in German in "Scheiße." "Weird Al" does not let her get away with it singing, "for no reason now I'll sing in French, Excusez-moi, Qui a pété?" He points out the unmotivated and unnecessary diversion from English and then undermines it even further for those who are, it fact, educated enough to know that he has really sung, "Excuse me, who farted?" There is also an implied critique that such a display is the artistic equivalent of "breaking wind." After this, he sums up what is his version of Lady Gaga's response to her critics, one that is perhaps typical of the confrontational and entitled attitude of many popular performers. "I'm sure my critics will say it's a grotesque display. Well, they can bite me, baby — I perform this way." Further, narcissism and the pursuit of money and fame are often closely related. They are character traits which appear repeatedly throughout the song. "Now on red carpets, well, I'm hard to miss, the press follows everywhere I go." He also shows himself reading a paper with a title referencing Lady Gaga, much like she does in her video for "Paparazzi." This self-aggrandizing narrative trope is not uncommon in Lady Gaga's own work where she mentions her stage name in multiple songs. He also points out a sense of entitlement that comes along with this fame and status as an artist by singing, "don't be offended" and "don't call the cops" because he should be afforded special status as a performer. He also speaks to how Lady Gaga "will honestly do anything" in the search for fame. It is not just the pursuit of fame that he criticizes, but also the mercenary pursuit of money that accompanies it. The parody points out the fact that although in real life she seems to care for her fans and has a seemingly sincere interest in them, she ultimately exploits them for the money they pay her to attend her concerts and buy her music.

Perhaps the most scathing attack on Lady Gaga in "Weird Al's" parody and among her critics in general is Gaga's apparent lack of originality. This critique, while present in the lyrics, is more obvious in the "Perform This Way" music video. As "Weird Al" sings, he is dressed in an outfit reminiscent of Madonna's Jean-Paul Gaultier designed golden cone-shaped bra that she wore on her Blonde Ambition tour. A Madonna look-alike dressed in the same outfit complete with a mole on her upper lip shows up, looks at "Weird Al's" Lady Gaga figure, then at the camera in disbelief. "Weird Al" then pushes her out of frame and continues singing. Later in the video, the Madonna figure pops up again and sings "Express Yourself" before being pushed off screen again. This is a reference to the major controversy that surrounded Lady Gaga's "Born This Way" when it was first unveiled. Although Lady Gaga has been accused of copying Madonna on many levels including origin, marketing strategy, and look, this was considered even more blatant. Marche suggested, "When she emerged from an egg at the Grammy Awards to sing 'Born This Way,' wasn't everybody thinking that the song sounded just like Madonna's 'Express Yourself,' only emptier?" (78). Ryan Tedder, an accomplished songwriter for modern pop singers further commented on the musical similarities between Madonna's "Express Yourself" and "Born This Way." He stated, "We were singing 'Express Yourself' over the melody [of 'Born This Way']! If I wrote 'Express Yourself' and I heard that song, I would be calling my manager five minutes later.... If Madonna's not getting credit on it, then I would just say, be careful" (qtd. in Halperin). The similarities between the songs are extensive, even to the point of both songs starting with a spoken motivational message. Also like Madonna, "Weird Al" suggests, Lady Gaga is willing to expose herself as much as it takes to obtain fame, even if she is treading on the same ground as Madonna.³ Lady Gaga's performance of parody can be fairly subtle and unexpected. Many of her fans appreciate her as an "original" artist, for they are not aware of how she imitates or parodies her precursors because the clues that she is performing parody remain more subtle than in parodies that "Weird Al" creates. However, when examining Lady Gaga's body of work and her self-referential inclusions, it becomes obvious that she exhibits a critical ironic awareness of herself and the artists whom she imitates.

As described earlier, I am employing a broader definition of parody, one that is not necessarily against the text, but which exists alongside it. As Hutcheon argues, much of parody today falls into this second category: "In fact the closest mode to present practice was not called parody at all, but imitation.... Imitation, however, offers a striking parallel to parody in terms of intent" paying a kind of homage to the original (10). Lady Gaga is hyperaware of where her artistic tradition has come from and consistently imitates the tradition's style to copy its success. However she also copies it with some of the critical separation or ironic transcontexualization. This form of parody, a kind of imitation/parody, is useful in understanding how Lady Gaga addresses her artistic heritage. Many of the same categories of originality, fashion, narcissism, and performance apply to Lady Gaga's imitation/parody of other artists and even of herself. As mentioned earlier, part of the definition of parody is that it must have some intentionality either on the part of the artist or on the spectator. Lady Gaga is self-aware enough to understand the effects of her work. When she imitates Madonna, she creates a self-conscious parody:

> And it's from Madonna that Gaga has stolen just about everything: the sexual and cultural provocations that made her generic pop music that much more interesting; the constant, very serious invocation of "my art"; the cultivation of the gay audience and vocal activism for their cause; the incessant reinvention and reincarnations [Callahan 88].

The appropriation of Madonna's image goes beyond mere imitation into the realm of parody. For instance, on the surface the idea of Lady Gaga's song "Beautiful, Dirty, Rich" seems nothing more than the warmed over materialism of the original "Material Girl," but it does have an ironic distance and self-awareness. It takes materialism to a new level in the video where Lady Gaga actually smokes and eats money. She is therefore subsisting entirely off of money as a parodic embodiment of materialism. Another parodic "dig" at Madonna occurred on tour when one of her backup singers dressed like Madonna for a performance, which had the effect of symbolically subordinating Madonna to Lady Gaga. The very end of the video for "Born This Way" provides another example of this parody where Lady Gaga, in her close-up, has re-created Madonna's signature gap between her front teeth. Callahan states, "If there's one thing Gaga can't stand, it's the idea that she's aggressively copied someone else's look. Because she so obviously, inarguably *has*, her outrage is almost funny" (59). This outrage and denial are symptomatic of parody in the modern era which is highly self-reflexive and self-referential. By blatantly imitating and yet vociferously denying the imitation and by incorporating the critique within her own artwork, Gaga seeks to recast the critical discussion of her work. In essence this strategy creates a kind of parody of the critical dialogue itself.

With each of Lady Gaga's works, the imitative text, whether it is music or fashion style, becomes a parody of the original and ultimately of itself as it tries simultaneously to copy the original and still form a revolutionary new artwork. This idea of imitation as revolution or homage as parody can perhaps best be seen in the video for Lady Gaga's song "Alejandro." This video is a high concept piece that, like many of Lady Gaga's videos, has very little to do with the rather pedestrian lyrics in her song. Directed by one of Madonna's frequent collaborators, Steven Klein, the music video clearly shows some of the same artistic influences as Madonna. The defining parodic moment of the video, and the one that often convinces viewers that Lady Gaga has pushed into the realm of parody, occurs near the end. While her outfit clearly pays homage to Madonna and her history of *fashion* extremism, Lady Gaga's outfit could be better described as a reference to *fascist* extremism in a video filled with people wearing retro neo–Nazi outfits. She marches down a ramp with a pointed bra much like Madonna's. Instead of being cone shaped, however, Lady Gaga's bra has "assault rifles thrusting out of her breasts" (Strauss 66). She demonstrates an awareness of and copies Madonna's daring fashion style in an effort to create similar controversy, but she pushes it over the edge into a parodic depiction. Madonna's pointed bra could be considered daring or in poor taste depending on one's point of view; Lady Gaga's can only be parody.

Lady Gaga moves from parody of her artistic forbearers into self-parody when she represents her own image in a way that goes well beyond narcissism. Lady Gaga references herself incessantly in her work. She frequently puts in signs reading "Gaga" and uses the word "Gaga" in many of her songs including "Eh Eh (Nothing Else I Can Say)," "Judas," and "Bad Romance." The pinnacle of this seems to be in her video for "Paparazzi." It is filled with visual references to Lady Gaga from newspaper headlines about her fame to pictures of her face on the money in the video. She is parodying her own fame and how it is taken to a ridiculous extreme, not only by her fans and the media, but by herself as well. One telling real-world incident appeared in an article in *Rolling Stone* in June 2011. The author of the article described a scene between Lady Gaga and one of her producers in which Gaga was working on a piece of her song, "Electric Chapel," which she described as being about "Seventies rock." Her producer argued that it was not about "Seventies rock," but about "Lady Gaga," to which Gaga replied, "I know ... But I can't reference myself. Not yet" (qtd. in Hiatt "Monster Goddess" 41). This is Lady Gaga, a parodic conglomeration of the new and the old, the prosaic and the original.

Lady Gaga is aware of and makes fun of her own image as a performance artist and the idea of becoming her own artistic image: "I don't want people to see I'm a human being. I don't even drink water onstage in front of anybody, because I want them to focus on the fantasy of the music and be transported from where they are to somewhere else. People can't do that if you're just on Earth. We need to go to heaven" (qtd. in Strauss 69). Her habit of reworking and releasing various versions of her songs is also indicative of this parodic self-awareness. For instance, in her appearance on *American Idol*, "Lady Gaga tore up 'Poker Face' and short-circuited the conventions of the show by splitting the song into a drunken solo-piano ballad and an up-tempo truncated version of itself" (Frere-Jones 64). This kind of behavior deconstructs her own image as a performance artist even as she is publicly constructing it.

Lady Gaga walks a dangerous line in the way she performs self-parody. She has stated, "I'm quite a schizophrenic person" (qtd. in Strauss 70) and indeed has fabricated alter egos that include a mermaid named Yüyi and a chain-smoking male named Jo Calderone. The sincerity of these alter egos remains questionable in light of her carefully crafted stage image. However, these alter egos are the clearest indication that Lady Gaga has become a simulacrum in the Baudrillardian sense. Although it is easy to lose sight of this fact, Lady Gaga, herself, is an alter ego for a woman named Stefani Germanotta. Yüyi and Jo are also alter egos of an alter ego:

> It is no longer a question of imitation, nor of reduplication, nor even of parody. It is rather a question of substituting signs of the real for the real itself; that is, an operation to deter every real process by its operational double, a metastable, programmatic, perfect descriptive machine which provides all the signs of the real and short-circuits all [of] its vicissitudes [Baudrillard 170].

There is still a real person somewhere in the parody of a parody that Lady Gaga has become. However, she risks the real metaphysical danger of unmasking the image of her own image. Baudrillard described this danger when he was talking about the Iconolaters, those who opposed the iconoclasts. They knew "that it is dangerous to unmask images, since they dissimulate the fact that there is nothing behind them" (172).

For Lady Gaga, the performance is the reality. It is a self-conscious performance and construction of reality. Using our expanded definition of parody, one that includes consciously working against an original text as well as a critically aware imitation of a text, Lady Gaga is both the object of parody and the creator of it. She exhibits characteristics of ironic critical awareness in her parodic imitations of others in her own performance. She becomes a nexus of parodic transformation, being parodied and parodying others. While this kind of parody is common in the modern era, Lady Gaga has taken it a step further, parodying her own self-created image in its various incarnations. Parody becomes a real danger to Lady Gaga who constantly risks having her image, unmasked which would reveal what, in fact, lies beneath it. To a certain extent, even the threat of this from "Weird Al" Yankovic's parody becomes superfluous in its quest to unmask and deconstruct the phenomenon that is Lady Gaga, because Lady Gaga has become a parody of herself.

Notes

1. Although free speech laws would allow "Weird Al" to make his parodies without permission, out of respect for the artists involved, he always secures permission to create parodies. He shortened a tour and a family vacation to complete the track only to have his request to create the parody rejected (Itzkoff AR16). After lamenting this on his Twitter account, word reached Lady Gaga who publicly reversed her manager's decision stating that the request had never been forwarded to her (Hiatt 44, Itzkoff AR16).

2. The choice of putting a man's head on a woman's body also references some of the controversy that surrounds the gender of Lady Gaga. There have been rumors that she is a transsexual or even a hermaphrodite, rumors that she may not have actively courted but, at the same time, she has done relatively little to dispel. These rumors help to gain public attention and contribute to her celebrity.

3. Yankovic's parody does not ultimately condemn Lady Gaga. Though he has parodied some of her pretensions, there seems to be a sincere appreciation of the music and dance. His parody works only because of Lady Gaga's original version and because of the sophistication of his own fans who appreciate what his parody is saying. This idea of cultural sophistication and the appreciation of parody becomes important as we consider Lady Gaga not only as the subject of parody, but as a perpetrator of it as well.

"I Hope When I'm Dead I'll Be Considered an Icon"

Shock Performance and Human Rights

KARLEY ADNEY

The cover of the September 2010 issue of *Vanity Fair* showcases Lady Gaga, posed like a modern-day Lady Godiva. Her lightly lilac-tinted, waist-long hair both shrouds her and billows from her face, while she sleepily gazes at the camera and flashes a peace sign. Written under the headline "Gaga for the Lady" are the questions "Who is she?" and "Why is she?" The interview, conducted by Lisa Robinson, revealed some unsettling (but not entirely unexpected) information about Gaga. She used to be a drug addict, who would regularly do lines of cocaine before performing or attending meetings. When Robinson asked her if she still used drugs, Gaga said "I won't lie; it's occasional. And when I say occasional, I mean maybe a couple of times a year. I really can't do [cocaine] anymore. I haven't done it in, oh, probably six months" (329). Gaga's casual revelation infuriated some readers, like former supermodel Janice Dickinson, who judged Gaga's comments as thoughtless, especially considering the millions of young women who idolize the music icon and her behavior.[1] Though Gaga's revelation spoke to another question framing her picture on the cover of *Vanity Fair*, "Should you worry?," her comments, made in shock-performance mode, required readers to consider the very real and significant problem of drug abuse in the music industry. Though notorious for her drug experimentation, Gaga remains best known for shocking her audiences with her amazing attire, ranging from sunglasses constructed of lit cigarettes to dresses made of bubbles to couture "Armadillo" shoes designed by the late Alexander McQueen (as seen in her "Bad Romance" video). She met Queen Elizabeth II dressed in a red vinyl version of a Renaissance-style gown sported by Queen Elizabeth I, and, when interviewed by Larry King, imitated his appearance, and later influenced King to imitate hers (he donned a pair of her staple round-framed black-lensed sunglasses). These incidents have undoubtedly earned her a permanent place in our collective consciousness and memory, and Gaga's shock performance tactics incur significant results. Whether on stage, at political rallies, or as she simply walks down the street, her performances create awareness for human rights. Already a cultural icon, Gaga shocks viewers and listeners into a socially just consciousness, promoting equality and respect for, in particular, women and members of the gay community with each performance.

Gaga desires to shock people into paying her some — and hopefully, their full — attention. Scholars and critics alike argue that, for Gaga, "Every appearance and every utterance is a tightly choreographed performance" (Stein and Michelson, "Lady Gaga: The Lady Is a Vamp"). Gaga describes herself as follows: "I was always a weird girl in school, who did theater and came to school with lots of red lipstick on or my hair perfectly curled, or whatever I was doing to get attention" (Morgan 23). Similarly, Gaga adds that "Nuns ran my school, so I was suppressing this part of myself for a long time. It wasn't until later that I realised [sic] my true passions were music, art and performance ... definitely shock art" (Herbert 21). Those acquainted with Gaga's work know that she no longer simply dons red lipstick or perfectly-sculpted curls to obtain attention. Instead, she creeps, more and more closely, to the monstrous in her work. A friend of Marilyn Manson and admirer of his work, Gaga "has always been drawn to the macabre and the monstrous," and finds great inspiration in fantasy and monster movies, especially of the 1950s (Stein and Michelson).[2] She revels in the unsettling nature of her performances, and flourishes as an artist while challenging herself to grow constantly: "My whole life is a performance [... and] I have to up the ante every day" (Stein and Michelson), and she adds that if she ever had to sacrifice her personal artistic style, she "would be kicking and screaming to [her] coffin" (Morgan 80). Gaga's entourage also applauds her daring, artistic nature. Gary Card, one of Gaga's trusted designers, told Anna Powers of *The Los Angeles Times* that Gaga is

> brave enough to let herself be a canvas for a designer to go and really express themselves. Nothing is off limits! With Rihanna and Beyoncé there is an end result of desirability and unattainable sexiness, whereas Gaga is a really interesting bridge between the desirable and the grotesque. She's not at all worried about looking ridiculous or hideous; actually, I think she thrives off it [Powers, "Frank Talk with Lady Gaga"].

Gaga's willingness to take risks places her in the company of other hailed shock performers like Alice Cooper, Ozzy Osbourne and Rammstein. Cooper loved to wear outrageous makeup and once threw a live chicken into his audience (and was actually appalled that the chicken was torn to pieces since he assumed the chicken could fly and would just soar over the screaming crowds to freedom); Osbourne bit the head off a bat (by accident; he did, however, bite the heads off of several doves intentionally at a business meeting); and the lead singer of Rammstein, Till Lindemann, is a certified pyrotechnician who regularly throws flames at his shows to excite his audiences. While some of Gaga's artistic choices place her in comparable standing to these outrageous artists, she also far surpasses them (and other typical shock performers) because she shocks to create social awareness. As Gaga says, "I want people to go to my show going 'What the fuck was that!?' In other words it's like a pop show fit for a museum" (Morgan 86). Much like an exhibit at a museum, Gaga's work makes viewers analyze, question, and often take action to affect change. She does not shock her fans for the sake of simple entertainment; she aims to educate them as well. She is, as Powers claims, "a monster — a monster talent, that is, with a serious brain" (Powers, "Frank Talk with Lady Gaga"). This mastermind has, undoubtedly, influenced the way her audiences (and possibly, her entire generation) think about members of the LGBT community and women via her shock performances.

Gaga has long been loved by the gay community because, as Michael Jones (a gay rights advocate writing for Change.org and author of "Lady Gaga as Gay Culture Warrior") argues, "the woman certainly loves her gays." Gaga explains that "When I started in the mainstream it was the gays that lifted me up. I committed myself to them and they committed themselves to me, and because of the gay community I'm where I am today" (Morgan 85). This reciprocation remains based on devotion and respect, which Gaga has held for the gay community since she was a child. She began playing the piano as a toddler, and during her training as a pianist, she received mentoring from several gay men. Gaga also reflects on her experiences in dance classes, in which she met and made many gay friends. Because of the countless friendships Gaga has had with gay men, she "feel[s] intrinsically inclined toward a more gay lifestyle" (Stein and Michelson "Lady Gaga: The Lady is a Vamp"), and even says with assurance, "I might as well be a gay man" (Raso 60). Beyond Gaga's respect for and commitment to the gay community, her life of glamour also appeals to certain sects of the gay community. Joshua David Stein and Noah Michelson assert that "a life of glamour is an ethos to which every gay — from the 17-year-old Dominican tranny voguing in his bedroom to the tanorexic middle-aged Miami circuit queen — can relate," but add that they love Gaga most because she "loves us [the gays] back. Gayness is in Gaga's DNA" (Stein and Michelson). Gaga proclaims that "I very much want to inject gay culture into the mainstream.... It's not an underground tool for me. It's my whole life" (Stein and Michelson). While some artists pledge allegiance to a cause for show or to garner more fame, Gaga remains a loyal supporter of gay rights, which she does not campaign for just to acquire fans or attention. As *The Huffington Post*'s Michael Solis argues, "Fortunately for the LGBT community, Lady Gaga is using her star power as a means to bring national attention to unresolved human rights issues. She has committed herself to being a staunch advocate, and she plans to become a representative for gay youth" (Solis, "Lady Gaga and Obama for Gay America"). Similarly, the editor of Advocate.com, Ross von Metzke, says that Gaga "puts her time and money where her mouth is" (Zak, "For Gay Activists the Lady is a Champ").

Gaga demonstrates her commitment to gay rights through various methods (including her music videos and appearances at political events), and creates awareness for this community's human rights in particular through shock performance. Her video for the single "Alejandro" provides a keen example of Gaga's shock performance at its best. Gaga, who believes no one "should have to hide who they are," confronts a major issue impacting the gay community in the video for her hit song "Alejandro," which, as she explains, has a "homo-erotic military theme" (King, Interview with Lady Gaga). The video opens with "GAGA" in white against a black background, then shifts to a soldier, who is naked save a black leather hat and fishnet tights, sleeping in a chair with his legs crossed (in the stereotypical pose of a woman). Seconds later, the camera focuses on a group of soldiers, wearing leather boots and small leather shorts, who march in unison. Gaga rests on an elaborate throne, surrounded by soldiers. She watches a scantily clad group of soldiers dance, as they perform a theatrical number with sharp movements that include gyrating on the ground and men grasping one another, pushing them to the ground and dominating each other, at times simulating anal sex. The video then incorporates numerous scenes in which the soldiers wear only black bikini briefs and black high heels; they writhe on beds, sometimes bonded to the bed frames with various forms of leather restraints. Gaga engages in this behavior as well, and but for her nude lingerie and black thigh-high stockings, appears androgynous as she and the soldiers mount and grasp each other. Scenes of Gaga dressed as a nun (in a red gown, white habit, and holding a black rosary) appear throughout the video, and at one point Gaga opens her mouth and dips the entire rosary into her mouth, presumably swallowing it. Shots of Gaga dressed akin to a knight — St. George, in particular — with a white tunic and red cross, also appear throughout the latter half of the video. At one point, video producers show Gaga on her knees before the men, facing them; she rips open her tunic to expose herself to them, and the soldiers appear aroused and lunge hungrily for her body.

Critics agree that Gaga's videos remain some of the most complex and convoluted videos produced today. While many interpretations of this video exist, some of the most convincing analyses of the video's content concern gay rights. Gaga, dressed as a nun and swallowing a rosary, clearly symbolizes the way in which religious institutions like the Catholic Church shun members of the gay community. The symbolism of Gaga as a knight in her tunic with several red crosses (one of which sits upside down over her genitals) emphasizes her role as crusader for gay rights, which explains, in part, why the soldiers lust for her; they become aroused by her symbolic cause.[3] The men in the video obviously represent gay soldiers; many times the men perform their dances in the shadows and always appear in the same attire. Relegating the soldiers to the shadows emphasizes their status as gay men — in the military, specifically — and how their rights as individuals remain ignored. That all the men wear the same attire seems to comment on how the military refuses to acknowledge how gay men are different from their fellow soldiers by denying them the opportunity to share who they truly are: in other words, the video demonstrates the effects of the "Don't ask, don't tell" policy, which, on June 1, 2010, Gaga told Larry King was one of the "archaic things floating around in the government" (King, Interview with Lady Gaga).

Due to the continued existence of these "archaic things" and a lack of action by President Obama on behalf of the gay community, gay people "grew jaded" and "wasted no time in adopting another star, Lady Gaga, as one of its unofficial icons.[4] Lady Gaga embraced the gesture with more gusto than any other woman in recent memory to hold the rainbow-colored spotlight" (Solis, "Lady Gaga and Obama for Gay America"). Only a few months after discussing the controversial "Don't ask, don't tell" policy with King, Gaga appeared at a political rally while roundly criticizing the military practice.[5] Though Gaga dressed the part (appearing in a modest black blazer, white blouse, a tie with stars and stripes and a simple, flowing coif), she continued in her role as shock performer by titling her speech "Equality is the Prime Rib of America." In the speech, Gaga calls soldiers who support the "Don't ask, don't tell" policy "cafeteria soldiers," who "choose some things from the Constitution to put on [their] plate, but not others" ("Lady Gaga's 'Don't Ask Don't Tell' Speech"). Gaga asks her listeners to consider other questions: "In the military, is it acceptable to be a cafeteria American? What I mean to say is, should soldiers and the government be able to pick and choose what we are fighting for in the Constitution or who we are fighting for? I wasn't aware of this ambiguity in our Constitution. I thought the Constitution was ultimate. I thought equality was non-negotiable" ("Lady Gaga's 'Don't Ask Don't Tell' Speech").

Besides making a surprising connection between equality and prime rib for her listeners, Gaga referenced one of her greatest examples of shock performance by closing her speech with "Equality is the prime rib of America. Equality is the prime rib of what we stand for as a nation. And I don't get to enjoy the greatest cut of meat that my country has to offer. Are you listening? Shouldn't everyone deserve the right to wear the same meat dress that I did? Repeal 'Don't ask, don't tell' or go home" ("Lady Gaga's 'Don't Ask Don't Tell' Speech"). Gaga wore the meat dress that she mentions (made entirely of meat, including her shoes and handbag) at the 2010 MTV Video Music Awards. The outfit served as a catalyst for controversy and remains one of her most shocking performances to date. When asked why she wore the dress, she explained that "If we don't stand up for what we believe in and if we don't fight for our rights, pretty soon we're going to have as much rights as the meat on our own bones. And, I am not a piece of meat" ("Lady Gaga Explains"). Many viewers, including loyal fans, questioned if Gaga had changed from the artist whose every outfit and utterance had a purpose to someone just yearning to incite discomfort, shock and even rage (on the part of some vegetarians). Instead, the gay advocate clearly planned to capitalize on the shocking effects of her meat dress in the speech she delivered in Maine exactly one week later, proving her ultimate goal was not just to create controversy but to simultaneously shock people into awareness about gay rights.

On October 10, 2009, Gaga attended and performed at the Human Rights Campaign[6] dinner in Washington, D.C. where Joe Solmonese, President of the Human Rights Campaign, said that Gaga was an "obvious invite" to the dinner because "she pushes boundaries and brings people along" (Zak, "For Gay Activists, the Lady is a Champ"). Solmonese recognizes and respects Gaga's shock performance tactics, and acknowledges that those tactics work. Dressed in a demure (but short and stylish) black gown with her hair curled loosely, Gaga took center stage. She told the crowd "I'm not going to play one of my songs tonight because tonight is not about me. It's about you" (Zak). Instead, she performed a revised version of John Lennon's peace-inspiring ballad "Imagine."

Gaga's performance lacked over-the-top costuming, elaborate staging, and provocative choreography, but some viewers remained shocked by her performance. Presenting herself to an audience already supportive of her cause, Gaga surprised her critics and detractors by her degree of seriousness. Many, still viewing her as an artist akin to Alice Cooper, Ozzy Osbourne, or Till Lindemann, found themselves unsettled by Gaga's reserved demeanor and her comment about refusing to perform her own material because the night belonged to those whose rights she champions.[7] Though her performance failed to shock her loyal fans, Gaga's choices during the Human Rights Campaign dinner resounded with others who still speculated about her sincerity and dedication.

The following day, Gaga spoke at the Gay Rights Rally in Washington, D.C. Gaga assured the crowd that speaking at the rally was the "single most important moment [of her] career" ("Lady Gaga Speaks"; Johnson, "Interview with Lady Gaga at Gay Rights Rally"; Solis, "Lady Gaga and Obama for Gay America"). On the lawns before the platform, people cheered and waved signs saying "Gay for Gaga" ("Lady Gaga Speaks") and "Lady Gaga {heart} Equality, U Should 2" (Zak, "For Gay Activists the Lady is a Champ"). Dressed professionally in simple black pants, a white blouse, black suspenders, and sunglasses, her hair hanging softly past her shoulders, Gaga took the stage while Penelope Williams, a bisexual activist, introduced Gaga as a woman who "has shown us all that performance art and pop music can indeed become a platform for LGBT activism" ("Lady Gaga Speaks"). Gaga's eloquence called attention to inequality, using the phrase "It's not equal if it's *sometimes*" again ("Lady Gaga Speaks," emphasis added). She later said "Obama, I know that you're listening," and unlike the preceding night, Gaga lapsed into shock performance mode for a matter of seconds when she screamed violently to the president "ARE YOU LISTENING!?" ("Lady Gaga Speaks," emphasis added). The crowd roared vehemently while Gaga assured Obama she and other gay rights activists would not relieve the pressure placed upon him until he made his "words of promise a reality." Many performers do not hesitate to address or criticize a president, but the fervor with which Gaga screamed, breaking her fixed composure, undeniably shocked her listeners and spurred even more of them to action, including political administrators who, within the coming year, made significant strides in obtaining and protecting gay rights.[8] Gaga's speech, says attendee Daniel Campbell, was "almost like Martin Luther King and the civil rights speeches. We [the gay community] have a voice" (Zak, "For Gay Activists the Lady is a Champ").

In the same speech, Gaga pledged to fight not only against homophobia, but misogyny as well: "I refuse to accept any misogynistic ... behavior in music, lyrics, or actions, in the music industry" ("Lady Gaga Speaks"). Gaga spoke with Corey Johnson of *Towleroad TV* after the rally and added that "artists are allowed to speak in a hateful way ... a misogynistic way ... and the press does not challenge them and ... I'm going to be taking a very strong stance against that and I am an artist that refuses to accept that behavior" (Johnson, "Interview with Lady Gaga at Gay Rights Rally"). And even though Gaga told Larry King "I am a feminist," critics still question the performer's commitment to women's rights, especially based on her employment of shock tactics to create awareness. Some feminists, says *The Atlantic Wire*'s John Hudson, feel "it's not clear whether she's advancing or regressing the feminist cause" (Hudson, "Lady Gaga's Ambiguous Feminism").

Some of her most well-known quotations about women's rights "rightfully [call] out a double standard that persists in the industry and beyond" (Landau). Gaga once said "I find that men get away with saying a lot in this business, and that women get away with saying very little" (Powers, "Frank Talk with Lady Gaga"; Morgan 122). Similarly, in a much debated comment made to interviewer Gjermund Jappee of the Norwegian website *Dagbladet.no*, Gaga said: "You see if I was a guy and I was sitting here with a cigarette in my hand, grabbing my crotch, talking about how I make music because I love fast cars and fucking girls, you'd call me a rock star. But when I [sing about sex] in my music videos, because I'm a female, because I make pop music, you are judgmental and say that it is distracting" (Williams, "Is Lady Gaga a Feminist, Or Isn't She?"). Moments later, however, Gaga told Jappee "I'm not a feminist. I hail men, I love men, I celebrate American male culture — beer, bars, and muscle cars" (Williams). These sentiments infuriated feminists, since the aforementioned statement equates feminism with hating men, a stereotype from which feminists have tried to free themselves for decades. One critic in particular asked if Gaga meant "to reduce American males to beer, bars, and muscle cars? And since when do feminists hate beer?" (Landau, "Grrrly Talk"). In sum, Erica Landau argues that Gaga "only seems to per-petuate feminist man-hating stereotypes" (Landau). An academic with a back-ground in feminism or Women's Studies may lean from the ivory tower, tongue clucking and head shaking, disapproving of Gaga's tendency to rely on stereotypes. But some staunch feminists *do* hate men, however, and without having studied the critical school of feminist thought in detail, Gaga speaks in generalities while confronting the negative stereotype of a feminist, which is what the majority of the young public believes — that feminists do not like men.[9] Saying that she "hails" and "loves" men may very well be Gaga's effort to show her listeners and viewers that one can champion women's rights and talk about double standards for men and women without hating or disgracing the other gender. In fact, some critics view Gaga as someone "on her way to becoming a feminist icon and a gender revolutionary" (Angyal, "Feminism's Unlikely Champion"), whose choices "[inch] her toward a new articulation of feminism" (Powers, "Frank Talk with Lady Gaga").

One of the most significant examples of Gaga's use of shock performance to create awareness about the status of women concerns her comments and stunts that implied that she had a penis. Since the beginning of her career, rumors swirled that Gaga was a member of the intersex community; in other words, she possessed both female and male genitalia. Gaga acknowledges the rumors with humor, stating that "we all know that one of the biggest talking points of the year was that I have a [penis], so why not give them [the rumor-mongers] what they want?" (Daly, "Lady Gaga Talks Penis Rumors"). At a music festival in Glastonbury, photographers caught Gaga in what they thought was a compromising position: shooting upward to the stage, they had a clear view under her dress and, as pictures revealed, Gaga appeared to have a penis. In an interview after the incident at Glastonbury, Gaga told reporters:

> It's not something that I'm ashamed of, [it] just isn't something that I go around telling everyone. Yes. I have both male and female genitalia, but I consider myself a female. It's just a little bit of a penis and really doesn't interfere much with my life. The reason I haven't talked about it is that it's not a big deal to me. Like come on. It's not like we all go around talking about our vags. I think this is a great opportunity to make other multiple gendered people feel more comfortable with their bodies. I'm sexy, I'm hot. I have both a poon and a peener. Big fucking deal [Szymanski, "That's Right, Lady Gaga Doesn't Have a Penis"].

These comments, however, functioned as a part of a larger agenda for Gaga, an agenda planned to catch those who supported the rumor. In the February 2010 issue of *Q* magazine, Gaga revealed that she merely wore a strap on, and intentionally carried herself like a man and spoke in lower tones to incite her fans at the Glastonbury music festival to believe she was indeed an intersex person (Daly), if not a drag queen.[10] Gaga refused to address the rumors at the time of the performance — instead she carefully planned how to confront the rumors, ultimately revealing she was only biologically female, and shamed those who had participated in the rumor mill for perpetuating stereotypes about gender. While simultaneously encouraging intersex persons to "feel more comfortable with their bodies" (Szymanski), Gaga claimed that some people assigned her male genitalia because they associated accomplishment, wealth, and power (of which she had obtained great amounts) with men. These people could not fathom a woman as successful as Gaga, and in turn decided she must be a man, a member of the gender naturally capable of amassing power. This episode of shock performance caused many viewers to doubt her biological gender, but regardless, Gaga achieved her desired result of making audiences think more carefully about gender and power.

Another medium in which Gaga's shock performance thrives while creating awareness about issues important to the women's community remains her music videos, which function like short films. Even Gaga argues that "There's certainly always a hidden message in my music videos, but I would say I'm mostly always trying to convolute everyone's idea of what a pop music video should be" (Morgan 154). The video for "Bad Romance" opens with Gaga on a white throne, surrounded by what seems to be her court. Once the track for "Bad Romance" begins playing, the scene shifts to a sterile looking room with a number of white pods and showers lining the wall; the room is part of the Bath Haus of Gaga. As the music grows in intensity, the pods open and women crawl from them, drenched in white vinyl, their faces covered and thus, indistinguishable. The scenes change rapidly, focusing on Gaga in other situations. One section in particular shows Gaga in a bath, with two nurses attending to her, forcing her to drink some concoction. Gaga (due to makeup) has oversized doe eyes, which advertise her innocence and feelings of horror at her situation. Another scene to which the video returns time and again shows Gaga in the sterile room, this time looking severely emaciated, each knob of her spine clearly visible. The video also shows Gaga being introduced to a room full of men who sip Nemiroff Ukrainian vodka. A group of women rip off Gaga's Burberry coat (revealed by the traditional beige, black, cream, and red plaid lining), exposing her silver panties and a diamond-encrusted chainmail bra. She wears an elaborate headpiece also constructed of diamonds; chains of diamonds cover her eyes.[11] She dances for the men, then crawls toward them. As she services one customer, in particular, with a lap dance, the scene cuts to a shot focused on a series of monitors with results of bids being placed (presumably for Gaga's sexual favors); as she dances, the number hits 1,000,000 and a sign displaying the word "sold" appears beneath the number. Gaga later enters a room wearing a white cape made from the skin of a bear. The creature's head drags on the floor behind her as she walks, its mouth frozen in a ferocious snarl. The man who "won" Gaga waits on the edge of a white bed; she approaches him, and his presence reflects on her sunglasses. After Gaga drops the cape and exposes herself to him (she wears a tiny white lace lingerie set) the room ignites in flames. The final scene of the video shows Gaga lying on the bed, now wearing black lingerie with sparks shooting from her breasts, the man nothing more than a scorched corpse beside her.

Like most of Gaga's other videos, the video for "Bad Romance" is convoluted and yields several interpretations. Perhaps the most viable interpretation of the video concerns women's rights and representations of women. Someone clearly intends the women in this video to do nothing more than satisfy the needs of men. When the women emerge from the space-like pods dressed in white, video makers emphasize the innocence and birth of these female creatures. The fact that none of them reveals distinct facial features (except for Gaga, whose lips show as she sings the lyrics) hearkens to the practice used in another of Gaga's most shocking videos: by making the women all look alike, they lose their individuality and become one of an ignored mass, much like the gay dancing soldiers in "Alejandro." The men drink their premium alcohol as women are presented to them; they bid on these women as if they are purchasable goods. Their behavior symbolizes the sexual objectification of women. When Gaga meets with the male patron who won her in the bidding war, however, she subverts the power dynamics of the situation. Similar to the ending of *Hostel: Part II* (2007), the bought woman seizes control and instead destroys the man she was about to serve.[12] The video for "Bad Romance," Gaga claims, represents "how the entertainment industry can, in a metaphorical way, simulate human trafficking — products being sold, the woman perceived as a commodity" (Morgan 134; Powers, "Frank Talk with Lady Gaga"). Even so, this shocking video remains a cause of concern for some viewers: "I love the originality of people like Lady Gaga (and other quirky girls that have come before her), but I don't think that my generation should confuse the right to amble about sans pants with the right to be an equal person" (Teal, "Young Women and Feminism in the Lady Gaga Age"). Though Gaga may be "sans pants," she is not without power.

Another powerful example of Gaga's shock performance creating awareness about women occurs in the videos (both the traditional music video and one of the live versions) for the hit song "Paparazzi." The traditional music video once again emphasizes Gaga's shock performance skills. Producers set the video at a glorious, decadent, ocean-side mansion. The audience sees various views of the mansion, leading eventually to the bedroom in which Gaga lies with her boyfriend. Money with Gaga's face printed on it adorns the floor and tabletops. Newspaper headlines advertise Gaga's success and wealth. An altercation occurs, and Gaga's boyfriend throws her from a balcony; reporters appear, claiming Gaga is "so over." Seconds later, a limousine bearing a paralyzed Gaga arrives. One of her servants places her in a wheelchair. Gaga regains the movement of her arms and head, and as her servants remove her neck brace, she strips to show her bra, then staggers monstrously and jaggedly to her feet on a pair of crutches. With eerily halting movements, she thrusts herself forward, still unable to move her legs. Random shots then show women of various professions dead throughout the mansion. The focus returns to Gaga, who has now mastered the use of her legs, as she dances through one of the mansion hallways. Fully healed, Gaga prepares a glass of poisoned drink for the man who threw her from the balcony. He dies, and when Gaga calls 911, she says quite calmly (and even somewhat sweetly), "I just killed my boyfriend" (Lady Gaga, "Paparazzi"). As the police drag her from the mansion, headlines flash on the screen championing Gaga and assuring readers that "she's back" and that "we love her again." The final headline reads "She's Innocent: Police Investigate Lady Gaga" (Lady Gaga, "Paparazzi").

Much like in the video for "Bad Romance," Gaga retains the power and kills the man.[13] The video chronicles the Hollywood star's fall (both literal and figurative) from and eventual rise back to Hollywood fame and glamour. One message relayed via Gaga's shock performance concerns the fickleness of the media, and how paparazzi care only about stories that center on women in disastrous situations (like when Gaga sustains awful injuries after plummeting from the balcony in her home, or after she murders her boyfriend). Gaga says that part of her inspiration for the "Paparazzi" video came from one of her fascinations: "I thought watching the celebrity fall apart is so fascinating to everybody, why don't I just fall apart for seven minutes and see what happens" (Robinson 330). Likewise, Gaga adds

> I had this incredible fascination with how people love watching celebrities fall apart, or when celebrities die; I wanted to know, what did they look like when they die? Marilyn Monroe, Princess Diana, JonBenét Ramsey ... I think about all these dead girls, these blonde, dead icons. What did they look like when they died? So then I thought, Well, maybe if I show what I look like when I die, people won't wonder. Maybe that's what I want people to think I'll look like when I die [Robinson 330].

Gaga's macabre fascination with blonde dead icons was not the only inspiration for "Paparazzi." The work of some of her fellow celebrities also influenced the video: "I thought about performance art and shock art and how Paris Hilton and her sister and Lindsay Lohan and Nicole Richie are shock artists in their own way.[14] They're not necessarily doing fine arts — something they put in museums — but it's an art form" (Morgan 126). In sum, Gaga's shock performance in "Paparazzi" creates awareness about the tragic aspects of celebrity life, specifically female celebrities who encounter trouble or tragedy, and earn fame and notoriety from those incidents.

On the other hand, the video also sends some significant messages about sexual and domestic violence. While she kisses her boyfriend on the mansion balcony at the beginning of the video, he asks her "Do you trust me?" She answers "Of course," and a paparazzo begins to photograph them. He begins to kiss her more violently, and she begs him to stop. He refuses to yield, and instead kisses her more forcefully. She slaps him. He touches his fingers to the spot on his mouth where Gaga slapped him, then hooks his arm under her knees and tosses her from the balcony. He watches her fall for a few seconds, then he simply walks away. Though the fall paralyzes Gaga, the video chronicles her return to physical strength and freedom; by the end of the video she walks and dances as if no injury had occurred, which suggests that women can and will overcome their abusers. Furthermore, this shocking performance also comments on a trend in women who suffer from domestic or sexual abuse: women who kill their abusers. Some may suspect that the Gaga in the "Paparazzi" video killed her boyfriend to gain the attention of the photographers, but the last newspaper headline shown near the close of the video entitled "She's Innocent" creates an awareness of and encourages viewers to think more critically about battered women who kill their abusers and if, as in some cases, such women deserve lighter penalties than other murderers, if not complete forgiveness.[15]

One of Gaga's live performances of "Paparazzi" serves as another fine example of shock performance that, in turn, creates awareness about concerns facing women. Gaga performed a montage of songs at the 2009 MTV Video

Music Awards. In the section devoted to "Paparazzi," her voice turns desperate and as she sings, she grasps and lunges awkwardly around the stage. By the end of the number, Gaga is completely drenched in fake blood (some viewers thought Gaga had actually been injured). *The New York Times*' Nancy Bauer argues that Gaga's "fondness for dousing herself in what looks like blood [... complicate] what are otherwise conventionally sexualized performances" (Bauer, "Lady Power). This live rendition highlights the dangerous effects the media—and paparazzi, specifically—have on women. One of Gaga's influences and idols, Princess Diana of Wales, met her death as the result from a frantic paparazzi chase through Paris. Similarly, some female stars (like Kristen Stewart of the *Twilight* series) have compared the aggressive behaviors of the media towards women, in particular, to sexual assault.[16]

In response to a discussion of her shock performance methods, Gaga told Larry King "I'm trying to push boundaries as much as I can" and "I hope when I'm dead I'll be considered an icon" (King, Interview with Lady Gaga). One cannot help but reflect of the icons Gaga herself lauds in her song "Dancing in the Dark": Marilyn Monroe, JonBenét Ramsey, and Princess Diana, among others. These blonde icons touted sexuality and beauty, and served as the catalyst for scandal. The scandals surrounding Gaga do not end with her sexual encounters, her pageantry, or her fashion like the aforementioned women. Instead, it is with these elements that Gaga's scandals—her shock performances—begin. Appearing as female characters ranging from a quadriplegic recovering movie star to a woman swathed in meat, Lady Gaga arrests her audience's attention and both creates awareness and encourages advocacy through her shock performances. Her performances (in videos, shows, and even rallies) force audience members to question both their understanding of and their beliefs about the gay community and women, in particular. Gaga has obtained and will retain iconic status as a sex symbol, fashion mogul, and humanitarian. Though attributes of Marilyn, JonBenét, and Diana present themselves in Gaga, she has achieved iconic status in her own right by championing civil rights and advocating for social justice through every performance, shocking or not.

NOTES

1. Dickinson failed to acknowledge Gaga's further comments to Robinson several paragraphs later: "If you print that, I do not want my fans to ever emulate me or be that way. I don't want my fans to think they have to be that way to be great. It's in the past. It was a low point, and it led to disaster" (329).

2. The 1950s witnessed some crucial developments in horror including Hammer Horror, which found great popularity in the latter part of the decade. Horror films with a science-fiction aspect also grew in popularity during the 1950s; one of the most popular films remains the classic alien-versus-human battle, *The War of the Worlds*.

3. The tale of Saint George slaying a dragon became immensely popular during the crusades of the eleventh-thirteenth centuries and continued throughout the Renaissance.

4. Gaga openly challenged the President in an advertisement she made as part of Pepsi's RefreshEverything.com campaign. Her open letter to the president reads as follows:

> Dear Mr. President, congratulations! I want to sing love songs, and breaking up with a jerk songs, and songs about having a good time, and letting the chips fall where they may. I want to sing tough songs, and songs that make you want to just dance, I mean really dance. What I really wish, is that I didn't have to write a protest song, so my true hope for the future is that there is no need.
> Sincerely, yours truly, Lady Gaga — Manhattan, New York.

5. The speech occurred on September 20, 2010, in Portland, Maine. Four days earlier Gaga sent a message to politicians in the video "A Message From Lady Gaga to the Senate," in which she sits in front of a United States flag and educates viewers on the "Don't ask, don't tell" policy, and why it should be repealed.

6. The Human Rights Campaign (HRC) is the largest grassroots organization devoted to advocating for the LGBT community.

7. That is not to say that Gaga does not capitalize on her ability to shock listeners at possibly inappropriate venues. Consider, for instance, one of Gaga's performances at a Six Flags Amusement Park. Park administrators clarified for Gaga the park's atmosphere was family-friendly and that she should avoid certain topics. In the middle of singing "Poker Face," Gaga stopped and said, "They gave me a pretty specific laundry list of all the things I wasn't allowed to say today [because] this was a family show [because] I am notorious for being provocative" ("Lady Gaga Sings"). Disregarding the wishes of park staff, Gaga went on to say, "But I decided that there is always one thing that I talk about in my show that some people might not want me to talk about but I think it's very relevant to your generation [...] and it's very important that we all band together to legalize gay marriage.... So my apologies, but not really." While Gaga's unwavering commitment to creating awareness about gay rights deserves praise, the many young children at the park may have been confused, and their parents and guardians may have been angered by discussing a topic possibly viewed as inappropriate for young park visitors.

8. Consider, for instance, the repeal of the "Don't ask, don't tell" policy discussed earlier.

9. Based on personal experience and stories relayed to me from colleagues, difficulty still persists in discussing the concept of feminism in various higher education courses, especially with Gaga's target audience — more specifically, those between the ages of 15 and 23. I can think of numerous instances in which I would ask my class how many people considered themselves feminists and only several students would raise their hands. When asked why more students did not consider themselves feminists, many female students responded by saying "I don't hate men." Likewise, scores of male students have explained to me that they cannot consider themselves feminists because they feel it is unfair to other men. This is precisely the notion to which Gaga responds in her interview.

10. Gaga graced the cover of this issue of *Q*, and the picture — yet another example of Gaga's shock performance at work — caused major controversy. The cover shows Gaga "in true lads' mag style, the image is of a topless blonde, in black leather-like trousers, one gloved hand coyly positioned over her boobs, the other not so coyly rammed against her crotch. Jutted hip, parted lips and vacuous expression tick the remaining boxes that constitute the image of sexy" (Hoby, "So Much for Lady Gaga's Feminist Credentials"). *The Guardian*'s Hermione Hoby adds that "I'm loath to say that [Gaga's] feminist self-determining shtick was all talk and no trousers." Hoby's analysis neglects to mention that Gaga also has an enormous dildo shoved in the front of her pants, no doubt to play off the Glastonbury incident. Many *Guardian* readers commented on Hoby's neglecting to acknowl-

edge the depth and complexity of the picture when one considers the dildo in Gaga's pants. Chloe Angyal, in "Feminist's Unlikely Champion," offers that "By wholeheartedly embracing the grotesque, [Gaga's] doing everything she can to be naked without being sexy." I do not mean to suggest a woman with a dildo is grotesque, but Angyal's comment applies to Gaga's *Q* cover because she subverts the stereotypical sexy image Hoby discussed with the inclusion of the dildo in the photograph. Likewise, Gaga says "The last thing a young woman needs is another picture of a sexy pop star writhing in sand, covered in grease, touching herself" (Morgan 102).

11. Gaga appears a bit majestic in her headwear, which resembles more a piece of bondage than an ornate headpiece. One critic suggests that one of Gaga's major influences, Madonna, "employed bondage imagery, and it felt sexual. Gaga does it, and it looks like it hurts" (Powers, "Frank Talk with Lady Gaga"). Indeed, Gaga's diamond headwear does more to emphasize her subservient status than her sexuality.

12. Eli Roth's *Hostel: Part II* follows the story of three young women lured to a hostel from which they are eventually sent to their deaths. People bid on the girls and the winner gets to execute the "prize" in any method he or she chooses. One girl, won by a completely emasculated man, manages to reverse the situation and instead of dying herself, cuts off the man's genitals and leaves him to die.

13. Gaga's pattern of killing men in her videos has not gone unnoticed. When *Vanity Fair*'s Robinson asked Gaga about the recurring theme, Gaga responded by saying, "Someone recently texted me, 'Why do you keep killing all your boyfriends in your videos? Are you going to kill me?' I'm like ... I don't know why, I don't really know" (330). Robinson responded by saying "You poison a boyfriend in 'Telephone,'" to which Gaga added the clarification "I don't actually kill him in that video. Beyoncé does. I'm just assisting her."

14. Lindsay Lohan posed in the January–February 2012 issue of *Playboy* for which the magazine reportedly paid her nearly $1 million.

15. Consider the case of Emma Humphreys, who murdered her abusive boyfriend, who was also her pimp, in 1984. After serving a decade for murder she was released, with officials claiming that "Her case changed the law for battered women who kill [their abusers]. It established that provocation could be cumulative and did not have to occur immediately before a murder to form a legitimate defence [sic]" ("Diary of a Teenage Killer" 8). Another similar case concerns Heather Thornton, a battered woman who stabbed her viciously abusive husband to death. She was convicted of murder but after a retrial was convicted of manslaughter. Her case, in particular, allowed that "judges could reflect some sympathy upon battered women driven to kill" (Mills, "Sara Thornton Granted Murder Case Appeal").

16. Stewart told *British Elle* in July 2010 that watching the media assault women for information and photographs is like "looking at someone being raped" ("Kristen Stewart in *Elle UK*"). After being roundly criticized by rape support and sexual assault advocacy groups, Stewart did apologize for her comment.

Whiteness and the Politics of "Post-Racial" America

LAURA GRAY-ROSENDALE, STEPHANIE CAPALDO,
SHERRI CRAIG *and* EMILY DAVALOS

Ever since President Obama's election, it seems that conversations about race in America have become more heated, further polarizing the right and the left. Many conservatives — from the jowl-jiggling Glenn Beck of *Fox News* fame to various right-leaning academicians of note like Dinesh D'Souza — have contended that we are now living in a "post-racist" America. According to D'Souza (who further outlines his argument in *The End of Racism*), this term suggests that "racism, which once used to be systematic" has "now become episodic" (1). In other words, the thinking goes, though racism still exists, it no longer controls or greatly affects the lives of African-Americans and other minorities. Many leftist public figures such as Jesse Jackson have challenged this view, however, asserting that racism is still very much alive, that electing a black president far from signals its demise. Instead it now operates in ever more subtle ways, ways that are becoming harder to name and thus overtly challenged. Likewise, scholars such as Kimberle Crenshaw, professor of law at UCLA and Columbia law schools, have argued against the idea that we live in a "post-racial" period. Crenshaw indicates that the term "post-racism" is being used now to ignore real charges of racism, in effect to "silence those who want to talk about race" (1).

We agree with Jackson and Crenshaw. Even though time has passed since segregation as well as the Civil Rights movement, and our country's official policy on race is certainly more inclusive, racist practices continue to hold sway. The term "post-racism" is functioning as little more than a smokescreen, a way to smuggle in racist discourses without getting caught. Or, as Joel Anderson writes so eloquently in his essay "Burying Post-Racial," "Post-racial is a figment of the imagination. Post-racial America is Utopia. Atlantis. Unicorns. Aerocars. It simply doesn't exist" (2).

It is within this larger historical, political, and racialized context that Lady Gaga has gained inordinate popularity. And while it is clear that the Gaga phenomenon has been fruitfully analyzed by those inside and outside the academy for its innovative visual rhetoric, transgressive discourses of sexuality, and fluid gender constructions, exactly how Gaga is operating discursively within this charged racial atmosphere has been left relatively unexamined. One main reason for this lack of analysis, as scholars such as Mike Hill have articulated in his crucial *Whiteness: A Critical Reader*, is due to the fact that constructions of whiteness have historically remained "the invisible" and therefore less open to critique. This invisibility is possible precisely because of cultural privilege. In *Identifying Race and Transforming Whiteness in the Classroom*, Virginia Lea and Judy Hefand define whiteness as "a constellation of social practices, knowledge, norms, values and identities that maintain a race and class hierarchy in which white people disproportionately control power and resources," and argue that "naming whiteness as invisible is the first step to making it visible" (23).

As Alfred J. Lopez suggests in his introduction to the collection *Postcolonial Whiteness: A Critical Reader on Race and Empire*, now "whiteness finds itself to some extent caught in the other's gaze: it has come to be aware of itself as a race-object among other race-objects" (15), resulting in discomforts around discussions of race in American culture that loom ever larger on our horizon. Likewise, Gwendolyn Audrey Foster clarifies in *Performing Whiteness: Postmodern Re/constructions in the Cinema*, "white performances are simulacra, falsely stabilized by master narratives that themselves are suspect and whiteness itself is a concept that needs constant upkeep. It is in the cracks and fissures of performative whiteness that we can begin the dismantling of whiteness as a norm" (2). However, the very fact that Lady Gaga is not often read in these terms, in spite of the numerous books now published about whiteness, suggests something crucial: Not only do we not reside in a "post-racial" America, the fact that no scholars interrogate Gaga in terms of race simply reveals how far we still have to go.

This chapter traces some of the key discourses concerning race and Lady Gaga by analyzing Gaga's music videos, specifically "Bad Romance" and "Telephone." Gaga's media prominence is largely the result of how she embodies as well as deploys and subverts powerful historical discourses about whiteness and racism. Analyzing Lady Gaga's complex deployment of contradictory discourses about whiteness in our classrooms might be key to initiating fruitful larger cultural conversations about race. As Leda Cooks and Jennifer S. Stinson assert in *Whiteness, Pedagogy, and Performance*, "Teaching about whiteness is about exposing contradictions, about pulling away layers of rhetoric and sense-making that have maintained white privilege" is more important than ever

(14). We must increasingly find new ways to examine how whiteness is played out "through relations of dominance, inclusion, exclusion, marginality, and resistance; and as always interacting with other identity markers such as gender, sexuality, and class" (17).

Reading the Lady

While our own classroom conversations about Lady Gaga have covered almost all subjects imaginable, the most intriguing ones for us focused upon issues of race. The diverse backgrounds and pressing concerns that today's students bring to this conversation make for compelling interrogations. We have considered the extent to which race plays a fundamental role in how Lady Gaga's sexuality is interpreted by the public.[1] Oftentimes her popularity is predicated upon her perceived challenges to traditional ideals of whiteness and white womanhood specifically. But these challenges need careful examination. In what ways exactly does Lady Gaga subvert constructions of whiteness? In what ways does she fail to interrogate them fully, instead of simply using them to her own ends? Lady Gaga's whiteness shapes how her audience views her. While Gaga is often interpreted as a feminist for her brazen actions and costumes that seem to assert women's sexual empowerment, historically women of color who have portrayed similar images, such as Lil' Kim or Foxy Brown, have been lambasted as sexually licentious. Without her whiteness, one wonders whether Gaga's "challenge" might not be little more than simple reinforcement of stereotypical images of over-sexualized women of color, such as the exotic Asian or the black jezebel. Undoubtedly, Lady Gaga receives more attention in the media for her outrageous behavior precisely because popular culture has different expectations for white women and women of color. Perhaps Gaga's whiteness — alongside her dress, dance, lyrics, and her makeup — make her more shocking than women of color who have pushed definitions of gender appropriateness in terms of public displays of sexuality further both musically and visually. Lady Gaga's whiteness affords her many freedoms and privileges not available to female performers of color. As Gayle Wald claims in *Crossing the Line: Racial Passing in 20th-Century U.S. Literature and Culture*, music is a space within which white women can play with and challenge femininity (152). As we have explored with our students, Lady Gaga constantly enacts such "play." Gaga's music falls within the normative ranges of expected white female pop music, yet her image contrasts this. Although Gaga has a reputation for challenging traditional notions of proper femininity in her image and videos, she is able to "reclaim" her whiteness if and when she chooses.

Consider the now infamous interview with a Norwegian journalist, the one in which Lady Gaga grossly misrepresented feminism by proclaiming: "I'm not a feminist. I hail men, I love men. I celebrate American male culture, beer and bars and muscle cars" (as if feminists could not make these claims). Here Gaga performs her most recognizable character, that which she is both acclaimed and criticized for, her rebellious, "I don't give a fuck" persona. She sits relaxed, legs crossed high where her black leather boots meet her black fishnet covered-thighs. Hair from her purple wig rests on the drastically raised shoulder pads of her black form-fitting jacket while her gaze is hidden by very large black sunglasses. Clearly indifferent, she appears bored and even annoyed with the questions posed to her by the interviewer. Her confidence borders on arrogance when asked if she fears that the attention she gets for her sexuality overshadows her music. She responds proudly: "Nope, not at all. I've got three number one records and I've sold almost four million albums worldwide." Obviously irritated by the interviewer, Lady Gaga exclaims that she loves the gay community because "they don't ask her questions like that," and they "love sexual, strong women who speak their mind." Rightfully challenging the obviously gendered double standard in the music industry, Gaga uses her tough, gritty voice to describe the media's acceptance of males who grab their crotches and sing about f**king girls yet question women who display similar behavior. Here Gaga offers an astute gender analysis yet neglects to acknowledge how her racial privilege allows her to use vulgar language, dress provocatively, and nonchalantly brag of her success in one interview, while completely reinventing herself and reclaiming her whiteness for different audiences in other events. After all, she's "just a rock star."

Consider Lady Gaga's April 24, 2011 interview with Ellen DeGeneres. Here Gaga clearly performs her whiteness both through her language choices and her actions. While Gaga remains true to her *avant-garde* image, wearing a white latex dress, tall white leather boots and silver sparkly makeup around her eyes, on the "Ellen DeGeneres Show," her visual performance stands in stark contrast to the interview with the journalist mentioned earlier. Instead, Gaga sits erect and attentive, with her legs appropriately crossed at the ankles, her dress conservatively hanging below the knee and her hands properly folded in her lap. She leans forward, hanging on Ellen's every word, smiling, nodding and laughing at all the right moments. She is soft-spoken, cheerful, witty, sweetly giggling at Ellen's jokes while gently brushing her long blond hair over her shoulder. When Ellen complements her success, adoringly exclaiming: "look at you, you're huge! In one year!" Gaga interrupts her, looks demurely at the crowd and says "Not as big as Ellen!" which receives approving applause. Humbly continuing, Gaga says "It happened really fast but I just really love my fans so much and I'm really grateful and I thank God every day." This is a drastic contrast to her almost pompous list of accomplishments in the previously analyzed interview. Gaga appears very family oriented, exclaiming that her mom is backstage "freaking out because she loves Ellen so much!" Gaga also shares the story behind the song "Speechless" she performs later in the show, confessing that it was written for her father who recently had open-heart surgery. Tugging on the heartstrings of Ellen's mostly white, female, middle-aged audience, Gaga performs "Speechless" Norah Jones-style at a solo white piano. Gaga demonstrates her very talented vocal skills without the distraction of electro-pop beats and disco remixes commonly found in her more popular radio hits, also without the disturbing or provocative dance moves performed in her videos. In effect, Gaga deploys her whiteness because she can, offering up a song, a persona, a performance appropriate for and accepted by a mostly white middle-class audience made up of many stay-at-home moms who watch day-time talk shows.

In both interviews, the public accepts Lady Gaga. She can be taken seriously as the outlandishly shocking, sexually provocative pop star, but also as the sweet singer/song writer who composes pieces for her family, who giggles girlishly on the couch next to Ellen. In doing so, Gaga embodies the privileges of whiteness. Her ability to choose to separate herself from dominant white culture and dissent from the norm, thereby otherizing herself, demonstrates this privilege. Race Studies critic Daniel Traber argues in *Whiteness, Otherness, and the Individualism Paradox from Huck to Punk* that one's ability to distinguish oneself as an individual, a loner, misfit, rebel, a "freak" perhaps, can come only through the privilege of being a member of the dominant culture, something afforded by the privilege of whiteness (13). By appropriating a marginalized identity, Gaga achieves autonomy. On the other hand, non-whites are often represented as the Other. Oftentimes they do not have the liberty to choose Otherness. Lady Gaga's whiteness enables her to "play" Other, appropriating signs of Otherness to her own ends. As such, she can appear to contradict the norm. White privilege allows her to effortlessly move between the norm and the Other in her "performance art." Non-whites, the perpetual Other, do not often have the privilege of negotiating between such identities.

As such, Lady Gaga easily moves in and out of her "shocking" and "offensive" personae to suit her agenda or mood. White privilege permits her to move in and out of these spaces without consequence, without invalidating her rebellious persona to her fans and the media, yet still not preventing her from entertaining middle class white women watching *Ellen*. Both personae are performances for Gaga, both are performances of white privilege: one a liberal challenge to traditional ideas of gender, the other a reinforcement of traditional white feminine stereotypes. Gayle Wald argues that whiteness provides an entitlement to "experiment with identity," and Lady Gaga exemplifies that experimentation (153). In effect, Gaga subverts traditional notions of gender by breaking what critic Shannon Sullivan in *Revealing Whiteness: The Unconscious Habits of Racial Privilege* refers to as "white habits" (2). Gaga successfully rejects ideals of romantic love, gendered divisions of proper conduct and cultural norms surrounding sexuality. Yet, in an attempt to challenge traditional gender roles, Gaga risks reinforcing dominant notions of white privilege, along with the racial hierarchies that sustain uneven power relations. The concept of whiteness has an aesthetic: popular, rich, beautiful, thin, and adorned in jewels. Gaga wields all of these weapons. Lady Gaga's Nordic female body reinforces feminine whiteness with her pale skin, often white or platinum blond hair and European features. Sullivan further argues that a white person's choice to be with non-white people, to go to non-white places, or to participate in non-white bodily expressions are further demonstrations of white privilege. Non-whites, on the other hand, do not always have the choice to venture into white spaces (13). It is also important to note that in many of her videos, not only does Lady Gaga consistently express her own self-worth and importance, but she is also repeatedly branding the Lady Gaga image in conjunction with other popular brands (Smirnoff Vodka, Diet Coke, etc.). This excessive appearance of fortune and wealth expresses whiteness in predominantly commercial terms. In effect, Gaga opts to become part of American culture in which "flaunting wealth ... is the accepted norm of the American consumer. Whites are trained by television commercials, magazine promotions, radio spots, internet "spam," and web "banner" advertisements to be good consumers.... Whiteness is a commodity that can be bought and faked; and, to perform whiteness correctly, increasingly one is expected to be a gluttonous American consumer" (Foster 102).

In her music videos, Lady Gaga conveys this whiteness through her use of jewelry, fashion, and environment. Lady Gaga, who has an acute awareness of self, performs her whiteness successfully, whether it is "bought or faked." Interestingly, in an interview for Elle magazine, Lady Gaga quips "But you know, I can be whoever ... I want to be. That's what artists do. We choose what you see and we tell a story" (3). However, Gaga's whiteness and her performance of it allow her to tell stories many people of color may be less able to tell. And the stories Gaga creates are oftentimes predicated upon white dominance, dominance reinforced and secured by the world of elaborate possessions she owns and/or represents. Turning to several music videos that we have examined with our students and including our own analyses based upon such conversations, we will now see how Lady Gaga uses discourses about race and whiteness to these ends. Analyzing "Bad Romance" and "Telephone" in such a light — and within our contemporary political moment — can be quite telling.

"Bad Romance" and Performative White Femininity

Lady Gaga's music videos use race in striking and complicated ways. While she often employs long-standing problematic discourses and representations of whiteness and race privilege, at other moments she radically debunks them. This paradox makes Lady Gaga such a captivating and potentially problematic figure within our contemporary cultural landscape. Beginning with a detailed description of the video for "Bad Romance, we see whiteness a symbol throughout (all-white set, white outfits, platinum-white Gaga hair), though its performative function seems to operate in radically different ways at different moments in the visual text. In the beginning, Gaga sits on a white throne in a gold dress and high heels in a *tableau vivant*, women in white with shimmery masks surrounding her — at her feet or in a bathtub — men on the outskirts in all black. Lady Gaga does not face the camera but instead stares off screen, wearing starburst sunglasses reminiscent of old film clips, obscuring her eyes from view. Gaga then presses a button, her fingernails covered in wire mesh. Then the viewer is introduced to The Bath Haus of Gaga, a strange futuristic landscape in which people wearing head-to-toe white vinyl with only their lower faces visible, emerge from white "Monster"-brand pods. Interspersed with these images are other visuals of Lady Gaga, wearing dark contacts that fill her whole eyes; she is sitting in a white bathtub, wearing a white plastic sheath and headphones. In brief moments we also see Gaga in front of a mirror, dressed in all black, wearing dark sunglasses. Soon the big-eyed Gaga is forcibly lifted from the tub by two women and she is made to drink a clear liquid. Whether this liquid is vodka or poison, the viewer is left to wonder. It is precisely at this point in the visual text — as Gaga is dragged out of the bathtub — that a new set of clips emerge, those featuring a sad, demure, feminine and teary-eyed Gaga. And this feminine counter-point, this alternative Gaga, will appear again and again at key points throughout the rest of the video.

Next, other women in the video shove Gaga in front of an all-male audience. Gaga's coat is removed from her gruffly by the other women. She is revealed to be wearing a dress and headpiece made entirely of white, diamond-like jewels. Gaga — pushed and prodded by the other women in white leotards — dances alongside them. The images of Gaga and the other female dancers appear between two black male pant-legs. Next, Gaga crawls on hands and knees toward the men, giving one a robotic lap dance. In the next shot, men are bidding on Gaga with remotes, bets appearing in bright green on a long line of black computer screens. Gaga, wearing black, is frozen in time and space, jewels all around her and on her, shot from every angle as the male bidders watch. These images of wealth and consumption are interspersed with others of Gaga in a shiny, reptilian outfit or wearing a series of silver rings — like those of Saturn — around her body. Then, dressed all in white with bright red lipstick and wearing a bear skin on her back, complete with head and teeth, Gaga slowly makes her way toward her new "owner." The dance montages feature Gaga and all of her dancers in red, their hair whipped around by wind. The other Gaga — the one always in soft-focus and hyper-feminine — makes more frequent and more desperate appearances now. Gaga screams inconsolably at the camera. Faced with her new "owner" wearing a gold chin piece, Gaga throws off her coat, presenting herself to him like a gift dolled up in white lingerie. Now the red dancers' gyrations become more frenetic and a fire erupts behind the man. More and more soft-focus images of the feminine Gaga appear, more and more pleading and broken. Suddenly a fire erupts behind Gaga and engulfs the entire set. Only Gaga appears unharmed, standing there in her bear skin, fire shooting ferociously behind her. Next there is a flash back to Gaga and her red dancers, her outfit now little more than a few scraps of red tape and lace. The final image in the video features Gaga wearing black lingerie, lying on a burnt bed. Next to her is a skeleton, presumably that of her "owner." She lays there covered in soot, a cigarette dangling nonchalantly from her mouth, sparks shooting from a gun-like object that she holds in her hands.

How exactly is Gaga deploying discourses of whiteness and femininity in this video? It is clear that at some moments, Lady Gaga functions in her "performance art" mode — wearing white spandex, almost disappearing into the set itself, or donning full-face masks. In such instances she utilizes contorted dance moves, wears dark makeup with bright red lipstick, and dons jewels or scanty lingerie. In her book *The Myth of Aunt Jemima: White Women Representing Back Women*, Diane Roberts argues that these particular sorts of performative vixen images, ones that are strongly sexual, have been historically relegated primarily to women of color (115). Whiteness, in other words, has depended upon passive sexuality or virginal purity.

Significantly, in the "Bad Romance" music video, such vixen images are consistently contrasted with a much softer, traditionally "feminine" Gaga. In these soft-focus shots she adheres almost entirely to the historical ideals of white femininity. We see close-ups of Lady Gaga's crying face, her powdered, porcelain pale white skin, and lightly colored pink lips. We see a distraught, submissive Gaga, cupping her hands and white polished nails to her face, occasionally looking away from the camera as if distracted by whatever is bringing her to tears. Just as in the two interviews discussed earlier, Lady Gaga is once again able to both utilize the vixen images as well as employ traditional discourses about whiteness and femininity as the embodiment of goodness and beauty. As Richard Dyer contends in his text *White*, "[i]n Western tradition, white is beautiful because it is the color of virtue. This remarkable equation relates to a particular definition of goodness" (72). This frail, delicate, submissive, sexually pure or virginal Gaga, passive and in desperate need of help, often wearing white, depends upon discourses that have traditionally defined female attractiveness and white womanhood. And, as Roberts asserts, historically such constructions of white femininity depend greatly on the link between white femininity and sexual repression, a sexual repression that Gaga overtly challenges throughout the other visual narratives of the video (35). While Gaga fights the repression of female sexuality through her own outfits and dance moves, the video's narrative is all about white women's sexual repression. She is a prize for purchase. In addition, the men are not the only ones forcing her to become a slave. A host of other white women facilitate this bidding, first by drugging her and then by pushing her to perform in front of the men. This dynamic leaves the viewer to ponder the extent to which white femininity and sexual repression are not only exercised by patriarchal culture, but also reinforced by white women — perpetuating it amongst it themselves, then forcing it upon each other. If so, do these moments in the video not expose the true complexity of these myths of white femininity and how they function?

As previously stated, it is mainly because of Lady Gaga's white privilege that can move easily in and out of spaces commonly held by both white women and women of color. However, the music video accomplishes much more than simply revealing the ways in which Lady Gaga's racial privilege enables her easy movement between traditional female roles and how white women facilitate such movement. The visual text also reveals white femininity to be little more than a commodity traded amongst men. The video plays out a well-worn patriarchal narrative. The men effectively steal Gaga's virginal purity from her as a sex trade ensues — one that incidentally looks very much like an electronic stock exchange interaction — her virtue sold like a commodity to the highest bidder.

But Lady Gaga does not only expose white femininity as a myth. She goes one step further. By the video's conclusion, Gaga effectively turns this old narrative on its head, potentially challenging all representations of femininity foisted upon women — whether based in white privilege or not. Once "sold," Lady Gaga proceeds neither to accept her "slave status" nor to acquiesce to the desires of a man. By the end of the video for "Bad Romance," the viewer begins to believe that Gaga might, in effect, deploy and manipulate constructions of white femininity for her own ends. If she accomplishes this, certainly her white privilege enables it in large part. The myths of white femininity and the discourses surrounding it have had real, practical and disempowering results for women of color historically. White women have also been complicit in their own subordination and have helped to perpetuate the myths. And yet still one might rightly argue that the result of Gaga's challenge to traditional discourses of femininity is a valuable one. In effect, the outcome suggests the destabilization of constructions of femininity. This outcome leaves the viewer to think about new questions: If women are able to utilize and deploy problematic constructions of femininity themselves — working within racist and sexist narratives in order to dismantle them — is this not another very valuable form of empowerment? As she sets her male "owner" on fire, leaving the viewer to stare at the sparking, smoking corpse, the viewer is left to think about who exactly has controlled white femininity in this narrative. Has Gaga, in fact, exposed the basic tenets of femininity as merely part and parcel of a larger patriarchal mythos, dismantling this false femininity? Indeed, who in the end has suffered most in this "bad romance"? While Gaga's race privilege enables her to easily move between the traditional feminine roles of virgin and vixen, in the end one sees that she may be using this privilege, at least in part, to destabilize traditional notions of femininity.

In the end, the video is far more complex than it would first appear. It reveals fascinating aspects about our conflictual contemporary discourses around femininity and race. It raises critical concerns and questions such as the following: What exactly constitutes whiteness in an American culture that is more and more homogeneous in its heterogeneity? How do we define what constitutes femininity and what role do women themselves play in such definitions? What role do women play in their own oppression? What can and does contemporary female empowerment for all women look like? Is it fair for Gaga to move between constructions of femininity relegated to women of color as well as those associated with white privilege? In doing so, does Lady Gaga expose white privilege and implicitly challenge it? Or, does she, in fact, have a greater responsibility than she actually assumes?

"Bad Romance" never offers definitive answers. Instead, the video leaves us all to struggle with and consider the possibilities. As such, the video provides a crucial jumping off point for discussions about the complicated nature of contemporary sexist and racist discourses. Instead it shows how complex and multi-layered they are, the extent to which we must increasingly use the master's tools to dismantle the master's house, as it were. It also exposes the extent to which women can be complicit in their own oppression and oppress one another. It reveals that whiteness and racism operate in disturbing, complex ways. But it does not overtly tell us exactly what we should do to combat or subvert such discourses. Instead — and this is what makes Lady Gaga so very captivating in an age where the term "post-racism" is continually asserted as little more than a thin justification for covert racism — she leaves us to figure out the answer to this question ourselves. If we are to challenge racism amidst these slippery discourses of "post-racism," what will we need to look like? What new tactics — and even uses of traditionally racist and sexist discourses — will we have to employ?

White Privilege, Democracy and "Telephone"

Perhaps in an attempt to overcome charges of using her white privilege without fully interrogating it, however, Lady Gaga has recently involved herself more in non-white environments within some of her videos. "Telephone" features Gaga and Beyoncé Knowles, the African-American pop and hip-hop superstar. Much like many of Gaga's previous music videos, "Telephone" opens like a film with credits, panning across razor wire and cityscapes. Gaga, wearing a revealing black and white striped dress, is brought into an all-female prison by female guards, themselves wearing two piece leather outfits. The camera pans across a series of scantily clad female prisoners, seductively mugging and pouting before the camera, occasionally licking the bars. Quickly, in a move not unlike the one made by those dancers from "Bad Romance," Gaga is stripped of her clothes and tossed onto a bed by the female guards. The video cuts to the prison exercise yard in which buff, hardcore female prisoners are lifting weights. The camera moves between a fuzzy black and white surveillance film observing the prisoners and the slick music video footage. Gaga, now wearing chains and glasses made of smoking cigarettes, is led into the yard where the rest of the prisoners gawk at her. They proceed to taunt her. We see her kissing one female prisoner with a short, dark haircut, clad in all-black leather. In the next scene, however, the female prisoners are back inside. A fight breaks out as the guards look on casually, doing nothing to stop it. During this fight, Gaga, wearing black-lingerie and creative curlers made of Diet Coke cans, answers the telephone on the cell wall.

Suddenly the female prisoners, now clad in glittering bikinis, mysteriously emerge from their cells, performing a dance number as they strut down the prison halls. Once again, the video cuts between the black and white prison surveillance footage and the high production quality of the music video itself. And each of these narrative strands interspersed between images of Gaga dressed in little more than yellow and black crime scene tape, trapped in her prison cell. Next, Gaga is allowed to leave the prison, clad in a black and white dress, her trademark dark sunglasses, and a big black hat. Beyoncé is waiting for her there in a brightly-painted pick-up. They escape together through the desert "Thelma and Louise"-style. As they drive, Beyoncé begins to sing while Gaga shoots Polaroid snapshots of her. In the next scene, we see Beyoncé in a diner, now wearing all yellow. Two men of color begin to fight over her and, as they do, she pours a blue poison liquid into the African-American man's coffee. After smacking a woman on the butt, this man returns to the booth and Beyoncé. As the man begins to choke, the video cuts to Gaga-as-chef, working in a kitchen in an apron, surrounded mainly by men of color. They gyrate and dance around her, holding phallic baguettes, making and slicing sandwiches. Next, we see images of Gaga mixing the poison in the kitchen while a recipe for it flashes on the screen. Gaga then appears, now all in white, and presents the food to this same African-American man who Beyoncé has already poisoned. As he eats it, he falls over dead onto his plate. It becomes clear that all of the diners have been poisoned as, one by one, they fall over dead. Upon their death another dance number breaks out, both of women now clad in patriotic red-white-and blue leotards, moving behind the dead bodies that frame their actions. This dancing intermingles with clips of Beyoncé on the telephone in a hotel room. The next shots in the video feature the two women speeding away in a truck, with the label "The Pussy Wagon." Occasionally, these shots are interrupted by clips of Gaga dancing in front of the truck in a leopard-patterned skin-tight outfit. Again, we see grainy television footage, this time on a television screen. The footage describes the murders, featuring a smug shot of Gaga and a grainy surveillance still of Beyoncé. Finally, we see the two escaping, Gaga wearing a long periwinkle dress and Beyoncé all in black, promising one another they will never return, driving off into the desert. The final screen shot features a heart and the words "To be continued."

What are we to make of how discourses about whiteness and race are deployed by Gaga in this video? Here Lady Gaga takes on the persona of a tough, seasoned criminal, yet curiously she is still clad mostly in underwear. She walks with a "gangsta" swagger, slowly brushing her hair back with a plastic comb — "James Dean"-style — strutting with shoulders back, chin up, scanning the room side to side as if preparing for an inevitable violent altercation with another prisoner. Even her dance routines involve fighting moves such as punches and kicks. Scowling angrily at the camera she seems to yell the lyrics instead of singing them. The prison scenes also seek to represent an "authentic" tough, urban, street image. In portraying prison in this way, one might argue, the video effectively romanticizes this lifestyle (Traber 115). Gaga appropriates non-white cultures in order to accomplish this. Once again, it is crucial to note that it is white privilege that allows Gaga to perform non-white prison culture, without having to truly experience racial or class oppression.

By "playing" prison inmate and imitating what she understands to be prison behavior, Lady Gaga assumes that she has unlimited access to spaces, or to represent spaces un-commonly held by upper-class white women. As a white woman, she is not familiar with racialized obstacles to space (Sullivan 91–92, 103). The video's seeming assumption that prison is racially and class neutral reinforces notions of white privilege. In point of fact, according to The State University of New York-Binghamton's Center for Interdisciplinary Studies in Philosophy, Interpretation, and Culture, the number of nonwhite prisoners in the United States is significantly disproportionate to the number of white prisoners: 70 percent of prisoners in the United States are non-white (1).

In addition, the cinematic format of the "Telephone" music video reinforces systems of white privilege and racist discourse. In *Performing Whiteness*, Gwendolyn Foster contends that film historically has occupied space as "a living record of the performances of whiteness, class, gender and myriad identity markers, such as sexuality, nationality, and ethnicity" (1). When examined more closely, the viewer sees how "Telephone" prominently features whiteness, class and ethnicity issues. As noted earlier, the beginning of the video centers on this white privilege as the fashionable Gaga in designer prison stripes is paraded past groups of female prisoners behind bars — many of whom are women of color — before she hands the white guards her designer sunglasses to hold. Later, as Gaga enters the exercise yard wearing sunglasses made of jail currency cigarettes, segregated racial groups look on. Gaga maintains the focus of the gaze when her name is announced over the loudspeaker indicating she has a phone call. When Gaga answers her call in the larger cell, she is once again surrounded by women, grouped according to race, now fighting one another. Once the music begins, Gaga continues to make a spectacle of the prison system by presenting a group of white women in black, studded bikinis freely dancing outside of their cells while scantily clad, non-white prisoners watch from behind bars. A white female prison guard also freely surfs internet dating sites. As if this were not enough, Gaga repeatedly appears in what Foster describes as "whiteface" (4). Foster contends that whiteface "not only includes [...] unnaturally white makeup but also careful lighting and an insistence on the binaries of black and white" (1). This binary opposition appears in Gaga's dress as she enters the jail as well as in the black and white prison uniforms; her unnaturally white makeup, platinum blond hair and the bright lighting during the all-white dance scene further emphasize it. It continues in her subsequent interactions with Beyoncé. The flaunting of white privilege and the spectacle of the jail inevitably foreground institutionalized systems of power. One might rightly argue that this video mocks the prison system as an institution. Whether this satire brings productive ends or not remains debatable. However, the video shows white privilege at an institutional level and provides important conversational opportunities.

Whiteness and blackness continue to function as key visual tropes with

Beyoncé's arrival in the video. Gaga's white face contrasts with a black and white dress complete with an oversized black hat. Meanwhile, Beyoncé is clad in black, long black hair and black lipstick. Likewise, the dark lighting surrounding Beyoncé and her boyfriend directly contrasts the bright lighting surrounding Gaga, dressed in almost transparent clothing, as she prepares the poisoned food in a white kitchen. The men of color (who are apparently working for Gaga) also wear white. Interestingly, these deep color contrasts shift once Gaga and Beyoncé succeed in their murderous plot. Previously segregated racial groups immediately integrate. Once the people in the diner are successfully poisoned, the camera flashes to multiracial dancers clothed in variations of the American flag. Now the once all-white and all-black visual binary is replaced with red, white and blue. In fact, even Beyoncé's nail polish switches from pink and white to American flags once her boyfriend dies. The fact that Gaga appears in leopard print in a cutaway as the women make their getaway can be read in multiple ways as well. Historically, racist discourses have represented non-whites as savage, animalistic. Now, it is Gaga who sports the leopard outfit. The viewer is once again left to wonder — is this in fact a challenge to that racist discourse or a further reinforcement of it?

Much as with "Bad Romance," in "Telephone" Lady Gaga clearly destabilizes traditional discourses around sexuality and race. But what message is she sending? Once again, white women are oppressing other white women. Racial groups are segregated. Racism and sexism only seem to begin to disintegrate once men are out of the way (and a lot of other people, it would seem). This disintegration is not necessarily an overthrow of racist and sexist discourses, however, but rather an embracing of American patriotism. Discourses of American patriotism frequently obscure the ways in which racist and sexist discourses operate. Should we view this video as Lady Gaga's suggestion that only full democracy — a real patriotism — can dismantle racism and sexism? Yet again, the viewer faces a conundrum.

Pedagogical and Political Implications

The popularity of Lady Gaga creates crucial discursive spaces through which to examine white privilege and power relations operating at personal and institutional levels. Certainly Gaga's outrageous performative choices, from product placement and self-aggrandizement to extreme fashion and sexuality, draw attention to the problematic functions of fame, celebrity and pop culture in the United States. They also force us to consider the complex discourses around race in contemporary culture. Lady Gaga asserts that no one should think that her work is a simple celebration in the pursuit of every single aspect of fame. She is not celebrating these cultural aspects but rather, as she explains to Larry King, making an attempt to "put everything on the table and then reject it." Whether or not she is successful in her attempt to challenge traditional discourses of oppression, however — particularly claims about whiteness and racism — does not diminish the contradictions she embodies nor the crucial controversial conversations she ignites.

Often our cultural examinations of racial discourses are not only extremely difficult but can also become rather limited and circumscribed. We need to challenge racist representations of people of color in the mainstream media. We must also examine exactly how white privilege enables us to elide crucial questions about how whiteness operates to reinforce privilege and perpetuate the othering of non-whites. Some people may be tempted to claim that while they are not at all opposed to interrogating how whiteness grants privilege and tends to minimize the insidious operation of racist discourses, their "whiteness" makes it hard for them to know how to most effectively enter the conversation. Foster describes this reaction, contending that white students too often simply "opt out as if they have no race, no ethnicity, and no investment in the stakes of race as social discourse" (5). And yet the invisibility of whiteness and the ways in which white privilege operates are some of the most vital discussions that we can have, spaces within which we can have great social growth. Lady Gaga is a crucial pop culture icon at this historical moment, surrounded as we are by these troubling discourses about post-racism. Gaga reflects white privilege and yet also challenges it, practicing it through her visual choices and by accentuating as well as playing with the satirical mirror of her own whiteness. In doing so — whether she finally succeeds in subverting white privilege or not — she brings the operation of this spectacle's systematic inner workings into sharp relief. Gaga draws unspoken aspects of privilege to the forefront of public scrutiny. Responses to Lady Gaga's videos also reflect the polarized nature of the political conversation. In a blog focusing on "the intersection of race and pop culture," the authors respond to the Lady Gaga phenomenon. They argue that Gaga reinforces oppressive white/black power relations and that she undeservedly receives attention over transgressive nonwhite performers because "they are already seen as non-normative" (1). As a result of such charged reactions, Lady Gaga's work offers a fertile source of classroom analysis. Her portrayal of whiteness as normative through satirical elements such as whiteface attempts to make visible that which typically operates invisibly and systematically as the norm. Focusing on Lady Gaga and how she takes up issues of race then may furnish a space to move past such restrictive binaries and toward a more complex focus of racial discourse, enabling us all to interrogate myriad, complex perspectives about discourses of race in our contemporary moment.

Lady Gaga has oftentimes admitted that she purposefully courts and cultivates contradictions. Yet it is amidst and within such contradictions that we can work to build bridges — even if sometimes only temporary — across racial divides. Examining Gaga's videos — "Bad Romance," "Telephone," and others — may afford teachers the opportunities to move discussions about discourses of racism in the classroom beyond dualism and opposition. Close examination affords the opportunity to observe how systems of privilege operate at larger social, political, and institutional levels. As Lea and Hefhand emphasize, abstract discussions about discourses of racism — ones rooted in amorphous theories or outside popular culture — are sometimes too vague to result in any form of empowerment or political change. Increasingly, we need for "students to exchange stories with each other and engage in critical dialogue in order for learning to occur" (23). Conversations about Lady Gaga — and contemporary popular culture in general — offer such possibilities. Since such discussions about discourses about race tend to be unnerving or polarizing, bringing such conversations into the realms of experience and the study of popular culture can have dramatic, political effects. As Foster maintains, "only by coming to a full awareness of the ways in which an artificially crafted identity [is] constructed to maintain hierarchy and divisiveness can any meaningful and useful dialogue on race begin" (23).

Lady Gaga's videos serve as a terrific point of departure. As Foster notes, it is only by "challenging the visual systems that result in othering" that we can begin to effectively de-center whiteness, revealing the problematic discourses that make it possible as well as how it constructs the "other" (4). This investigation of performative whiteness allows the conversation to move past limiting binaries that further polarize racial discourse, instead making what systematically operates at an invisible level a central focus of analysis. Only by making white privilege visible — something that Lady Gaga seems to both deploy and subvert — can any antiracist strides be made. Sullivan explains that "while rational, conscious argumentation has a role to play in the fight against racism, antiracist struggle ultimately will not be successful if the unconscious operations of white privilege are ignored" (22). Lady Gaga's videos encourage conversations about the operation of whiteness at an historical time when, as Shelly Tochluk argues in *Witnessing Whiteness: The Need to Talk About Race and How to Do It* and Melanie Bush asserts in *Everyday Forms of Whiteness: Understanding Racism in a Post-Racial World*; the very existence of overt racism is being challenged in our mainstream political and social discourses. Interestingly, in the video for "Telephone" when Beyoncé and Gaga make their transition to the diner scenes, they recite an idiom that has great value for how we need to view today's discourses of racism. They say that "trust is like a mirror; you can fix it when it's broken but you can still see the cracks in that mother fucker's reflection" ("Telephone"). This imagery is particularly apt with regard to satire and making white privilege visible. As Foster rightly contends, "it is in the cracks and fissures of performative whiteness that we can begin the dismantling of whiteness as a norm" (2). It is in the spaces in between — between privileging whiteness and dismantling it, between asserting the presence of racist practices and undermining them — in which our best conversations will emerge. It is here that we can best begin to challenge the troubling claims of "post-racism" in our time. The Lady — our Mother Monster — gives us a crucial place to start.

NOTES

1. For thirteen years, Laura Gray-Rosendale has been directing and designing the curriculum for the Northern Arizona University's S.T.A.R. (Successful Transition and Academic Retention). The foundational course in the curriculum is "Rhetoric in the Media," a class in which students learn about critical thinking, reading and writing; rhetorical analysis; and argumentation through the study of popular culture. All students in this program fulfill one or more criteria — lower income, racial or ethnic minority, and/or first generation college. Co-authors Stephanie Capaldo, Sherri Craig and Emily Davalos also teach in this program. At the end of the program each year, they design several final events that bring all of the program's students together for an energetic, analytic discussion about popular cultural texts. Recently, their conversations have centered upon the work of Lady Gaga.

Works Cited

Aesop. *Aesop's Fables*. Trans. Mons De Meziriac. Chicago: The Henneberry Co., 1897. Print.

"The Age Old Question: Is Lady Gaga a Feminist?" *Community.Feministing.com*, Feministcupcake. 7 July 2011. Web. 10 Nov. 2011.

Alien. Dir. Ridley Scott. Perf. Sigourney Weaver, Tom Skerritt, John Hurst. 20th Century–Fox, 1979. DVD.

Alien Quadrilogy: Alien, Aliens, Alien 3, Alien Resurrection. FOX. 1979–1997. DVD. 2003.

Alphonso, Doris Rita. "Introduction." *French Feminism Reader*. Ed. Kelly Oliver. Lanham: Rowman & Littlefield, 2000. 253–57. Print.

Altmann, Dennis. *Gore Vidal's America*. Cambridge: Polity, 2005. Print.

Amos, Tori. *Strange Little Girls*. Atlantic, 2001.

Anderson, Joel. "Burying 'Post-Racial.'" *Prospect.org*. The American Prospect, 28 July 2010. Web. 15 Oct. 2010.

Andsager, Julie and Kimberly Roe. "'What's Your Definition of Dirty, Baby?' Sex in Music Video." *Sexuality & Culture* 7.3 (2003): 79–97. Print.

American Idol. Prod. Simon Cowell. Fox. 2002. Television.

"Androgyny in Dada and Surrealism: From Marcel Duchamp to Lady Gaga." *awindowintomodernism.blogspot.com*. A Window Into Modernism, 26 Jan. 2011. Web. 26 Nov. 2011.

Angyal, Chloe. "Feminism's Unlikely Champion." *SpliceToday.com*. Splice Today, 24 Feb. 2010. Web. 5 Dec. 2010.

Aronowitz, Nona W. "Lady Gaga: Celebrity Feminist?" *OntheIssuesMagazine.com*. On the Issues Magazine, Winter (2011). Web. 1 Oct. 2011.

Artaud, Antonin. *Artaud le Mômo*. Paris: Bordas, 1947. Print.

_____. *Œuvres complètes*. XIII. Paris: Gallimard, 1974. Print.

_____. *Pour en finir avec le jugement de Dieu*. Paris: K Éditeur, 1948. Print.

_____. *Le Théâtre et son double*. Paris: Éditions Gallimard, 1964. Print.

Axon, Samuel. "Lady Gaga First Artist with One Billion Online Video Views." *Mashable.com*. Mashable, Mar. 2010. Web. 26 Mar. 2010.

Babuscio, Jack. "Camp and Gay Sensibility." *Camp Grounds: Style and Homosexuality*. Ed. David Bergman. Amherst: University of Massachusetts Press, 1993. 19–37. Print.

Bacon, Francis. *Self Portrait*. 1973. Collention of Richard Nagy, London.

Badder Romance. By Lady Gaga. Perf. Britnee Bloschichak, Ian Gonzales, Nikki D'Albora, and Kayla Chin. *YouTube*. 8 Jan. 2010. Web. 22 Nov. 2010.

Baker, Philip J. *Assessment in Psychiatric and Mental Health Nursing*. London: Stanley Thorns, 2004. Print.

Bakhtin, Mikhail. *Problems of Dostoevsky's Poetics*. Trans. Caryl Emerson. Minneapolis: University of Minnesota Press, 1984. Print.

_____. *Rabelais and His World*. Trans. Hélène Iswolsky. Bloomington: Indiana University Press, 1984. Print.

Barton, Laura. "'I've Felt Famous My Whole Life': Lady Gaga May Be No 1 in the Charts Right Now. But, as she tells Laura

Barton her ambitions stretch way beyond being a one-hit wonder." *Guardian.co.uk*. Guardian News and Media Limited, 21 Jan. 2009. Web. 12 Jan. 2010.

Baudelaire, Charles. *Œuvres complètes*. Paris: Éditions du Seuil, 1968. Print.

Baudrillard, Jean. *Selected Writings*. Mark Poster Ed. 2nd ed. Stanford: Stanford University Press, 2001. Print.

Bauer, Nancy. "Lady Power." *New York Times*. Opinionator, 20 June 2010. Web. 19 Dec. 2010.

Beckett, Sandra L. *Red Riding Hood for All Ages: A Fairy-Tale Icon in Cross-Cultural Contexts*. Detroit: Wayne State University Press, 2008. Print.

Beckman, Rachel. "'Thirty Two Kilos': A Stark Look at Anorexia." *WashingtonPost.com*. Washington Post Company, 8 Jan. 2009. Web. 30 Nov. 2009.

Bedard, Ella. "'Can't Read My Poker Face': The Postmodern Aesthetic & Mimesis of Lady Gaga." *Gaga Stigmata: Critical Writings and Art About Lady Gaga*. Eds. Kate Durbin and Meghan Vicks. 17 Aug. 2010. Web. 7 Jan. 2011.

bell hooks. *Black Looks: Race and Representation*. Boston: South End Press, 1992. Print.

Bennett, Andy. "Towards a Cultural Sociology of Popular Music." *Journal of Sociology* 44 (2008): 419–32. Print.

Berger, Peter L. and Thomas Luckmann. *The Social Construction of Reality*. New York: Anchor, 1967. Print.

Bergman, David. *Camp Grounds: Style and Homosexuality*. Amherst: University of Massachusetts Press, 1993. Print.

Beyhar, Joy. Interview With Kara Dioguardi; Interview With Alice Cooper. *Joy Behar Show*. CNN. 6 May 2011.

Beyoncé. "Video Phone." *I Am ... Sasha Fierce*. Columbia, 2008. Dir. Hype Williams. Music Video.

Blalock, Meghan. "2010: A Gagadyssey." *Gaga Stigmata: Critical Writings and Art About Lady Gaga*. Eds. Kate Durbin and Meghan Vicks. 10 May 2010. Web. 7 Jan. 2011.

Blau, Herbert. *The Audience*. Baltimore: Johns Hopkins University Press, 1990. Print.

Bliss, Jeff. "Being Al Yankovic: Getting Inside his Weirdness' Head." *Cal Poly Magazine*. Spring 2000: 2–5. PDF file.

Bolton, Lesley. *The Complete Book of Baby Names*. Naperville: Sourcebooks, Inc., 2009. Print.

Booker, Keith M. *Joyce, Bakhtin, and the Literary Tradition: Toward a Comparative Cultural Poetics*. Ann Arbor: University of Michigan Press, 1998. Print.

Boorstin, Daniel J. *The Image: A Guide to Pseudo-Events in America*. New York: Atheneum, 1961. Print.

Booth, Mark. "*Campe-toi!*: On the Origins and Definitions of Camp." *Camp: Queer Aesthetics and the Performing Subject—A Reader*. Ed. Fabio Cleto. Edinburgh: Edinburgh University Press, 2008: 66–79. Print.

Bordo, Susan. *Unbearable Weight: Feminism, Western Culture, and the Body*. Tenth Anniversary Ed. Berkeley: University of California Press, 2004. Print.

Bourke, Philippa. "Lady Gaga's Granny Shaper out in the Open." *Monstersand-Critics.com*. 29 Jan. 2010. Web. 10 Feb. 2011.

Braidotti, Rosi. *Nomadic Subjects: Embodiment and Sexual Difference in Contemporary Feminist Theory*. New York: Columbia University Press, 1994. Print.

Breton, André. "*Manifeste du surréalisme*." *Œuvres complètes*. Vol. 1. Paris: Gallimard, 1988. Print.

Breton, André, Hugo Valentine, Nusch Éluard and Paul Éluard. *Exquisite Corpse*. 1934. Crayon on paper. Musée d'Art et d'Histoire, Saint-Denis.

Broberg, Anders G., Ingrid Hjalmers, and Lauri Nevonen. "Eating Disorders, Attachment and Interpersonal Difficulties: A Comparison Between 18-to 24-Year-Old Patients and Normal Controls." *European Eating Disorders Review* 9 (2001): 381–96. Print.

Brockett, Oscar. *Century of Innovation: A History of European and American Theatre and Drama since 1870*. Englewood Cliffs, Prentice-Hall, 1973. Print.

Brottman, Mikita. *High Theory/Low Culture*. New York: Palgrave Macmillan, 2005. Print.

Brown, Tina. *The Diana Chronicles.* New York: Doubleday, 2007. Print.

Buckland, Fiona. *Impossible Dance: Club Culture and Queer World Making.* Middletown: Wesleyan University Press, 2002. Print.

Bush, Melanie E. *Everyday Forms of Whiteness: Understanding Racism in a Post-Racial World.* New York: Rowman and Littlefield, 2011. Print.

Butler, Judith. "Against Proper Objects." *Feminism Meets Queer Theory.* Ed. Elizabeth Weed and Naomi Schor. Bloomington: Indiana University Press, 1997. 1–30. Print.

_____. "Critically Queer." GLQ: A Journal of Lesbian and Gay Studies 1.1 (1993): 17–32. Print.

_____. *Gender Trouble: Feminism and the Subversion of Identity.* New York: Routledge, 1990, 2006, 2008, 2010. Print.

Caged. Dir. John Cromwell. Perf. Eleanor Parker, Agnes Moorehead, and Ellen Corby. Warner Bros., 1950. Film.

Caged Heat. Dir. Jonathan Demme. Perf. Juanita Brown, Erica Gavin and Roberta Collins. New World Pictures, 1974. Film.

Callahan, Maureen. *Poker Face: The Rise and Rise of Lady Gaga.* New York: Hyperion, 2010. Print.

Camp, Kevin. "Lady Gaga and Emergent Feminism." *Examiner.com.* Examiner, 14 Mar. 2010. Web. 10 Oct. 2011.

Campbell, Joseph. *Reflections on the Art of Living.* San Anselmo: Joseph Campbell Foundation, 2011. N. pag. EPUB file.

Carpenter, Elle. "Lady Gaga Unleashes "Monster" With Dr. Dre: Headphones First, Song Next? Singer on New Tracks." *RollingStone.com.* Rolling Stone, 1 Oct. 2009. Web. 18 Nov. 2011.

Cavanagh, Kristie. "Lady Gaga Thought to be SHOWstudio's Male Model Jo Calderone Seen in *Vogue Hommes* Japan." *NYDailyNews.com.* New York Daily News, 1 July 2010. Web. 1 Sep. 2010.

Cher. "Believe." *Believe.* Warner Bros., 1998. CD

_____. "If I Could Turn Back Time." *Heart of Stone.* Geffen Records, 1989. Dr. Marty Callner. Music Video.

Cho, Alex. "Lady Gaga, Balls-Out: Recu-perating Queer Performativity." *FlowTV.* Department of Radio, Television, and Film, University of Texas at Austin, 7 Aug. 2009. Web. 29 Jan. 2010.

Christian, Elizabeth Barfoot. "Rev. of *Poker Face: The Rise and Rise of Lady Gaga,* au. Maureen Callahan." *Journal of American Culture* 34.2 (2011): 209. *Academic Search Complete.* EBSCO. Web. 21 Sep. 2011. Print.

City of Lost Children. Dir. Marc Caro. Perf. Ron Perlman, Daniel Emilfork and Judith Vittet. Sony Pictures, 1995. Film.

Cixous, Hélène. "The Laugh of the Medusa." *French Feminism Reader.* Ed. Kelly Oliver. Lanham: Rowman & Littlefield, 2000. 257–75. Print.

Clapp, Rodney. "From Shame to Fame." *The Christian Century,* 128.15 (2011): 45. Print.

Clery, E. J. *The Rise of Supernatural Fiction, 1762–1800.* Cambridge Studies in Romanticism. 12. 1999 ed. Cambridge, Cambridge University Press, 1995. Print.

Cleto, Fabio. *Camp: Queer Aesthetics and the Performing Subject—A Reader.* Edinburgh: Edinburgh University Press, 2008. Print.

Clott, Sharon. "Was Lady Gaga's Meat Dress Real?" *Style.MTV.com.* MTV Style, 13 Sep. 2010. Web. 15 Oct. 2010.

Cobb, Ben. "AnOther Thing I Wanted to Tell You: Alejandro Jodorowsky on Lady Gaga & Surrealism." *AnotherMag.com.* Another, 13 Apr. 2011. Web. 26 Nov. 2011.

Cochrane, Kira. "Is Lady Gaga a Feminist Icon." *TheGuardian.com.* Guardian, 16 Sep. 2010. Web. 5 Jan. 2011.

Cohan, Steven. *Incongruous Entertainment: Camp, Cultural Value, and the MGM Musical.* Durham: Duke University Press, 2005. Print.

Cohen, Jeffrey Jerome. "Monster Culture (Seven Theses)." *Monster Theory: Reading Culture.* Ed. Jeffrey Jerome Cohen. Minneapolis: University of Minnesota Press, 1996. 3–25. Print.

Cohen, Sara. 2001. "Popular Music, Gender and Sexuality." *The Cambridge Companion to Pop and Rock,* eds. S. Frith, W. Straw and J. Street. Cambridge: Cambridge University Press (2001). 226–42. Print.

Common Sense Media. "Common Sense Media: Celebrity Role Models." *YouTube*. Web. 7 Sep. 2010.

Connan, Frances, Nick Troop, Sabine Landau, Iain C. Campbell, and Janet Treasure. "Poor Social Comparison and the Tendency to Submissive Behavior in Anorexia Nervosa." *International Journal of Eating Disorders* 40:8 (Dec. 2007): 733–39. Print.

Connell, Robert W. *Gender and Power: Society, the Person, and Sexual Politics*. Stanford: Stanford University Press, 1987. Print.

Cooks, Leda M., and Jennifer S. Simpson, eds. *Whiteness, Pedagogy, Performance: Dis/Placing Race*. Boston: Lexington Books, 2008. Print.

Coppinger, Raymond and Lorna Coppinger. *Dogs: A Startling New Understanding of Canine Origin, Behavior, & Evolution*. New York: Scribner, 2001. Print.

Core, Philip. *Camp: The Lie that Tells the Truth*. London: Plexus, 1984. Print.

Corona, Victor P. "Memory, Monsters, and Lady Gaga." *Journal of Popular Culture* 44 (2011): 1–19. Print.

Cronberg, Anja. "Interview with Lady Gaga." *H&M Magazine* (Winter 2009): 78–80. Print.

Cronin, Melissa. "Inside Lady Gaga's Twisted World." *Star* 13 Oct. 2010: 42–45. Print.

Crowe, Lauren Goldstein. *Isabella Blow: A Life in Fashion*. New York: Thomas Dunne, 2010. Print.

Dahl, Roald. "Little Red Riding Hood and the Wolf." *The Classic Fairy Tales*. Ed. Maria Tatar. New York: W.W. Norton, 1999. 21–22. Print.

Dalí, Salvador. *Geopolitical Child Watches the Birth of the New Man*. 1943. Sculpture. Dalí Theatre-Museum, Figueres.

Daly, Bridget. "Lady Gaga Talks Penis Rumors." *Hollyscoop.com*. Hollyscoop, 23 Feb. 2010. Web. 15 Dec. 2010.

Däwes, Birgit. "Sound Tracks to the Frontier: Gender, Difference and Music in the American Road Movie." *Dichotonies: Gender and Music*. Ed. Beate Neumeier. Heidelberg: Winter, 2009. 321–39. Print.

DeLamotte, Eugenia C. *Perils of the Night: A Feminist Study of Nineteenth-Century Gothic*. Oxford: Oxford University Press, 1990. Print.

Denisoff, Dennis. *Aestheticism and Sexual Parody: 1840–1940*. Cambridge: Cambridge University Press, 2001. Print.

Desperately Seeking Susan. Dir. Leora Barish. Perf. Rosanna Arquette, Madonna and Aidan Quinn. Orion Pictures, 1985. Film.

Devitt, Rachel E. "Girl on Girl: Passing, Ambivalence, and Queer Musical Time in Gender Performative Negotiations of Popular Music." Diss. University of Washington, 2009. *ProQuest Dissertations and Theses*. Web. 3 Jan. 2011.

_____. "Girl on Girl: Fat Femmes, Bio-Queens, and Redefining Drag." *Queering the Popular Pitch*. Eds. Sheila Whiteley and Jennifer Rycenga. New York: Routledge, 2006. 27–39. Print.

"Diary of a Teenage Killer: Emma Humphreys." *The Guardian* 10 Nov. 2003: 8. Print.

Dickinson, Kay. "'Believe?' Vocoders, Digitalised Female Identity and Camp." *Popular Music* 20.3 (2001): 333–47. Print.

Dinh, James. "Lady Gaga Reveals *The Fame: Monster* Re-Release Details." *MTV.com*. MTV Networks, 8 Oct. 2009. Web. 17 Jan. 2009.

_____. "Lady Gaga Says 'Born This Way' Video Shows 'The Birth of A New Race.'" *MTV.com*. MTV Networks, 28 Feb. 2011. Web. 26 Nov. 2011.

Ditzian, Eric. "Lady Gaga Reveals Real Meaning of 'Dance in the Dark.'" *MTV.com*. MTV Networks, 16 Dec. 2009. Web. 22 Jan. 2010.

Dodds, Sherril. "From Busby Berkeley to Madonna: Music Video and Popular Dance." *Ballroom, Boogie, Shimmy Sham, Shake: A Social and Popular Dance Reader*. Ed. Julie Malnig. Champaign: University of Illinois Press, 2009. 248–59. Print.

Dowd Hall, Jacqueline. "The Mind that Burns in Each Body: Women, Rape, and Racial Violence." *Powers of Desire*. Eds. Ann Snitow, Christine Stansell, and Sharon Thompson. New York: Monthly Review Press, 1983. 328–49. Print.

D'Souza, Dinesh. "Obama and Post-Racist America." *Townhall.com*. Townhall, 28 Jan. 2009. Web. 15 Oct. 2010.

Dyer, Jennifer. "The Metaphysics of the Mundane: Understanding Andy Warhol's Serial Imagery." *Artibus et Historiae* 25.49 (2004): 33–47. Print.

Dyer, Richard. *The Culture of Queers.* London: Routledge, 2002. Print.

_____. *Heavenly Bodies.* New York: Routledge, 2004. Print.

_____. "Judy Garland and Gay Men." *Queer Cinema: The Film Reader.* Ed. Harry M. Benshoff. New York: Routledge, 2005. 153–65. Print.

_____. *White.* New York: Routledge, 1997. Print.

Dyhouse, Carol. *Glamour: History, Women, Feminism.* London: Zed Books, 2010. Print.

Eager, Sophie. "Lady Gaga Talks about Hermaphrodite Rumors." *Monstersand-Critics.com.* WotR Ltd., 25 Jan. 2010. Web. 30 Jan. 2010.

Eco, Umberto. "Frames of Comic Freedom." *Carnival!* Ed. Thomas A. Seebeok. Berlin: Mouton, 1984. 1–9. Print.

Edwards, Posy. *Lady Gaga: Me & You.* London: Orion, 2010. Print.

"Eh Eh (Nothing Else I Can Say)." *Lady-gaga.com.* LadyGaga, 5 Feb. 2009. Web. 28 Sep. 2011.

Eisner, Douglas. "*Myra Breckinridge* and the Pathology of Heterosexuality." *The Queer Sixties.* Ed. Patricia Juliana Smith. New York: Routledge, 1999. 255–70. Print.

Eleveld, Kerry. "View From Washington." *Advocate.com.* Here Media, Inc., 18 Sep. 2010. Web. 12 Jan. 2011.

Elliot, Patricia and Katrina Roen. "Transgenderism and the Question of Embodiment: Promising Queer Politics?" *GLQ: A Journal of Lesbian and Gay Studies* 4.2 (1998): 231–61. Print.

Emerson, Caryl. *The First Hundred Years of Mikhail Bakhtin.* Princeton: Princeton University Press, 1997. Print.

Emert, Allison. "Lady Gaga Promotes Anorexia." *Examiner.com.* Examiner, 12 Dec. 2009. Web. 12 Jan. 2010.

Ernst, Max. *Men Shall Know Nothing of This.* 1923. Oil on canvas. Tate Gallery, London.

Esther, John. "The Wild and Beautiful Entertaining Life of Lady Gaga." *Lesbian News* 34.8 (2009): 28–31. Print.

Everett, Cristina. "In the flesh: Lady Gaga dons raw meat on the cover of *Vogue Hommes* Japan." *NYDailyNews.com.* NY Daily News, 7 Sep. 2010. Web. 12 Jan. 2011.

"Extravagant Lady Gaga Broke, Homeless." *DailyTelegraph.com.* Daily Telegraph, 18 Feb. 2010. Web. 18 Dec. 2010.

Fame. Prod. Christopher Gore. NBC. 1982. Television.

Feil, Ken. "Queer Comedy." *Comedy: A Geographic and Historical Guide.* Ed. Maurice Charney. Westport: Praeger, 2005. 477–92. Print.

Ferreday, Debra. "Showing the Girl: The New Burlesque." *Feminist Theory,* 9.1 (2008): 47–65. Print.

Ferris, Kerry O. "The Sociology of Celebrity." *Sociology Compass* 1 (2007): 371–84. Print.

"Feud of the Week." *Us Weekly* 13 June 2011: 14. Print.

Forte, Jeanie. "Women's Performance Art: Feminism and Postmodernism." *Performing Feminisms: Feminist Critical Theory and Theatre.* Ed. Sue-Ellen Case. Baltimore: The Johns Hopkins University Press, 1990. 251–69. Print.

Foster, Gwendolyn Audrey. *Performing Whiteness* (SUNY Series in Postmodern Culture). Albany: SUNY, 2003. Print.

Foucault, Michel. *Abnormal: Lectures at the Collège de France, 1974–1975.* New York: Picador, 2003. Print.

Frank, Lisa and Paul Smith, eds. *Madonnarama: Essays on Sex and Popular Culture.* Pittsburgh: Cleis Press, 1993. Print.

Frankenberg, Ruth. *White Women, Race Matters: The Social Construction of Whiteness.* Minneapolis: University of Minnesota Press, 1993. Print.

Frere-Jones, Sasha. "Ladies Wild." *New Yorker* 85.11 (2009): 62–64. *Academic Search Complete.* EBSCO. Web. 21 Sep. 2011.

Fricke, John. *Judy Garland: A Portrait in Art & Anecdote.* New York: Bullfinch Press, 2003. Print.

Frith, Simon, Will Straw, and John Street, eds. *The Cambridge Companion to Pop and Rock*. Cambridge: Cambridge University Press, 2001. Print.

Fry, Stephen. "Lady Gaga Takes Tea with Mr Fry." *FT.com*. Financial Times, 27 May 2011. Web. 30 May 2011.

Fury, Alexander. "ShowStudio.com Interview with Lady Gaga." *SHOWstudio.com*. SHOWstudio, 30 May 2010. Web. 10 June 2010.

Gaffield-Knight, Richard. "Antonin Artaud: In Theory, Process and Praxis." MA thesis. State University of New York at Binghamton, 1993. Print.

"Gaga: We've Found Our Fierce Advocate." *Advocate.com*. Advocate, 21 Sep. 2010. Web. 12 Jan. 2011.

Gamson, Joshua. *Claims to Fame: Celebrity in Contemporary America*. Berkeley: University of California Press, 1994.

Gardner, Elysa. "Lady Gaga, Truly 'Born' to be Fame's Mistress." *USA Today*. 24 May 2011: Life 1d. *Academic Search Complete*. EBSCO. Web. 21 Sep. 2011.

Garrard, Mary D. "Feminism: Has It Changed Art History?" *Heresies* 4 (1978): 59–60. Print.

Gentlemen Prefer Blondes. Dir. Howard Hawks. Perf. Jane Russell, Marilyn Monroe and Charles Coburn. 20th Century–Fox, 1953. Film.

George, Lianne. "Going Gaga." *Maclean's* 122.21 (2009): 47–49. *Academic Search Complete*. EBSCO. Web. 21 Sep. 2011.

Gill, Rosalind. "Postfeminist Media Culture: Elements of a Sensibility." *European Journal of Cultural Studies*, 10.2 (2007): 147–71. Print.

Gillray, James. "Tales of Wonder!" *The History of Gothic Fiction*. Ed. Markman Ellis. Edinburgh: Edinburgh University Press, 2003. 95. Print.

Girl, Interrupted. Dir. James Mangold. Perf. Winona Ryder, Angelina Jolie and Whoopi Goldberg. Columbia Pictures, 1999. Film.

Glazer, Eliot. "'Bad Romance' Parody Sweeps the Web–Badder Romance, Better Romance?" *Urlesque*. Urlesque, 11 Jan. 2010. Web. 2 Feb. 2010.

Gliatto, Tom. "Lady Gaga and Camille Paglia." *TheHuffingtonPost.com*. Huffington Post, 24 Sep. 2010. Web. 15 Oct. 2011.

Goodman, Lizzy. *Lady Gaga: Critical Mass Fashion*. New York: St. Martin's, 2010. Print.

Gorgan, Elena. "Lady Gaga Stays Slim by Starving Herself." *Softpedia.com*. Softpedia, 23 May 2009. Web. 15 Jan. 2010.

Graham, Elyse. "Interview Request, American Scholar." Message to the author. 1 Nov. 2010. E-mail.

_____. "Monster Theory." *The American Scholar*. 80.4 (2011): 12–13. Print.

Grease. Dir. Randal Kleiser. Perf. John Travolta, Olivia Newton-John, and Stockard Channing. Paramount, 1978. Film.

Griffin, Sean. *Tinker Belles and Evil Queens: The Walt Disney Company from the Inside Out*. New York: New York University Press, 2000. Print.

Grigoriadis, Vanessa. "Growing Up Gaga." *NewYorkMagazine.com*. New York Magazine, 28 Mar. 2010. Web. 7 Jan. 2011.

Grimm, Jacob and Wilhelm Grimm. "Little Red Cap." *The Classic Fairy Tales*. Ed. Maria Tatar. New York: W.W. Norton and Company, 1999. 13–16. Print.

_____. "Snow White." *The Classic Fairy Tales*. Ed. Maria Tatar. New York: W.W. Norton and Company, 1999. 83–89. Print.

Guisinger, Shan. "Adapted to Flee Famine: Adding an Evolutionary Perspective on Anorexia Nervosa." *Psychological Review* 110:4 (Oct. 2003): 745–61. Print.

_____. "Competing Paradigms for Anorexia Nervosa." *American Psychologist* 63.3 (Apr. 2008): 199–200. Print.

Halberstam, Jack. "You Cannot Gaga Gaga." *Gaga Stigmata: Critical Writings and Art About Lady Gaga*. Blogger, 6 Apr. 2010. Web. 1 Sep. 2010.

Halberstam, Judith. *In a Queer Time and Place: Transgender Bodies, Subcultural Lives*. New York: New York University Press, 2005. Print.

_____. *Skin Shows: Gothic Horror and the Technology of Monsters*. Durham: Duke University Press, 1995. Print.

Halperin, Shirley. "Lady Gaga's 'Born This Way' Is Madonna's 'Express Yourself,' Says Ryan Tedder." *Hollywood Reporter*. 13 Feb. 2011. Web. 30 Sep. 2011.

Hamilton, Anna. "The Transcontinental

Disability Choir: Disability Chic? (Temporary) Disability in Lady Gaga's 'Paparazzi.'" *BitchMagazine.org*. Bitch Media, 20 Nov. 2009. Web. 16 Dec. 2010.

Harcourt, Wendy. "Editorial: Lady Gaga Meets Ban Ki-Moon." *Development* 53.2 (2010): 141–43. Print.

Hardt, Michael and Antonio Negri. *Multitude: War and Democracy in the Age of Empire*. New York: Penguin, 2004. Print.

"Has Lady Gaga Killed Off Sex? Top Feminist Claims Biggest Pop Star on the Planet Is All Style and no Substance." *DailyMail.com*. Daily Mail, 14 Sep. 2010. Web. 10 Oct. 2010.

Hazel, Witch. "Brew Bits: Toni Braxton's Sister & Lady Gaga?" *WitchesBrewOnline.com*. Witches' Brew, 24 May 2010. Web. 10 Oct. 2010.

Hedges, Chris. *Empire of Illusion: The End of Literacy and the Triumph of Spectacle*. New York: Nation Books, 2009. Print.

Hegel, Georg Wilhelm Friedrich. *Phenomenology of Spirit*. Trans. A.V. Miller. Oxford: Oxford University Press, 1979. Print.

Hennessy, Rosemary. "Queer Theory: A Review of the *differences* Special Issue and Wittig's *The Straight Mind*." *SIGNS* 118.4 (1993): 964–973. Print.

Herbert, Emily. *Lady Gaga: Behind the Fame*. New York: Overlook Press, 2010. Print.

Hiatt, Brian. "Monster Goddess. (Cover story)." *Rolling Stone* 1132 (2011): 40–47. *Academic Search Complete*. EBSCO. Web. 21 Sep. 2011.

_____. "New York Doll." *Rolling Stone* 11 June 2009: 56. Print.

Hill, Mike. *Whiteness: A Critical Reader*. New York: New York University Press, 1997. Print.

Hintz-Zambrano, Katie. "Lady Gaga Plays Pantless Witch in Vogue's Fashion Fairy Tale." *StyleList.com*. AOL Inc., 14 Nov. 2009. Web. 12 Jan. 2011.

Hoby, Hermione. "So Much For Lady Gaga's Feminist Credentials." *Guardian. co.uk*. Guardian, 27 Feb. 2010. Web. 5 Jan. 2011.

Höch, Hannah. *Mutter: Aus einem ethnographischen Museum*. 1930. Photomontage with watercolor and magazine illustrations cut out and pasted on paper. Centre Pompidou, Musée national d'art moderne, Paris.

Homans, Margaret. "'Women of Color' Writers and Feminist Theory." *Feminisms: An Anthology of Literary Theory and Criticism*. Eds. Robyn R. Warhol and Diane Price Herndl. Houndmills: Macmillan, 1997. 406–24. Print.

Hostel: Part II. Dir. Eli Roth. Perf. Lauren German, Heather Matarazzo and Bijou Phillips. Lionsgate, 3007. Film.

Hsu, Hua. "The End of White America." *TheAtlantic.com*. Atlantic, Jan. 2009. Web. 10 Dec. 2010.

Hudson, John. "Lady Gaga's Ambiguous Feminism." *TheAtlanticWire.com*. Atlantic Wire, 25 Feb. 2010. Web. 12 Dec. 2010.

TheHuffingtonPost.com. Huffington Post, 25 Aug. 2010. Web. 1 Oct. 2010.

Hunt, Carol. "This Lady Will Never Be a Tramp." *Independent.ie*. Independent, 26 Sep. 2010. Web. 15 Oct. 2010.

Hutcheon, Linda. *Irony's Edge: The Theory and Politics of Irony*. London: Routledge, 1994. Print.

_____. *A Theory of Parody: The Teachings of Twentieth-Century Art Forms*. New York: Methuen, 1985. Print.

Huysmans, Joris-Karl. *À Rebours*. Paris: Gallimard, 1977. Print.

Imam, Jareen. "Crenshaw Discusses Issues with 'Post-Racial' Worlds." *EmoryWheel. com*.

Emory Wheel, 25 Jan. 2010. Web. 2 Jan. 2011.

Interscope Records. "Lady Gaga Returns With 8 New Songs on The Fame Monster." Press Release. PR Newswire. United News Media, 8 Oct. 2009. Web. 21 Dec. 2010.

Interview by Larry King. *CNN Larry King Live*. CNN. New York: 1 June 2010. Television.

"Interview with Lady Gaga." *SHOWstudio. com*. SHOWstudio, 30 May 2010. Web. 22 Dec. 2010.

Interview with Neil Strauss. "The Broken Heart and Violent Fantasies of Lady Gaga." *Rolling Stone* 1108/1109 (2010): 66–74. Print.

Interview with Touré. "Lady Gaga: On the

Record." *On the Record with Fuse.* Fuse. 3 Nov. 2009.

Interview with Touré. "Lady Gaga: The Lost Tapes." *On the Record with Fuse.* Fuse. 28 Apr. 2010.

Isherwood, Christopher. *The World in the Evening.* Minneapolis: University of Minnesota Press, 1999. Print.

Itzkoff, Dave. "Serving Pop Stars, but on a Skewer." *NewYorkTimes.com.* New York Times, 9 June 2011. Web. 28 Sep. 2011.

Jackson, Michael. "Thriller." *Thriller.* Epic Records, 1982. Music Video. 27 Nov. 2011.

Jaffe, Sarah. "Lady Gaga: Pop Star for a Country and an Empire in Decline." *AlterNet.com.* AlterNet: Media & Culture, 26 July 2010. Web. 22 Dec. 2010.

James, Robin. "From Dance in the Dark, Little Monsters: On Gaga's Post-Goth Posthumanism." *Gaga Stigmata: Critical Writings and Art About Lady Gaga.* Ed. Kate Durbin and Meghan Vicks, 29 Nov. 2010. Web. 7 Jan. 2011.

Jameson, Fredric. "Postmodernism and Consumer Society." *Postmodernism and Its Discontents.* Ed. E. Ann Kaplan. London/New York: Verso, 1988. 13–29. Print.

Jennings, Wade. "The Star as Cult Icon: Judy Garland." *The Cult Film Experience: Beyond All Reason.* Ed. Jay P. Telotte. Austin: University of Texas Press, 1991. 90–105. Print.

"Jo Calderone, Likely Lady Gaga in Disguise, Models for *Vogue Hommes* Japan."

Johnson, Corey. "Interview with Lady Gaga at Gay Rights Rally." *YouTube.* 11 Oct. 2009. Web. 5 Jan. 2011.

Jones, Amelia. *The Feminism and Visual Culture Reader.* New York: Taylor and Francis, 2002. Print.

Jones, Michael. "Lady Gaga as Gay Culture Warrior." *News.Change.org.* Gay Rights/Change, 14 Aug. 2009. Web. 3 Jan. 2011.

Jurgensen, John. "The Lessons of Lady Gaga." *The Wall Street Journal.* Dow Jones & Company, Inc., 29 Jan. 2010. Web. 1 Feb. 2010.

Kaufman, Gil. "Lady Gaga's 'Born This Way' Is Fastest-Selling Single in iTunes History." *MTV.com.* MTV Networks, 18 Feb. 2011. Web. 13 Sep. 2011.

Keats, John. "Lamia." *John Keats: The Major Works.* Oxford World's Classics. Ed. Elizabeth Cook. 2001 ed. Oxford: Oxford University Press, 1990. 305–23. Print.

Keller, Jessalynn. "'I'm Not a Feminist ... I Love Men': Rethinking Lady Gaga's Postfeminist Rhetoric and Its Potential for Social Change." *Mediacommons.futureofthebook.org.* in media res, 2 Aug. 2010. Web. 20 Oct. 2011.

Kelly, Kevin. "Becoming Screen Literate." *nytimes.com/pages/magazine.* New York Times Magazine, 21 Nov. 2008. Web. 26 Jan. 2010.

Kill Bill: Vol. 1. Dir. Quentin Tarantino. Perf. Uma Thurman, David Carradine and Daryl Hannah. Miramax, 2003. Film.

Kimmel, Michael. *The Gendered Society.* 4th ed. New York: Oxford University Press, 2011. Print.

King, Larry. Interview with Lady Gaga. *Larry King Live.* CNN. 1 June 2010. Print.

Kinser, Jeremy. "Portrait of a Lady." *Advocate.com.* Advocate, 5 July 2011. Web. 22 Oct. 2011.

Klinger, Barbara. *Melodrama and Meaning: History, Culture, and the Films of Douglas Sirk.* Bloomington: Indiana University Press, 1994. Print.

Knapp, Bettina L. *Antonin Artaud: A Man of Vision.* New York: Avon Books, 1969.

Koch, Eileen. "Lady Gaga Becomes a 'Billion-Hit' Artist." *BBC World Service.* BBC, 26 Mar. 2010. Web. 30 Mar. 2010.

Komitee, Shana. "A Student's Guide to Performance Studies," Web. University of Harvard I-sites, 2011.

Kreps, Daniel. "'Alejandro' Director Breaks Down Lady Gaga's Racy Video." *RollingStone.com.* Rolling Stone, 8 June 2010. Web. 26 Nov. 2011.

_____. "Lady Gaga Premiers 'Bad Romance,' Her Craziest Video Yet." *Rollingstone.com.* Rolling Stone, 10 Nov. 2009. Web. 18 Jan 2010.

_____. "Lady Gaga Protests Arizona Immigration Law in Phoenix." *Rollingstone.com.* Rolling Stone, 2 Aug. 2010. Web. 21 Dec. 2010.

"Kristen Stewart in *Elle UK*: Fame is Like Rape." *TheHuffingtonPost.com.* Huffington Post. 2 June 2010. Web. 12 Jan. 2011.

Kumbier, Alana. "One Body, Some Genders: Drag Performance and Technologies." *Journal of Homosexuality* 43.3–4 (2002): 191–200. Print.

Kurzman, Charles, Chelise Anderson, et al. "Celebrity Status." *Sociological Theory* 25 (2007): 347–67. Print.

Lady Gaga. "Alejandro." *The Fame Monster.* Interscope Records, 2009. CD.

_____. "Alejandro." *Ladygaga.com.* Lady-Gaga. 6 Aug. 2010. Music Video.

_____. "Bad Romance." *The Fame Monster.* Interscope Records, 2009. CD.

_____. "Bad Romance." Dir. Francis Lawrence. *YouTube.com.* 23 Nov. 2009. Web. 10 Jan. 2011. Music Video.

_____. "Beautiful, Dirty, Rich." *The Fame.* Interscope Records, 2008. CD.

_____. "Beautiful, Dirty, Rich." Dir. Melina Matsoukas. *YouTube.com.*13 Dec. 2009. Web. 12 Jan. 2011. Music Video.

_____. "Born This Way." *Born This Way.* Streamline Records, 2011. CD

_____. "Born This Way." Dir. Nick Night. *Ladygaga.com.* 28 Feb. 2011. Web. 28 Sep. 2011. Music Video.

_____. "Dance in the Dark." *The Fame Monster.* Interscope Records, 2009. CD.

_____. "The Edge of Glory." *Born This Way.* Streamline Records, 2011. CD

_____. "Fashion of His Love." *Born This Way.* Streamline Records, 2011. CD

_____. "Hair." *Born This Way.* Streamline Records, 2011. CD.

_____. "Highway Unicorn." *Born This Way.* Streamline Records, 2011. CD.

_____. "Judas." *Born This Way.* Streamline Records, 2011. CD.

_____. "Judas." Dir. Lady Gaga and Laurieann Gibson. *Ladygaga.com.* 3 May 2011. Web. 28 Sep. 2011. Music Video.

_____. "Just Dance." *The Fame.* Interscope Records, 2008. CD.

_____. "LoveGame." *So You Think You Can Dance*, Los Angeles. 31 July 2008. Live Performance.

_____. "LoveGame." Dir. Joseph Kahn. *YouTube.com*, 16 June 2009. Web. 22 Dec. 2010. Music Video.

_____. "Marry the Night." *Born This Way.* Streamline Records, 2011. CD.

_____. "Monster." *The Fame Monster.* Interscope Records, 2009. CD.

_____. *The Monster Ball Tour.* May 21 2010, Palais Omnisports de Paris-Bercy, Paris; July 31, 2010, US Airways Center, Phoenix; Sept. 7, 2010 Verizon Center, Washington, D.C.; Sept. 16, 2010, XL Center, Hartford; Feb. 26, 2011, Consol Energy Center, Pittsburgh. Live Performance.

_____. "Paparazzi." *The Fame.* Interscope Records, 2008. CD.

_____. "Paparazzi." Dir. Jonas Åkerlund. *Ladygaga.com.* 29 May 2009. Web. 28 Sep. 2011. Music Video.

_____. "Paparazzi." *MTV Video Music Awards.* New York, Radio City Music Hall, 13 Sept. 2009. Live Performance.

_____. "Poker Face." *The Fame.* Interscope Records, 2008. CD.

_____. "Scheiße." *Born This Way.* Streamline Records, 2011. CD

_____. "So Happy I Could Die." *The Fame Monster.* Interscope Records, 2009. CD.

_____. "Speechless." *The Fame Monster.* Interscope Records, 2009. CD.

_____. "Teeth." *The Fame Monster.* Interscope Records, 2009 Records. CD.

_____. "Telephone." *The Fame Monster.* Interscope Records, 2009. CD.

_____. "Telephone." Dir. Jonas Åkerlund. 2010. *YouTube.* Web. 7 Jan. 2011. Music Video.

_____. "Yoü and I." *Born This Way.* Streamline Records, 2011. CD

"Lady Gaga." *Entertainment Weekly* 1053/ 1054 (2009): 60–61. *Academic Search Complete.* EBSCO. Web. 21 Sep. 2011.

"Lady Gaga." *Rollingstone.com.* Rolling Stone, 16 Nov. 2010. Web. 1 Dec. 2010.

"Lady Gaga: A Dissenting Opinion." *Enjoy-your-style.com.* Enjoy Your Style, n.d. Web. 5 Jan. 2011.

"Lady Gaga & the Art of Fame." *60 Minutes, Interview with Anderson Cooper.* CB-SNewsOnline. Web. 13 Feb. 2011.

"Lady Gaga–Attacked by the Fame Monster & Singing 'Paparazzi' Live @ O2 Arena 30th May 2010." *YouTube.* 1 June 2010. Web. 2 Jan. 2011.

"Lady Gaga Confused by Personas." *femalefirst.co.uk.* Female First: Celebrity Gossip and Lifestyle Magazine, 8 July 2011. Web. 21 July 2011.

"Lady Gaga Explains Her VMA Raw Meat Dress." *USAToday.com*, Gannet Co., Inc., 13 Sep. 2010. Web. 8 Jan. 2011.

"Lady Gaga Headscarf—Red." *Ladygaga. shop.bravadousa.com*. Lady Gaga Official Store, 2011. Web. 12 Jan. 2011.

"Lady Gaga: 'I'm not a feminist. I hail men, I love men.'" *BitchMedia.com*. BitchMedia, 4 Aug. 2009. Web. 8 Sep. 2010.

"Lady Gaga Interview." 2009. *YouTube*. Web. 27 Nov. 2010.

"Lady Gaga Lesbian Photos With Lady Starlight." *PopCrunch.com*. PopCrunch, 3 Apr. 2009. Web. 10 Nov. 2011.

"Lady Gaga On Sex, Fame, Drugs, and Her Fans." *VanityFair.com*. *VF Blog*. 2 Aug. 2010. Web. 20 Dec. 2010.

"Lady Gaga Performs 'Paparazzi' at the 2009 Video Music Awards." *YouTube.com*. 13 Sep. 2009. Web. 15 Aug. 2010.

"Lady Gaga Sings 'Poker Face' and Talks about Gay Marriage." *YouTube.com*. 4 May 2009. Web. 5 Jan. 2011.

"Lady Gaga Speaks at Gay Rights Rally." *C-SPAN*. 11 Oct. 2009. Web. 8 Jan. 2011.

"Lady Gaga Talks About Music and Fashion: Singapore." *KosFusion.net*. Kosfusion, 18 Sep. 2009. Web. 27 Nov. 2010.

"Lady Gaga Tells All." *Elle.com*. Elle, 21 June 2010. Web. 16 Nov. 2010.

"Lady Gaga: The Singing Sensation on Stress, Sexuality, and Her Romantic Future." *Elle.com*. Elle, 1 Dec. 2009. Web. 12 Jan. 2010.

"Lady Gaga to Perform at Belfast MTV Awards." *BBC*.com. BBC, 17 Oct. 2011. Web. 8 Nov. 2011.

"Lady Gaga Writes 'Love Song' to Alexander McQueen." *Independent.co.uk*. Independent Print Limited, 7 June 2011. Web. 2 July 2011.

"Lady Gaga. The Singing Sensation on Stress, Sexuality, and Her Romantic Future." *Elle.com*. Elle, 2 Dec. 2009. 10 Nov. 2011.

"Lady Gaga's (Controversial) 'Bad Romance' Video—We Want Your Views." *Female First: Celebrity Gossip and Lifestyle Magazine*. First Active Media Ltd., 21 Nov. 2009. Web. 23 Jan. 2010.

"Lady Gaga's 'Don't Ask Don't Tell' Speech: The Full Transcript." *MTV.com*. MTV Networks, 20 Sep. 2010. Web. 8 Jan. 2011.

"Lady Gaga's Extreme Looks." *BeautyRiot. com*, Total Beauty Media, n.d. Web. 12 Jan. 2011.

"Lady Gaga's Message to the President." *Pepsi Refresh Campaign*. n.d. Web. 5 Jan. 2011.

"Lady Gaga's New Album Will 'Change The World.'" *MTV.co.uk*. MTV, 16 Sep. 2010. Web. 18 Nov. 2011.

"Lady Gaga's Technical Rider." *TheSmokingGun.com*. Smoking Gun. 4 Jan. 2010. Web. 28 Nov. 2011.

Lager, E. Grace and Brian R. McGee. "Hiding the Anorectic: A Rhetorical Analysis of Popular Discourse Concerning Anorexia." *Women's Studies in Communication* 26.2 (Sep. 2003): 266–96. Print.

Landau, Erica. "Grrrly Talk: Anti-Feminist Lady Gaga 'Hails,' 'Loves' Men, Performs New Year's Eve." *blogs.miaminewtimes. com*. Miami New Times, 16 Oct. 2009. Web. 17 Dec. 2010.

Lange, Karen L. "Wolf to Woof: The Evolution of Dogs." *NationalGeographic.com*, National Geographic Society, 2001. Web. 14 Jan. 2011.

Langellier, Kristin M. "Voiceless Bodies, Bodiless Voices: The Future of Personal Narrative Performance." *The Future of Performance Studies: Visions and Revisions*. Ed. S.J. Dailey. Annandale: National Communication Association, 1998: 207–13. Print.

Larosa, Brad. "How Stefani Germanotta Became Lady Gaga." *ABCNews.go.com*. ABC News, 21 Jan. 2010. Web. 10 June 2010.

Lawrence, Tim. *Love Saves the Day: A History of American Dance Music Culture, 1970–79*. Durham: Duke University Press, 2003. Print.

Lee, Ken, and Liz Raftery. "Lindsay Lohan Will Appear in *Playboy*: Mom." *People. com*. People, 25 Oct. 2011. Web. 29 Oct. 2011.

Lester, Paul. *Lady Gaga: Looking for Fame: The Life of a Pop Princess*. London: Omnibus Press, 2010. Print.

"Little Red Riding Hood Topsy Turvey

Doll." *WorthPoint.com*, Worth Point Corporation, 2009. Web. 13 Jan. 2011.

Lea, Virginia and Judy Hefand. *Identifying Race and Transforming Whiteness in the Classroom.* New York: Peter Lang, 2004. Print.

Leedom, Kathryn. "Grab Your Old Girl with Her New Tricks: Lady Gaga and Reflective Performance." Web log post. *Gaga Stigmata*. Blogger, 6 June 2010. Web. 9 Sep. 2010.

Lim, Thea and Andrea Plaid. "A Contrarian View of Lady Gaga for Racialicious Blog." *Racialicious.com*. Racialicious, 5 May 2010. Web. 10 Nov. 2010.

Livi, François. *Futurisme et surréalisme.* Lausanne: L'Âge d'homme, 2008. Print.

Lloyd, Jo Ann. "Weird Al: Where Rock 'N' Roll Meets 'Fiddler on the Roof.'" *Cal Poly Magazine.* Fall 2007: 12–14. Web. 20 Oct. 2011.

Lobel, Michael. "Warhol's Closet." *Art Journal* 55.4 (1996). 42–50. Print.

Lopez, Alfred J. *Postcolonial Whiteness: A Critical Reader on Race and Empire.* Albany: SUNY Press, 2005. Print.

Madonna. "Express Yourself." *Like a Prayer.* Sire Records, 1990. CD.

_____. "La Isla Bonita." *True Blue.* Sire Records, 1987. CD.

_____. "Like a Prayer." *Like a Prayer.* Sire Records, 1990. CD.

_____. "Like A Virgin." *Blonde Ambition Tour.* 1990. Live Performance.

_____. "Material Girl." *Like a Prayer.* Sire Records, 1990. CD.

_____. *Madonna Celebration: The Video Collection.* Dir. Various. Warner Bros., 2010.

_____. "Oh Father." *Blonde Ambition Tour.* 1990. Performance.

_____. "She's Not Me." *Hard Candy.* Warner Bros., 2008.

_____. *Sticky & Sweet Tour.* 2008–2009. Performance.

"Manifesto of Little Monsters." *Gagapedia*, 2009. Web. 8 Sep. 2010.

Marche, Stephen. "Lady Gaga Fifty-Nine Questions." *Esquire* 155.5 (2011): 78–80. Web. 21 Sep. 2011.

Marks, Craig. "Producer Rob Fusari Dishes on Lady Gaga, Beyoncé." *Billboard.com.* Billboard, 24 Feb. 2010. Web. 10 July 2010.

Marshall, Elizabeth. "Stripping for the Wolf: Rethinking Representations of Gender in Children's Literature." *Reading Research Quarterly* 39.3 (2004): 256–70. Print.

Marshall, P.D. *Celebrity and Power: Fame in Contemporary Culture.* Minneapolis: University of Minnesota Press, 1997. Print.

Martin, Peter J. *Sounds and Society: Themes in the Sociology of Music.* Manchester: Manchester University Press, 1996. Print.

Maselli, Morganne. "Masking the Human Face in Dadaism and Surrealism." Cloaking and Masking in Dada and Surrealism, n.d. Web. 26 Nov. 2011.

Massumi, Brian. *A User's Guide to Capitalism and Schizophrenia: Deviations from Deleuze and Guattari.* Cambridge: MIT Press, 1992. Print.

Matlack, Tom. "Poker Face: Don't Ask, Don't Tell." *TheHuffingtonPost.com.* Huffington Post, 22 Jan. 2010. Web. 25 Jan. 2010.

Matthews, Kyle. "Great Ideas Lecture: Beauty." Carson-Newman College. First Baptist Church, Jefferson City, TN. 27 Oct. 2011. Presentation.

Mayne, Judith. *Framed: Lesbians, Feminists, and Media Culture.* Minneapolis: University of Minnesota Press, 2000. Print.

McCormick, Neil. "Lady Gaga's Telephone Video," *DailyTelegraph.com.* Daily Telegraph, 17 Mar. 2010. Web. 10 Oct. 2011.

McLean, Don. "American Pie." *American Pie.* United Artists, 1971. CD.

"A Message from Lady Gaga to the Senate Sept 16 2010." *YouTube.* 17 Sep. 2010. Web. 10 Dec. 2010.

"Meet Lady Gaga's Little Monsters: The Singer's Super Fans Feel a Special Connection to Her." *ABCNews.go.com.* ABC News, 24 May 2011. Web. 19 July 2011.

Michelson, Noah. "Heather Cassils: Lady Gaga's Prison Yard Girlfriend." *OutMagazine.com.* Out Magazine, 16 Mar. 2010. Web. 7 Jan. 2011.

Miller, Erin. "Is Fame Catching Up with GaGa?" *Celebrity Tracker.* NineMSN, Nov. 2009. Web. 19 Dec. 2010.

Milligan, Lauren. "Klein Time." *British*

Vogue. n.p., 23 Mar. 2010. Web. 30 Sep. 2011.

Mills, C. Wright. *The Power of the Elite.* Oxford: Oxford University Press, 1956. Print.

Mills, Heather. "Sara Thornton Granted Murder Case Appeal." *Independent.co.uk.* Independent, 5 May 1995. Web. 10 June 2011.

Mitchell, John. "Lady Gaga Doesn't Need to Be a Sex Object to Be An Awesome Pop Star." *PopEater.com.* PopEater, 13 Sep. 2010. Web. 10 Nov. 2011.

Moran, Caitlin. "Why We Are Gaga for Lady Gaga." *TimesOnline.com.* Times Newspapers Ltd., 29 Jan. 2010. Web. 1 Feb. 2010.

Morgan, Johnny. *Gaga.* New York: Sterling, 2010. Print.

Morrison, Toni. *Playing in the Dark: Whiteness and the Literary Imagination.* Cambridge: Harvard University Press, 1992. Print.

Moskin, Julia. "A Dollop of Salami, Spreading from Calabria." *NYTimes.com.* New York Times Company, 22 Dec. 2009. Web. 3 Feb. 2010.

Mulvey, Laura. *Fetishism and Curiosity.* Bloomington: Indiana University Press, 1996. Print.

_____. *Visual and Other Pleasures.* Houndmills: Macmillan, 1989. Print.

_____. "Visual Pleasure and Narrative Cinema." *Screen* 16.3 (1975): 6–18. Print.

_____. "Visual Pleasure and Narrative Cinema." In *Film Theory and Criticism: Introductory Readings.* Eds. Leo Braudy and Marshall Cohen. New York: Oxford University Press, 1999: 833–44. Print.

Murfett, Andrew. "Lady Gaga." *The Sydney Morning Herald.* 15 May 2009. Web. 16 Dec. 2010.

Murphy, Blair. "Leaving Something to the Imagination: Neo-Burlesque, Gendered Spectacle and New Subcultural Forms." Diss. Georgetown University, Washington, D.C., 2009. *ProQuest Dissertations and Theses.* Web. 13 Nov. 2010.

Myra Breckinridge. Dir. Michael Sarne. Perf. Mae West, John Huston and Raquel Welch. 20th Century–Fox, 1970. Film.

Needham, Alex. "Camille Paglia's Attack on Lady Gaga is Way Off the Mark." *Guardian.co.uk.* Guardian, 13 Sep. 2010. Web. 10 Nov. 2011.

Nelson, Maggie. *The Art of Cruelty: A Reckoning.* New York: W. W. Norton & Company, 2011. Print.

Newton, Mandi, Sheryl Boblin, Barbara Brown, and Donna Ciliska. "'An Engagement-Distancing Flux': Bringing a Voice to Experiences with Romantic Relationships for Women with Anorexia Nervosa." *European Eating Disorders Review* 13 (2005): 317–29. Print.

Nietzsche, Friedrich Wilhelm. *Basic Writings of Nietzsche.* Trans. Walter Kaufmann. New York: Random House, 2000. Print.

Nur, Lolla Mohammed. "Female objectification isn't empowerment." *MNDaily.com.* Minnesota Daily, 15 Nov. 2010. Web. 13 Jan. 2011.

Nyong'o, Tavia. "Iphone, U-Phone ... Or Is Gaga the new Dada? ... Or Roll Over Andy Warhol..." *Bully Bloggers.* Ed. Lisa Duggan et al., 22 Mar. 2010. Web. 20 Mar. 2011.

O'Brien, Daniel. "Why It's Time to Stop Paying Attention to Lady Gaga." *Cracked.com: America's Only Humor Site Since 1958.* Demand Media, Inc., 10 Sep. 2010. Web. 11 Dec. 2010.

Odell, Amy. "Lady Gaga Seems to Be Taking Her Jo Calderone Alter Ego Pretty Seriously." *NYMag.com.* New York Magazine, 25 Aug. 2010. Web. 10 Nov. 2011.

Orenstein, Catherine. "Dances With Wolves: Little Red Riding Hood's Long Walk in the Woods." *MsMagazine.com.* Ms Magazine Online, Summer 2004. Web. 4 Aug. 2010.

_____. *Little Red Riding Hood Uncloaked: Sex, Morality, and the Evolution of a Fairy Tale.* New York: Basic Books, 2002. Print.

Paglia, Camille. "Lady Gaga and the Death of Sex." *TheSundayTimes.co.uk.* Sunday Times Magazine, 12 Sep. 2010. Web. 20 Dec. 2010.

_____. "Madonna: Finally, a Real Feminist." *NYTimes.com.* New York Times, 14 Dec. 1990. Web. 10 Nov. 2011.

_____. *Sexual Personae.* New York: Vintage Books, 1990. Print.

Paré, Ambrose and Janis L. Pallister. *On Monsters and Marvels.* Chicago: University of ChicagoPress, 1982. Print.

Parks, Gregory and Matthew Hughey. *The Obamas and a (Post) Racial America?* Oxford: Oxford University Press, 2011. Print.

Parker, James. "The Last Pop Star." *TheAtlantic.com.* Atlantic Monthly Group, June 2010. Web. 1 Sep. 2010.

Patch, Nick. "Lady Gaga announced as performer at MuchMusic Video Awards in June." *CP24.com.* Toronto's Breaking News, 26 May 2009. Web. 23 Dec. 2010.

Patterson, Sylvia. "She's the Man." *Q Magazine* Apr. 2010: 44–52. Print.

Patton, Cindy. "Emodying Subaltern Memory: Kinesthesia and the Problematics of Gender and Race." *The Madonna Connection: Representational Politics, Subcultural Identities, and Cultural Theory.* Ed. Cathy Schwichtenberg. Sydney: Allen and Unwin, 1993. 81–105. Print.

Pearlman, Ellen. "The World of the Body According to Lady Gaga." *syneme.ucalgary.ca/blogpost340.* Web blog post. Syneme, 24 Feb. 2010. Web. 26 Nov. 2011.

Perrault, Charles. "Little Red Riding Hood." *The Classic Fairy Tales.* Ed. Maria Tatar. New York: W.W. Norton, 1999. 11–13. Print.

Peter Pan. Dir. Clyde Geronimi et al., Disney, 1953. Film.

Polivy, Janet and C. Peter Herman. "Causes of Eating Disorders." *Annual Review of Psychology* 53 (2002): 187–213. Print.

Powell, Alison. "Gaga, Inc." *Billboard* (2011): 62–65. 11 May 2011. *Academic Search Complete.* EBSCO. Web. 21 Sep. 2011.

Powers, Ann. "Frank Talk with Lady Gaga." *LATimes.com.* Los Angeles Times, 13 Dec. 2009. Web. 16 Dec. 2010.

_____. "Lady Gaga's Multi-Pronged Campaign for Self-Awareness." *Post-Gazette.com.* PG Publishing Co., Inc., 24 Dec. 2009. Web. 2 Feb. 2010.

Psycho. Dir. Alfred Hitchcock. Perf. Anthony Perkins, Janet Leigh and Vera Miles. Paramount, 1960. Film.

"Purple Face." *TheSun.co.uk.* The Sun, 10 Mar. 2010. Web. 16 Dec. 2010.

Quinlan, Andrea. "Lady Gaga is Always Lady Gaga." *Gaga Stigmata: Critical Writings and Art About Lady Gaga.* Ed. Kate Durbin and Meghan Vicks. 6 Sep. 2010. Web. 7 Jan. 2011.

Rad Bromance. By Hiimrawn. Perf. Hiimrawn and Kassemg. *YouTube.* 27 Nov. 2009. Web. 22 Nov. 2010.

Raso, Anne. *Faces: Lady Gaga.* Poughkeepsie: Loki Publications, 2010. Print.

Rawles, Simon. "Why More Men Are Becoming Victims of Bigorexia." *MailOnline.com.* Associated Newspapers Ltd., 31 Dec. 2010. Web. 2 Jan. 2010.

"Re: Gaga = Jo Calderone!!? "*Lady Gaga Forum.* Web. 27 Aug. 2010.

Rear Window. Dir. Alfred Hitchcock. Perf. James Stewart, Grace Kelly and Wendell Corey. Paramount, 1954. Film.

Reilly, Elizabeth A. "From Calorie-Counting to Relationships." *Group Analysis* 39.3 (2006): 375–89. Print.

"Resisting the Prison Industrial Complex." Center for Interdisciplinary Studies in Philosophy, Interpretation, and Culture. *Binghamton.edu.* The State University of New York–Binghamton, 2011. Web. 5 Aug. 2011.

Richards, Chris. "Gaga Turns Verizon into a self-love camp meeting." *The Washington Post.* 9 Sep. 2010. C1+.

Richardson, Niall. *The Queer Cinema of Derek Jarman: Critical and Cultural Readings.* London: Tauris, 2009. Print.

Roach, Joseph. *It.* Ann Arbor: University of Michigan Press, 2007. Print.

Roberts, Diane. *The Myth of Aunt Jemima: White Women Representing Black Women.* New York: Routledge, 1994. Print.

Robertson, Pamela. *Guilty Pleasures: Feminist Camp from Mae West to Madonna.* London: Tauris, 1996. Print.

Robinson, Lisa. "Lady Gaga's Cultural Revolution." *Vanity Fair* 601 (Sep. 2010): 280–87, 329–31. Print.

Sawdey, Evan. "Lady Gaga's 'Bad Romance' Video: WTF?" *PopMatters.com.* PopMatters, 12 Nov. 2009. Web. 22 Dec. 2010.

Scaggs, Austin. "Lady Gaga." *Rolling Stone* 1072 (2009): 34. *Academic Search Complete.* EBSCO. Web. 21 Sep. 2011.

Schaefer, Jenni. *Goodbye Ed, Hello Me: Recover from Your Eating Disorder and Fall in Love with Life*. New York: McGraw-Hill, 2009. Print.

_____, and Thom Rutledge. *Life Without Ed: How One Woman Declared Independence from Her Eating Disorder and How You Can Too*. New York: McGraw-Hill, 2004. Print.

Schechner, Richard. *Between Theater and Anthropology*. Philadelphia: University of Pennsylvania Press, 1985. Print.

_____. *The Future of Ritual: Writings on Culture and Performance*. London: Routledge, 1995. Print.

Sellers, Susan. "Introduction." *The Hélène Cixous Reader*. New York: Routledge, 1994. xxvi–xxxiv. Print.

Seltzer, Sarah. "Lady Gaga, Grrrl Power, and Rock 'n' Roll Feminism." *RHRealityCheck.org*. RH Reality Check, 22 Mar. 2010. Web. 10 Nov. 2011.

Sendak, Maurice. *Where the Wild Things Are*. 25th Anniversary Ed. n.p.: HarperCollins, 1988. Print.

Senelick, Laurence. *The Changing Room: Sex, Drag, and Theatre*. New York: Routledge, 2000. Print.

Serpe, Gina. "Watch Lady Gaga's Music Video Premiere of 'Marry the Night.'" *EOnline.com*. EOnline, 1 Dec. 2011. Web. 2 Dec. 2011.

Shakespeare, William. *King Lear*. The New Shakespeare Series, G.I. Duthrie & J. Dover Wilson, eds. Cambridge: Cambridge University Press, 1960. Print.

Shakira. *She Wolf*. Epic Records, 2009. CD.

Sharkey, Willow. "Manifesting Love: 'Born This Way' and Surrealist Art." *GagaJournal.Blogspot.com*. Gaga Journal, 7 Mar. 2011. Web. 25 Nov. 2011.

Sheffield, Rob. "Lady Gaga Spanks the Planet: She's a Free Bitch, Baby." *RollingStone.com*. Rolling Stone, 20 July 2010. Web. 21 Dec. 2010.

Shelley, Mary. *Frankenstein, Or, The Modern Prometheus*. Ed. J. Paul Hunter. New York: Norton, 1996. Print.

Shiva, Vandana. *Biopiracy: The Plunder of Nature and Knowledge*. Cambridge: South End Press, 1997. Print.

Sigel, Tego. "Lady Gaga Thinks Her New Album Will Change the World." *RWD.com*. RWD, 17 Sep. 2010. Web. 18 Nov. 2011.

Silverman, Debra. "Making a Spectacle: Or, Is There Female Drag?" *Critical Matrix: The Princeton Journal of Women, Gender, and Culture* 7.2 (1993): 69–89. Print.

Slosar, J.R. *The Culture of Excess: How America Lost Self-Control and Why We Need to Redefine Success*. Santa Barbara: ABC CLIO, 2009. Print.

Smith, Patricia Juliana. "Icons and Iconoclasts: Figments of Sixties Queer Culture." *The Queer Sixties*. Ed. Patricia Juliana Smith. New York: Routledge, 1999. xii–xxvi. Print.

Smith, S.E. "Push(back) at the Intersections: Lady Gaga and Feminism." *Bitch-Magazine.org*, Bitch Media, 13 Sep. 2010. Web. 14 Jan. 2011.

Smith, Sidonie. "Identity's Body." *Autobiography and Postmodernism*. Eds. Kathleen Ashley, Leigh Gilmore, et al. Amherst: University of Massachusetts Press, 1994: 263–92. Print.

Solis, Michael. "Lady Gaga and Obama for Gay America." *TheHuffingtonPost.com*. The Huffington Post, 12 Oct. 2009. Web. 4 Jan. 2011.

Sontag, Susan. *Against Interpretation and Other Essays*. New York: Picador, 2001. Print.

Spines, Christine. "Lady Gaga Wants You." *Cosmopolitan* (Apr. 2010): 30–34. Print.

Staley, Gregory A. *Seneca and the Idea of Tragedy*. New York: Oxford University Press, 2010. Print.

Star Wars: The Phantom Menace. Dir. George Lucas. Perf. Ewan McGregor, Liam Neeson and Natalie Portman. 20th Century–Fox, 1999. Film.

Steele, Michael, et al. *Lady Gaga: From the Editors of Us Weekly*. Us Weekly: New York, 2011. Print.

Stein, Joshua David and Noah Michelson. "Lady Gaga: The Lady is a Vamp." *Out.com*. Out Magazine, 7 Aug. 2009. Web. 5 Jan. 2011.

Sterbak, Jana. *Chair Apollinaire*. 1996. Sculpture. Barbara Gross Galerie. Munich.

_____. *JanaSterbak.com*. n.p., n.d. Web. 29 Sep. 2011.

Stevenson, Robert Louis. *The Strange Case of Dr. Jekyll and Mr. Hyde.* Ed. Richard Dury. *The Collected Works of Robert Louis Stevenson.* Edinburgh: Edinburgh University Press, 2004. Print.

StilettoREVOLT. "Lady Gaga on Double Standards & Feminism." *YouTube.* 4 Aug. 2009. Web. 10 Nov. 2011.

Stoker, Bram. *Dracula.* Ed. Glennis Byron. Peterborough: Broadview, 1998. Print.

"The Story of Grandmother." The Classic Fairy Tales. Ed. Maria Tatar. New York: W.W. Norton, 1999. 10–11. Print.

Strauss, Neil. "Lady Gaga Tells All." *Rolling Stone* 8–22 July 2010: 68–73. Print.

_____. "The Broken Heart and Violent Fantasies of Lady Gaga." *Rolling Stone* 8 July 2010: 66–74. Print.

Suárez, Juan Antonio. *Bike Boys, Drag Queens & Superstars: Avant-Garde, Mass Culture, and Gay Identities in the 1960s Underground Cinema.* Bloomington: Indiana University Press, 1996. Print.

Sullivan, Shannon. *Revealing Whiteness: The Unconscious Habits of Racial Privilege.* Bloomington: Indiana University Press, 2006. Print.

Summers, Anthony. *Goddess: The Secret Lives of Marilyn Monroe.* New York: New American Library, 1986. Print.

Surgenor, Lois, Sarah Maguire, Janice Russell, and Stephen Touyz. "Self-Liking and Self-Competence: Relationship to Symptoms of Anorexia Nervosa." *European Eating Disorders Review* 15 (2007): 139–40. Print.

Surkan, Kim. "Drag Kings in the New Wave: Gender Performance and Participation." *Journal of Homosexuality* 43.3–4 (2002): 161–85. Print.

"Surréalisme." *La Quinzaine littéraire* 977 (1 Oct. 2008): 16. Print.

Syzmanski, Mike. "That's Right, Lady Gaga Doesn't Have a Penis." *Examiner.com.* Examiner, 2010. Web. 15 Dec. 2010.

Tasker, Yvonne. *Working Girls: Gender and Sexuality in Popular Culture.* London: Routledge, 1998. Print.

Tatar, Maria, ed. *The Classic Fairy Tales.* New York: W.W. Norton, 1999. Print.

Teal, Whitney. "Young Women and Feminism in the Lady Gaga Age." *Change.org.* Change, 23 Feb. 2010. Web. 5 Jan. 2011.

Terzieff, Juliette. "Fashion World Says Too Thin Is Too Hazardous." *WomenseNews.org.* Women's eNews, 24 Sep. 2006. Web. 9 Nov. 2010.

Thein, Ivonne. "Thirty-Two Kilos." *IvonneThein.com.* Ivonne Thein/VG Bild-kunst, 9 Jan. 2009. Web. 12 Jan. 2010.

Thelma & Louise. Dir. Ridley Scott. Perf. Susan Sarandon, Gina Davis, and Harvey Keitel. MGM, 1991. Film.

"Three Models Cut from Alexander McQueen Show After Refusing to Wear Armadillo Shoes." *TheHuffingtonPost.com.* Huffington Post, 22 Dec. 2009. Web. 8 Jan. 2011.

Thurber, James. "The Little Girl and the Wolf." *The Classic Fairy Tales.* Ed. Maria Tatar. New York: W.W. Norton, 1999. 16–17. Print.

Tinkcom, Matthew. *Working Like a Homosexual: Camp, Capital, and Cinema.* Durham: Duke University Press, 2002. Print.

Tochluk, Shelly. *Witnessing Whiteness: The Need to Talk About Race and How to Do It.* New York: Rowman and Littlefield, 2010. Print.

Tong, Rosemarie Putnam. *Feminist Thought: A More Comprehensive Introduction.* Boulder: Westview Press, 1998. Print.

Traber, Daniel. *Whiteness, Otherness, and the Individualism Paradox from Huck to Punk.* New York: Palgrave Macmillan, 2007. Print.

Turner, Victor. *From Ritual to Theater: The Human Seriousness of Play.* New York: PAJ Publications, 2001. Print.

Twain, Shania. "That Don't Impress Me Much." *Come On Over.* Mercury Nashville, 1998. Dr. Paul Boyd. Music Video.

"20/20 Lady Gaga Interview with Barbara Walters." *YouTube.* 22 Jan. 2010. Web. 10 Sep. 2010.

Twitter.com. @ladygaga. 7 Aug. 2009: 30 Oct. 2011; 20 Oct. 2010: 9 Sep. 2011;19 Dec. 2010: 30 Oct. 2011; 31 Dec. 2010: 9 Sep. 2011; 14 Nov. 2011: 18 Nov. 2011;15 Nov. 2011: 17 Nov. 2011:17 Nov. 2011: 17 Nov. 2011;1 Dec. 2011: 1 Dec. 2011.

Tyrangiel, Josh. "Auto-Tune: Why Pop Music Sounds Perfect." *Time.com.* Time Magazine, 5 Feb. 2009. Web. 21 July 2011.

Van Meter, Jonathan. "Our Lady of Pop." *Vogue* (Mar. 2011): 514–20, 570–71. Print.

Vena, Jocelyn. "*Born This Way* Is Lady Gaga's *Like A Prayer*, Perez Hilton Says." *MTV.com*. MTV Networks, 3 Feb. 2011. Web. 18 Nov. 2011.

_____. "Lady Gaga, Johnny Depp Top *Entertainment Weekly* Power List." *MTV.com*. MTV Networks, 7 Oct. 2010. Web. 18 Nov. 2011.

_____. "Lady Gaga Plans To Battle Her 'Monsters' During Monster Ball Tour." *MTV.com*. MTV Networks, 6 Nov. 2009. Web. 19 Nov. 2011.

_____, and Sway Calloway. (2009–11–23). "Lady Gaga Gets 'Dark' On *The Fame Monster*." *MTV.com*. MTV Networks, 23 Nov. 2009. Web. 10 Nov. 2011.

_____. "Lady Gaga Says 'Bad Romance' Video Is About 'Tough Female Spirit.'" *MTV.com*. MTV Networks, 9 Nov. 2009. Web. 12 Jan. 2010.

Vertigo. Dir. Alfred Hitchcock. Perf. James Stewart, Kim Novak and Barbara Bel Geddes. Paramount, 1958. Film.

Vicks, Meghan. "The Icon and the Monster: Lady Gaga is a Trickster of American Pop Culture." *Gaga Stigmata: Critical Writings and Art About Lady Gaga*. Blogger, 19 Mar. 2010. Web. 1 Sep. 2010.

Villiers de l'Isle-Adam, Auguste. *L'Ève future*. Paris: GF-Flammarion, 1992. Print.

Volcano, Del LaGrace, and Indra Wrath. "Gender Fusion." *Queer Theory*. Eds. Iain Morland and Annabelle Willox. New York: Palgrave Macmillan, 2005: 130–41. Print.

Waddell, Ray. "Lady Gaga's Monster Ball Tour Breaks Record for Debut Headlining Artist." *Billboard.com*. Billboard Magazine. 5 May 2011. Web. 17 Nov. 2011.

Wald, Gayle. *Crossing the Line: Racial Passing in 20th-Century U.S. Literature and Culture*. Durham: Duke University Press, 2000. Print.

Walls, Seth Colter. "The Blah-Blah of Gaga." *Newsweek* 154.22 (2009): 57. *Academic Search Complete*. EBSCO. Web. 21 Sep. 2011.

Walters, Barbara. "The 10 Most Fascinating People of 2009." Interview with Lady Gaga. 29 Dec. 2009. ABC. Print.

Warner, Kara "Lady Gaga's 'Alejandro': Video's Religious Imagery Gets Mixed Reactions From Fans," *MTV.com*. MTV Networks. 10 June 2010. Web. 9 Sep. 2011.

War of the Worlds. Dir. H.G. Wells. Perf. Gene Barry, Ann Robinson and Les Tremayne. Paramount, 1953. Film.

Weber, Max. "Class, Status, Party." *From Max Weber*. H.H. Gerth and C. Wright Mills, eds. and trans. New York: Oxford University Press, (1922) 1958. 180–95. Print.

Wharton, Amy S. *The Sociology of Gender: An Introduction to Theory and Research*. Malden: Blackwell, 2005. Print.

Whitehead, Gregory, "Holes in the Head: Theatres of Operation for the Body in Pieces." *UBU Papers*. 2003. Print.

Whitesell, Lloyd. "Trans Glam: Gender Magic in the Film Musical." *Queering the Popular Pitch*. Eds. Sheila Whiteley, Jennifer Rycenga. New York: Routledge, 2006. 263–77. Print.

Williams. *Luxury or the Comforts of a Rump Ford*. London: S. W. Fores, 26 Feb. 1801. British Museum. *The History of Gothic Fiction*. By Markman Ellis. Edinburgh: Edinburgh University Press, 2003. 97. Print.

Williams, Noelle. "Is Lady Gaga a Feminist, or Isn't She?" *MsMagazine.com*. Ms. Magazine, 11 Mar. 2010. Web. 4 Jan. 2011.

Wills, Clair. "Upsetting the Public: Carnival, Hysteria and Women's Texts." *Bakhtin and Cultural Theory*. 2nd ed. Eds. Ken Hirschkop and David Shepherd. Manchester: Manchester University Press, 2001. 85–108. Print.

Winterman, Denise. "What Would a Real Life Barbie Look Like?" *bbc.co.uk/news/magazine*. BBC News Magazine, 6 Mar. 2009. Web. 23 Dec. 2010.

_____, and Jon Kelly. "Five Interpretations of Lady Gaga's Meat Dress." *bbc.co.uk/news/magazine*. BBC News Magazine, 14 Sep. 2010. Web. 3 Jan. 2011.

The Wizard of Oz. Dir. Victor Fleming. Perf. Judy Garland, Frank Morgan and Ray Bolger. MGM, 1939. Film.

"The Wizard of Oz: An American Fairy Tale." *Library of Congress,* 27 July 2010. Web. 10 Dec. 2010.

Wolf, Naomi. *The Beauty Myth: How Images of Beauty Are Used Against Women.* New York: HarperCollins, 2002. Print.

Wolk, Douglas. "Monsters Inc." *Time* 177.21 (2011): 58–60. *Academic Search Complete.* EBSCO. Web. 21 Sep. 2011.

Woody, Erik Z. Rev. of *Anorexia Nervosa: A Multidimensional Perspective,* by Paul E. Garfinkel and David M. Garner. *Canadian Psychology/Psychologie Canadienne* 25:2 (Apr. 1984): 150. Print.

Yankovic, "Weird Al." "Perform This Way." *YouTube,* 20 June 2011. Web. 24 June 2011.

_____. *Alpocalypse.* New York, NY: Volcano, 2011.

_____. "The Saga Begins." *YouTube,* 2 Oct. 2009. Web. 24 June 2011.

_____. *Straight Out of Lynnwood.* New York, NY: Volcano, 2006.

_____. *"Weird Al" Yankovic.* Los Angeles, CA: Rock 'n Roll Records, 1983.

Zak, Dan. "For Gay Activists, the Lady Is a Champ." *WashingtonPost.com.* Washington Post, 12 Oct. 2009. Web. 5 Jan. 2011.

Zinoman, Jason. "For Lady Gaga, Every Concert Is a Drama." *New York Times* 23 Jan. 2010: C3. Print.

About the Contributors

Karley **Adney** is the program chair of the General Studies Program for ITT Technical Institute-Online. Adney specializes in 16th and 17th-century British literature. Her primary research interest is adaptations of Shakespearean plays for children, but she also focuses her work on representations of gender in popular culture.

David **Annandale** teaches literature and film at the University of Manitoba. He is writing a book on video games and has written chapters for *Roman Catholicism in Fantastic Film; Reframing 9/11: Film, Popular Culture and the "War on Terror"* and *The Meaning and Culture of Grand Theft Auto.*

Stephanie **Capaldo** is a doctoral candidate in U.S. environmental history and environmental legal studies at the University of Arizona. She teaches in the department of history at the University of Arizona and in the STAR Program at Northern Arizona University. Her research interests include environmental justice on the U.S.–Mexico Border.

Sherri **Craig** teaches composition and STAR English at Northern Arizona University. Her research interests include the study of African-American rhetoric and cultural studies.

Emily **Davalos** teaches freshman composition at Northern Arizona University and introductory Latin courses at Coconino Community College. Her research interests include classics and gender studies.

Mathieu **Deflem** is a professor of sociology at the University of South Carolina. His main research areas are sociology of law, crime and social control, social theory, and popular culture. He teaches the undergraduate course "Lady Gaga and the Sociology of Fame" and privately maintains a fan site at www.gagafrontrow.net.

Richard J. **Gray** II is a visiting associate professor of French at Denison University in Granville, Ohio. He is the coeditor with Betty Kaklamanidou of

The 21st Century Superhero: Essays on Gender, Genre and Globalization in Film and is the coauthor of an essay in the collection *The Comedy of Dave Chappelle*, ed. Kevin Wisniewski. His work on Lady Gaga is cited in the autumn 2011 *The American Scholar* magazine.

Laura **Gray-Rosendale**, a professor of English at Northern Arizona University and President's Distinguished Teaching Fellow, specializes in rhetoric, composition, and cultural studies. She is the director of the Multicultural Summer Writing Program for STAR. Her books include *Rethinking Basic Writing, Alternative Rhetorics, Fractured Feminisms, Radical Relevance,* and *Pop Perspectives.*

Katrin **Horn** is a doctoral candidate in the American Studies department of Friedrich-Alexander-University, Erlangen-Nuremberg, where she has taught courses on queer studies, camp, and the gender politics of Neo-Burlesque. Her musings on Lady Gaga can be found in several German publications as well as her dissertation, "Deconstructing Gender Hegemony, Queering the Cultural Mainstream...."

Heather Duerre **Humann** teaches a variety of writing, literature, and special topics courses in the English Department at the University of Alabama. Her writing has been published in *African American Review; Clues: A Journal of Detection; South Atlantic Review; Black Warrior Review;* and *Home Girls Make Some Noise! Hip Hop Feminism Anthology.*

Rebecca M. **Lush** is an assistant professor of literature and writing studies at California State University, San Marcos. Her interests include early colonial and U.S. American literature, women's studies, and Native American literature. She has an essay on Aphra Behn in *Early Modern Women: An Interdisciplinary Journal* 6 (2011) and wrote on Cooper's *The Prairie* in *Literature in the Early American Republic* 2.1 (April 2010).

Jennifer M. **Santos** is an assistant professor in the Department of English and Fine Arts at Virginia Military Institute, where she teaches 19th-century British literature. Intrigued by that period's "pop culture," she is writing a book on reader response to Gothic fiction. She has also published several papers on popular culture, reception, and pedagogy.

Elizabeth Kate **Switaj** is a doctoral candidate at Queen's University Belfast and an editorial assistant for *Irish Pages: A Journal of Contemporary Writing.* Her first collection of poetry, *Magdalene & the Mermaids,* was published in 2009. More recently, her article "'The Sisters,' 'The Dead,' and Ron Butlin's Night Visits" appeared in *Hypermedia Joyce Studies.*

Ann T. **Torrusio** is currently a Ph.D. candidate in English literature at Saint Louis University. She is also a lecturer for the Pierre Laclede Honors College at the University of Missouri–St. Louis and has contributed articles for *The Encyclopedia of Women and American Popular Culture; Music in American Life: An Encyclopedia of Women of the Songs, Styles Stars, and Stories That Shaped Our Culture* and *Up Jumped the Devil: Explorations of Evil in Popluar Music.*

Matthew R. **Turner** is an assistant professor of communication at Radford University in Radford, Virginia. His article "Arrr!!!: Performing Piracy and the Origin of International Talk Like a Pirate Day" appears in *Popular Culture Review* (2012) and an article on the Orpheus legend appears in *Hogar, Dulce Hogar* (2012). He has also published articles on comedy westerns and the Marx Brothers.

Jennifer M. **Woolston** teaches in the English Department and in the Women's Studies Program at Indiana University of Pennsylvania. Her academic essays appear in *Let the Games Begin! Engaging Students with Field-Tested Interactive Information Literacy Instruction; Studies in the Novel; Hispanic Culture Review; Grace Under Pressure: Grey's Anatomy Uncovered;* and *Persuasions Online.*

Index